Acing

Property

Second Edition

**A Checklist Approach to
Solving Property Problems**

Colleen E. Medill

Robert and Joanne Berkshire Family Professor of Law
University of Nebraska
College of Law

Series Editor
A. Benjamin Spencer

WEST®

A Thomson Reuters business

Mat #41264814

© 2009 Thomson Reuters
© 2012 Thomson Reuters
  610 Opperman Drive
  St. Paul, MN 55123
  1–800–313–9378

Printed in the United States of America

ISBN: 978–0–314–28095–4

This book is dedicated to my first-year Property students—
past, present and future.

About the Author

COLLEEN E. MEDILL is the Robert and Joanne Berkshire Family
Professor of Law at the University of Nebraska College of
Law. She has taught first-year Property for over fifteen
years, beginning at The University of Tennessee College of Law
(1997–2004) and currently at the University of Nebraska College of
Law. Professor Medill has won the Outstanding Teacher Award at
both institutions. She also is the author of *Developing Professional
Skills: Property* (West 2011), a book designed to teach legal practice
skills to law students. In addition to teaching Property, Professor
Medill teaches advanced courses on real estate transactions and
mortgage financing, wills, trusts and estates, and employee benefits
law.

Professor Medill graduated first in her law school class at the
University of Kansas, where she was an Articles Editor for the
Kansas Law Review. Upon graduation, Professor Medill served as a
law clerk for the Honorable Deanell Reece Tacha on the United
States Tenth Circuit Court of Appeals. After her clerkship, Profes-
sor Medill practiced corporate and tax law in Kansas City, Missouri,
before joining the law school faculty at The University of
Tennessee.

Introduction

During the course of teaching first-year Property for over fifteen years, I have read all of the student study aids in the area. This book is *different*. It does not present lengthy lists of detailed rules to memorize. Rather, this book *organizes* the rules for you so that you can analyze and answer Property problems. It shows you how to *think* about Property.

The first-year Property course is difficult for many students for two reasons. First, the material is difficult to organize in a systematic way because, unlike most first-year law school subjects, Property lacks an overarching meta-theory. Second, some of the material (e.g., present and future interests and the Rule Against Perpetuities) is notoriously difficult to teach and to learn due to the archaic nature of the legal vocabulary.

These inherent difficulties are compounded if your Property teacher tends to hide the ball. Your casebook may not clearly identify the fundamental concepts and rules that you must understand to perform well on the exam. You easily may find yourself wandering, lost in the proverbial Property forest of the historical, the obscure, or the irrelevant. Students who ace their Property course know how to navigate the Property forest in an efficient manner.

This book provides you with a navigational roadmap. Each chapter begins with a student-friendly summary (the "Review") of the fundamental rules for a specific area of Property law. The Review only talks about the important rules and shows you how these rules fit together. The Review also highlights for you those key points of intersection where the rules in one area of your Property course may intersect with the rules in other areas. Some Property professors highlight these points of intersection for their students. Others do not, and award the best grades to those few students who spot these points of intersection on the exam.

After the Review, the rules are organized in the form of an outline-like checklist (the "Checklist"). At a minimum, you can compare your own outline with the Checklist to determine if your outline is missing a key rule or principle of Property law. Ideally, you can use the Checklist as a tool to train your brain for the exam. The Checklist shows you the order in which you should consider and apply the rules of Property to solve problems. Studying the organizational structure of the Checklist and using it to develop your own course outline will train you how to think about Property issues in a systematic, efficient, and thorough fashion—the hallmarks of an "A" Property student.

After the Checklist, each Chapter contains Problems (with answers) so that you can test your understanding of the material. Finally, each Chapter concludes with a suggested list of Points to Remember so that you can avoid making silly mistakes on the exam.

To help you understand present and future interests and the Rule Against Perpetuities, the Review portion of Chapters 3 and 4 has been expanded. Chapters 3 and 4 also contain lengthy lists of practice problems so that you can approach present and future interests and Rule Against Perpetuities questions on your Property exam with confidence, not dread.

This book is not intended to be a scholarly treatise on Property law, or even a comprehensive student study aid. Coverage in the first-year Property course varies widely, and so your particular professor may or may not teach all of the topics addressed in this book. This book is a teaching and learning tool that focuses on the *most difficult* parts of the typical Property course. After listening to and learning from my own Property students for many years, I have taken my teaching methods and incorporated those methods into this book. These methods simplify and distill Property law down to its essence so that you can at least understand, and may even come to enjoy, Property.

Colleen E. Medill
July 24, 2012

Table of Contents

CHAPTER 1

Captured and Found Property

Many students begin Property law by studying cases involving captured or found items of tangible personal property. Captured property has no original or true owner—it typically consists of things found in nature, such as wild animals, minerals, and other natural resources. In contrast, found property is assumed to have had a prior owner, who either lost, mislaid or abandoned the item. The underlying theme of captured and found property cases is the concept of possession, and how possession determines who has the superior legal right to the captured or found property.

CAPTURED AND FOUND PROPERTY REVIEW

Captured Property Analysis

In a dispute between two persons over an item of tangible personal property, the plaintiff may bring a claim for **conversion** against the defendant who presently holds the item. The plaintiff may seek either damages for the value of the converted property, or may seek the return of the converted item.

To assert a conversion claim, the plaintiff must prove that the defendant has: (1) exercised dominion and control (2) over personal property (3) that belongs to (or is owned by) the plaintiff. Note carefully that the defendant's state of mind is irrelevant to proof of the plaintiff's claim. The defendant's mistaken or good faith belief that the defendant is entitled to possess the disputed property is not a defense to a conversion claim.

Generally, the first two elements of a conversion claim are undisputed. Proof of the third element often turns on whether the plaintiff possessed the disputed property before the defendant did. For captured property (which has no original owner), prior possession of the disputed property gives the plaintiff the superior legal right to the property under the fundamental Property law rule of **first in time, first in right** ("FTFR").

Given that the success of the plaintiff's conversion claim usually turns on who "possessed" the disputed property first, it is important to understand how courts analyze possession issues. The concept of possession has two component parts, both of which must be satisfied (to a greater or lesser degree, as we will see) before a court will conclude that a party has obtained possession of the property. For possession to occur, there must be: (1) a physical act of control over the object; and (2) the intent to control the object, or the intent to exclude possession of the object by others.

Although breaking down the concept of possession into its physical act and state of mind components is useful, judges still must apply these components to actual facts. In close cases, a judge may turn to two other Property law doctrines—**occupancy theory** (a close cousin to the principle of FTFR) and **labor theory**—to justify the court's ultimate decision. Although the cases you read in Property class might only hint at these two doctrines, your professor may spend significant time on these doctrines during class. It is at this point that some students wander off into the Property law forest. Your task is to remain focused on *why* the doctrinal theory matters, and how each theory may or may not apply to the parties' dispute. The diagram on the following page provides a roadmap so that you can place a classroom discussion of various doctrinal theories into context.

Captured Property Analysis

CLAIM

Elements of Conversion Claim:
(1) Defendant controls
(2) Personal property
(3) Belonging to (owned by) the plaintiff

INTERPRETATION OF ELEMENT (3)

Under the Rule of FTFR, ownership of captured property with no original owner is determined by who possessed the property first.

ISSUE & ANALYSIS

Possession requires:
• Physical act of control AND
• Intent (state of mind) to control or exclude possession by others

---

THEORY AND PUBLIC POLICY

To resolve the issue of who had first possession, courts may consider theory and public policy:
• Occupancy Theory
• Labor Theory
• Economic Theory
• Public Policy

In addition to occupancy and labor theory, courts also may consider economic theory and general public policy in ruling on close cases. Your professor may use captured and found property cases as a vehicle to introduce several important Property-related economic theories, such as:

- the concept of **externalities** (actions have consequences that may be either beneficial or harmful to other members of society);

- the **tragedy of the commons** (the tendency of individuals to overdeplete natural resources owned collectively); and

- the **Coase Theorem** (absent transaction costs, individuals would freely bargain to an optimal resource allocation irrespective of how the law allocates property rights and liabilities).

Public policy justifications for awarding superior property rights to one claimant over another may be based on policies such as:

- promoting established societal norms and expectations;

- deferring to the custom and practice among experts in the field;

- promoting or protecting a business or industry that has come to depend on awarding superior property rights under certain circumstances for its operations;

- the impact on future societal behavior, such as discouraging violence, encouraging the peaceful resolution of disputes, or encouraging honesty; and

- the impact on the administration of justice and judicial resources (clear rules discourage parties from litigating lawsuits, but may create unfair results in some cases).

Theory and public policy are fun and engaging to discuss in class, but do not lose sight of the role of theory and policy in your legal analysis. The legal rule of FTFR is based on the concept of first possession. Only where it is difficult for the court to determine which claimant had first possession will the court look to theory and public policy to resolve the possession issue.

Captured Property Cases

The classic captured property cases illustrate how courts apply the steps of the above analysis. Again, the main point is that different judges may resolve the issue of first possession differently. For example, in *Pierson v. Post*,[1] the majority required a very strong physical act of control over the fox—killing it and "occupying" (holding) the carcass. The minority preferred to award the fox to the initial hot pursuer—requiring a lesser degree of physical control because of the "labor" invested in spotting and chasing the fox and the societal norms and expectations ("custom") that the pursuer acquires the right to the pursued fox. In *Ghen v. Rich*,[2] the outcome is reversed. The majority awarded ownership based on first "possession" of the whale's carcass to the harpooner of the whale over the person who found the carcass on the shoreline based on the labor expended and industry custom. To rule otherwise would discourage an economic activity—the whaling industry—that was socially desirable.

Found Property: Additional Factors For Consideration

In the classic capture cases, the rule of first possession as conveying superior legal rights to the disputed property is simplified. No one has held prior ownership of the disputed object, and the object is captured on public property. The fox is chased and killed on a public beach; the whale is harpooned in the open ocean and washes ashore.

In found property cases, however, three new factors are introduced that potentially complicate the court's analysis of which claimant should be awarded the superior legal right to a disputed item of property. First, a found item may have had a **prior true owner**, whose rights must be considered and protected if possible. Second, the disputed item may have been **found on private property**, in which case the rights of the private landowner (the owner of the "locus") must be considered. Third, the **status or conduct of the finder** may affect whether the court will reward the finder with the superior legal right to the disputed item.

---

1. 3 Cai. Rep. 175 (N.Y. Sup. 1805).   2. 8 F. 159 (D. Mass. 1881).

Rights Of The True Owner

Whether a court will consider the rights of the true owner of the disputed item depends on the state of mind of the true owner at the time she became separated from her property. Obviously, drawing a conclusion about what the true owner must have been thinking (or not thinking) when she became separated from her property is pure fiction. Nevertheless, this is what courts routinely do in resolving disputes over found items. The court's characterization of the true owner's state of mind is based on the physical circumstances ("circumstantial evidence") under which the property was found.

If the court characterizes the property as **abandoned** by the true owner (e.g., a home run ball at a Major League Baseball game), the true owner has voluntarily relinquished her legal rights to the found property. For abandoned property, courts rely exclusively on the second and third judicial factors (rights of the owner of the locus and the conduct of the finder) to determine which claimant has the superior legal right to the property.

If the court characterizes the property as **mislaid**, the law assumes that the true owner *intentionally* placed the item in a particular spot. Eventually (so the law assumes), the forgetful true owner will remember where the found property was placed and will return to retrieve it. For mislaid property, courts favor leaving possession of the property with the owner of the locus where the item was found over awarding possession to the finder.

If the true owner does remember and returns to claim the item, the owner of the locus must return the mislaid item to the true owner. Until then, however, the owner of the locus where the mislaid item was found retains physical possession of the item. If the true owner fails to return and claim the mislaid property after a reasonable period of time, the found item may be recharacterized as lost or abandoned property and awarded to the finder.

If the court characterizes the property as **lost**, the law assumes that the true owner did *not* intentionally place the item in a particular spot, but rather was careless and accidentally lost the item. If the property was lost accidentally (so the law assumes), the true owner will not be able to remember and retrieve the item. For lost property, the courts struggle with whether to award the lost property to the owner of the locus or to the finder of the lost item. Here, judicial decisions tend to rely heavily on the conduct of the finder and whether that conduct in finding the item involved a trespass on privately owned land.

Rights Of The Owner Of The Locus

Consideration of the rights of the owner of the locus is consistent with Property law's strong tendency to protect the rights of private landowners. One of these rights is the landowner's right to exclude entry onto his land by others. Another right is reflected in the general rule that the owner of real estate is deemed to own anything that is under, attached to, or on the surface of his land.

In reading the classic cases on found property, you may encounter *Hannah v. Peel*.[3] The outcome in *Hannah v. Peel* is an anomaly because the finder, who discovered a broach stuck behind the top of a windowsill in the owner's house, was awarded possession of the broach over the competing claim of the home's owner. Normally, as a general rule the private landowner would be awarded possession of the broach in this situation.

To understand *Hannah v. Peel*, you must focus on the unusual background of the case. The British government had requisitioned the vacant house for quartering solders during World War II. Significantly, the home's owner had never set foot in the house. If the owner had occupied the house prior to its requisition, under the general rule described above the home owner most likely would have been awarded the broach over the competing claim of the soldier who found it.

Private property, such as a store or business, that is open to the public ("quasi-public property") presents a more difficult problem. Here, if the item found is characterized as lost or abandoned,

---

3. [1945] K.B. 509.

courts generally award the item to the finder. If, however, the found property is characterized as mislaid, courts generally rule that the owner of the store or business must hold the item for safekeeping in case the true owner remembers where she mislaid the property and returns to claim it. The above rules for items found on quasi-public property are subject to criticism, of course, because the characterization of the property as "lost" or "mislaid" is a fiction. The true owner's state of mind is determined solely by the circumstantial evidence, in particular the location or condition of the found item.

Conduct Of The Finder

Consideration of the conduct of the finder is a crucial factor used by courts to resolve claims involving found property. Trespassers who enter onto privately owned land (or a private area of quasi-public property, such as the "no customers allowed" area of a store) without the permission of the owner as a general rule are not rewarded for their misconduct with the superior legal right to any captured, lost or abandoned property found by the trespasser. Ownership generally is awarded to the private landowner to discourage trespassing.

In contrast, when a person who finds a lost item on quasi-public property is honest and turns the lost property over to the owner of the locus, the courts often reward the honest finder with the superior legal right to possess the item if the true owner does not return to claim it within a reasonable amount of time. This general rule is based on public policy. It encourages and rewards honesty by other finders in the future. This general rule also protects the rights of future true owners, who may remember where the item became lost or misplaced and return to the locus to claim their missing property.

Exam Tip: Property Captured On A Private Locus

Recall that the fox in *Pierson v. Post* was captured on a public beach. This crucial fact limited the court's analysis to the issue of first possession. Now assume that the fox had been captured on a private beach. Changing this fact requires you to expand your analysis beyond the issue of first possession. You also must analyze and weigh the rights of the owner of the beach and the conduct of the capturer (was the capturer trespassing?) in deciding who should be awarded the superior legal right to the fox.

The purpose of this exam tip is to alert you that the "rules" for captured and found property are really principles that the courts apply in specific factual situations. On the exam, you should look for points of intersection where two or more of the principles governing captured or found property may apply, and then use the facts on the exam to reason by analogy to the cases you have studied. Is a fox that is chased and killed on a private beach like finding a ring at the bottom of a pool? O is it more like finding someone's wallet on a table in a store? Problem 1.1 at the end of Chapter 1 allows you to practice this type of legal reasoning by analogy.

Damages For A Conversion Claim

A plaintiff who successfully asserts a conversion claim against the defendant recovers as damages the value of the converted personal property.[4] If the disputed property cannot be appraised because the defendant no longer possesses the item, the law presumes that the item is of the highest quality of its kind. For example, if the disputed item was a jewel, it would be valued for purposes of assessing damages against the defendant as the highest quality stone of a comparable shape and size.[5]

The defendant who converts the plaintiff's personal property may further enhance the property's value by adding the defendant's own labor to create a more valuable product. This situation is illustrated by the modern case of *Moore v. Regents of the University of California*,[6] where the plaintiff claimed that his doctors removed his diseased spleen and used it to develop a valuable patented cell line. The *Moore* court avoided the difficult issue of how to measure

---

4. A replevin claim seeks the return of the found property itself; therefore, the measure of damages is not in dispute.

5. *Armory v. Delamirie*, Str. 505 (1772).

6. 793 P.2d 479 (Cal. 1990).

the plaintiff's damages by holding that, once removed from the body, the diseased spleen was no longer the plaintiff's personal property. If the court had held that the removed spleen was the plaintiff's property, the possibilities for measuring damages ranged from the value of the "raw material" (the diseased spleen) to the value of the "final product" (a patented cell line). A different situation (as on your exam) could force a court (or you) to address this type of difficult measure of damages issue and discuss the corresponding public policies involved.

CAPTURED AND FOUND PROPERTY CHECKLIST

With the above Review in mind, the Captured and Found Property Checklist is presented below.

A. DETERMINE THE DISPUTED ELEMENTS OF THE PLAINTIFF'S CONVERSION CLAIM. Determine if the plaintiff should bring a claim for conversion and identify the disputed elements of the plaintiff's claim.

    1. Elements For Proof Of Claim. To bring a claim for conversion, the plaintiff must prove the following three elements:

        a. Defendant Exercised Dominion And Control. Did the defendant possess the item? If the defendant no longer possesses the item, the plaintiff's remedy is damages, not the return of the disputed item.

        b. Over Personal Property. A claim for conversion applies only to personal property.

        c. Belonging To (Owned By) The Plaintiff. Did the plaintiff own or possess the disputed item *before* the defendant exercised dominion and control over the item?

B. CHARACTERIZE THE DISPUTED PROPERTY AND STATE THE APPROPRIATE GENERAL RULE. Characterize the disputed property using Parts B.1 and B.2 of the checklist and state the appropriate general rule. Where the characterization is questionable, identify all possibilities for analysis. Further consider whether the complicating factors described in Parts B.3 and B.4 of the checklist should be considered in awarding the superior legal right to the disputed property to a particular claimant.

1. **Captured Or Abandoned Property.** Captured property has no true original owner. For abandoned property, the true owner has voluntarily relinquished (either expressly by words or implicitly by conduct) all rights to the property. The general rule is FTFR. The property belongs to the first person who obtains possession of the property.

2. **Lost Or Mislaid Property.** Circumstantial evidence is used to determine whether the true owner accidentally has lost the property, or whether the true owner mislaid the property and therefore is likely to remember and return to claim it.

   a. **Circumstantial Evidence.** Do the circumstances indicate that the true owner *intentionally* placed the property in the location where the property was found and then forgot to retrieve it?

      i. **If yes**, characterize the property as mislaid.

      ii. **If no**, characterize the property as lost.

   b. **General Rule For Lost Property.** Lost property generally is awarded to the finder because the true owner is unlikely to return and claim it.

   c. **General Rule For Mislaid Property.** Mislaid property generally is awarded to the owner of the locus for safekeeping for the true owner, who may return to claim it. If the true owner fails to claim the mislaid property after a reasonable period of time, the property may be recharacterized as lost or abandoned property and awarded to the finder.

3. **Disputes Concerning First Possession Between Capturers Or Finders.** If there is a dispute between two competing capturers or two competing finders, proceed to Part C of the checklist to determine who has the superior legal right under the rule of FTFR by virtue of obtaining first possession of the disputed property.

4. **Property Captured Or Found On A Privately Owned Location.** If the property was found on exclusively private land or quasi-public land, proceed to Part D of the checklist to determine whether the court should award the superior legal right to the disputed property to the owner of the locus over a capturer or finder.

C. **DETERMINE WHO HAD FIRST POSSESSION.** As between two competing capturers or finders, the party who obtained possession first has the superior legal right to the disputed property under the rule of FTFR. Consider the elements of possession, occupancy and labor theory, economic theory, and public policy (if applicable) to determine which claimant should prevail.

1. **The Elements Of Possession.** Possession requires both a physical act and a certain state of mind.

   a. **Physical Act.** To what extent was the claimant successful in physically controlling the captured or found property, or excluding possession of the captured or found property by others?

   b. **State Of Mind.** Did the claimant intend to control and possess the captured or found property, or intend to exclude possession of the property by others?

2. **Occupancy And Labor Theory.** Where either or both of the two elements of possession are in doubt, further consider whether occupancy or labor theory justifies awarding the superior legal right to the disputed property to one claimant over the other.

a. **Occupancy Theory.** Did one claimant have a reasonable expectation of ownership based on his occupation of the site where the property was captured or found, or based on his physical control over the captured or found property? **If yes**, occupancy theory supports awarding the superior legal right to the claimant who first occupied or controlled the property.

      b. **Labor Theory.** Did one claimant invest more time and effort in capturing or finding the property than the other claimant? **If yes**, labor theory supports awarding the superior legal right to the claimant who has invested more time and labor in capturing or finding the property.

3. **Economic Theories.** Do one or more of the economic theories below support a ruling that the captured or found property should be awarded to a particular claimant?

      a. **Externalties.** Would the ruling reduce harmful side effects or increase beneficial side effects for other members of society?

      b. **Tragedy Of The Commons.** Would the ruling encourage overdepletion of scarce resources?

      c. **Coase Theorum.** Would the ruling reduce transaction costs or free rider problems in the future and thereby encourage private bargaining that could more efficiently allocate resources?

4. **Public Policy.** Do one or more of the public policies below support awarding the captured or found property to a particular claimant?

      a. **Promoting Established Societal Norms And Expectations.** Does how society has dealt with similar disputes in the past support awarding the superior legal right to a particular claimant?

    b. **Deferring To Custom And Practice Among Experts In The Field.** Will awarding the disputed property to a particular claimant be consistent with the custom or practice among experts?

    c. **Promoting Or Protecting Business Or Industry Expectations Or Reliance.** Has a business or industry come to rely on a rule that awards the disputed property to one claimant over the other?

    d. **Impact On Future Societal Behavior.** Will awarding the superior legal right to a particular claimant discourage violence and/or encourage honesty among members of society?

    e. **Impact On Justice And Judicial Resources.** Will the precedent established in awarding the disputed property create a "bright line" rule that is easily understood and applied by judges in the future? Could the precedent lead to unfair or harsh results in subsequent cases?

D. PROPERTY CAPTURED OR FOUND ON A PRIVATE LOCUS. When property is captured or found on a private locus, the rights of the private landowner must be considered in awarding the superior legal right to the disputed item.

    1. **General Rule Of Ownership.** The general rule for property that is captured or found on a private locus is that the private landowner is presumed to own anything that is under, attached to, or on the surface of the land.

        a. **Private Owner's Knowledge, Control Or Intent Irrelevant.** The private landowner does *not* need to know that the item is on the owner's land, control the item, or intend to possess the item of property in order to prevail over a competing capturer or finder.

        b. **Public Policy Underlying General Rule.** The general rule described above is based on the public policy of preserving and protecting the private landowner's rights, particularly the right to exclude trespassers from the owner's land.

2. **Exceptions For Property Found In A Quasi–Public Location.** When property is found on premises that are privately owned, but that are open to access by the public or the owner has given permission to enter (a "quasi-public" locus), the analysis requires balancing the rights of the true owner, the rights of the private landowner and the policy of encouraging an honest finder.

    a. **Mislaid Property.** The general rule is that possession of mislaid property is awarded initially to the private owner of the locus for safekeeping in case the true owner remembers and returns to claim it. This rule gives paramount weight to protecting the rights of the true owner of the mislaid property.

        i. **Recharacterization After Passage Of Time.** If the true owner fails to claim mislaid property after a reasonable period of time, the property may be recharacterized as lost or abandoned property and awarded to the finder.

    b. **Captured, Abandoned and Lost Property.** The general rule is that, so long as the capturer or finder is not a trespasser, possession of captured, abandoned or lost property on a quasi-public locus is awarded to the capturer or finder.

        i. **True Owner's Rights.** The true owner's rights are not weighed in the analysis because either there is no original owner (captured property), the true owner has voluntarily relinquished property rights (abandoned property), or the true owner is unlikely to remember and return to the locus to claim the item (lost property).

ii. **Encouraging Honest Finders.** The public policy of encouraging honesty by rewarding the finder with the superior legal right to property that is abandoned or lost by the true owner is *given paramount weight* for a "good faith" finder who is not a trespasser.

iii. **Rights Of Private Landowners.** The rule that a private landowner is presumed to own any item that is under, attached to, or on the surface of the land is of lesser weight in the analysis when the property is captured or found on private property that is open to entry by the public or found by someone who is on the private owner's property with permission.

c. **Trespassers.** The public policy against trespassing on privately owned land weighs heavily against rewarding a trespasser with the superior legal right to captured or found property.

i. **Permission To Enter?** Did the capturer or finder have permission (either express or implied) from the landowner to be on the premises where the property was captured or found? **If no**, the capturer or finder is a *trespasser* and should not be rewarded with the superior legal right to the disputed item.

ii. **Scope Of Permission?** Were the actions or conduct of the capturer or finder within the scope or purpose of the permission to be on the land granted by the private landowner? **If no**, the rule that property that is under, attached to, or on the surface of privately owned land is presumed to be owned by the landowner is given paramount weight and supports awarding the superior legal right to disputed item to the landowner.

E. **DETERMINE DAMAGES (IF APPLICABLE).** If the plaintiff seeks a damages award based on a conversion claim, determine the value of the converted property as the measure of damages.

1. **Defendant No Longer Possesses The Converted Property.** If the defendant no longer possesses the converted property, in awarding damages to the plaintiff the law assumes the highest quality, and therefore the highest value as damages, for an item of like kind.

2. **Defendant Has Added Labor.** If the defendant's labor has been added to the converted property and increased its value, the damages awarded to the plaintiff will be based on the following factors.

    a. **The Range Of Possible Values.** Consider as possibilities a range from the value of the converted property in its original form to the value of the finished product with the defendant's labor added.

    b. **Deterrence And Public Policy.** Did the defendant *know* that the converted property belonged to the plaintiff? A higher damages award acts as a greater deterrent to conduct similar to the defendant's in the future.

ILLUSTRATIVE PROBLEMS

Here are two problems that illustrate how the Checklist can be used to resolve captured and found property questions.

■ PROBLEM 1.1 ■

Sammy Slammer of the Arizona Diamondbacks came to bat in the ninth inning. In his first three at bats, Sammy had hit a single, a double, and a triple. With a home run, Sammy would join an elite group of Major League Baseball players who had hit for the cycle in a single game.

With a full count, the opposing pitcher threw a blazing baseball over the outside corner of the plate. Sammy connected, and the "cycle ball" soared into the sky. The cycle ball cleared the right field bleachers, landed in the parking lot, and bounced high into the air. The ball came to rest in the front seat of Frank Fan's convertible, which was parked on a public street outside of the parking lot.

The parking lot attendant, Paul Parker, who had been following the game on his radio, saw the cycle ball bounce into Fan's car. Parker ran to the car, reached inside, took the cycle ball and put it into his pocket. Parker's co-worker saw the incident and left a note on Fan's windshield telling Fan what happened. Fan read the note after the game ended and learned that the cycle ball had landed inside his car before Parker took the ball from the front seat.

Assume that Paul Parker still has possession of the cycle ball. Frank Fan has filed a conversion claim against Paul Parker seeking the return of the cycle ball. How should the court rule on Fan's conversion claim?

Analysis

By custom and practice, a Major League Baseball home run ball is characterized as abandoned property. Ownership of abandoned property normally belongs to the first person to possess the abandoned property under the rule of first in time, first in right ("FTFR"). The court may, however, consider other public policy factors in deciding whether Fan or Parker has the superior legal right to the cycle ball.

To prevail under the rule of FTFR, Fan must show that he had first possession of the abandoned cycle ball. Possession requires an act of physical control by Fan and the intent to exercise control over the cycle ball. If construed strictly, neither element appears to be satisfied here. Fan was unaware that the cycle ball had landed in his car until *after* Parker had taken the ball.

A court may, however, consider other public policies in determining which claimant should be awarded possession of the cycle ball. Persons generally expect that items inside of their parked cars will not be taken by others. Awarding the cycle ball to Parker may encourage theft by others in the future.

A court also may characterize the location where the cycle ball was found, the inside of a private vehicle, as analogous to the situation where abandoned property is found on exclusively private land. A private landowner is deemed to possess anything that is on his land, even if the landowner does not know the item is there. Just as a private landowner is deemed to possess any item of property found underneath, on, or attached to his land, a court may rule that a car owner like Fan is deemed to possess any tangible personal property inside of his private vehicle.

Finally, the court may consider the conduct of Parker in ruling on Fan's replevin claim. If the inside of Fan's car is like an owner's private land, then by reaching inside of Fan's car to retrieve the cycle ball Parker's conduct was similar to that of a trespasser. Parker did not have permission to reach inside Fan's car. The law generally does not reward trespassers, even those trespassers who are first to possess and capture an item of abandoned property.

For these policy-based reasons, the court is likely to rule in favor of Fan and order Parker to return the cycle ball to Fan.

■ PROBLEM 1.2 ■

In the mountains of Colorado, summer rains can literally wash bits of turquoise from the slag heaps outside of old abandoned mines down the mountain and into the streets of the town of Cripple Creek. One June morning, after a particularly heavy rain the night before, Trisha Tourist found a large rock of raw turquoise in a pile of mud that had collected in the middle of a public road. She put the stone in the pocket of her jeans and continued on her hike.

That night, Trisha went to a local laundromat to wash her clothes. As she went through her pockets, she found the turquoise stone. Trisha set the stone on a counter in the laundromat. She then sat down to read a book while she waited on her laundry.

After reading a few chapters, Trisha decided she needed a cup of coffee. Forgetting about the turquoise stone on the counter, Trisha went next door to the coffee shop. She ran into a few friends in the coffee shop and stayed much longer than she originally intended.

While Trisha was visiting with her friends in the coffee shop, Jim Jeweler came into the laundromat. Jim saw the turquoise stone on the counter, put the stone in his pocket and walked out. Jim cut the stone into bits and made an elaborate necklace and earring set, combining the bits of the turquoise stone with other semi-precious gems.

When Trisha returned from the coffee shop to reclaim her clean and dry clothes and her turquoise stone, she discovered that the stone was gone. Trisha contacted the owner of the laundromat, who reviewed the video surveillance tape of the inside of the laundromat. The owner identified Jim Jeweler, who was a well-known character around town, based on the surveillance tape.

Accompanied by a police officer, Trisha went to Jim Jeweler's house to reclaim her turquoise stone. Jim admitted that he took the stone from the laundromat counter. He showed Trisha the necklace and earring set, which was made in part from bits of Trisha's turquoise stone.

You are the judge. Trisha has brought a conversion claim in your court against Jim seeking damages. The testimony at trial was that the value of the raw turquoise stone is $100 and the value of Jim's necklace and earring set is $1,000. Write a brief judicial opinion ruling on the merits of Trisha's conversion claim and, if applicable, the damages to be awarded to Trisha.

Analysis

Opinion by Judge Student:

To prevail on her conversion claim, Trisha must satisfy the following elements: (1) Jim exercised dominion and control (2) over personal property (the turquoise stone) (3) that was owned by Trisha. The first two elements are undisputed on the facts. The issue in this case concerns whether Trisha had established ownership of the stone by her possession of it.

The raw turquoise stone was captured property when Trisha picked it up from the public road. Trisha became the owner of the stone when she secured possession by picking the stone up and putting it in her pocket. This first possession was sufficient to give Trisha ownership of the stone.

Trisha did not lose or abandon her ownership right to the stone when she placed it on the counter at the laundromat. The stone was mislaid property. Upon seeing the stone on the counter, Jim Jeweler should have acted more honestly by at least turning the stone in to the owner of the laundromat for safekeeping. By taking the stone, Jim converted Trisha's property by (1) exercising control over (2) tangible personal property (3) owned by Trisha, who clearly had established ownership by her first possession of the stone.

In determining the amount of the damages award, the court must weigh the fact that Jim was lawfully on the laundromat premises as a potential customer when he found the stone on the counter. The court also must weigh the fact that a laundromat is the type of business that would suffer if conduct such as Jim's is rewarded. The court further must weigh the fact that Jim's own labor and materials added significantly to the value of the necklace and earring set. Weighing all these factors, the court rules that Jim must pay Trisha $500 (50% of the value of the finished jewelry) as damages on her successful conversion claim.

[Author's Note: The amount of the damages awarded here is presented merely as an example. The important point is the discussion.]

POINTS TO REMEMBER

- Professors play exam games with critical facts. Beware the factual situation that seems similar to a case you read for class, but with a few different facts. Focus on these changes in the facts. The changed facts are likely to suggest that a different rule may apply and a different outcome may result.

- It is wrong to assert that a finder of lost property has superior legal rights against everyone except the true owner. Always remember that, as between two subsequent finders, the first finder who later loses or mislays the found item has the superior legal right over the second finder of the item under the rule of FTFR. The first finder does not forfeit his superior legal right to the found article by subsequently misplacing or losing the item.

- To successfully establish a claim of conversion, the plaintiff is not required to show that the defendant knew that the property belonged to someone else. The defendant's state of mind is irrelevant to proving a claim of conversion or replevin. The defendant's state of mind (bad faith or good faith) may be relevant, however, when determining the measure of damages for a conversion claim.

- If your exam question involves a novel situation with potentially significant consequences for future societal behavior or economic activity, this is your opportunity to discuss theory and public policy. Otherwise, characterize the property as either lost, mislaid or abandoned, apply the appropriate general rule, and move on to solve the problem. Do not waste valuable exam time by overanalyzing straightforward questions involving captured or found property.

CHAPTER 2

Gifts

The concept of a gift arises in three distinct areas of the first-year Property course. For many Property students, the concept is introduced through gifts of tangible personal property. Gifts arise again in the study of partial ownership interests in property, where a donee may receive a present, a future, or a co-ownership interest in the gifted property. Finally, gifts of real property involve unique issues. This chapter addresses the concept of a gift in all three areas.

Although your Property professor may cover gift issues intermittently throughout the course, on the exam (where it really counts) these issues often fit together. Chapter 2 collects the rules on gifts in one place so that you can see how the rules are connected and could be tested on the exam.

GIFTS REVIEW

Elements For A Valid Gift

As with the concept of possession discussed in Chapter 1, a valid gift has two elements. These elements focus on the donor's state of mind and the donor's physical actions. To make a valid gift, the donor must (1) have donative intent and (2) must physically manifest this donative intent by the act of delivery of the gift.

Donative Intent And Gifts Of Future Interests

The donative intent necessary for a valid gift is an intent by the donor to make a *present* (not in the future or at the donor's death), *irrevocable* (not conditional) *transfer* of the gifted property. Although a gift usually entitles the donee to immediate possession of the gift, the donor may gift a future interest in property.[1] In this situation, although the donee does not have the right to present physical possession of the property, the gift of the future interest in the property nevertheless presently is operational and therefore satisfies the donative intent element.

Donative Intent And Conditional Gifts

The donor presently may transfer property to a donee, but with an express or implied condition attached that must be satisfied before the donee will own the property transferred. In these conditional gift situations, the donative intent element is not satisfied until either the condition is fulfilled, or the condition is not fulfilled but the donor fails to revoke the gift within a reasonable period of time.

Methods Of Delivery

The **traditional common law rule** is that manual delivery of the property itself is required for a valid gift. Manual delivery requires the actual physical delivery of the property to the donee.

The **modern view** is that manual delivery is not always required for a valid gift. Rather, delivery must be as perfect as practicable under the circumstances.

Under the modern view, courts have recognized constructive delivery and symbolic delivery as valid types of delivery. Constructive delivery occurs when the donor provides the donee with the sole means of access to the gifted property. The classic example of a constructive delivery is when the donor gives the donee the sole

---

1. *E.g.*, Gruen v. Gruen, 68 N.Y.2d 48, 505 N.Y.S.2d 849, 496 N.E.2d 869 (1986) (father gifts to his son a vested remainder interest in a valuable painting).

key to a safe deposit box or a vault that holds the gift. Symbolic delivery occurs when the donee receives a document or other item that is symbolic of the gifted property itself. The classic example is a writing that declares the donor is giving a valuable item of tangible personal property to the donee along with a photograph of the gifted property.

Special Rule: Delivery Of Gifts Of Real Property

A special rule applies for the delivery of a gift of real property. A gift of real property is valid only if the donor executes a written deed presently conveying the real property (or a partial interest therein, such as a future interest) to the donee. The deed must comply with the execution requirements of the Statute of Frauds[2] and validly be delivered to the donee using manual or constructive delivery.

Delivery Issues

When analyzing delivery issues, the key is to focus on the point of relinquishment of dominion and control by the donor over the gifted property. So long as the donor has the ability to revoke the gift, a valid delivery has not yet occurred.

Note that the donee does not necessarily have to control the gifted property in order for the delivery element to be satisfied. For example, a donor's irrevocable transfer of the gifted property (or, in the case of real estate, the written deed) to an agent of the donee satisfies the delivery element. Handing the gifted property or the deed to an agent of the donor, however, does not satisfy the delivery element. Why? Because the donor's agent is a fiduciary of the donor. If the donor decides to revoke the gift while the gift or the deed is still in the agent's possession, the donor's agent must return the gift or the deed to the donor. Similarly, the donee's control over the sole key to a safe deposit box that holds the gifted property or the deed satisfies the delivery element. But if the box has two keys,

---

2. See Chapter 7, Real Estate Transactions, for the execution requirements for deeds   under the Statute of Frauds.

one for the donor and one for the donee, the delivery element is not satisfied until the donee goes to the box and takes physical control of the gifted property or the deed. Why? Because until the donee takes control of the box's contents, the donor may change her mind, race to the safe deposit box before the donee, and remove the contexts of the box first.

Exam Tip: Analyzing Ambiguous Cases

In ambiguous cases, the donative intent element and the delivery element for a valid gift may interact. For example, very clear and strong evidence of donative intent bolsters the case for a valid gift when delivery has been accomplished by means other than a manual delivery. Conversely, actual manual delivery of the gift provides support for less than compelling evidence of donative intent. On the exam, consider using the stronger element to support the weaker one when analyzing ambiguous circumstances.

Void Testamentary Gifts

The delivery element must be satisfied while the donor is alive. Final and absolute relinquishment of dominion and control over the gift by the donor cannot occur at or as the result of the donor's death. If delivery is not completed while the donor is alive, a court will treat the gift as an invalid **testamentary gift**. A testamentary gift is *void* unless the donor has executed a valid will that devises the "gifted" property to the "donee."

Consequences Of A Failed Lifetime Gift

As a general rule, if the donor fails to satisfy the donative intent and delivery elements while the donor is alive, the property that is the subject of the gift will continue to be owned by the donor. The donor may (while still alive) gift or sell the property that was the subject of a failed lifetime gift to someone else. If the donor dies without gifting or selling the property to someone else, the property that was the subject of a failed lifetime gift will become part of the donor's estate. The personal representative[3] of the donor's estate will distribute the property in the donor's estate to the donor's will beneficiaries (if the donor has a valid will that distributes the property) or to the donor's intestate heirs (if the donor dies without a will that distributes the property).

Gifting Back By The Donee

Once a valid gift has been made, the donee owns the gifted property and the donor cannot later revoke the gift. For the donor to reacquire the gifted property, the donee must validly gift the property back to the donor by independently satisfying the two elements for a valid gift.

So-called "gifting back" issues often arise in the context of gifts of real property. Once the donor gifts an interest in real property to the donee by delivering a properly executed written deed, the donee cannot transfer the real estate back to the donor by merely tearing up the deed. The donee must properly execute and deliver to the donor another written deed that conveys the gifted interest in the real estate from the donee back to the donor.

Gifts of Real Property and Bona Fide Purchasers

On the exam, a gift of real property is easily intertwined with a subsequent transfer (either by the donor or the donee) of the previously gifted real estate to a third party. To understand how these disputes over "Who owns Blackacre?" arise, you must first understand a fundamental rule of real estate transfers. As between a grantor and a grantee (including a donor and a donee) of real estate, the deed *does not need to be recorded* to transfer title to the real estate (or a partial interest therein) from the grantor to the grantee. When applied in the context of a gift, this fundamental rule means

---

3. Modern state probate codes use the generic term "personal representative" to describe the person appointed by the probate court to handle the estate of a decedent who is either testate (died with a will) or intestate (died without a will). Older probate codes use the terms "executor" (male version) or "ex- ecutrix" (female version) to describe the person appointed by the probate court to handle the estate of a testate decedent, and the terms "administrator" (male version) and "administratrix" (female version) to describe the person appointed by the probate court to handle the estate of an intestate decedent.

that the transfer is effective as of the date when both the donative intent and delivery elements are satisfied. This may occur before, on, or after the date written on the deed, and before the deed is actually recorded.

This fundamental rule of real estate transfers means that so long as the donor delivers the deed while the donor is still alive, the donee may record the deed *after* the donor's death. Because recording of the deed is not necessary for a valid gift of real property as between the donor and the donee, recording the deed after the donor's death does *not* make the transfer invalid as a testamentary gift.

When the donor's deed is recorded can matter greatly, however, if a third party **bona fide purchaser** ("BFP") later claims title to the same real estate. Determining whether a BFP holds superior title to the real estate may require analyzing whether the BFP has satisfied the requirements of the jurisdiction's recording act statute.[4]

To analyze real estate title disputes involving donors, donees and BFPs, begin by determining whether the BFP acquired title from the *donor* or the *donee*. These two scenarios (and their possible variations) are summarized in the diagram on the following page. The analysis for each scenario is explained following the diagram.

---

4. *See infra* Chapter 8, Recording Acts and
Adverse Possession.

Analyzing Donor-Donee-BFP Issues

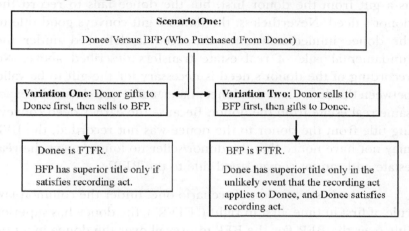

Scenario One:

Donee Versus BFP (Who Purchased From Donor)

Variation One: Donor gifts to Donee first, then sells to BFP.

Variation Two: Donor sells to BFP first, then gifts to Donee.

Donee is FTFR.

BFP has superior title only if satisfies recording act.

BFP is FTFR.

Donee has superior title only in the unlikely event that the recording act applies to Donee, and Donee satisfies recording act.

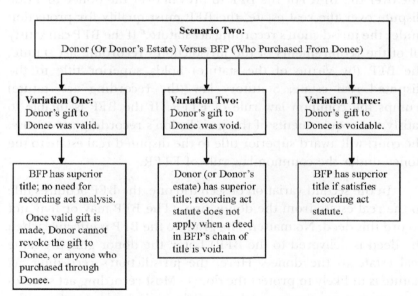

Scenario Two:

Donor (Or Donor's Estate) Versus BFP (Who Purchased From Donee)

Variation One: Donor's gift to Donee was valid.

Variation Two: Donor's gift to Donee was void.

Variation Three: Donor's gift to Donee is voidable.

BFP has superior title; no need for recording act analysis.

Once valid gift is made, Donor cannot revoke the gift to Donee, or anyone who purchased through Donee.

Donor (or Donor's estate) has superior title; recording act statute does not apply when a deed in BFP's chain of title is void.

BFP has superior title if satisfies recording act statute.

Scenario One: Donee Versus BFP (Who Purchased From Donor)

Scenario one involves a challenge brought by a donee against a BFP who purchased the real estate from the donor. Scenario one has two possible variations depending upon who acquired title to the real estate from the donor first—the donee or the BFP.

In the first variation, the donee acquires title to the real estate as a gift from the donor first, but the donee fails to record the donor's deed. Nevertheless, the donor's gift conveys good title to the donee immediately once the deed is delivered under the fundamental rule of real estate transfers described above. No recording of the donor's deed is necessary for the gift to be valid between the donor and the donee. Later, a BFP purchases the exact same real estate from the donor. Because the earlier deed conveying title from the donor to the donee was not recorded, the BFP may not have notice that the donor/seller no longer owns the real estate and cannot convey good title to the BFP.[5]

In the first variation of scenario one, under the common law rule of first in time, first in right ("FTFR"), the donee has superior title over the BFP. For the BFP to prevail over the donee in a title dispute over the real estate, the BFP must qualify for protection under the jurisdiction's recording act statute.[6] If the BFP can satisfy all of the requirements of the jurisdiction's recording act statute, the BFP (by virtue of the statute) holds superior title to the disputed real estate. Statutory law (the recording act statute) trumps the common law rule of FTFR. If the BFP is unable to satisfy the requirements of the jurisdiction's recording act statute, the court will award superior title to the disputed real estate to the donee under the common law rule of FTFR.

In the second variation of scenario one, the BFP acquires title to the real estate from the donor first. (The BFP may or may not record this deed. No matter. The grant to the BFP is effective when the deed is delivered to the BFP.) Later, the donor gifts the same real estate to the donee. Here, the jurisdiction's recording act statute is unlikely to protect the donee. Most recording act statutes only protect purchasers and expressly exclude donees from the protection of the recording act statute. Assuming the recording act

---

5. Notice may be actual, constructive (from the records system), or inquiry notice. *See infra* Chapter 8, Recording Acts and Adverse Possession. If the donee is physically occupying the real estate, then the BFP will be deemed to have inquiry notice. *See id.*

6. *See infra* Chapter 8, Recording Acts and Adverse Possession.

statute does not protect donees, then the BFP holds superior title to the disputed real estate under the common law rule of FTFR.

Scenario Two: Donor (Or Donor's Estate) Versus BFP (Who Purchased From Donee)

Scenario two involves a challenge brought by the donor (or the personal representative of a deceased donor's estate) to title held by a BFP who purchased the real estate from the donee. Scenario two has three variations, depending on whether the original gift from the donor to the donee is valid, void, or merely voidable.

In the first variation, the original gift transferring title to the real estate from the donor to the donee is determined to be valid.[7] Because the gift to the donee is valid, the donee conveys good title to the real estate to the BFP, who holds superior title if later challenged by the donor or the personal representative of the donor's estate. Remember that as a general rule under the law of gifts, once property has been validly gifted away, the donor cannot revoke the gift from the donee, or from anyone else who purchased through the donee.

Note carefully that in the first variation of scenario two, you do *not* rely on a recording act statute as part of your analysis. The first variation of scenario two is simply a straightforward application of the general rule for a valid gift. Once a valid gift is made, it cannot be revoked by the donor.

A more complex analysis is required for the second variation of scenario two. In the second variation, the original gift of the real estate is determined to be void. If the original gift is void, the donee did not acquire good title to the real estate from the donor. The donor's deed purporting to transfer the real estate to the donee may be void because:

- the deed was not delivered to the donee while the donor was still alive (a testamentary gift is void); or

---

7. To determine whether the original gift is valid, you would apply the elements for a valid gift discussed *supra*.

- the donor's signature on the deed is a forgery.

Although the donor's deed gifting the real estate to the donee is void, the deed may have been recorded and relied upon by a BFP who purchased the property from the donee. A popular exam question on this point involves a deed that is not validly delivered to the donee until after the donor's death. Although the attempted gift of the real estate is void as a testamentary gift, the donee nevertheless records the donor's deed.[8] Once the deed to the donee is recorded, in the exam question a BFP may purchase the real estate from the donee/seller in reliance on the recorded deed. Note that under these circumstances, the BFP is unlikely to have notice that the donor's deed conveying title to the donee/seller is void.

In this situation, another fundamental rule of real estate transfers applies. A deed that is void cannot convey good title to anyone. Not to the grantee (here, the donee/seller), or to anyone else who purchases from the grantee, including a subsequent BFP without notice that the prior deed in the donee/seller's chain of title is void. How does the law resolve the void deed situation? Unless a statutory exception[9] applies, the BFP loses in a title dispute over the real estate to the donor (or the donor's estate). This result really stinks for the innocent BFP. Does the innocent BFP have any claim or remedy? Perhaps. The BFP may be able to sue the donee/seller for breach of the covenants in the donee/seller's deed that purported to convey the real estate to the BFP.[10]

In the third variation of scenario two, the donor's original deed gifting the real estate to the donee is voidable. A deed that gifts real estate is voidable (not void) if the element of donative

---

8. This act of recording does not necessarily prove that the donee is a deceitful person. The donee may not know the rule that a testamentary gift is void.

9. To mitigate the harsh effect of this fundamental rule concerning void deeds, some jurisdictions have incorporated as part of the state's recording act statute a conclusive presumption that a deed, once recorded, has been validly delivered. In these conclusive presumption jurisdictions, a BFP without notice is fully protected against a claim that the seller acquired title through an undelivered, and therefore void, deed.

10. *See infra* Chapter 7, Real Estate Transactions (claims based on a breach of deed covenants).

intent for a valid gift is not satisfied. For example, the donor may lack the donative intent necessary for a valid gift because the donor was not of sound mind when the deed was executed by the grantor, or the grantor executed the deed while being unduly influenced (coerced) by the donee, or the donee tricked or defrauded the donor into signing the deed. (Note: If the donor actually signed the deed, the donor's signature is not a forgery, even if the signature was obtained through fraud or deceit.)

To say that a deed is voidable means that the donor (or the personal representative of the donor's estate) can revoke the conveyance of the real estate so long as title is still held by the donee. But what happens if the donee already has conveyed the real estate to someone else? Variation three assumes that the donee has already sold the real estate to a BFP, who acquired title to the real estate without knowledge of the circumstances that make the deed voidable as between the donor and the donee. In this situation, if the BFP satisfies the requirements of the jurisdiction's recording act statute, the court will award superior title to the disputed real estate to the BFP.

Exam Tip: Make Connections Throughout The Course

If you are reading this book at the beginning of your Property course, you may be thinking, "I don't understand this very well." Of course not! You have not yet learned about real estate transactions, the recording act system, BFPs, or deed covenants. These areas of Property law usually are not covered until much later in your Property course. But you are now aware of how these later topics may fit together with the law of gifts. Once you study this more advanced material in class, you can focus on these points of intersection with the law of gifts.

If you are reading this book toward the end of your Property course, you may be thinking, "I have studied real estate transactions, recording acts, and deed covenants, and I do not think I could have made those connections on the fly during the exam." Perhaps you might have, but why leave it to chance? The student who aces Property identifies these types of connections before the

exam. If you think through these points of intersection beforehand, when you spot the issue on the exam you can nail the analysis
and advance yourself to the top of the class.

GIFTS CHECKLIST

With the above Review in mind, the Gifts Checklist is presented
below.

A. ANALYZE THE ELEMENTS FOR A VALID GIFT. Determine if
the gift is valid by analyzing the donative intent and physical
delivery elements.

    1. Donative Intent. Did the donor intend to make a present
and irrevocable transfer of the gifted property? Look to
the oral statements or written words of the donor as
evidence of the donor's state of mind.

        a. Present Transfer. Did the donor indicate that
the transfer of the gifted property was effective
immediately, or did the donor indicate that the
transfer would take place in the future or at the
donor's death instead?

        b. Irrevocable Transfer. Did the donor indicate
that the gifted property absolutely and uncon-
ditionally belonged to the donee, or did the
donor attach conditions that must be satisfied
first?

        **c. Donative Intent And Deeds Conveying Real
Property.** Consider both the written language
on the face of the deed and the circumstances
surrounding execution of the deed by the
donor to determine if the donative intent element is satisfied.

            i. Deed Language. Does the deed lan-
guage itself indicate the donor in-
tended to make a present and irre-

vocable transfer of the real estate (or an interest therein) to the donee? Or, does the language of the deed suggest that the transfer will take place sometime in the future?

    ii. Surrounding Circumstances. Even if the deed language indicates the donor intended to make a present irrevocable transfer, do the surrounding circumstances indicate that the donor did not intend for the transfer to be effective immediately, that the transfer was conditional or revocable, or that the transfer was effective only upon the donor's death?

2. Physical Delivery. Did the donor relinquish physical dominion and control over the gifted property (or a written deed conveying an interest in real property) while the donor was alive? Look to the surrounding circumstances and the type of delivery to determine if the gifted property was validly delivered.

    a. Donor's Lack Of Physical Control. Is there any possibility that, while still alive, the donor had the power to revoke the gifted property? **If yes**, a valid lifetime delivery did not occur (even if the donor never actually asserted such power).

    b. Donee's Physical Control Not Always Necessary. Depending on the circumstances and the type of property interest transferred, the donee's physical control over or receipt of the gifted property may not be necessary for a valid delivery by the donor.

        i. Delivery To Donee's Agent. Delivery to an agent of the donee satisfies the delivery element once the agent of the donee acquires control of the gifted property.

ii. **Delivery Of Future Or Co–Ownership Interest Without Present Possession.** The donee's present physical possession of the gifted property is not required for a valid delivery of a future or co-ownership interest.

c. **Rule Against Testamentary Gifts.** Was the act of delivery finalized or completed at or due to the donor's death? **If yes**, the attempted transfer of the gifted property is void as a testamentary gift (unless the donor also executed a valid will devising the property to the donee).

d. **Method of Delivery.** The traditional rule is that manual delivery is required. The modern view is that delivery must be as perfect as practicable under the circumstances. If constructive or symbolic delivery is involved, focus on the donor's relinquishment of dominion and control as the touchstone for a valid delivery.

i. **Manual.** Manual delivery requires actual physical delivery of gifted personal property or, for real property, the deed itself, to the donee or the donee's agent.

ii. **Constructive.** Constructive delivery requires that the donor must provide the donee with the sole means of accessing the gifted property.

iii. **Symbolic.** In a symbolic delivery, the donor provides the donee with a symbol of the gifted property in lieu of the gifted personal property itself. Symbolic delivery cannot be used for gifts of an interest in real estate.

3. **Interrelationship Between Evidence Of Donative Intent And Physical Delivery.** Consider whether strong evi-

dence of delivery can be used to bolster ambiguous or weak evidence of donative intent, and vice versa.

4. **General Rule For Failure To Make A Valid Lifetime Gift.** If the gift is invalid, the donor still owns the property and can transfer the property (by gift or sale) to someone else while the donor is alive. If no subsequent transfer occurs while the donor is alive, at the donor's death the property becomes part of the donor's estate. The personal representative of the donor's estate will distribute the estate property to either the donor's will beneficiaries or intestate heirs.

5. **Gifting Back By The Donee.** Once the donor makes a valid gift to the donee, the donor cannot revoke the gift. To return ownership of the gifted property back to the donor, the donee independently must satisfy the donative intent and delivery elements for a valid gift. For real property, this requires proper execution and delivery of a written deed that conveys the gifted real estate interest from the donee as grantor back to the donor as grantee.

B. **CHALLENGES TO TITLE INVOLVING DONORS, DONEES AND BONA FIDE PURCHASERS OF REAL ESTATE.** For disputes between the donor and the donee, proceed to Part B.1 of the checklist. For disputes between a donee and a BFP who purchased from the donor, proceed to Part B.2 of the checklist. For disputes between a donor (or the donor's estate) and a BFP who purchased from a donee, proceed to Part B.3 of the checklist.

1. **Disputes Between Donor And Donee.** If title to the gifted real estate is still held by the donee, the donor (or the personal representative of the donor's estate) may revoke the gift if the donor's deed conveying the real estate to the donee is *voidable*. A deed is voidable if the element of donative intent necessary for a valid gift is not satisfied. A deed may be voidable if the donor executed the deed while of unsound mind, under duress or undue influence by the donee, or through fraud or trickery.

   a. **Recording Of Deed Not Required.** As between the donor and the donee, the deed does not need to be recorded to be a valid transfer of title to the donee. The transfer is effective as of the date that the elements for a valid gift are satisfied (not the date of the deed or the date of recording).

b. **Recording Of Delivered Deed After Donor's Death.** A deed that is validly delivered to the donee during the donor's lifetime may be recorded by the donee after the donor's death.

c. **Common Law Rule On Void Testamentary Gifts.** A deed conveying an interest in real property that is not validly delivered to the donee while the donor is alive is void and cannot convey good title to the donee.

d. **Effect Of Failed Delivery Or Lack Of Donative Intent If Donee Has Not Transferred The Real Estate.** If the attempted gift of the real estate to the donee is invalid due to a failed delivery or lack of donative intent, refer to Part A.4 of the checklist for the consequences of failing to make a valid gift of the real estate.

2. **Disputes Involving Donee Versus BFP Who Bought From Donor.** Determine who acquired title to the disputed real estate first in time from the donor.

a. **Donee Is First.** Did the BFP have notice of the prior transfer of title to the donee? If the BFP lacked notice, the BFP holds superior title to the disputed real estate if the BFP can satisfy the requirements of the jurisdiction's recording act statute. If the BFP cannot satisfy the recording act statute, then the donee holds superior title to the disputed real estate under the common law rule of FTFR.

b. **BFP Is First.** Assuming the jurisdiction's recording act statute does not cover donees, then the BFP has superior title to the disputed real estate under the common law rule of FTFR.

3. **Disputes Involving Donor (Or Donor's Estate) Versus BFP Who Bought From Donee.** Determine if the donor's gift to the donee is valid, void, or voidable.

    a. **Donor's Gift Is Valid.** The donor's gift is valid if the donative intent and delivery elements are satisfied. Refer to Part A of the checklist to determine if these elements are satisfied. If the donor's gift is valid, the donee acquired good title to the real estate via the gift from the donor and therefore transferred superior title to the disputed real estate to the BFP.

    b. **Donor's Gift Is Void.** The donor's gift is void if the deed was not delivered to the donee while the donor was still alive, or if the donor's signature on the deed is a forgery. A deed that is void cannot convey good title to the donee. If the donee has no title due to a void deed, then the BFP cannot acquire good title from the donee, even if the BFP purchased the property from the donee without notice of the prior void deed in the donee/seller's chain of title. The donor (or the donor's estate) holds superior title to the disputed real estate.

    c. **Donor's Gift Is Voidable.** The donor's gift of the real estate to the donee is voidable (and can be revoked so long as title is held by the donee) if the element of donative intent required for a valid gift is not satisfied. A deed may be voidable if the donor executed the deed while of unsound mind, under duress or undue influence by the donee, or through fraud or trickery. As between the donor and the BFP, the BFP holds superior title to the real estate if the BFP can satisfy the requirements of the jurisdiction's recording act statute.

ILLUSTRATIVE PROBLEMS

Here are two problems that illustrate how the Checklist can be used to resolve gift questions.

■ **PROBLEM 2.1** ■

Donor maintained a mailbox at a local retail store. The mailbox, which was located in the lobby of the store, was opened by dialing a sequence of numbers. Donor kept $1,000 in cash inside of the mailbox.

Donor and her best friend, Donee, were driving together in a winter snow storm. Their vehicle slid off the road and became stuck in a ditch. They decided to remain in the car and wait out the storm. Donee confessed to Donor that Donee was having financial difficulties that could be solved for $1,000. Donor told Donee the combination necessary to open her mail box, saying, "As soon as we get this car back on the road, I'll give you the $1,000." A few hours after this conversation, the State Highway Patrol rescued the pair.

One week later, Donor had a heart attack and died intestate (without a will). When Donee learned the news, she went to the store, opened the mailbox using the combination, and removed the $1,000 in cash.

You have been appointed as the personal representative of Donor's estate. Should you bring a claim seeking the return of the $1,000 held by Donee on behalf of Donor's estate? State "yes" or "no" and briefly explain the reasoning for your decision.

Analysis

Yes, as the personal representative of Donor's estate I will file a claim against Donee seeking the return of the $1,000. My legal theory is that Donor did not make a valid gift of the $1,000 to Donee while Donor was still alive.

The conversation in the car between Donor and Donee indicated that Donor lacked the donative intent necessary for a valid lifetime gift. Donor's statements while in the car indicated that Donor intended to make a gift of the $1,000 to her friend Donee in the future ("as soon as we get this car unstuck"), rather than to make a presently effective transfer.

The delivery requirement for a valid gift also is not satisfied under these circumstances. Although under the modern rule manual delivery is not necessarily required for a valid gift, delivery of the gift of $1,000 in cash must be as perfect as possible under the circumstances. Donor could have manually delivered the $1,000 cash gift to Donee during the week before Donor died, but failed to do so.

Donee is likely to argue that a constructive delivery occurred when Donor told Donee the combination to open the mailbox. Donor, however, also had access to the mailbox and could have withdrawn the $1,000 at any time until Donor's death one week later. Donor did not relinquish dominion and control over the $1,000 cash in the mailbox while the Donor was alive. Therefore, the transfer of the $1,000 to Donee is void as a testamentary gift, and the money belongs to the Donor's estate.

■ **PROBLEM 2.2** ■

At age 85, Grandmother Jessica Sanders still lived alone in her house. Her grandson, Joe Jones, visited her frequently and helped his grandmother by mowing the yard and doing repairs and improvements around the house. Grandmother Jessica was very grateful for Joe's help and often told him, "This house will be yours when I die."

One Saturday night, after Joe had been working at the house all day, Joe told his grandmother that he could not help her anymore "unless I'm getting something for the work." Grandmother Jessica started to cry because she had become so emotionally and physically dependent on Joe's help. Without Joe around, she was afraid that she would have to live in a nursing home. Grandmother Jessica took out a pen and paper and wrote the following:

DEED

I, Jessica Sanders, hereby give my house, located at 236 Hunt Court in Blueview, California, to my grandson Joe Jones.

/date/   /signature of Jessica Sanders/

(Assume that this writing satisfied the jurisdiction's Statute of Frauds).

As Joe was leaving for the night, Grandmother Jessica handed him the above-described Deed and a spare set of keys to the house, telling Joe, "I want you to have something now so you will keep taking care of me and my house. Joe thanked his grandmother and told her, "Granny, I hope you can live here forever."

A few weeks later, Grandmother Jessica fell and broke her hip. After surgery and a lengthy hospital stay, she moved into a rehabilitation facility for therapy. Believing that his grandmother would never be able to return to live at the house, Joe recorded the Deed and sold the house to Bert and Beju Buyer. The Buyers were without notice of the earlier conversation between Grandmother Jessica and Joe or the circumstances surrounding the delivery of the Deed. The Buyers promptly recorded their deed from Joe after the closing. (Assume that these facts are sufficient for the Buyers to be protected as bona fide purchasers under the jurisdiction's recording act statute.)

Grandmother Jessica miraculously made tremendous progress at the rehabilitation facility. One day, the physical therapist told her that she could return home. Grandmother Jessica called Joe and told him to come get her and take her back to live at her house. Joe explained that he had sold the house to the Buyers.

Grandmother Jessica has come to you for legal advice. She wants to know whether she successfully can sue the Buyers and recover title to and possession of her house. Advise Grandmother Jessica.

Analysis

Whether Grandmother Jessica can recover the title to her house depends on whether the Deed gifting the house to Joe was void, valid or voidable. Here, a court is likely to find that the Deed was valid or merely voidable. Consequently, a court is likely to rule that the Buyers have superior title to the house.

A deed purporting to convey the title to real estate is void if it is delivered after the grantor's death or if the grantor's signature is a forgery. A void deed in the chain of title cannot convey good title to subsequent grantees, even grantees that are bona fide purchasers such as the Buyers. The facts indicate that Grandmother Jessica executed the Deed conveying the title to the house to Joe, and that she manually delivered the Deed to Joe. Therefore, a court is unlikely to rule that Grandmother Jessica's Deed to Joe was void.

A court is likely to rule that the Deed was either a valid gift to Joe, or that the Deed was merely voidable as between Grandmother Jessica and Joe, but not as to the Buyers. A valid gift requires that the donor must intend to make the present irrevocable transfer of the gifted property and must deliver the gift. Gifts of real estate can only be delivered by the manual or constructive delivery of a properly executed deed. Here, the Deed was manually delivered to Joe. Therefore, the delivery requirement for a valid gift of the house was satisfied. The issue is whether Grandmother Jessica intended to make a present and irrevocable transfer of title to the house to Joe at the time the Deed was delivered, and whether she was unduly influenced by Joe to make the gift.

The words of the Deed ("I hereby give") indicated an intent to make a presently effective transfer of title to the house to Joe. The oral statements made at the time of the delivery of the Deed to Joe ("here's something now") indicate a present intent. Joe's reply, ("I hope you can live here forever") suggests that there might have been an understanding that the transfer of title to the house to Joe would not take effect until sometime in the future. Thus, the circumstantial evidence of Grandmother Jessica's intent is ambiguous. A court may find that the Jessica's dependence on Joe, coupled with Joe's threat to stop his visits, unduly influenced Jessica's decision to make the gift and rendered the gift to Joe voidable.

Assuming that the court finds that the Deed purporting to convey title to the house to Joe was either valid or voidable, the Buyers will prevail in a title dispute over the house with Grandmother Jessica. If the Deed was valid, then Joe later conveyed superior title to the Buyers. Grandmother Jessica cannot revoke a valid gift by attempting to revoke the title acquired by the Buyers from Joe. If the Deed was voidable, the Buyers are bona fide purchasers who are protected by the jurisdiction's recording act statute. Thus, in a title dispute with Grandmother Jessica, even if the Deed is voidable due to undue influence the Buyers will prevail by virtue of the recording act statute in a title dispute with Grandmother Jessica.

POINTS TO REMEMBER

- Once made, a valid gift is irrevocable. The donor can reacquire the gifted property only if the donee, in turn, validly gifts the property back to the donor.

- A present (immediately effective) transfer of a future interest or a co-ownership in property satisfies the donative intent element, even though the donee may not have physical possession of the property.

- A valid gift of real property can only be accomplished by the execution and delivery of a written deed conveying the real property (or a partial interest therein) to the donee. Oral statements and destruction of the donor's deed do not transfer interests in real estate.

- A deed gifting real property is immediately effective upon delivery of the deed to the donee; recording of the deed is not required for a valid transfer as between a grantor and a grantee. The transfer of title to the donee is effective when both elements for a valid gift (donative intent and delivery) are satisfied (not as of a contrary date on the deed, or a later date of recording).

CHAPTER 3

Present and Future Interests

Present and future interests are the Achilles' heel of many first-year Property students. For this reason, Chapter 3 contains an expanded Review and multiple charts to help you visualize present and future interests.

To excel in this area of your Property course, focus on developing the two skills you must perform on the final exam. First, learn how to classify the various types of present and future interests based on the language of the grant. Second, master the attributes and characteristics of each type of present and future interest.

If you can acquire these two fundamental skills, and perform a Rule Against Perpetuities ("RAP") analysis,[1] you will move to the top of your Property class. (This is, of course, much easier said than done, so read on.)

PRESENT AND FUTURE INTERESTS REVIEW

Let's begin with an overview of the universe of present and future interests and a system for reducing the cumbersome

---

1. *See infra*, Chapter Four, The Rule Against Perpetuities.

vocabulary. In the summary below, main categories are marked by squares (■) and subtypes within a main category are marked by dots (•). The shorthand abbreviation for each interest is in parentheses.

Summary Of Present Interests

■ Fee Simple Absolute (FSA)

■ The Defeasible Fee Simples

   • Fee Simple Determinable (FSD)

   • Fee Simple Subject to Condition Subsequent (FSSCS)

   • Fee Simple Subject to Executory Limitation (FSSEL)

■ Fee Tail (FT)

■ Life Estate (LE)

■ Term of Years (TY)

Summary Of Future Interests Retained By The Grantor

■ Possibility of Reverter (PR)

■ Right of Entry (RE)[2]

■ Reversion (REV)

Summary Of Future Interests Created In Third Parties

■ Remainders

   • Contingent Remainder (CR)

   • Vested Remainder (VR)

   • Vested Remainder Subject to Open (VRSO)[3]

   • Vested Remainder Subject to Total Divestment (VRSTD)[4]

---

2. This future interest is also known as a power of termination.

3. This future interest is also known as a vested remainder subject to partial divestment.

4. A VRSO can be combined with a VRSTD to create the VRSO and STD.

■ Executory Interests (EI)

  • Springing Executory Interest

  • Shifting Executory Interest

Pairings Of Present And Future Interests

Present and future interests come in certain types of combinations. You should approach the grant language by classifying each interest in sequence, starting with the present interest.

Every year, my first-year Property students ask me, "Isn't there an easier way to learn future interests?" The charts on the following page respond to this request, but not exactly in the manner you may hope. To utilize the charts effectively, you need to have a firm grasp on the underlying theory. After a brief explanation of how the charts work, the Review will explain the underlying theory and provide exam strategies and tips. As you read the Review, periodically refer back to these summary charts.

The first summary chart shows the pairings for a present interest (first column) and its corresponding first future interest. The second column shows the pairing if the first future interest is retained by the grantor (expressly or implicitly, as we will see). The third column shows the pairing if the grantor transfers the first future interest to a third party other than the grantor.

Pairings Of The Present And The First Future Interest

Present	Future (Grantor)	Future (Third Party)
FSA	None	None
FSD	PR	None[5]
FSSCS	RE	None
FSSEL	None	EI (shifting)
FT, LE,[6] TY	REV	Remainder[7]
Determinable FT, LE, TY	REV	EI (shifting)
None (Grantor retains present interest)	REV	EI (springing)

The language of the grant may contain more than one future interest. The second summary chart below shows the combinations for the first and second (and sometimes a third) future interest. Further explanation follows this chart. Although this second chart may be a bit intimidating at first, it will be enormously helpful once you understand the theory that underlies the chart.

Combinations Of Multiple Future Interests

1st Future Interest	2nd Future Interest (Third Party)	2nd or 3rd Future Interest (Grantor)
CR	CR	REV
VRSTD or VRSO and STD	EI (shifting)	REV or None if EI is held in FSA
	VR/VRSO in FSA	None
VRSO or VR in LE, TY, or FT	CR (of any duration)	REV
	VR/VRSO in LE, TY, or FT	REV
	None	REV
VRSO or VR in FSA	None	None

---

5. Some student study aids may indicate that an EI can follow a FSD. This is not correct. The FSD must be classified as a FSSEL for the future interest to be classified as an EI. *See* THOMAS F. BERGIN & PAUL G. HASKELL, PREFACE TO ESTATES IN LAND AND FUTURE INTERESTS, 112 (1984) ("Bergin & Haskell").

6. References to a LE include the life estate pur autre vie. *See infra* Categories of Present Interests.

7. The possible types of remainders are the CR, the VR, the VRSO, and/or the VRSTD. *See infra* Remainder Subtype Analysis.

The pairings in the first two rows of the second chart are the ones that students tend to have the most difficulty in recognizing. Because a CR always follows a CR, and a shifting EI always follows a VRSTD (including a VSRO that is also subject to total divestment, the key is to classify correctly the first future interest as either a CR or a VRSTD.[8]

The third row of the second chart is more complex because it summarizes multiple possible pairings that can arise when the *first future interest* conveyed to an individual (VR) or a not-yet-closed class of individuals (VRSO) is *limited in duration to something less than a FSA*. If the second future interest in the sequence is held by a third party, this second future interest must be some type of remainder. Let's work down the various boxes in the second column of the third row of the chart (the boxes identifying the *second* future interest held by a third party) in order.

If the second future interest to a third party is a VR or a VRSO held in FSA, then the grantor does not hold any future interest. If the second future interest to a third party is a CR (of any duration), then the grantor holds a REV. If the second future interest is a VR or a VRSO of limited duration (it is held in something less than FSA), then the grantor holds a REV. Finally, if the grant creates a first future interest of limited duration (something less than FSA), but there is no second future interest granted to a third party, the grantor holds a REV.

This discussion assumes, of course, that the grant contains only one present interest and two future interests. A grant having more than two future interests is most likely going to be a string of remainders, each held in life estate.

The fourth row of the chart shows the obvious. If the first future interest is to an individual (VR) or to a not-yet-closed class of individuals (VRSO), but the duration is in FSA, then there are no more future interests. The grantor has conveyed away the entire FSA.

---

8. *See infra* Exam Tip: Distinguishing Pre-conditions (CR) From Conditions Subsequent (VRSTD).

Illustrations And Identification Tips For Classifying Present Interests

The explanation below uses the "code" for how professors usually discuss present and future interests. "O" is the grantor. "A" has the present interest. "B" holds the first future interest. "C" holds the second future interest. A, B, and C may be individuals, or they may be a group of individuals (a "class").

Some of the illustrations below tell you to assume certain facts about who is alive and who is dead "at the time the grant is made." The grant is made when it becomes effective to transfer a property interest. For property rights transferred by a will (a "devise"), the grant becomes effective at the time of the death of the testator O. For property rights created by inter vivos transfer (a transfer made by the grantor O while O is still alive), the grant becomes effective when the transfer becomes irrevocable, either under the property law of gifts[9] or under the law of contracts in the case of a sale.

■ Fee Simple Absolute (FSA)

Common law language: "to A and his heirs"
                      "to A and her heirs"
                      "to the children of A and their heirs"
Modern language: "to A"

Under the common law rule, a conveyance by O "to A" granted only a LE to A, not a FSA. For O to convey a FSA to A, the magical words of limitation ("and his heirs," "and her heirs," or "and their heirs") had to be added. Modern statutes create a rebuttable presumption that if O owns a FSA in the property and grants the property "to A," then O conveyed a FSA to A (thereby making the cumbersome "and his/her/their heirs" language unnecessary).

Your professor may be a stickler for the common law rule, or may prefer the modern statutory presumption for conveyance of a FSA. For the exam, know your professor's idiosyncrasies and pay

---

9. *See supra*, Chapter 2, Gifts.

careful attention to the exam instructions concerning the governing law (common law or modern statute).

■ Life Estates (LE)

Common law language: "to A"
Modern language: "to A for life"

At common law, a grant "to A" was presumed to convey only a LE and not a FSA. In jurisdictions that have adopted the modern statutory presumption that a grant "to A" conveys a FSA (and not a LE), to convey a LE the granting language must be "to A for life" (or similar words to that effect).

The life estate pur autre vie (literally, "for the life of another"), is created by the language "to A for the life of B." When B dies, A's present interest is extinguished, because it lasts only for the duration of B's life.

What happens if O conveys the property "to A for life" and A later transfers her life estate interest to B? A cannot change the original duration of A's interest by conveying A's life estate to someone else.[10] In this situation, B has a life estate pur autre vie, which lasts for the life of A. B's present interest will terminate and be extinguished at A's death.

■ Fee Tail (FT)

Common law language: "to A and the heirs of A's body"

Modernly, most jurisdictions by statute have abolished the FT. Jurisdictions that have abolished the FT generally construe the above language in one of two ways. Either the language is construed as creating a FSA in A, or the language is construed as creating a life estate in A, followed by a VR in FSA in A's heirs.[11]

---

10. This is just one of many illustrations of the fundamental Property rule that a grantor cannot convey more property rights, or a different set of property rights, than the grantor actually owns. The grantor can, however, always convey a lesser property right

than the grantor owns and retain a REV in the property.

11. *Heirs* is a technical term that describes those individuals who, as of the moment of the decedent's death (and not before), are

■ Term of Years (TY)

Common law language: "to A for ten years"

The TY provides an intellectual bridge from present and future interests to landlord and tenant law. The TY present interest is a lease giving exclusive possession of the real estate to A for a fixed period.[12]

■ The Defeasible Fee Simples (FSD, FSSCS, FSSEL)

The three defeasible fee simples have one attribute in common. The fee interest held by A is not absolute, but rather may be divested and could belong to someone else if a specified event occurs. At early common law, only two defeasible fee simples could be created—the FSD and the FSSCS. After the enactment of the Statute of Uses in 1536, a third defeasible fee simple—the FSSEL— became possible.

Examples Of Language Creating Defeasible Fee Simples

The grants below illustrate language that creates each type of defeasible fee simple.

FSD: "to A and his heirs so long as the property is used as a farm. Once the property ceases to be used as a farm, title shall revert back to O."

FSSCS: "to A and his heirs, but if the property ceases to be used as a farm, then O has a right of reentry."

FSSEL: "to A and his heirs so long as the property is used as a farm, but if the property ceases to be used as a farm, then to B and his heirs."

Many students have difficulty distinguishing between the three defeasible fee simples. Below are two exam tips to assist you in correctly identifying a FSD, a FSSCS and a FSSEL.

---

identified as succeeding to ownership of the decedent's property under the state's intestate succession statute. Thus, a living person has no ascertainable heirs.

12. *See infra*, Chapter 6, Landlord and Tenant.

Exam Tip: FSSEL Versus FSD/FSSCS

When examining grant language, begin by distinguishing the FSD or the FSSCS from the FSSEL. To do this, determine who will receive the property after A's present interest is terminated by the occurrence of the defeasing event. If the future interest holder who is next in the line of succession is a third party (B) (not the grantor O), then A's present interest is a FSSEL.[13]

If the grant language is silent concerning who owns the property next after the defeasing event occurs, the property automatically reverts back to the grantor O. In this situation, A's present interest must be either a FSD or a FSSCS.

Exam Tip: FSD Versus FSSCS

If you have ruled out the FSSEL because O holds the future interest that follows A's defeasible fee simple, there are three classic signals that will help you to determine whether A holds a FSD or a FSSCS. These signals are: (1) the punctuation of the grant language; (2) the ("magic") words used in the grant; and (3) the characteristics of the grantor O's retained future interest.

Signal: Punctuation

Is the defeasing event in the same clause as the grant to A (a FSD signal)? Or, is the defeasing event separated from the clause granting the property to A by some sort of punctuation (a FSSCS signal)? To illustrate, in each of the examples below the "granting clause" ends with the comma.

Example of a defeasing event in the granting clause to A: "to A as long as the land is used for a church,"

Example of a defeasing event separated by punctuation from the granting clause to A: "to A, on the condition that the land must be used for a church."

Signal: "Magic" Words

The law of Property strongly associates the following "magic" words with the creation of either a FSD or a FSSCS. The FSD magic

---

13. The third party (B) holds a shifting EI.
See infra Executory Interests.

words suggest duration or the passage of time. The FSSCS magic words suggest a condition, limitation, or restriction on the nature or use of A's present interest.

FSD Magic Words	FSSCS Magic Words
so long as	if
as long as	but if
until	provided
while	however
during	on the condition
	subject to the condition

The above lists of magic words provide only a starting point for analysis. The words of a grant on your exam may be different from the magic words on the above lists. In that case, focus on the similarities and differences between the grant language on the exam and the classic magic words listed above. Try to make linguistic arguments that the exam language suggests either the duration or passage of time (FSD), or instead suggests a condition, limitation, or restraint on the use of the property (FSSCS).

Signal: O's Retained Interest

Does the grant indicate that upon the occurrence of the defeasing event, O's retained interest automatically reverts back to O (a FSD signal)? Or does the grant indicate that O must take some type of action (enter upon the property, or affirmatively terminate A's interest) to reclaim present possession of the property upon the occurrence of the defeasing event (a FSSCS signal)?

Example of an automatic PR: "then ownership of the property *shall return* to O"

Example of a RE: "then O *may reclaim and retake* ownership of the property"

If O's future interest is not expressly described in the language of the grant, then O's future interest is implied. If O's future interest is implied, you must determine whether A has a FSD (O has a PR) or a FSSCS (O has a RE) using only the first two signals–punctuation and magic words.

Exam Tip: Ambiguous Grant Language

On an essay question, you should expect to see ambiguous or "mixed" signals that indicate either a FSD or a FSSCS may have been created. In this situation, recognize that there are two possibilities, make the best argument for each possible classification (FSD or FSSCS), and then move on to do an attributes and characteristics analysis for each possibility. Problem 3.3 at the end of Chapter 3 provides an opportunity for you to practice analyzing a grant that may have created either a FSD or FSSCS.

Sometimes the grant language on the exam is designed to ferret out students who have just memorized words and phrases. Consider the following grant:

"to A until March 31, 2020"

The Property student who just memorized the lists of magic words may seize upon the word "until" and conclude that this grant conveys a FSD to A. The more thoughtful Property student will recognize that this grant language creates a TY because A's present interest lasts for a fixed period and terminates at a set time, rather than terminating upon an indeterminate event or occurrence.

Key Attributes And Characteristics: FSD Versus FSSCS

When performing an attributes and characteristics analysis for a FSD or a FSSCS, focus on the statute of limitations and the transferability of the future interest (PR or RE) as distinguishing characteristics. Finally, always consider the possibility that the defeasible fee simple may be void as a restraint on alienation. These attributes and characteristics are described below.

- **Statute of Limitations.** Distinguishing correctly between the FSD and the FSSCS may be important because the triggering event that starts the statute of limitations differs for each defeasible fee simple. Let's begin with the common law rules. If A holds a FSD, once the defeasing event occurs the statute of limitations immediately begins to run against the grantor O, who holds the corresponding future interest (the PR). O must claim her right to ownership of the fee estate against A within the statute of limitations period. If O fails to do so and the statute of limitations expires, then O is forever barred from claiming the property, and A effectively owns the property in FSA.

In contrast, the statute of limitations for the FSSCS does not begin to run against the grantor O until O asserts her right to enter and take the property (or, exercises the power to terminate A's present interest) and is rebuffed by A. As a practical matter, the grantor O may not learn that the defeasing event or condition has occurred until many years after the fact. Thus, the characterization of A's defeasible fee as a FSD or a FSSCS can mean the difference between a claim by O that is barred by the statute of limitations (FSD), and a claim by O that is successful (FSSCS).

Modernly, some jurisdictions by state statute establish a "cut-off" that voids O's PR or the RE if the defeasing event does not occur within a set period of years after the creation of A's FSD or FSSCS. For example, the jurisdiction by statute may invalidate O's PR or a RE (thereby awarding a FSA to A by operation of law) if the defeasing event has not occurred within 30 years after the creation of A's defeasible fee.[14] If your professor highlights a jurisdiction-specific statutory rule such as this one, pay attention. Be prepared to discuss both the common law rule and the jurisdiction-specific statutory rule on the exam.

  • **Transferability.** Distinguishing between a FSD and a FSSCS may be important because the jurisdiction could have different rules for whether the future interest held by O (or O's estate, if O is deceased) is *alienable*[15] and *devisable*,[16] or only *inheritable*.[17] This is another area where the common law may be superceded by a jurisdiction-specific statutory rule.

---

14. *See, e.g.*, Neb. Rev. Stat. § 76–107(b).

15. If the future interest is alienable, O can gift or sell the interest to someone else during O's lifetime.

16. If the future interest is devisable, O's will can direct who owns the future interest at O's death (assuming that O has not otherwise

gifted or sold the future interest away while O was alive).

17. If the future interest is only inheritable, then O cannot gift or sell the future interest to someone else during O's lifetime. A future interest held by O that is solely inheritable must pass to O's statutory intestate heirs at O's death.

The **common law rule** is that O only may transfer a PR or a RE during O's lifetime to the owner of FSD or the FSSCS. The technical term for this type of permitted lifetime transfer by O is a release. Under the common law rule, any attempt by O to transfer a PR or a RE during O's lifetime to someone else is void. Similarly, under the common law rule at O's death any attempt to devise a PR or RE under O's will is void. At O's death, the PR or RE must go to O's statutorily-determined intestate heirs if O has not released the PR or RE to A while O was still alive.

The **modern trend** is to change the common law rule governing the transferability of a PR or a RE by statute. Again, jurisdictions vary. Both the PR and the RE may, by statute, be made freely alienable and/or devisable by the grantor O. Or, the jurisdiction may modify the common rule for only one or the other of these two future interests. If your professor highlights a jurisdiction-specific statutory rule, pay attention. Be prepared to discuss both the common law rule and the jurisdiction-specific statutory rule on the exam.

• **Restraints on Alienation**. A FSD or FSSCS conveyed to a charitable organization or a governmental entity with a defeasing event tied to use of the property for charitable, public, or governmental purposes generally will not be struck down as an invalid restraint on alienation. If a FSD or a FSSCS is conveyed to a private owner, however, and the defeasing event is unrelated to use of the property for charitable or public purposes, then the owner may be successful in having the defeasible event struck from the title as an invalid restraint on alienation.

Whether a court will strike a defeasing event as an invalid restraint on alienation turns on the market pool of buyers who are willing to continue to use the property in a manner that is consistent with the terms of the defeasing event. The smaller the market pool of potential buyers, the more likely a court will be to void the defeasing event as invalid restraint on alienation, and rule that A holds a FSA.

Illustrations And Identification Tips For Classifying Future Interests

Until now, Chapter 3 has focused primarily on the present interest held by A. The remainder of Chapter 3 focuses on the types of future interests that may be retained by the grantor O or conveyed by O as part of the language of the grant to a third party (B, C, etc.).

Future Interests Retained By The Grantor O

Two of the three possible future interests that may be retained by the grantor O, the PR and the RE, were discussed above in the context of the defeasible fee simple. The PR always is paired with the FSD, and the RE always is paired with the FSSCS. The third future interest that may be retained by the grantor O—the "catch-all" reversion (REV)—is explained below.

■ Reversion (REV) Versus PR And RE

A REV is the name given to any future interest retained by the grantor O whenever O transfers (either as a present interest or as a combination of present and future interests) *something less than the estate originally held by O.* For example, if O has a FSA, and transfers a LE to A, then O retains a REV.

The exception to this general rule is where O has a FSA and transfers a FSD or a FSSCS to A. In this situation, O's retained future interest is not a REV. Why? Because the "estate" O transferred to A was a "fee simple"—the same basic type of estate that O originally possessed. O's retained future interest is either a PR or a RE, depending on whether A's defeasible fee simple is a FSD or a FSSCS.

Unlike the PR and the RE, a REV is almost always implied from the language of the grant rather than being expressly retained by O. The law assumes that you can add up the total duration of the interests conveyed by O and determine whether or not O has retained an interest in the property conveyed.[18]

In most instances, O will have started out with a FSA. But suppose O started out with something less than a FSA, such as a 50 year TY. If O conveys a 20 year term of years to A, O's retained future interest is called a REV, not a "30 year future term of years." Why? A TY can only be a present interest; it can never be a future interest. Thus, O's retained future interest must be classified as a REV.

Transferability Of A REV

Unlike the PR and a RE, under the **common law rule** a REV is freely *alienable* during O's life and *devisable* by O's will at O's death. A REV is *inheritable* by O's intestate heirs if O dies without a will.

Future Interests Created In Third Parties

There are two main categories of future interests that may be created in a third party other than the grantor O. These two main categories are **remainders** and **executory interests**.

Within the main category of remainders, there are four subtypes:

- Vested Remainder (VR)

- Contingent Remainder (CR)

- Vested Remainder Subject to Open (VRSO)

- Vested Remainder Subject to Total Divestment (VRSTD)

Within the main category of executory interests, there are two subtypes:

- Shifting Executory Interest (Shifting EI)

- Springing Executory Interest (Springing EI)

---

18. As a guide, the Summary of Present Interests section at the beginning of Chapter 3 lists present interests in order from longest to shortest duration.

Starting Point: Distinguishing Remainders From Executory Interests

The secret to correctly classifying any future interest created in a third party is to learn the fundamental rule for a remainder. Any future interest that only can come into present possession immediately upon the "natural" termination of the prior interest must be a remainder (and cannot be an executory interest).

The three types of present interests that terminate "naturally" (and, therefore, *always* are followed by a remainder) are the LE, the TY, and the FT.[19] Remainders following the natural termination of a LE or a TY are by far the most common in the practice of law. The natural termination rule also applies if a second future interest follows the first future interest. If the first future interest can only terminate naturally (because it is held in LE, for a TY, or in FT), then the second future interest must be some type of remainder.[20]

What if the prior interest is defeasible or determinable (i.e., it *either* can terminate naturally *or* if a specified event occurs)?[21] Here, the fundamental rule for an executory interest applies. A future interest that follows a prior interest that could terminate other than "naturally" must be an executory interest (and cannot be a remainder).

These fundamental rules governing remainders and executory interests are imbedded in the two charts at the beginning of Chapter 3 (Pairings Of The Present And The First Future Interest and Combinations Of Multiple Future Interests). You may find it helpful to refer back to these two charts as you review the examples below.

Assume the grant reads: "to A ['for life' or 'for 50 years' or 'and the heirs of A's body'] or until A remarries, then to B." We call A's present interest a determinable LE, TY, or FT (depending on

---

19. *See supra* Chart: Pairings Of The Present And The First Future Interest.

20. *See supra* Chart: Combinations Of Multiple Future Interests.

21. Examples are the FSSEL and the determinable LE, TY, or FT.

which phrase in the brackets is used). A's present interest is determinable because it can either terminate naturally at death (LE), at the end of the term (TY), or at the death of A's last lineal descendant (FT), or A's present interest could terminate earlier upon remarriage. Because B's future interest could come into present possession prior to the natural termination of A's present interest, B's future interest cannot be a remainder. Therefore, B's future interest must be classified as a shifting EI.[22]

Now assume instead the grant reads: "to A so long as A uses the land for a farm, but if A ceases to use the land as a farm, then to B and his heirs." A's present interest is a FSSEL that will not terminate naturally. Therefore, B's future interest must be classified as a shifting EI.

Suppose the grant reads: "to A for life, then to B for life, then to C and her heirs." The first future interest in this grant held by B can only come into present possession immediately upon the natural termination of A's LE. Therefore, B's future interest must be some type of remainder.[23] The second future interest held by C can *only* come into present possession immediately upon the natural termination of either B's life (if B survives A), or A's life (if B predeceases A). Therefore, C's future interest must be some type of remainder.[24]

Compare this grant: "to A for life, then to B for life or until B remarries, then to C and her heirs."[25] Although B may in fact never remarry and therefore C's future interest may come into present possession naturally at B's death, the law does not care what actually happens in this situation. The law cares only what could happen. What could happen is that B could remarry, which would cut short B's interest prior to its natural termination at B's death.

---

22. *See supra* Chart: Pairings Of The Present And The First Future Interest.

23. In this grant, B has a VR in LE.

24. In this grant, C has a VR in FSA.

25. In this grant, B's future interest is a VRSTD in LE.

Merely because this possibility exists, C's future interest must be classified as an executory interest[26] and cannot be classified as a remainder.

It may be useful for you to visualize this analysis of future interests held by third parties as a decision tree.

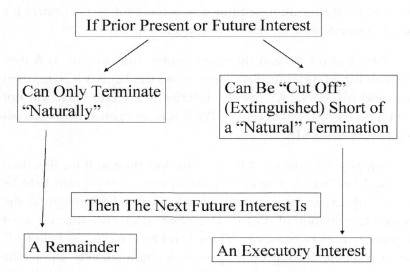

Once you have determined whether a future interest is a remainder or an executory interest, then you can determine the appropriate subtype of remainder (VR, CR, VRSO or VRSTD) or subtype of executory interest (shifting or springing). The next section of Chapter 3 reviews the four subtypes of remainders and the two subtypes of executory interests.

Remainder Subtypes

• **Vested Remainder (VR)**

    Example: "to A for life, then to B and his heirs"

    In this grant, A has a LE. B has a VR in FSA. B's "heirs" have nothing. The words "and his heirs" are of limitation indicating that

---

26. Technically, C holds a shifting EI in FSA.

B's future interest is held in FSA. The same interests would be created in a modern jurisdiction if the grantor O had a FSA in the property being conveyed and the grant read: "to A for life, then to B."

Note carefully that the law does *not* consider the death of A (the preceding LE holder) to be a "precondition" for B's future interest to come into present possession. Why? Because death is a certainty. Eventually, A's LE must naturally terminate.

Three Requirements For A Vested Remainder

For a remainder to be a VR, the following three requirements must be satisfied:

(1) At least one of the future remainder holders (B) must be born, alive and ascertainable;

(2) there are no preconditions that must be satisfied before B's interest can come into present possession,[27] or all preconditions have been satisfied; and

(3) there are *no* subsequent events that may divest B of his interest, either partially[28] or totally,[29] before B comes into present possession.

Transferability Of A VR

A VR is alienable, devisable and inheritable. To illustrate, assume that B dies one month after the above grant is made by O. A is still alive. Does B's VR die with B, or does B's estate now own the VR? B's estate owns the VR, which will pass to either B's designated beneficiary under B's will, or if B has died intestate, to B's statutory intestate heirs. Because B held a VR, no survival by B to the time the remainder comes into present possession is necessary.

---

27. Don't forget: the death of A (the preceding LE holder) is not considered a "precondition" for the remainderman B to come into present possession.

28. Partial divestment occurs when the grant is to a class and the class is still open. If B could be partially divested by a new class member, B's future interest is a VRSO.

29. If B could be totally divested, B's future interest is a VRSTD.

- **Contingent Remainder (CR)**

    B has a CR if one or both of requirements (1) or (2) described above for a VR are not satisfied.

    Example: "to A for life, then to B's children and their heirs"

    Assume that B has no children at the time the above grant is made. B's (yet to be born) children have a CR in FSA. The "heirs" referenced in the grant language have nothing. Why? The words "and their heirs" are words of limitation indicating that the future interest held by B's children is in FSA. The same interests would be created in a modern jurisdiction if the grantor O originally held a FSA in the property being conveyed and the grant read: "to A for life, then to B's children."

    Example: "to A for life, then to B and his heirs if B is alive at A's death"

    In this example, B's survival of A is a true precondition for B's future interest to come into present possession. B has a CR in FSA. The same interests would be created in a modern jurisdiction if the grantor O had a FSA in the property being conveyed and the grant read: "to A for life, then to B if B is alive at A's death."

    Example: "to A for life, then to the heirs of B and their heirs"

    In this example, it is the "heirs of B" who hold the future interest. The word "heirs" has a specialized meaning in Property law. Heirs are the persons identified by the state's statute of intestate succession as the owners of B's estate if B dies without a will. Due to how intestate succession statutes operate in every jurisdiction, the heirs of a living person (here, B) are never ascertainable until that person has died. Thus, B's "heirs" in the above grant (whoever they will be once B dies) hold a CR in FSA. The same interests would be created in a modern jurisdiction if the grantor O had a FSA in the property being conveyed and the grant read: "to A for life, then to the heirs of B."

Key Attributes: Survivorship As A Precondition And The Doctrine Of Destructibility Of CRs

    Survivorship until present possession is the classic precondition that makes a remainder a CR. The grantor O may want the grantee personally to enjoy the property rather than someone else, such as the grantee's spouse, stepchildren, or a friend, who might succeed to ownership pursuant to the grantee's will if the grantee were to hold a VR interest in the property. If the grantee does not live to enjoy the present possession of the property, then the CR is extinguished.

But survivorship is not the *only* type of precondition that may create a CR. Study the terms of the precondition carefully to ascertain when the precondition will be satisfied. It is at that point that the CR turns into a VR, which will become part of the grantee's estate if the grantee dies prior to attaining present possession of the property. The grants in Problem 3.1 at the end of Chapter 3 allow you to practice identifying preconditions.

Another key attribute of a CR is the Doctrine of Destructibility. At common law, if a CR had not turned into a VR before or at the natural termination of the prior estate, the CR was destroyed. Modernly, the Doctrine of Destructibility has been abolished by statute in many jurisdictions. If the jurisdiction has abolished the Doctrine of Destructibility, a more complex analysis is required.

To illustrate and compare the Doctrine of Destructibility under the common law with the modern approach abolishing the Doctrine, consider the following grant:

"to A for life, then to B and his heirs when B attains age 25"

Assume that A and B are both alive at the time the grant is made. Later, A dies when B is only age 20. What happens to B's CR?

The answer depends on whether the governing jurisdiction follows the Doctrine of Destructibility or has abolished the Doctrine. In a jurisdiction that follows the Doctrine of Destructibility, if B's CR has not become some type of "vested" remainder (VR, VRSO and/or VRSTD) at or before the termination of the immediately preceding estate (here, at A's death), then B's CR is destroyed. O (or O's estate) holds a REV, which comes into present possession at A's death because B's CR has been destroyed. Applying these common law rules to the example, the Doctrine of

Destructibility would destroy B's CR at A's death because B has not yet satisfied the precondition of obtaining age 25. After A's death, O (or O's estate) will own the property in FSA based on O's retained REV interest.

In a modern jurisdiction that has abolished the Doctrine of Destructibility, upon A's death present possession of the property reverts back to O, and B's CR turns into a springing EI.[30] O holds present possession of the property, but O's present interest is subject to a springing EI held by B. Present possession of the property will "spring forth" from O to B once B attains age 25. If B dies prior to attaining age 25, B's springing EI is extinguished at B's premature death, and O owns the property in FSA.

"Secondary" Life Estates

Assume the grant reads: "to A for life, then to B for life." If A and B are alive at the time of the grant, what interest does B have? Is it a VR of a limited duration (only for B's life), or is it a CR (because B must survive A to attain present possession of the property)?

Technically, the better classification is that B has a VR in LE, not a CR.[31] Read strictly, the words "for life" are structured as words of limitation defining the duration of B's estate, not as a precondition that B must be "living" to attain a present interest in the property at A's death.

All that being said, it is easy to see why one might be tempted to call B's interest a CR, because present possession is what really counts, and if B's estate is limited in duration to B's life, B's interest functions like a CR.[32] To avoid quibbles and arguments, experi-

---

30. *See infra* Executory Interests.

31. *See* Bergin & Haskell, *supra,* at 73 & n. 37 ("If O had meant to give B a vested remainder, he could have done so by transferring 'to A for life, then to B for life' ").

32. In the real world, the only harm in misclassifying B's future interest as a CR is that one would have to perform a Rule Against Perpetuities analysis to test the CR. No such testing is required of a VR in LE. If tested as a CR, a secondary life estate held by B always will be valid under the Rule Against Perpetuities if B is a life in being at the time of the grant. *See infra,* Chapter 4, The Rule Against Perpetuities.

enced estate planners finesse the issue of what to call B's future interest by simply labeling this future interest as a "secondary" life estate.

What matters on the exam, however, is how your professor categorizes a secondary life estate. If the proper characterization of a secondary life estate is not covered during your Property class, be sure to know your professor's view about how to classify this future interest before the exam.

• Vested Remainder Subject To Open (VRSO)

The VRSO (also known as the vested remainder subject to partial divestment) is created in a class of future interest holders whose members may increase in number before the future interest comes into present possession.

Example: "to A for life, remainder to B's children and their heirs"

At the time the above grant is made, assume that A and B are both alive and B has one child, B1. B1 has satisfied the first two criteria for a VR because at least one member of the class of B's children (B1) is born,[33] and there are no preconditions.[34] B1 has a VRSO because at the time of the grant B is alive and could have more children before the VRSO comes into present possession at A's death.[35] If B has a second child (B2) before A dies, the class of B's children opens to admit B2. Now, B1 must share. B1's 100% interest in the property conveyed by the grantor O has been partially divested (reduced to 50%) by B2's birth.

---

33. If no children of B were born as of the time of the grant, the remainder interest held by the members of the class of B's unborn children would be a CR and not a VRSO. *See infra* Special Rules: Class Members Who Share A CR.

34. If there were an unsatisfied precondition, the remainder interest held by the members of the class of B's children would be a CR and not a VRSO. *See infra* Special Rules:

Class Members Who Share A CR.

35. In the eyes of the common law, it did not matter if B were 80 years old and, as a practical matter, could not physically have more children. Under the "fertile octogenarian" assumption of the common law, if B was alive, the law assumed that B could have more children. This assumption may create Rule Against Perpetuities issues. *See infra*, Chapter 4, The Rule Against Perpetuities.

When A VRSO Closes

Once a VRSO closes, only individuals who are class members at the time of the closing will share in the present ownership of the property. When the class is closed, the class members hold a VR.

A VRSO closes at the earlier of two possible events. Using the example above, either: (1) B will die[36] and therefore no more class members can be born; or (2) A will die, at which point the VRSO closes, turns into a VR, and the class members come into present possession of the property (this all happens instantaneously at A's death).[37] This rule for when a class closes is extremely important. Why? Because if, under option (2) above, the VRSO must close because the time has come for present possession by the class members, any afterborn members of the class will *not* share in ownership of the property.

"Shutting out" afterborn class members once the time arrives for the VRSO to come into present possession is known as the Rule of Convenience. The Rule of Convenience promotes certainty in property ownership. Closing the class of property owners once the property interest comes into present possession avoids the uncertainty and related inconvenience of giving afterborn class members a share (and a say) in the ownership of the property.

Special Rules: The Contingent Remainder Held By An Unborn Or Unascertainable Class

Special rules apply if a class holds a CR because the members of the class are unborn or are unascertainable. Recognizing the unborn or unascertainable class is easy. Applying the special rules is tedious. If you find yourself becoming overwhelmed in reading this

---

36. At common law and today, if B is a male, the class of "B's children" will remain open for approximately ten months following B's death to definitively determine whether B will have any more children.

37. Note that the same analysis would apply if A's present interest were a TY or a FT instead of a LE. The natural termination of a prior LE, TY, or FT will close a VRSO. Further note that if the LE, TY, or FT can terminate other than naturally (i.e., it is a determinable LE, TY, or FT), the following future interest must be classified as a shifting EI, *not* a remainder. *See infra* Executory Interests Following A Determinable LE, TY Or FT.

material, skip this section of the Review and proceed to the section on Vested Remainder Subject to Total Divestment (VRSTD). Return to this material later if you have the time.

Recognizing The Unborn Or Unascertainable Class Situation

If the remainder is held by a class of individuals, but none of the class members are born or otherwise ascertainable, then the class holds a CR and not a VRSO. Below are two examples of grant language that creates an unborn or unascertainable class.

> **Example 1:** The grant from O reads: "to A for life, then to the children of B and their heirs." B is alive, but no children of B have been born at the time of A's death.

> **Example 2:** The grant from O reads: "to A for life, then to the heirs of B and their heirs." B is still alive at A's death; consequently, B's heirs are not yet ascertainable.

In each of the above examples, what happens when A dies and there is still *not one class member* who is born, alive, and ascertainable? How does the law address this problem of uncertain ownership of the property at A's death?

The answer depends on whether or not the governing jurisdiction has abolished the Doctrine of Destructibility. If the jurisdiction follows the Doctrine of Destructibility, the CR held by the class in each of the above examples is destroyed immediately upon A's death because there is not one class member who is able to take present possession of the property at A's death. The grantor O, who retained a REV interest in the property in each of the above examples, would own the property in FSA at A's death.[38]

In a jurisdiction that has abolished the Doctrine of Destructibility, upon A's death present possession of the property would be held by O pursuant to O's retained REV interest. O's present possessory interest is subject, however, to a springing EI held by the

---

38. Recall that a REV is alienable, devisable and inheritable. If O has not transferred the REV to someone else during O's lifetime, then at O's death the REV would be owned by O's estate.

members of the unborn or unascertainable class. Using the above examples, this springing EI is held by B's unborn children, or B's unascertainable heirs (assuming B is still alive at A's death).

Returning to Example 1 above (the CR to B's unborn children), what happens in a jurisdiction that has abolished the Doctrine of Destructibility to ownership of the property once the first child of B (B1) is born? Here, B1's birth creates yet another ownership issue. Now that one member of the class of B's children has been born, does the class close under the Rule of Convenience so that B1 holds sole ownership of the property? Or, does B1 have to share the property if more children of B are born?

In this situation, a special exception to the Rule of Convenience applies. Because *none* of B's children were born as of the time of A's death, *all* of B's children born after A's death (not just the firstborn B1) will be entitled to share in ownership of the property.[39] The rationale for this special exception is that if the law is going to be inconvenienced by waiting for the first child of B to be born, then there is little additional harm in waiting to vest ownership of the property until all of B's children are born. Once B dies, present ownership will vest in all of B's children. Until B dies, however, O will retain present possession of the property.

The analysis for Example 2 above (the CR to B's unascertainable heirs) is similar. In a jurisdiction that has abolished the Doctrine of Destructibility, at A's death the present possession of the property is held by O until B dies. The class of B's heirs holds a springing EI.

Once B dies, the class of B's heirs is immediately ascertainable. Unlike the class of unborn children in the Example 1, there is no possibility of an afterborn intestate heir. The class of B's heirs is determined conclusively by the state's statute of intestate succession as of the moment of B's death. At B's death, title and present possession of the property springs forth from O and vests in B's statutory heirs.

---

39.   *See* Bergin & Haskell, *supra*, at 146 & n. 28.

- **Vested Remainder Subject To Total Divestment (VRSTD)**

The VRSTD is created when the holder of the future interest (B) has satisfied the first two criteria for a VR,[40] but the grant contains a condition subsequent that may totally divest B of the remainder interest before B comes into present possession of the property.

> **Example:** "to A for life, then to B and his heirs, but if B fails to attain age 21, then to C and his heirs"

Assume that B is age 18 at the time the grant is made. In the above example, the granting clause that creates B's remainder interest is the phrase "then to B and his heirs". The granting clause ends with the comma after the word "heirs". This grant language is construed as an absolute (not a preconditional) grant of the remainder interest to B.[41]

Following the absolute grant of the remainder interest to B (marked by the comma after the word "heirs") is a divesting condition (a condition subsequent) that will sweep away B's remainder and give it instead to C. The condition subsequent in this grant is the requirement that B must have attained the age of 21 in order to come into present possession of the property at A's death.

Exam Tip: Distinguishing Preconditions (CR) From Conditions Subsequent (VRSTD)

Many students have difficulty in distinguishing between a precondition (that creates a CR) and a condition subsequent (that creates a VRSTD). Some students attempt to cope with this difficulty by simply memorizing the examples presented during class and hoping that nothing different shows up on the exam. Other students rely on the false heuristic that a precondition always comes before B's name in the grant language, and a condition

---

40. These criteria are: (1) B (or at least one member of the class of "B") is born, alive, and ascertainable; and (2) there are no preconditions that must be satisfied before B's remainder can come into present possession. *See*

supra Three Requirements For A Vested Remainder.

41. *See* Bergin & Haskell, *supra*, at 71.

subsequent always comes after B's name. Both coping strategies are ill-advised. Here are two exam tips to use instead.

Exam Tip: Study The Granting Clause[42]

A better approach is to look closely at the punctuation of the granting clause, and analyze how that punctuation relates to the condition or event that affects B's remainder. Is the condition or event in the same clause or phrase as the grant to B? If so, B's remainder is more likely to be construed as a precondition (CR) and not as a condition subsequent (VRSTD). To illustrate, compare the punctuation in the following two grants.

Example 1 (condition precedent): "to A for life, then to B and his heirs if B survives A, but if B does not survive A, then to C and his heirs"

Example 2 (condition subsequent): "to A for life, then to B and his heirs, but if B does not survive A, then to C and his heirs"

In Example 1, the granting clause is the phrase "then to B and his heirs if B survives A". Here, the condition that affects B's remainder is *inside* the granting clause, which ends with the comma after the phrase "if B survives A". Because the condition is inside the granting clause, it is more likely to be construed as a precondition. B most likely holds a CR in Example 1.

In Example 2, the granting clause is the phrase "then to B and his heirs". The granting clause ends with the comma after the word "heirs". The condition that affects B's remainder is *outside* of the granting clause, which ends with the comma after the word "heirs". Because the condition is outside of the granting clause, it is most likely to be construed as a condition subsequent. B most likely holds a VRSTD in Example 2.

Exam Tip: Strategies For Ambiguous Language

On your exam, the language of a grant that is part of an essay question is likely to be subject to more than one possible

---

42. *See generally* Bergin & Haskell, *supra*, at 71–73.

construction. A typical ambiguous language issue concerns whether B's future interest should be classified as a CR or a VRSTD.[43] Resolution of this threshold issue has two potential implications for further analysis. First, your classification of B's future interest will likely determine your classification of a subsequent future interest held by C.[44] Second (to preview Chapter 4), if B's future interest is classified as a CR, it must be tested for compliance with the Rule Against Perpetuities ("RAP"). If, however, B's future interest is classified as a VRSTD, it is not tested under the RAP.

Dealing with ambiguous exam language concerning present and future interests causes many students to lose their concentration (in other words, they blow it). The entire first year of law school is about learning to recognize and debate the multiple possible outcomes for a given legal issue. Yet, when faced with ambiguous future interest grant language on a first-year Property exam, most of the class will discuss only one possible interpretation of the grant's language. The students who ace their Property exam approach ambiguous grant language just like any other garden-variety legal issue on a law school exam. They:

- identify the possible interpretations of the language;

- provide arguments for each interpretation; and

- analyze the consequences that flow from each possible interpretation.

To be successful, you must be able to classify present and future interests rapidly so that the bulk of your time on the Property exam may be spent on this sort of higher-level legal analysis. The Problems at the end of Chapter 3 allow you to practice classifying present and future interests quickly so that you will have time to engage in higher-level legal analysis of ambiguous grant language on the exam.

---

43. The other typical essay question involving ambiguous grant language is the distinction between the FSD and the FSSCS. An ambiguous grant often will contain "mixed" signals concerning the nature of the defeasible fee simple. *See supra* Exam Tip: FSD Versus FSSCS and Exam Tip: Ambiguous Grant Language.

44. If B has a CR, then C has a CR. But if B has a VRSTD, then C has a shifting EI.

Combination: The VRSO And STD

A VRSO and a VRSTD are not mutually exclusive. They both can co-exist in the same future interest, thereby creating the combination VRSO and STD.

> **Example:** "to A for life, then to B's children and their heirs. Provided, however, that if B predeceases A, the property shall go instead to C and her heirs."

Assume that B is alive at the time the above grant is made and has three children. In the above example, B's children have a VRSO and STD. Why? So long as B is alive, the class of B's children remains open (the VRSO). In addition, because A and B are both alive at the time the grant is made, B may predecease A. If this happens, B's children will be totally divested of their VRSO, and present ownership of the property at A's death will go to C instead (the VRSO is also STD).

What future interest does C hold? C holds a shifting EI, which always follows a VRSTD (in this case, a VRSO that is also STD).[45]

Executory Interests (EI)

The EI is a future interest that became possible under the common law only after the British Parliament enacted the Statute of Uses in 1536. The EI must be created in a third person and cannot be created or retained by the grantor O. If the grantor O holds a future interest, O's future interest is classified as either a PR, RE, or a REV, but never as an EI.

There are two subtypes of EIs. The **shifting EI** comes into present possession by divesting (before its natural termination) the prior interest of another third party. The **springing EI** comes into present possession by divesting the grantor O, who holds present possession of the property.

---

45. *See supra* Chart: Combinations Of Multiple Future Interests, and *infra* Executory Interests.

• Shifting EIs

Both remainders and shifting EIs are held by third parties, which can make the proper classification of a shifting EI difficult. When classifying remainders and executory interests, remember the fundamental rule that distinguishes a remainder from an executory interest.[46] If the prior interest (it could be a present FSSEL or a future VRSTD) can be extinguished prior to its natural termination, then the next future interest in the sequence must be a shifting EI and cannot be a remainder.

> **Example 1:** "to A and her heirs until the property is no longer used for a farm, but if the property ever ceases to be used for a farm, then to B and her heirs"

In Example 1, A's present interest is a defeasible fee simple (a FSSEL) that can be cut short by a specified event (cessation of use as a farm). B holds a shifting EI, not a remainder.

> **Example 2:** "to A for life, then to B and his heirs, but if B does not survive A, then to C and her heirs"

Example 2 is more difficult because it requires correctly classifying B's future interest as a VRSTD and not as a CR. The granting clause to B ends with the comma after the word "heirs". The condition that extinguishes B's interest (B's failure to survive A) is more likely to be construed as a condition subsequent because it is *outside* of the granting clause to B. Therefore, B's future interest is better classified as a VRSTD and not as a CR. A shifting EI always follows a VRSTD that is held in FSA. Therefore, in Example 2 C most likely has a shifting EI and not a remainder.[47]

Distinguishing Between Shifting EIs And CRs

You may be wondering why C's interest in Example 2 is not classified as a CR. For historical reasons, only a shifting EI (not a CR) can divest a "vested" interest held by another third party when

---

46. *See supra* Starting Point: Distinguishing Remainders From Executory Interests.

47. *See* Bergin & Haskell, *supra*, at 113.

both interests are created simultaneously as part of the same grant or devise.[48] The "vested" fee simple interest that precedes the shifting EI could be a present interest (a FSSEL) or it could be a future interest (a VRSTD held in FSA). Thus, in Example 1 above, B's shifting EI follows A's FSSEL. In Example 2 above, C's shifting EI follows B's VRSTD (a "vested" interest) in FSA.

Exam Tip: Shifting EIs That Belong To A Class Or Are Subject To A Precondition

B's shifting EI can be held by a class rather than an individual. If granted to a class of person, B's future interest must be classified as a shifting EI and not as a VRSO if the future interest may come into present possession prior to the natural termination of the prior estate. Once the EI comes into present possession, the class of owners closes.

B's shifting EI also can be subject to a precondition. Nevertheless, B's future interest must be classified as a shifting EI and not as a CR if the future interest may come into present possession prior to the natural termination of the prior estate.

Executory Interests Following A Determinable LE, TY Or FT

A shifting EI is the future interest that cuts short a preceding LE, TY or FT prior to its natural termination. Note carefully in the examples below that the present interest held by A can terminate naturally, but it also can be divested prior to its natural termination. It is this mere possibility (not what actually happens) that makes B's future interest a shifting EI and not a remainder.

Example 3: "to A for life or if A remarries, then to B and her heirs"

Assume that A is alive and divorced at the time the above grant is made. In Example 3, the present interest held by A is a determinable life estate. B's future interest could come into present possession (cut off A's life estate) before A's life estate naturally

---

48. *See id.*

terminates at A's death. Because of this mere possibility, B has a shifting EI in FSA and not a remainder.

Example 4: "to A for 15 years or if A resumes drinking alcohol, then to B and his heirs"

Assume that A is alive and does not drink alcohol at the time the grant is made. In Example 4, A's present interest is a determinable TY. B's future interest could come into present possession (cut off A's 15 year term) before A's term expires naturally at the end of the 15th year. Because of this mere possibility, B has a shifting EI in FSA and not a remainder.

Example 5: "to A and the heirs of her body, but if A or a descendant of A ever fails to occupy the family farmhouse at Greenacre, then to B and his heirs"

Assume that A is alive and occupying the family farmhouse at the time the grant is made. You know the drill. A has a determinable FT and B has a shifting EI in FSA.

• **Springing EIs**

A springing EI arises in a unique situation that is easy to spot on an exam. In a springing EI situation, the grantor O holds present possession of the property. The springing EI held by B will come into present possession ("spring forth") from the grantor O upon the occurrence of a specified event or condition in the future.

Under the **common law rule**, a springing EI could be created only where the grantor O retained the present interest in the property, but gave a future interest to a third party.

Examples: "$10,000 to B when B marries"
"$10,000 to B when B graduates from law school"

In each of the above examples, the grantor O has retained present possession of the property. B's entitlement to the property depends on whether or not the stated event ever occurs in the future. At common law, B has a springing EI. The common law did not have a special name for O's retained present interest. O's retained present interest is simply described as a FSA that is "subject to" a springing EI held by B.

The **modern rule** is that a springing EI also can arise in a jurisdiction where the Doctrine of Destructibility for CRs has been abolished. For examples of springing EIs created in a modern rule jurisdiction, refer back to the previous section entitled Key Attributes: Survivorship As A Precondition And The Doctrine Of Destructibility Of CRs.

A Final Word About Ancient Rules

In addition to the Doctrine of Destructibility, there are three other ancient common law rules that are still covered in some Property casebooks. These rules are:

- the Rule in Shelley's Case;[49]

- the Rule in Wild's Case;[50] and

- the Doctrine of Worthier Title.[51]

Modernly, almost all jurisdictions have abolished these ancient rules by adopting the Uniform Property Act. For this reason, many Property professors no longer cover these ancient rules. If your Property professor is still teaching these ancient rules, see the excellent treatise by Bergin and Haskell referenced in footnote 5 of Chapter 3 for a comprehensive explanation.

PRESENT AND FUTURE INTERESTS CHECKLIST

With the above Review in mind, the Present and Future Interests Checklist is presented below.

---

49. *See* Bergin & Haskell, *supra*, at 93–98. **51.** *See id*. at 118–19.
50. *See id*. at 235–36.

A. DETERMINE WHEN THE GRANT BECOMES EFFECTIVE.
Before classifying the present and future interests in the grant, determine the point in time when the transfer of these property interests became effective. Then proceed to Part B of the checklist to classify the present and future interests created by the grant.

    1. Grant Made While Grantor Is Alive? The property interests in the grant are classified as of the point in time when the transfer becomes irrevocable.

    2. Grant Made Under A Will? The property interests created under the will are classified as of the moment of the testator's death.

B. CLASSIFY THE PRESENT AND FUTURE INTERESTS. Identify the present interest by selecting the appropriate description using Parts B.1 to B.5 of the checklist. The classification of the first future interest follows the description of the present interest.

    1. Present Defeasible Fee Simple Held By A; Future Interest Held By Third Party B. A holds a FSSEL. B holds a shifting EI. Proceed to Part D.1 to perform further analysis.

    2. Present Defeasible Fee Simple Held By A; Future Interest (Express or Implied) Held By The Grantor O. After determining the type of defeasible fee simple created by the grant, proceed to Part D.1 to perform further analysis.

        a. FSD And PR? A holds a FSD and the grantor O holds a PR if the signals below are predominant.

            i. Punctuation. Is the defeasing event inside the granting clause? **If yes**, A is more likely to hold a FSD.

            ii. Magic Words Indicating Duration Or The Passage Of Time. Do the words describing the defeasing event connote duration or the passage of time (so long as, as long as, until, while, during)? **If yes**, A is more likely to hold a FSD.

        iii. O's Retained Interest Is Automatic. Do the words of the grant indicate that upon the defeasing event, title to and present possession of the property automatically reverts back to the grantor O? **If yes**, A is more likely to hold a FSD.

     b. FSSCS And RE? A holds a FSSCS and the grantor O holds a RE if the signals below are predominant.

        i. Punctuation. Is the defeasing event outside the granting clause? **If yes**, A is more likely to hold a FSSCS.

        ii. Magic Words Indicating Condition, Limitation Or Restriction. Do the words describing the defeasing event suggest a condition, limitation or restriction on A's use of the property (if, but if, provided, however, on the condition, subject to the condition)? **If yes**, A is more likely to hold a FSSCS.

        iii. O Must Act To Retake Possession. Do the words of the grant indicate that O must act (enter or terminate) to reclaim title to and present possession of the property from A upon the occurrence of the defeasing event? **If yes**, A is more likely to hold a FSSCS.

3. Present LE, TY, Or FT Held By A; Future Interest (Express Or Implied) Held By Grantor O.

     a. A's LE/TY/FT Can Only Terminate Naturally. A's present interest is a LE/TY/FT. O holds a REV.

     b. A's LE/TY/FT Interest Can Be Cut Off Short Of A "Natural" Termination. A's present interest is a determinable LE/TY/FT. O holds a REV.

4. **Present LE, TY, Or FT Held By A; Future Interest Held By Third Party B.**

    a. **A's LE/TY/FT Can Only Terminate Naturally.** A's present interest is a LE/TY/FT. B holds a remainder. Proceed to Part C of the checklist to determine the type of B's remainder and any subsequent future interests.

    b. **A's LE/TY/FT Interest Can Be Cut Off Short Of A "Natural" Termination.** A's present interest is a determinable LE/TY/FT. B holds a shifting EI. If B's shifting EI is of less than FSA duration (for an interest in real property) or is not held in absolute ownership (for an interest in personal property), then the grantor O holds a REV.

5. **Present Interest Held By The Grantor O; Future Interest Held By B.** O holds present possession subject to a springing EI. B holds a springing EI. If B's shifting EI is of less than FSA duration (for an interest in real property) or is not held in absolute ownership (for an interest in personal property), the grantor O holds a REV.

C. **DETERMINE THE TYPE OF THE FIRST REMAINDER AND ANY SUBSEQUENT FUTURE INTERESTS.** If the first remainder is held by an individual, proceed to Part C.1 of the checklist. If the first remainder is held by a class of persons, proceed to Part C.2 of the checklist. After classifying the first remainder, proceed to Part C.3 of the checklist to classify any subsequent future interests. Conclude the analysis by proceeding to Part D of the checklist to determine the attributes and characteristics of the future interests created by the grant.

1. **First Remainder Is Held By An Individual.** If the first remainder is held by an individual, determine whether it is a CR, VRSTD, or VR using the checklist. Proceed to Part C.3 of the checklist to classify any subsequent future interests that follow the first remainder.

    a. **Is The Individual Who Holds The First Remainder Born, Alive, And Ascertainable?**

    i. No. The first remainder is a CR.

    ii. Yes. Continue to Part C.1.b of the checklist.

  b. Is There A Precondition That Must Be Satisfied Before The Individual Can Take Present Possession Of The Property?

    i. Yes, But The Precondition Is Not Yet Satisfied. The first remainder is a CR.

    ii. Yes, But The Precondition Is Satisfied. The individual has some type of vested remainder. Continue to Part C.1.c of the checklist to determine the exact type of vested remainder.

    iii. If There Is No Precondition, the individual has some type of vested remainder. Continue to Part C.1.c to determine the exact type of vested remainder.

  c. Can The Individual's Vested Remainder Be Divested By A Condition Subsequent?

    i. Yes. The first remainder is a VRSTD.

    ii. No. The first remainder is a VR.

2. First Remainder Is Held By A Class Of Persons. If the first remainder is held by a class of persons, determine whether it is a CR, a VRSO, a VRSO and STD, or a VR using the checklist. Proceed to Part C.3 to classify any future interests after the first remainder. Conclude the analysis by proceeding to Part D of the checklist to determine the attributes and characteristics of the future interests created by the grant.

  a. Is There At Least One Member Of The Class Who Is Born, Alive, And Ascertainable?

    i. No. The first remainder is a CR.

ii. **Yes.** Continue to Part C.2.b of the checklist.

b. Is There A Precondition That Must Be Satisfied Before Members Of The Class Can Take Present Possession Of The Property?

      i. **Yes, But The Precondition Is Not Yet Satisfied By Any Member Of The Class At The Time The Grant Is Made.** The first remainder is a CR.

      ii. **Yes, But The Precondition Is Satisfied By Only Some Members Of The Class At The Time The Grant Is Made.** Distinguish between those members who have and who have not satisfied the precondition at the time the grant is made.

      • **The members of the class who have satisfied the precondition** have some type of vested remainder. Continue to Part C.2.c to determine the exact type of vested remainder.

      • **The members of the class who have not yet satisfied the precondition** have a CR.

      iii. **If There Is No Precondition,** the class members have some type of vested remainder. Continue to Part C.2.c to determine the exact type of vested remainder.

c. Can Any Or All Of The Class Members Who Hold A Vested Remainder Be Divested By A Condition Subsequent?

        i. **Yes.** The class members who are subject to being totally divested[52] have a VRSTD.

       ii. **No.** The class members who cannot be totally divested have either a VRSO (class is still open) or a VR (class is closed).

- **Has The Class Closed?** The class closes and turns into a VR at the earlier of: (1) no more class members can be born, or (2) the time arrives for the class members to come into present possession of the property because the prior present interest has naturally terminated.

- **Effect Of Rule Of Convenience?** Under the Rule of Convenience, once the VR comes into present possession at the natural termination of the prior present interest, any afterborn class members (or members who afterwards satisfy all preconditions) do *not* share in the present ownership of the property.

3. Determine Subsequent Future Interests After First Remainder. Classify any subsequent future interests after the first remainder by selecting the appropriate description of the first remainder from the list below. Once you have classified the first remainder, the classification of subsequent future interests follows from the classification of the first remainder.

    a. The First Remainder Is A CR. If the first

---

52. "Totally divested" means that a class member's share is extinguished, not merely diluted by the addition of more class members.

remainder is a CR, look to whether or not the grant expressly creates a second future interest in a third party.

    i. **If The Grant Expressly Creates A Second Future Interest In A Third Party,** then the second future interest will be some type of remainder. Repeat the analysis in Part C.1 (second remainder is held by an individual) or Part C.2 (second remainder is held by a class of persons) above to determine the type of the second remainder, and any additional future interests created by the grant in third parties.

    ii. **If The Grant Does Not Create A Second Future Interest In A Third Party,** then O holds a REV. If the precondition later is satisfied, the first remainder turns into a VR. If the VR is held in FSA, then O's REV is extinguished. If the CR-turned-VR is not of FSA duration, then O still holds a REV (if O began with a FSA).

  b. **The First Remainder Is A VRSTD.** If the first remainder is a VRSTD, then look to whether or not the grant expressly creates a second future interest in a third party.

    i. **If The Grant Expressly Creates A Second Future Interest In A Third Party,** then the second future interest is a shifting EI. The grantor O holds a REV if the VRSTD and the shifting EI are not both held in FSA duration.

    ii. **If The Grant Does Not Create A Second Future Interest,** then O holds a REV. If the divesting condition or event is extinguished and the first remainder turns into a VR in FSA, then O's REV is extinguished. If the VRSTD-turned-VR is not of FSA duration, then O still holds a REV.

c. **The First Remainder Is A VR Or VRSO.** Determine any subsequent express or implied future interests created by the grant according to whether the VR/VRSO is held in FSA duration.

  i. **If The First VR/VRSO Is Held In FSA,** there are no subsequent future interests.

  ii. **If The First VR/VRSO Is Held In Less Than FSA,** then:

  • **If the grant expressly creates a second future interest in a third party**, that interest will be some type of remainder. Repeat the analysis in Part C.1 (second remainder is held by an individual) or Part C.2 (second remainder is held by a class of persons) above to determine the type of the second remainder, and any additional future interests created by the grant in third parties.

  • **If the grant does not expressly create a subsequent future interest in a third party**, then O holds a REV.

D. **ANALYSIS OF ATTRIBUTES AND CHARACTERISTICS OF PRESENT AND FUTURE INTERESTS.** Once the present and future interests have been classified, the final step is to apply the factual events that occurred after the grant became effective to determine how these subsequent events may have affected the ownership interests in the property. Key attributes and characteristics of the various present and future interests to consider in performing this analysis are described in Part D of the checklist. Apply the Part D checklist as appropriate based on the factual circumstances.

- For a defeasible fee simple (FSD, FSSCS, FSSEL), proceed to Part D.1.

- For a contingent remainder (CR), proceed to Part D.2.

- For a vested remainder subject total divestment (VRSTD), proceed to Part D.3.

- For a vested remainder (VR), proceed to Part D.4.

1. Attributes And Characteristics Of Defeasible Fee Simples (FSD, FSSCS, FSSEL).

    a. Statute Of Limitations (SOL) Barring O's Future Interest? If the present interest is a FSD, the SOL for O to claim FSA title based on O's PR interest begins to run immediately upon the occurrence of the defeasing event. If the present interest is a FSSCS, the SOL for O to claim FSA title based on O's RE interest begins to run only after O has asserted the right to present possession of the property.

    b. Transferability Of The Corresponding Future Interest (PR, RE, EI)?

        i. The Grantor (O) Holds A PR Or RE. Under the common law rule, a PR or RE is not alienable by O during O's lifetime (unless O releases the PR/RE to the holder of the FSD/FSSCS). O's PR or RE is not devisable at O's death and can only be inherited by O's intestate heirs. Absent a release, O's intestate heirs must own the PR or RE at O's death.

        ii. A Third Party (B) Holds A Shifting EI. B's shifting EI is freely alienable, devisable and inheritable by B (unless the grant language specifies otherwise).

c. **Invalidation Of Defeasing Event As A Restraint On Alienation?** Determine if the defeasing event or condition should be struck by a court as void because it is a restraint on alienation. If the defeasing event is void as a restraint on alienation, reclassify the present interest.

   i. **FSD Or FSSCS To Charity Or Government.** A defeasing event tied to use of a property for charitable, public, or governmental purposes is unlikely to be struck down by a court as a restraint on alienation.

   ii. **FSD Or FSSCS To Private Owner.** Look to the marketability of the property based on the size of the market of potential buyers who could continue to use the property consistent with the restrictions imposed by the defeasing event. The smaller the market pool of potential buyers, the more likely a court may strike the defeasing event as a restraint on alienation.

2. **Attributes And Characteristics Of Contingent Remainders.** Determine if the CR is extinguished due to failure of a precondition, or by the application of the Doctrine of Destructibility.

   a. **Nature Of The Precondition: Survivorship To Present Possession Or Something Else?** Scrutinize the nature of the precondition to determine when the precondition will be satisfied. If the precondition is something other than survivorship to present possession, the precondition, once satisfied, turns the CR into a VR. Proceed to Part D.4 of the checklist for further analysis of a VR.

b. Does The Doctrine Of Destructibility Of CRs Apply? If the jurisdiction applies the Doctrine of Destructibility, proceed to Part D.3.b.i. If the jurisdiction has abolished the Doctrine, proceed to Part D.3.b.ii.

i. Doctrine Of Destructibility Applies. Based on the facts, can the individual who holds the CR (or at least one member of a class who holds the CR) come into present possession when the prior present estate naturally terminates?

- **No CR holder is born, alive and ascertainable, and satisfies all precondition at the moment of present possession.** The CR is extinguished under the Doctrine of Destructibility. Strike the language creating the CR from the grant, reclassify the remaining future interest(s), and analyze who is entitled to present possession of the property.

- **At least one CR holder is born, alive and ascertainable, and satisfies all preconditions at the moment of present possession.** If the CR is held by an individual, the individual takes present possession of the property when the prior present estate naturally terminates. If the CR is held by a class, apply the Rule of Convenience. Once the prior present interest naturally terminates, the class closes and the holder(s) of the CR who are born, alive, and ascertainable and who have satisfied all preconditions take present ownership of the property. Any afterborn class members do not share in present ownership of the property under the Rule of Convenience.

ii. **Modern Rule: Doctrine Of Destructibility Abolished.** Based on the facts, can the individual who holds the CR (or at least one member of a class who holds a CR) come into present possession when the prior present estate naturally terminates?

- **No CR holder is born, alive and ascertainable, and satisfies all preconditions at the moment of present possession.** Present possession of the property reverts back to the grantor O, who holds fee title subject to a springing EI. The holder(s) of the CR now have a springing EI. If the CR is held by a class, under the exception to the Rule of Convenience no class members (who now together hold a springing EI) will take present ownership of the property until all class members have had the opportunity to satisfy all preconditions.

- **At least one CR holder is born, alive and ascertainable, and satisfies all preconditions at the moment of present possession.**

If the CR is held by an individual who has satisfied all preconditions, the individual takes present ownership of the property when the prior present estate naturally terminates. If at least one member of a class that holds a CR has satisfied all preconditions, under the Rule of Convenience those class members who have satisfied all preconditions take present ownership of the property when the prior present estate naturally terminates. Any afterborn class members (or members who afterwards satisfy all preconditions) do not share in present ownership of the property.

3. **Attributes And Characteristics Of Vested Remainders Subject To Total Divestment.** Based on subsequent events after the VRSTD is created, is the condition subsequent satisfied?

    a. **Yes.** Then the VRSTD becomes a VR, and any shifting EI that follows the VRSTD is extinguished. If there is no shifting EI held by a third party that follows the VRSTD-turned-VR, the grantor holds a REV if the VR is of lesser duration than a FSA.

    b. **No.** Then the VRSTD is extinguished. Any shifting EI that follows the VRSTD turns into some type of remainder. Repeat the analysis in Part C.1 (remainder held by an individual) or Part C.2 (remainder held by a class of persons) above to determine the type of remainder. If there is no shifting EI held by a third party that follows the extinguished VRSTD, the grantor takes present ownership of the property pursuant to the grantor's retained REV.

4. **Attributes And Characteristics Of Vested Remainders.** Based on the subsequent events after the VR is created, determine who owns the property when the time comes for the VR to come into present possession.

    a. **The VR Is Held In FSA.** Is the person (or each person if the VR is held by a closed class) who holds the VR alive at the time the VR comes into present possession?

        i. **Yes.** The person owns the property in FSA if the VR holder did not make a lifetime transfer of the VR to someone else. If the VR was transferred during life, the transferee owns the property in FSA.

        ii. **No.** The estate of a predeceased VR holder owns the VR at the person's death. Determine who succeeded to ownership of the VR as a result of probate of the estate (is the successor the will beneficiary or an intestate heir?). The successor through the estate owns the decedent's share in the property in FSA.

    b. **The VR Is Held In LE (Secondary Life Estate).** Did the second future life estate holder survive the first present life estate holder?

        i. **Yes.** The second life estate holder assumes present possession of the property when the first life estate holder dies. Present possession lasts only until the second life estate holder dies, and then passes to the next person(s) in the sequence of future interests created by the grant. If there are no more future interests created after the secondary life estate, then the grantor O owns the property in FSA at the death of the second life estate holder pursuant to the grantor's retained REV interest.

ii. **No.** The secondary life estate is extinguished. At the death of the first present life estate holder, present possession of the property passes to the person(s) in the sequence of future interests created by the grant. If there are no more future interests created after the secondary life estate, then the grantor O owns the property in FSA at the death of the first present life estate holder pursuant to the grantor's retained REV interest.

ILLUSTRATIVE PROBLEMS

Here are several sets of problems that illustrate how the Checklist can be used to solve present and future interests questions.

■ PROBLEM 3.1 ■

For each grant below, classify the present and future interests. Assume that the common law rules for conveyance of a FSA apply, unless otherwise indicated.

Problems On Life Estates, Vested Remainders And Related Inheritance Concepts

1. O, the owner of Blackacre, validly executed and delivered a deed conveying Blackacre "to A for life, then to B and his heirs." Assume that at the time of the grant, A, B and O are alive.

  a. What is the state of the title to Blackacre immediately after the deed is delivered?

  b. Assume A dies, then B dies. Who owns Blackacre upon B's death?

  c. Assume instead that B dies, then A dies. Who owns Blackacre upon B's death?

2. O, the owner of Blackacre, validly executed and delivered a deed conveying Blackacre "to A for life, then to B." Assume that at the time of the grant, A, B and O are alive.

  a. What is the state of the title to Blackacre immediately after the deed is delivered?

  b. Assume B dies, then A dies. Who owns Blackacre upon A's death?

  c. Assume instead that A dies, then B dies. Who owns Blackacre upon B's death?

  d. Assume B dies. B's will leaves all of B's property to Y. Next, O dies. O's will leaves all of O's property to X. Then A dies. A's will leaves all of A's property to Z. What is the state of the title to Blackacre upon A's death?

  e. Does your answer in 2.d above change if O died intestate (without a will)?

  f. Assume A dies, and then B sells Blackacre to C. Later, B dies. B's will leaves all of B's property to B's spouse. What is the state of the title to Blackacre upon B's death?

Problems On The Defeasible Fee Simples

3. Determine the state of the title to the property in each of the following grants by O, who originally owned the property conveyed in FSA. Does the language of the grant clearly

indicate the type of interest created, or is it ambiguous? Discuss all possible interpretations if the granting language is ambiguous.

a. "to the Lincoln Public Schools, on the condition that the land will always be used for school purposes, but if the land is not used for school purposes, O may reenter and reclaim title and possession."

b. "to the Lincoln Public Schools on the express condition that the land shall be used only for school purposes. If the land ceases to be used for school purposes, it shall revert to O."

c. "to the Lincoln Public Schools on the express condition that the land be used solely for school purposes."

d. "to the Lincoln Public Schools, so long as the land is used for school purposes, but if the land ceases to be used for school purposes within 21 years of the date of this grant, then to my daughter Briana and her heirs."

Problems On Future Interests Retained By The Grantor

4. Determine the state of the title to Blackacre in each of the following grants by O, who originally owned the property conveyed in FSA. Assume that all individuals named in the grant are alive.

a. "to A for life."

b. "to A for life, then to B and the heirs of his body."

c. "to A for 20 years."

Problems On Future Interests Held By Third Parties

5. Determine the state of the title to Blackacre in each of the following grants by O, who originally owned the property conveyed in FSA. In each grant, assume the modern statutory presumption for conveyance of a FSA applies, and that the jurisdiction has abolished the common law Doctrine of Destructibility of Contingent Remainders. Further assume that all individuals named in the grant are alive, unless otherwise indicated.

    a. "to A for 10 years, then to B for life."

    b. "to A for 10 years, then to B."

    c. "to A for life, then to B if B survives A."

    d. "to A for life or until A remarries, then to B."

    e. "to A for life, then to the children of B." Assume A and B are alive at the time the grant is made, but B has no children.

    f. Same grant language as in 5.e above, except assume B has one child, B1, at the time the grant is made.

    g. Same grant language as in 5.e above, except assume that A dies after the grant is made while B is still alive. At the time of A's death, B has one child, B1. What is the state of the title to Blackacre at A's death?

    h. Same grant language as in 5.e above, except assume that A dies after the grant is made while B is still alive. At the time of A's death, B has no children. What is the state of the title to Blackacre at A's death?

6. Determine the state of the title to Blackacre in each of the following grants by O, who originally owned the property conveyed in FSA. In each grant, assume the common law rules apply for conveyance of a FSA and that the Doctrine of Destructibility of Contingent Remainders is in effect. Further assume that all individuals named in the grant are alive, unless otherwise indicated.

    a. "To A for life, then to B and his heirs if B attains age 21." Assume that B is age 15 at the time the grant is made.

    b. Same grant language as in 6.a above, except B turns age 21 while A is still alive.

    c. Same grant language as in 6.a above, except B dies at age 25, then A dies.

    d. Same grant language as in 6.a above, except B dies at age 19, then A dies.

e.   Same grant language as in 6.a above, except A dies when B is age 19.

f.   "To A from today until December 1, 2020, then to B and his heirs beginning on December 3, 2020."

g.   "To A and his heirs once A has ceased smoking for one year." Assume that at the time the grant is made, A smokes.

7.   The grantor O, who owned Blackacre in FSA, made the following conveyance: "To A for life, then to B's children and their heirs who are living at A's death, but if B has no living children at A's death, then to C and her heirs." Assume that at the time the grant is made, A and B are alive and B has one child, B1. What is the state of the title to Blackacre after the conveyance is made?

8.   O's will devises Blackacre "to my wife Alice for life, then to Alice's children and their heirs."

a.   Assume that at the time of O's death, Alice and O have two adult children, B1 and B2. Two years after O's death, Alice remarries and has a third child, D. Then B1 dies. B1's will leaves all of her property to her husband, H. Then Alice dies. Who owns Blackacre upon Alice's death? Do you think O intended this result?

b.   If O intended that only his children own Blackacre upon the death of O's wife Alice, how should the devise language in O's will have been written?

9.   The grantor O, who owned Blackacre in FSA, made the following devise of Blackacre in O's will: "to my only daughter Amy for life, then to my grandchildren and their heirs, but if any grandchild dies while Amy is still alive, then that deceased grandchild's share shall go to the Red Cross and its heirs and assigns."

a.   Assume that at the time of O's death, Amy is alive and has two children, G1 and G2. Determine the state of the title to Blackacre upon O's death.

b.   Assume the grant language in 9 above reads: "to my only daughter Amy for life, then to my grandchildren and their heirs, but if any grandchild dies while Amy is still alive, then that deceased grandchild's share shall go to my grandchildren and their heirs who are living at Amy's death." Assume that at the time of O's death, Amy is alive and has two children, G1 and G2. Determine the state of the title to Blackacre upon O's death.

10. O, owner of Blackacre, wanted to convey Blackacre to his son A for life, and upon A's death O wanted Blackacre to go to A's children if any were alive or, if none were then alive, to O's daughter B.

   a. O conveyed Blackacre "to A for life, then to A's children and their heirs, but if at A's death A is not survived by any children, then to B and her heirs." At the time the conveyance was made, A had two living children, A1 and A2. What is the state of the title to Blackacre at the time of O's conveyance?

   b. Refer to the grant language in 10.a above. Two years after O's conveyance, A1 died. A1's will left all of A1's real property to A1's best friend, X. What is the state of the title to Blackacre upon A1's death?

   c. Refer to the grant language in 10.a and the additional facts in 10.b above. Assume that after A1 died, A died. What is the state of the title to Blackacre upon A's death?

11. O's will contained the following bequest: "$1 million to my daughter Marie, but only if she survives her husband Tim." Assume that Marie and Tim are both alive at O's death.

   a. How would you classify Marie's interest in the $1 million?

   b. Why would a parent like O make this type of bequest?

Analysis

Problems On Life Estates, Vested Remainders And Inheritance Concepts

  1.a. A has a LE; B has a VR in FSA. O has no remaining property rights to Blackacre.

    b. Upon A's death, A's LE is extinguished and B's VR in FSA comes into present possession. B owns Blackacre in FSA. Upon B's death, B's estate owns Blackacre in FSA. The new owner of Blackacre will be determined by the probate of B's estate.

    c. B has a VR, which is not extinguished by B's death, but rather passes to B's estate. The probate of B's estate will determine the new owner of the VR interest in Blackacre. Upon A's death, A's LE is extinguished and the VR in FSA held by the new owner (as determined by the probate of B's estate) will come into the present possession and own Blackacre in FSA.

  2.a. A has a LE; B has a VR in LE (secondary life estate); O retains a REV. B's VR is only in LE because the instructions indicate that the common law rules are to apply. Under the common law rules, the presumption is that a grant "to B" conveys only an estate of LE duration. B has a VR in LE and not a CR because there are no preconditions specified in the grant that must be satisfied before B can assume present possession. The fact that the duration of B's interest is limited to B's life, and may expire before B is able to take present possession of the property, does not make B's secondary life estate a CR.

    b. B's VR in LE is extinguished at B's death. A's LE is extinguished at A's death. Upon A's death, O owns Blackacre in FSA pursuant to O's retained REV interest.

    c. O owns Blackacre in FSA upon A's death. When A died, A's LE was extinguished and B's VR in LE came into present possession as a LE. Upon B's death, B's present LE was extinguished, and O's REV came into present possession as a FSA.

   d. X owns Blackacre in FSA. Although a VR can be devised under a will, B's VR in LE expired at B's death because it was limited in duration to B's life. Therefore, no property interest in Blackacre passed to Y under B's will. The REV held by O is devisable by O's will and therefore passed to X at O's death pursuant to O's will. A's death extinguished A's LE; therefore, no property interest in Blackacre passed to Z under A's will. Upon A's death, the REV now owned by X comes into present possession as a FSA.

   e. O's intestate heirs own Blackacre in FSA at A's death. A REV is inheritable. Therefore, if O died intestate the REV would pass to O's intestate heirs.

   f. O owns Blackacre in FSA. At A's death, A's LE is extinguished. B's VR in LE comes into present possession, but only for the duration of B's lifetime. When B "sold" Blackacre to C, the maximum property interest B could transfer to C was a LE. After the sale, C owned a life estate pur autre vie (for B's life) in Blackacre. The life estate pur autre vie is extinguished at B's death; therefore, no property interest in Blackacre passed to B's spouse under B's will. At B's death, O's REV comes into present possession as a FSA.

Problems On The Defeasible Fee Simples

   3.a. The Lincoln Public Schools have a FSSCS; O has a RE. This grant is not ambiguous. All three signals (punctuation, magic words, O's retained interest) line up as a FSSCS–RE.

   b. This grant is ambiguous. On the one hand, there are two signals that the grant should be construed as conveying a FSD to the Lincoln Public Schools. The defeasing event is inside the granting clause and the description of O's retained interest indicates an automatic transfer of title and possession back to O if the defeasing event occurs (consistent with a retained PR by O). On the other hand, the words describing the defeasing event—"on the express condition"—connote a condition or limitation on use that suggest the grant conveys a FSSCS to the Lincoln Public Schools. If the grant is construed as conveying a FSSCS to the Lincoln Public Schools, then O must retain a RE. Given the strong indication that O retains an automatic PR and not a discretionary RE, a court is more likely to construe this grant as creating a FSD–PR.

c. This grant is ambiguous. On the one hand, the words describing the defeasing event—"on the express condition"—suggest that the Lincoln Public Schools have a FSSCS. On the other hand, the defeasing event is contained within the granting clause, which suggests that the Lincoln Public Schools have a FSD. The retained interest held by the grantor O is implied rather than expressly stated, and therefore will be determined by how a court construes the present interest conveyed to the Lincoln Public Schools. Although this is a close call, a court would most likely rely on the conditional nature of the language describing the defeasing event, and construe this grant as conveying a FSSCS to the Lincoln Public Schools with a RE retained by O.

d. This grant is not ambiguous. Lincoln Public Schools have a FSSEL; Briana has a shifting EI in FSA.

Problems On Future Interests Retained By The Grantor

4.a. A has a LE; O has a REV.

b. A has a LE; B has a VR in FT; O has a REV.

c. A has a TY; O has a REV.

Problems On Future Interests Held By Third Parties

5.a. A has a TY; B has a VR in LE; O has a REV.

b. A has a TY; B has a VR in FSA (due to the modern rule presumption).

c. A has a LE; B has a CR in FSA (due to the modern rule presumption); O has a REV (because B may predecease A).

d. A has a determinable LE; B has a shifting EI in FSA (due to the modern rule presumption). B's future interest cannot be a remainder because it could come into present possession prior to the natural termination of A's present interest if A remarries.

e. A has a LE; the unborn children of B have a CR in FSA (due to the modern rule presumption); O has a REV (because B may never have any children).

f. A has a LE; B1 has a VRSO in FSA (due to the modern rule presumption); O has no retained property interest in Blackacre.

g. B1 owns Blackacre in FSA. A's death extinguishes A's LE, closes the class of B's children (thereby turning the VRSO into a VR held by B1), and causes the VR to come into present possession as a FSA. Any other children of B who are born after A's death do not share in ownership of Blackacre due to the Rule of Convenience, which permanently closes the class of B's children when B1 assumes present possession.

h. O has present possession of Blackacre, subject to a springing EI held by the class of B's unborn children. Because the governing jurisdiction has abolished the Doctrine of Destructibility of Contingent Remainders, the CR held by B's unborn children is not destroyed at A's death. The grantor O takes present possession of Blackacre, and retains present possession until all of B's children are born under the exception to the Rule of Convenience for the unborn class members scenario. At B's death, present possession of Blackacre will "spring forth" from O to B's children. If B dies never having had any children, then O takes ownership of Blackacre in FSA at B's death, and the springing EI is extinguished.

6.a. A has a LE; B has a CR in FSA; O has a REV (because B could die before age 21).

b. A has a LE; B has a VR in FSA; O has no retained property interest in Blackacre.

c. When B died, B's VR in FSA was not extinguished, but rather passed to B's estate. The probate of B's estate will determine the new owner of B's VR in FSA. At A's death, A's LE was extinguished, and the VR in FSA held by the new owner as a result of the probate of B's estate will come into present possession as a FSA.

d. O owns Blackacre in FSA. B's CR was extinguished when B died at age 19. Upon A's death, A's LE was extinguished and O's REV came into present possession as a FSA.

e. O owns Blackacre in FSA. When A died, B's CR must be capable of coming into present possession at the instant of A's death or else the CR is extinguished pursuant to the common law Doctrine of Destructibility of Contingent Remainders. Here, B is only age 19, which fails to satisfy the precondition. Therefore, B's CR is destroyed, and O's REV comes into present possession as a FSA.

f. This is a tricky problem that requires close reading of the grant language. A has a TY that expires on December 2, 2010. B's future interest, however, does not come into present possession until December 3, 2010—thereby leaving a one day "gap." This "gap" means that B's future interest cannot be classified as a remainder, which must come into present possession *immediately* upon the natural termination of the preceding term of years. Therefore, B holds a springing EI in FSA. During the one day "gap" period, O holds present possession of the property subject to B's springing EI. On December 3, 2010, present possession and title in FSA springs forth from O and goes to B.

g. O has present possession of the property, subject to a springing EI in FSA held by A.

7. A has a LE; B1 has a CR in FSA; C has an alternative CR in FSA. Your professor may insist that a CR–CR pattern must always be followed by a REV in O, even when the CRs are in the alternative and either one or the other is certain to come into present possession.

8.a. On this type of problem, it helps to draw a family tree to keep the facts straight.

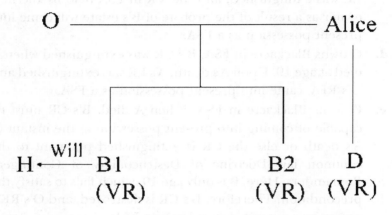

Begin by classifying the interests created by the terms of O's will as of the moment of O's death. Next, apply subsequent facts to determine how those interests change over time.

Classify the Interests: As of the moment of O's death, Alice has a LE; B1 and B2 have a VRSO in FSA. The class is still open because the grant conveys the future interest to "Alice's children" and Alice is still alive.

Analyze the Facts: When D is born, the VRSO is held by B1, B2 and D (who is Alice's child, too).

A VRSO is devisable, so when B1 dies, B1's VRSO passed to H pursuant to the terms of B1's will. Now the VRSO in FSA is held by H, B2 and D.

At Alice's death, the VRSO in FSA closes, turns into a VR, and comes into present possession as a FSA. H, B1 and D own Blackacre in FSA. (As you will see in Chapter 5, they each hold a 1/3 share as tenants in common.)

Did O intend that a son-in-law and another man's child own Blackacre at Alice's death? Probably not.

b. The wording of the grant was probably a drafting error. If the grant had been phrased as "to our children and their heirs who survive Alice," then B2 would be the sole owner of Blackacre at Alice's death.

9.a. Amy has a LE; G1 and G2 have a VRSO and STD in FSA; the Red Cross has a shifting EI in FSA. Note that the language of this grant makes the death of a grandchild before Amy a condition subsequent based on the punctuation of the granting clause. Only a shifting EI (not a CR) can fellow a "vested" fee simple interest held by another third party. Here, the "vested" interest is a combination VRSO and STD.

b. The interests in the grant are unchanged, except that now O's surviving grandchildren (a class) hold the shifting EI in FSA in lieu of the Red Cross. Note that the fact that a class holds this future interest does *not* change its character as a shifting EI.

10.a. A has a LE; A's children (A1 and A2) have a VRSO and STD in FSA; B has a shifting EI in FSA.

b. A has a LE; A2 and X have a VRSO and STD in FSA; B has a shifting EI in FSA. A1's VRSO and STD is not divested unless and until A dies without *any* surviving children. Therefore A1's VRSO and STD passes to X pursuant to the terms of A1's will at Al's death.

c. At A's death, A2 and X own Blackacre in FSA. (As you will see in Chapter 5, they each hold a ½ share as tenants in common.) The divesting condition subsequent is not triggered because one child of A (here, A2) survived A.

11.a. O's estate holds present possession of the $1 million, subject to a springing EI held by Marie. Marie's interest cannot be a remainder because it does not follow the natural termination of a prior present interest held by someone other than the grantor O.

   b. Have you ever heard of a "spendthrift" in-law? A bequest such as this one typically is used if the in-law Tim is a spendthrift (or is just intensely disliked by the grantor O). If O wants the $1 million to go to Marie's children (if any), but not to the spendthrift in-law Tim, this type of bequest typically would be followed by additional language in O's will that transfers the $1 million to a trust for the benefit of Marie's children in the event that Marie predeceased her husband Tim.

■ PROBLEM 3.2 ■

Assume that the modern statutory presumption for conveyance of a FSA applies in this jurisdiction.

On May 1st, O, the owner of Blackacre in FSA, properly executed and delivered a deed gifting the property "to A for life, then to B." B died intestate on May 31st. B's sole intestate heir is B1. What is the state of the title to Blackacre upon B's death? If O does not like B1, can O revoke the conveyance?

Analysis

When O delivered the deed, A had a LE and B had a VR in FSA in Blackacre. The grantor O retained no property interest in Blackacre. At B's death, B's VR in FSA passed to B's sole intestate heir, B1. Once validly executed and delivered, the gift of Blackacre is irrevocable by O (see Chapter 2).

■ PROBLEM 3.3 ■

O, the owner of Blackacre in FSA, conveyed Blackacre "to A and her heirs insofar as the premises are not used for gambling, but if gambling ever occurs on the premises then O shall reenter and terminate A's ownership."

A built a restaurant and a banquet hall on the property fifty years ago. From the beginning of the banquet hall's existence, each year a local high school rented the banquet hall for class reunions. At these reunions, bingo and poker games for cash prizes were part of the evening's entertainment.

O died testate last year. While O was alive, O never attempted to reclaim the property from A. O's will left all of O's property to a local charity ("Charity"). O's sole intestate heir is O1.

Your client wants to buy the property from A, tear down the restaurant and banquet hall, and build a neighborhood retail center instead. The retail center would include a convenience store that sells lottery tickets. Advise your client concerning the risks associated with acquiring title to the property, and how your client may attempt to mitigate these risks. In advising the client, assume that the statute of limitations for a PR or a RE is 20 years, and that it is unclear whether or not the jurisdiction follow the common law rules for transferability of these future interests.

Analysis

To analyze a complex problem such as Problem 3.3, begin by classifying the present and future interests created by the grant language. Second, analyze and apply the factual circumstances to determine what parties may hold property interests in Blackacre today. Third, for this particular problem you must determine what potential future interests your client needs to purchase, and from whom, in order for your client to acquire a FSA ownership interest in Blackacre under all possible scenarios. This third step will assure your client that, no matter how a court may construe this ambiguous grant language, your client is acquiring a FSA. Alternatively, this third step will warn your client of the potential risks associated with the client's proposed acquisition and development of Blackacre.

Classify the Present and Future Interests: This grant language is ambiguous. O's grantee A could have either a FSD or a FSSCS. The grantor O could have either a PR or a RE, depending on how A's present interest is classified.

One signal suggests a FSD because the defeasing event is inside the granting clause. "Insofar" is not a magic word phrase that is closely associated with either a FSD or a FSSCS. It could be read as suggesting either the passage of time (FSD), or as a limitation or restriction on A's use (FSSCS). The description of O's retained interest, with the words "reenter" and "terminate," suggests a discretionary RE, which conflicts with the mandatory nature of the preceding "shall."

Analyze the Facts: Visualize the ambiguity created by the grant language as a decision tree with two branches.

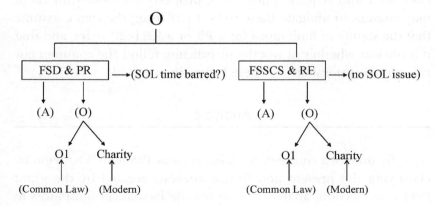

Issue: Has the Statute of Limitations expired?

A court could construe the grant as creating a FSD–PR. Did the bingo and poker games for cash prizes during the high school reunions (dating back at least fifty years) trigger the "gambling" defeasing event, and with it, the statute of limitations for O to assert his right to possession and ownership under the PR? If so, the 20 year statute of limitations on O's PR has expired. If the statute of limitations on O's PR has expired, A has the ability to sell Blackacre to the client free of the gambling restriction. Alternatively, a court could construe the grant as creating a FSSCS–RE. The statute of limitations for a RE does not begin to run until O asserts O's right to possession and ownership of the property under the RE. Here, O never attempted to enter and reclaim the property. Therefore, if the grant is construed as a FSSCS–RE, the RE would not be barred by the statute of limitations. The client would have to purchase the RE in order to acquire FSA title to Blackacre free of any use restrictions on gambling.

The other possibility on these facts is that the "gambling" defeasing event was *not* triggered by bingo and poker games for cash prizes during high school reunions. If the defeasing event has not been triggered, then the client must purchase the FSD/FSSCS from A and the PR/RE in order to acquire FSA title to Blackacre.

Issue: (Transferability) Can the client purchase the PR/RE, and if so, from whom?

At common law, a PR/RE is *not* alienable or devisable. If the jurisdiction follows the common law rule on transferability, then O1, O's intestate heir, owns the PR/RE, but cannot sell the PR/RE to the client. This creates an obvious problem for the client, who does not want to develop the retail center with the convenience store that sells lottery tickets and then later have O1 claim title to Blackacre because the sale of lottery tickets triggered the defeasing event. If the jurisdiction follows the common law rule, the client must either eliminate the convenience store from the development, or restrict the convenience store from selling lottery tickets.

The modern trend is to permit a PR/RE to be alienable and devisable as well as inheritable. If the jurisdiction follows the modern trend, O's PR/RE is now held by the Charity pursuant to the devise under O's will, not O1 as O's intestate heir. The client could negotiate with the Charity to buy the PR/RE, thereby giving the client FSA title to Blackacre free of the "no gambling" restriction.

Issue: Is the defeasing event void as a restraint on alienation?

It is unlikely that the client could buy the FSD/FSSCS from A and then successfully have a court invalidate the "no gambling" use restriction as an invalid restraint on alienation. Barring gambling on Blackacre is unlikely to so restrict the market pool of potential buyers that a court would consider the restriction void as a restraint on alienation.

POINTS TO REMEMBER

- In classifying the FSD and the FSSCS, look for how the classic signals (punctuation, magic words, and the nature of O's future interest) line up. In an essay exam, you will maximize your points by recognizing when the signals are inconsistent and explaining how the language could be construed as either a FSD or a FSSCS. Using the facts of the question, determine if the classification affects the ultimate outcome by focusing on the distinguishing attributes or characteristics (statute of limitations and transferability) of the FSD-PR and the FSSCS-RE alternatives.

- Classify a future interest as a remainder only if the future interest comes into prior possession upon the prior natural termination of a present LE, TY or FT. If a prior present LE, TY or FT can be "cut off" short of a natural termination, the present interest is a determinable LE, TY or FT. The future interest held by a third party that follows a determinable LE, TY or FT must be a shifting EI (not a remainder).

- A secondary life estate properly is classified as a VR in LE (not as a CR).

- Future interests held by third parties other than the grantor come in "paired" combinations. If the first future interest is a

CR, then the second future interest must be a CR. If the first future interest is a VRSTD, then the second future interest must be a shifting EI.

- An EI can be held by a class (it is still an EI, not a VRSO), or subject to a precondition (it is still an EI, not a CR). Don't be fooled. Focus on the fundamental rules for determining remainders and executory interests. If the prior present interest can be "cut off" short of a natural termination, the next future interest must be classified as a shifting EI.

- By definition, a VRSO must have at least one class member who immediately can take present possession. Otherwise, the class holds a CR. For a VRSO, class members who are born after the time for present possession arrives, or who have not satisfied a precondition to taking present possession, do not share in ownership of the property (they are "shut out" forever) based on the Rule of Convenience.

- A class that still holds a CR when the time arrives for present possession by definition has not one member who is capable of taking present possession. At common law, the CR is destroyed in this situation based on the Doctrine of Destructibility. Modern jurisdictions that have abolished the Doctrine of Destructibility suspend the Rule of Convenience in this particular scenario. The grantor O holds present possession of the property, subject to a springing EI held by the class. All class members eventually will share in ownership of the property under the exception to the Rule of Convenience created for this situation.

CHAPTER 4

The Rule Against Perpetuities

Many students punt learning the Rule Against Perpetuities ("RAP") and still pass Property. But it is unlikely you will ace Property without being able to perform a RAP analysis.

To get the most out of Chapter 4, read the Review below and then try to work the Problems at the end of Chapter 4. Do not struggle too much with the Problems on your first attempt. Focus instead primarily on the *solutions* to the Problems, then *reread* the Review section. This material takes time to absorb, and it cannot be learned in the abstract. By bouncing back and forth between the Problems, the solutions, and the concepts, principles and general rules described in the Review, you will learn to recognize the standard patterns that tend to make future interests valid or void under the RAP.

RULE AGAINST PERPETUITIES REVIEW

The common law version of the RAP provides that no future interest is valid unless it either vests or fails to vest within a life or lives in being plus twenty-one years.[1] To perform a RAP analysis,

---

1. Under the RAP, the 21 years period always is extended by ten months for gestation, if applicable.

the first step is to identify the future interests in the grant that must be tested under the RAP. The following diagram illustrates this part of the analysis.

Deciding What Future Interests Must Be Tested Under The RAP

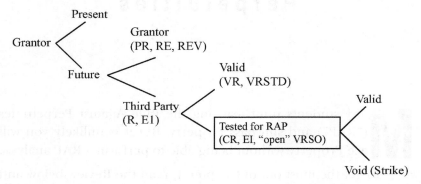

Only three future interests must be tested under the RAP. These three future interests are:

- ■ the Executory Interest (EI);

- ■ the Contingent Remainder (CR); and

- ■ the Vested Remainder Subject To Open (VRSO).

Note carefully that a VRSTD is treated as "vested" for purposes of the RAP and therefore is not tested. A shifting EI that follows a VRSTD, however, is subject to the RAP and must be tested for compliance. If the grant contains a CR–CR pattern, then both CRs must be tested under the RAP.

Watch For A Savings Clause

In the real world, attorneys who create future interests that are potentially void under the RAP also will incorporate a **savings clause** into the document or instrument that creates the future interests. A savings clause functions to vest all future interests that are subject to being voided by the RAP within the perpetuities period.[2]

On a multiple choice exam, the presence of a savings clause eliminates the need to do a RAP analysis by precluding the possibility that any of the three future interests subject to the RAP may be void. On an essay exam, to receive full credit for your answer the professor may expect you to do a full-blown RAP analysis, and then note that a void future interest is nevertheless "saved" from being struck as void under the RAP due to a savings clause.

RAP Analysis: Key Concepts

There are two key concepts involved in analyzing any RAP problem. The first key concept is when the perpetuities period begins and ends. The second key concept is when the future interest "vests" for purposes of the RAP (let's call this "RAP-vesting"). RAP-vesting has its own set of "vesting" rules, described in more detail later in Chapter 4,[3] for each of the three future interests (EI, CR, VRSO) that must be tested under the RAP.

As you apply these two concepts in performing a RAP analysis, you must remember that you have entered the "RAP Twilight Zone." Any woman, no matter how old, is assumed to be fertile and capable of having a child. Everyone who is alive at the time of the grant can die instantaneously afterwards. The RAP tends to void future interests based on the most improbable series of imagined future events, which at first blush may make a RAP analysis seem random and arbitrary. Once you gain experience with the RAP by solving problems, you will recognize patterns in the structure of grants that tend to make future interests either valid or void under

---

2. For example, if the grantor O is alive and desires to give O's grandchildren a VRSO interest in the property, the savings clause for the grandchildren's VRSO would provide as follows:

Notwithstanding any other provision of this document, each future interest created by this document shall vest and come into present possession not later than 21 years after the death of the last survivor of my children who are alive at the time that this document becomes irrevocable.

3. *See infra* Concept: RAP–Vesting.

the RAP. Learning to recognize these patterns takes practice, which is why there is a lengthy list of Problems, along with detailed solutions, at the end of Chapter 4.

Concept: The Perpetuities Period

After classifying the interests in the grant, the second step in a RAP analysis is to determine when the perpetuities period begins. The perpetuities period begins when the grant becomes effective to transfer a property interest (when the grant is "made").

For future interests created by the terms of a will (a devise), the grant is made and the perpetuities period begins on the date of death of the testator. (Memory Tip: Devise=Death of Testator.) For future interests created by an inter vivos transfer (a transfer made by the grantor while the grantor is still alive), the grant is made and the perpetuities period begins on the date the transfer becomes irrevocable under the law of gifts or the law of contracts for a bargained sale. (Memory Tip: Inter Vivos Transfer=Irrevocable.)

The duration of the perpetuities period combines a flexible element (the lives of persons who are alive at the time the grant is made) with a fixed period of 21 years. The concept of the perpetuities period is illustrated by the picture below.

The Perpetuities Period

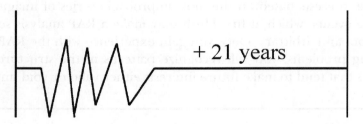

+ 21 years

Life or Lives in Being (persons who are alive at the time the grant becomes effective)

As the picture illustrates, the variable element in the duration of the perpetuities period is the lives in being—individuals who are alive at the time the grant is made ("LIB"). Note carefully that not all LIB matter. The only individual LIB who count (and you can ignore the rest of the world) are those persons whose actions during life, or by their death, can somehow affect the future interest being tested.

The third step in a RAP analysis is to identify those individuals who are the relevant LIB (i.e., the LIB who can affect the future interest that is being tested). Most of the time, the relevant LIB are expressly named or described as a group or class in the language of the grant. The most difficult RAP problems contain relevant LIB who are implied, but not stated expressly or described, based on the circumstances or the language of the grant.

The classic example of implied LIB is a future interest (a CR or a VRSO) given to a class of grandchildren of the grantor O. If the grant is a devise in O's will, the relevant LIB for the grandchildren's future interest will be those children of O who are alive when the grant is made at O's death. The death of the last to die of O's children terminates the "elastic" part of the perpetuities period, and simultaneously closes the class of O's grandchildren, thereby making the grandchildren's future interest valid under the RAP. If, however, the grantor O is alive at the time the grant is made, the future interest given to O's grandchildren most likely is void under the RAP.[4]

Methods For The Last Step Of A RAP Analysis

After identifying the future interests that are subject to RAP testing, determining when the grant is made, and identifying the relevant LIB, the fourth step in a RAP analysis is to determine if the future interest you are testing will be RAP-vested or destroyed before the perpetuities period ends. Professors generally use one or more of the following methods to help students in performing this last step in the RAP analysis. If your professor uses only one

---

4. *See infra*, Problem 4.3, Grant #19.

method and that method does not work for you, then try to use one of the other methods. All three methods, if properly applied, will lead you to the correct answer. The solutions to the Problems at the end of Chapter 4 illustrate all three methods so that you will have a better sense of how each method works.

1.   The Tether Method. The tether method helps students to visualize how the perpetuities period—with its elastic (relevant LIB) and fixed (21 years) components—operates. Imagine the perpetuities period as a tether that is anchored to the ground at the time the grant is made. The perpetuities period literally ties or tethers (it *connects*) ownership of the future interest being tested under the RAP. This "tether" is a *person*, a relevant LIB who is alive at the time the future interest is created, whose actions during life or whose death (plus 21 more years, if necessary) will determine if the future interest being tested is either RAP-vested or destroyed.

The tether method works particularly well for analyzing springing and shifting EIs. Future interests that lack a "tethering person" to anchor certainty in ownership of the future interest tend to fail the RAP.

2.   The Validating Life Method. The validating life method is featured in at least one popular casebook,[5] and is more fully explained (with additional examples) in a law review article written by the late Professor Jesse Dukeminier.[6] Unfortunately, perhaps only Professor Dukeminier himself could teach this method effectively so that all of his students could understand it. If your professor relies predominantly on this method, see the Appendix at the end of Chapter 4 for a more detailed explanation, along with tips and tricks for using the validating life method.

3.   The Diagram Or Timeline Method. Some students turn to the diagram or timeline method out of sheer frustration with the validating life method. The diagram or timeline method works

---

5.   JESSE DUKEMINIER, JAMES E. KRIER, GREGORY S. ALEXANDER, AND MICHAEL H. SCHILL, PROPERTY, 245–48 (6th ed. 2006) ("PROPERTY").

6.   Jesse Dukeminier, *A Modern Guide to Perpetuities*, 74 CAL. L. REV. 1867 (1986) ("Dukeminier").

particularly well for testing a VRSO or a CR that is a class gift. This method helps students to visualize the possibility of an afterborn child, which is the most likely reason that a class gift will be void under the RAP. The diagram or timeline method is easier to illustrate with a picture than to explain in words. The solutions to the Problems at the end of Chapter 4 contain pictures that show how the diagram or timeline method works.

Concept: RAP–Vesting

When does a future interest "vest" for purposes of the RAP? In other words, what is RAP-vesting?

RAP-vesting means that there is certainty concerning who (if anyone) owns the future interest being tested. To be "vested" for purposes of the RAP, we must know that the future interest will either (1) be owned by an identified individual or an identified class of individuals, or (2) the future interest will be permanently extinguished (so we know that no one ever will own it). A future interest whose ownership is still "in limbo" at the expiration of the perpetuities period (meaning that we do not know precisely who will own the future interest, or whether the future interest will be extinguished in the future) is struck as void under the RAP.

This need for certainty is why class gifts with an internal precondition are so vulnerable to being voided by the RAP. An example of a class gift with an internal precondition for the class members would be the following grant: "to A for life, then to the children of B who attain age 25." The attainment of age 25 is an internal precondition imposed on all of the members of the class of B's children. The RAP requires that we know exactly which individual members of the class have satisfied the precondition before the perpetuities period expires. If satisfying an internal precondition could still be in limbo for some class members, then the entire class gift is void, even for those class members who will have satisfied the internal precondition by the end of the perpetuities period. This principle is known as the **all-or-nothing rule for class gifts.**[7]

Depending on the type of future interest being tested, RAP-vesting may require that the future interest must come into present possession and turn into a present interest (this is called "vesting in possession") or be extinguished by the end of the perpetuities period. For other future interests, RAP-vesting only requires that the future interest being tested must turn into a VR within the perpetuities period. A VR can remain a future interest (not yet be vested in possession) at the end of the perpetuities period and still be valid under the RAP.

Let's look at the RAP-vesting requirements for the three future interests (EI, CR and VRSO) that are susceptible to being voided by the RAP. We'll start first with the easiest ones to analyze, and work up to the most difficult ones. In order from easiest to most difficult, the future interests that must be tested under the RAP are listed below.

- The EI
- The CR Held By An Individual
- The CR Class Gift With No Internal Preconditions
- The VRSO With No Internal Preconditions
- The CR Class Gift Or The VRSO With Internal Preconditions

■ **The Executory Interest**

An EI RAP-vests when the future interest comes into present possession and turns into a present interest. In testing an EI, your focus must be on when, if ever, the EI would turn into a present interest.

A so-called "one-way" or "open-ended" EI never has a set time to turn into a present interest. The EI simply remains in limbo as

---

7. *See* PROPERTY, *supra*, at 248; THOMAS F. BERGIN AND PAUL G. HASKELL, PREFACE TO ES- TATES IN LAND AND FUTURE INTERESTS, 194–95 (2d ed. 1984).

a future interest until the EI comes into present possession at some indefinite time in the future. A one-way EI is easy to spot on the exam, and it is always void under the RAP.

Problem 4.1 at the end of Chapter 4 allows you to practice analyzing grants that contain an EI for compliance with the RAP. The solutions also discuss how a grant that contains a void EI could be rewritten to comply with the RAP (a possible essay exam question by professors).

■ The CR Held By An Individual

Unlike an EI, a CR held by an individual does not have to come into present possession within the perpetuities period to be RAP-vested. The CR only needs to turn into a VR within the perpetuities period to be RAP-vested.

In testing a CR under the RAP, your focus should be on when the CR will turn into a VR, or, alternatively, when the CR will be forever extinguished or destroyed. For a CR held by an individual, the RAP analysis (specifically, the point in time where you must focus your attention) differs depending on whether or not the governing jurisdiction follows or has abolished the Doctrine of Destructibility.[8] Let's look first at the RAP analysis in a common law jurisdiction that applies the Doctrine of Destructibility. Next, we'll compare the RAP analysis in a jurisdiction that has abolished the Doctrine of Destructibility.

Individual CR: Doctrine of Destructibility Applies

If the jurisdiction applies the Doctrine of Destructibility, then the CR must either be "vested" (have turned into a VR) or "fail" (be forever destroyed) before or at the moment when the prior present estate naturally terminates.[9] In doing a RAP analysis, focus on the prior present interest, and whether the natural termination of that

---

8. See supra, Chapter 3, Key Attributes: Survivorship As A Precondition And The Doctrine Of Destructibility.

9. The present interest that precedes a CR and naturally terminates must be either a LE, TY or FT. See supra, Chapter 3, Distinguish-ing Remainders From Executory Interests. If the LE, TY or FT can terminate other than naturally, it is a determinable LE, TY or FT, and the future interest that follows is classi-fied (and tested under the RAP) as a shifting EI. See id.

prior present interest must occur either during the life or at the death of a person who is alive at the time the grant takes effect, or within 21 years thereafter.

Below is a summary of the principles for analyzing a CR held by an individual that follows each of the three naturally terminating prior present estates (LE, TY and FT). Be sure to study the application of these principles by reading the answers to the grants in Problem 4.2 at the end of Chapter 4.

Prior Life Estate

If the prior present interest is a LE, then the next CR will always be valid under the RAP if the prior LE is held only by a LIB (a person who is alive at the time the grant is made). If the prior LE is or could be held by a person who is not alive at the time the grant is made, then you cannot rely on the natural termination of the prior LE to prove that the CR satisfies the RAP. Instead, you must look to the precondition that makes the future interest a CR. If the ability to satisfy the precondition is held or controlled only by a relevant LIB, so that the precondition must be satisfied (if at all) within that relevant LIB's life, at death, or within 21 years after death, then the CR is valid under the RAP. If, however, the ability to satisfy the precondition is or could be held or controlled by a person who is not alive at the time the grant is made (and thus does not qualify as a LIB), then the CR is void under the RAP.

Prior Term of Years

If the prior present interest is a TY that must expire within 21 years after the grant becomes effective, then the next CR will always be valid. The CR will either turn into a VR and immediately come into present possession, or be forever destroyed, if the precondition is not satisfied when the TY expires. Either scenario occurs within 21 years (without the need to worry about who is and is not a LIB). Therefore, the CR is valid under the RAP.

If the prior present interest is a TY that will not expire within 21 years after the grant becomes effective, then you cannot rely on the natural termination of the prior TY to prove that the CR satisfies the RAP. Instead, you must look to the precondition that makes the future interest a CR. The ability to satisfy this precondition (so that the CR will turn into a VR) must be held or controlled only by a LIB, so that the precondition can be satisfied within the LIB's life, at death, or within 21 years after the LIB's death. If so, the CR is valid under the RAP. If, however, the ability to satisfy the precondition is or could be held by a person who is not alive at the time the grant is made, then the CR is void under the RAP.

Prior Fee Tail

By its very nature, the natural termination point for a FT always can occur after the death of all LIB at the time the grant is made plus 21 years. The FT expires when the last lineal descendant dies, which could be more than 21 years after all persons who were alive at the time the grant was made are dead. If the prior present interest is a FT, then the next CR will be void under the RAP unless, based on the precondition, the CR must turn into a VR within the perpetuities period.

Focus on how and when the precondition can be satisfied, and whether the ability to satisfy the precondition is held or controlled only by LIB at the time the grant is made. If so, the CR is valid under the RAP. If, however, the ability to satisfy the precondition is or could be held or controlled by a person who is not alive at the time the grant is made, then the CR is void under the RAP.

Individual CR: Doctrine of Destructibility Abolished

Recall from Chapter 3 that if the jurisdiction has abolished the Doctrine of Destructibility, then a CR that is not ready to turn into a present interest immediately at the moment of natural termination of the prior present interest will not be destroyed. Instead, the

CR will turn into a springing EI.[10] Consequently, CRs are much more vulnerable to being void under the RAP in jurisdictions that have abolished the Doctrine of Destructibility.

In analyzing a CR held by individual in a jurisdiction that has abolished the Doctrine of Destructibility, focus on who holds the CR and can control whether the precondition is satisfied. If the precondition involves a time element that is equal to or less than 21 years, or the ability to satisfy the precondition is held or controlled only by a person or persons who are LIB at the time the grant is made, then the CR is valid under the RAP.

For example, assume the grant is "to A for life, then to B if B attains age 21." B is a newborn child (a LIB) at the time the grant is made. The attainment of age 21 is a time element that will either be satisfied or B's CR will be extinguished within the perpetuities period.

If the ability to satisfy the precondition is or could be held by a person who is not alive at the time the grant is made, then the CR is void under the RAP. The CR also may be void if the grant contains a time element that exceeds 21 years. If the precondition contains a time element that exceeds 21 years, the CR is valid only if you determine the time element either must be satisfied, or the CR will be extinguished, within the perpetuities period.

Problem 4.2 at the end of Chapter 4 allows you to practice analyzing grants that create a CR held by an individual.

■ The CR Class Gift With No Internal Preconditions

The CR class gift with no internal preconditions arises in a unique (and thus easily recognized) situation. This situation arises only when, at the time the grant is made, no members of the class are born and ascertainable, and the class gift itself contains no other internal preconditions that the class members (once born) must satisfy. To illustrate, assume the grant is "to A for life, then to B for

---

10. *See supra*, Chapter 3, Key Attributes: Doctrine Of Destructibility.
Survivorship As A Precondition And The

life, then to the children of C and their heirs." At the time the grant is made, A, B and C are all alive (and are relevant LIB), but C has never had any children. The unborn children of C hold a CR class gift with no internal preconditions.

In testing a CR class gift with no internal preconditions, the CR class gift does not have to come into present possession and turn into a present interest within the perpetuities period to be RAP-vested. The CR class gift only must turn into a VR within the perpetuities period to be RAP-vested. As with an individual CR, the RAP analysis (specifically, the point in time where you must focus your analysis) differs depending on whether or not the governing jurisdiction follows or has abolished the Doctrine of Destructibility. Let's look first at the RAP analysis in a common law rule jurisdiction that applies the Doctrine of Destructibility, and then review the RAP analysis in a jurisdiction where the Doctrine of Destructibility has been abolished. You will notice similarities, but also a few key differences, from the RAP analysis of a CR held by an individual.

CR Class Gift With No Internal Precondition: Doctrine of Destructibility Applies

In analyzing a CR class gift with no preconditions in a jurisdiction that applies the Doctrine of Destructibility, look first to when the prior present estate (LE, TY or FT) must naturally terminate. This natural termination point controls the RAP analysis. In a jurisdiction that applies the Doctrine of Destructibility, only one of two things can happen to the CR class gift when the prior present estate naturally terminates. The CR class gift must either: (1) close, become a VR ("RAP-vest"), and turn into a present interest; or (2) be forever destroyed ("fail") because no class members have been born. If the prior present interest must naturally terminate within the perpetuities period, then the CR class gift with no internal preconditions is valid under the RAP. The CR class gift will either RAP-vest or be extinguished by the Doctrine of Destructibility at the moment of natural termination of the prior present interest. Either way, the RAP is satisfied.

If the prior present interest could naturally terminate beyond the perpetuities period, you cannot rely on the Doctrine of

Destructibility to extinguish the CR that follows the prior present interest within the perpetuities period. Consequently, you must focus on when the CR class will close. For example, a class of grandchildren closes upon the death of the last to die of their parent or parents. For purposes of illustration, assume that the parent or parents are the children of the grantor O. If the parent(s) are all LIB at the time the grant is made, the CR class gift to the grandchildren of the grantor O is valid under the RAP. If one or more parents could be born after the grant is made, then the CR class gift to the grandchildren is void under the RAP.[11]

To illustrate these principles in another context, consider the previous example of the grant "to A for life, then B for life, then to the children of C and their heirs" where C has never had any children. If the jurisdiction applies the Doctrine of Destructibility, then the CR class gift held by C's unborn children must either come into present possession at the moment in time when the prior life estate terminates (because at least one child of C has been born),[12] or must be destroyed forever at that moment (because no child of C has ever been born). Because both of the prior life estate holders (A and B) are LIB at the time the grant is made, the CR held by C's unborn children will (regardless of whether B predeceases or survives A) either conclusively RAP-vest or be extinguished by the Doctrine of Destructibility within the perpetuities period. Therefore, the CR held by C's unborn children satisfies the RAP.

CR Class Gift With No Internal Preconditions: Doctrine of Destructibility Abolished

A CR class gift created in a jurisdiction that has abolished the Doctrine of Destructibility is more vulnerable to being void under

---

11. *Compare* Problem 4.3, Grant #18 *with* Problem 4.3, Grant #19.

12. If one or more children of C are born before the prior life estate terminates, the CR turns into a VRSO. Under the Rule of Convenience, the class gift to C's children will come into present possession and be owned by C's children. Even if C is alive at the termination of the prior life estate, and there-

fore C could have more children, under the Rule of Convenience any children of C born after the class gift comes into present possession are forever "shut out" of sharing in the property. *See supra*, Chapter 3, When A VRSO Closes. *See also* Dukeminier, *supra*, 74 CAL. L. REV. at 1892–93 and illustrations 16–17 (explaining application of the Rule of Convenience).

the RAP. This increased vulnerability results from the exception to the Rule of Convenience for unborn class members.[13] Recall that under this exception, if the natural termination of the prior present interest occurs and no class members have been born or the class members are not yet ascertainable,[14] the CR is not destroyed in a jurisdiction that has abolished the Doctrine of Destructibility. Rather, when the prior present interest naturally terminates, the CR held by unborn or unascertainable persons becomes a springing EI. This springing EI will not come into present possession (and thereby RAP-vest) until all possible class members are born and ascertainable.

In testing a CR class gift with no internal preconditions in a jurisdiction that has abolished the Doctrine of Destructibility, focus on when the class will finally close. For example, if the class will close when a parent or parents die, determine whether *all* of the potential parents are LIB at the time the grant is made. If all of the parents are all LIB at the time the grant is made, the CR class gift is valid under the RAP because the class will close when the last LIB parent dies.[15] If one or more potential parents could be born after the grant is made, the CR class gift is void under the RAP. The class could close at the death of the afterborn parent, which may be more than 21 years after all of the LIB parents are dead and therefore after the perpetuities period ends.

A similar analysis applies if the CR class gift is held by the unascertainable heirs of a living person (let's call this living person "X"). Focus on X. If X is a LIB at the time the grant is made, the class of X's heirs must close at X's death, which is within the perpetuities period. If X is not a LIB at the time the grant is made, then the CR is void under the RAP.

The above discussion is admittedly abstract, so let's apply these principles to our familiar example of the grant "to A for life,

---

13. *See supra*, Chapter 3, Special Rules: Class Members Who Hold A CR.

14. The classic example of an "unascertainable" class is a grant to the heirs of a person who is still alive.

15. We do not need to know which parent will die last. All we need to know is that all parents are LIB, so that whatever parent dies last will be a LIB.

then to B for life, then to the children of C and their heirs." Assume that at the time the grant is made, A, B and C are all alive, but C has never had any children.

In this example, A could die, then B could die, but C could still be alive without yet having had any children. In a jurisdiction that has abolished the Doctrine of Destructibility, at the death of B the CR held by C's unborn children would not be destroyed, but rather would turn into springing EI. The springing EI would not come into present possession or be extinguished (recall that coming into present possession is required for an EI to RAP-vest) until the parent C dies and the class of C's (still unborn) children finally is closed.[16] At C's death, the springing EI is either extinguished (because C died never having had any children) or all of the children of C[17] take present possession of the property. Because C is a LIB, the CR-turned-EI is valid under the RAP.

To test your understanding, let's compare the grant "to A for life, then to A's grandchildren."[18] Assume that at the time the grant becomes effective, A is alive and has one child, A1, but A has no grandchildren. Thus, A's grandchildren have a CR class gift with no internal preconditions.

Focus your attention on when the class of A's grandchildren must close. This class of grandchildren will close only when the last

---

16. Note that here the special exception to the Rule of Convenience for a CR held by an unborn or unascertainable class applies. Under this exception, the springing EI does *not* come into present possession when the first child of C is born. Instead, the class is held open until C dies, and then all children of C share in present possession. *See supra*, Chapter 3, Recognizing The Unborn Or Unascertainable Class Situation.

17. If a child of C was born, but died prior to the time for taking present possession of the property because the class was being held open until C died under the exception to the Rule of Convenience, the personal representative of the deceased child's estate would take the predeceased child's share once the class closed and finally came into present

possession. *See* Dukeminier, *supra*, 74 CAL. L. REV. at 1892, Illustration 16.

18. If the governing jurisdiction follows the Doctrine of Destructibility, the RAP analysis of this grant is easy because you focus on the natural termination of A's prior life estate. The CR class gift either vests and comes into present possession under the Rule of Convenience (because at least one of A's grandchildren has been born by the time of A's death) or the CR class gift is destroyed under the Doctrine of Destructibility at A's death (because no grandchild of A has been born). Either way, the vesting or failing occurs at the moment of A's death. Because A is a LIB at the time the grant is made, the CR class gift is valid under the RAP in a jurisdiction that applies the Doctrine of Destructibility.

child of A (A's children are the parents who give rise to A's grandchildren) dies. On these facts, there is no assurance that the parents whose deaths will close the class of A's grandchildren will all be LIB at the time the grant is made. In addition to A1, A could have another child ("A2") who is born after the grant is made. Next, A could die, but A1 and A2 still do not have any children at A's death. In a jurisdiction that has abolished the Doctrine of Destructibility, the CR held by the class of A's still unborn grandchildren would not be destroyed at A's death, but rather would turn into a springing EI. Under the special exception to the Rule of Convenience, the springing EI would not RAP-vest by coming into present possession until all of A's grandchildren are born. This would occur when the last of A1 (the LIB parent) and A2 (the afterborn parent who is not a LIB) dies. A1 (the LIB parent) could die quickly, but the afterborn parent A2 could live to be 100 years old (much longer than 21 years after the death of A, A1 and all other persons who were alive at the time the grant was made). The potential longevity of the afterborn parent A2 makes the CR held by the class of A's grandchildren void under the RAP in a jurisdiction that has abolished the Doctrine of Destructibility.

Problem 4.3 at the end of Chapter 4 allows you to practice analyzing grants that contain a CR class gift with no internal preconditions in both a jurisdiction that follows the Doctrine of Destructibility and in a jurisdiction that has abolished the Doctrine of Destructibility.

■ VRSO With No Internal Preconditions

The type of grant language that creates a VRSO with no internal preconditions is exactly the same as a CR class gift with no internal preconditions. The only distinction (but an important one) is that, according to the facts of the problem, at the time the grant is made at least one class member is born, alive and ascertainable. This class members holds a VRSO.

Like a CR class gift with no internal preconditions, a VRSO with no internal preconditions does not have to come into present possession and turn into a present interest within the perpetuities

period. To be RAP-vested, the VRSO with no internal preconditions only needs to turn into a VR within the perpetuities period.

There are two possible ways that a VRSO with no internal
preconditions can RAP-vest by turning into a VR. The VRSO closes
and turns into a VR (thereby becoming RAP-vested) at the earlier
of:

(1) the moment of natural termination of the prior present
estate (LE, TY or FT). At the moment of natural termination,
the VRSO closes, turns into a VR (thereby RAP-vesting), and
immediately comes into present possession under the Rule of
Convenience;[19] or

(2) the moment when it becomes impossible for any more class
members to come into existence (typically, because a parent or
parents have died, and no more children or grandchildren can
be born.)

In testing a VRSO with no internal preconditions for compliance with the RAP, focus first on the prior present interest (LE, TY
or FT), and whether the natural termination of that prior present
interest must occur within the perpetuities period. Here, the
general rules described previously in the section entitled The CR
Held By An Individual for each of the three naturally terminating
prior estates (LE, TY or FT) govern. Under these general rules, if
the prior present LE or TY must naturally terminate within the
perpetuities period, then under the Rule of Convenience the
VRSO will turn into a VR and RAP-vest within the perpetuities
period. Note that a prior present FT is never assured of naturally
terminating within the perpetuities period.

If the prior present estate could terminate naturally beyond
the perpetuities period, focus on when the VRSO must turn into a
VR through the closing of the class because it is impossible for any
more class members to come into existence. If the VRSO with no

---

19. Recall that under the Rule of Convenience, the class closes and vests in possession
even though additional class members could
be born afterwards. These afterborn class
members are cut off and do not share in the
present ownership of the property.

preconditions is a class of children or grandchildren, focus on when the class closes due to the death of the last parent or parents who can generate the class members. If the parent(s) are all LIB at the time the grant is made, the VRSO is valid under the RAP. If one or more parents could be born after the grant is made, the VRSO is void under the RAP.

Problem 4.3 at the end of Chapter 4 allows you to practice analyzing grants that contain a VRSO with no internal preconditions for compliance with the RAP.

■ The CR Class Gift Or VRSO With Internal Preconditions

A CR class gift or a VRSO with internal preconditions is the most challenging type of future interest to analyze under the RAP. Classic examples of internal preconditions are that all class members must survive a specified individual, or that all class members must attain a certain age. Under the all-or-nothing rule for class gifts, a gift to a class of individuals is not RAP-vested in any member of the class until the interest of each and every class member has vested. This means that every class member (including class members who could be born after the grant is made, and therefore are not LIB) must be able to satisfy the precondition within the perpetuities period. The all-or-nothing rule greatly increases the likelihood of a RAP violation, particularly when the rule is combined with the possibility of a class member who could be born after the grant is made.

Like a class gift with no internal preconditions, a class gift with an internal precondition does not have to come into present possession and turn into a present interest within the perpetuities period to be RAP-vested. The class gift with an internal precondition only must turn into a VR (but under the all-or-nothing rule it must be a VR for all class members) within the perpetuities period.

The RAP analysis for determining whether a class gift with an internal precondition is valid or void is the same analysis used for a CR class gift or a VRSO with no internal preconditions, but with an extra analytical step due to the all-or-nothing rule. When the class gift contains an internal precondition, two criteria must be satisfied for the future interest being tested to be valid under the RAP:

(1) The class must close within the perpetuities period, and

(2) Each and every member of the class must be able to satisfy the precondition within the perpetuities period.

Problem 4.3 at the end of Chapter 4 allows you to practice analyzing grants that contain a class gift with an internal precondition for compliance with the RAP.

Striking A Void Future Interest

If you determine that a future interest is void under the common law version of the RAP, you must strike from the grant the language that creates the void future interest. The striking process is purely mechanical. No consideration is given to how the revised grant language, and the present and future interests that remain after the offending language is struck, may be inconsistent with the original intent of the grantor. In fact, on the exam you should not be surprised if the revised grant language is contrary to the grantor's original intent. Your analysis is not wrong. This is how the RAP operates (and why professors often criticize the RAP).

To strike the offending grant language, begin striking at the end of the granting clause that creates the void future interest, and work backwards to "line out" the offending language until you reach the end of the granting clause that creates the next prior valid interest. The Problems at the end of Chapter 4 allow you to practice striking void future interests.

Exam Tip: Striking And Re–Analyzing Grant Language

If the offending grant language is part of a larger essay question (with a description of events that occurred after the grant was made), then you must respond to the question in light of the revised grant language that remains after striking the void future interest. To respond to an essay question where a void future interest is involved, reclassify the present and future interests created under the language of the revised grant after striking the void future interests, and then treat this revised language as if it were the original grant. Analyze the subsequent events based on the revised grant language. Typically, the outcome of your analysis will be dramatically different from the intention of the grantor. C'est la vie in the crazy world of the common law RAP.

Modern Approaches To The Rule Against Perpetuities

Dissatisfaction with the common law version of the RAP has led jurisdictions to modify the RAP, either judicially or by statute, or to abolish the RAP altogether. The two predominant approaches to reform in jurisdictions that have retained the RAP are the wait-and-see approach and the Uniform Statutory Rule Against Perpetuities ("USRAP").

Under the wait-and-see approach, a future interest that is valid under the common law version of the RAP remains valid. A future interest that is void under the common law version of the RAP is not struck immediately from the grant language. Rather, one waits to see if the future interest does in fact RAP-vest[20] within the perpetuities period.

Under the USRAP approach, a future interest that is valid under the common law version of the RAP remains valid. If the future interest is void under the common law version of the RAP, one must wait for 90 years (measured from when the grant is made) to determine if the future interest does in fact RAP-vest within the 90–year period.

When analyzing a future interest under these modern approaches to the RAP, your first step is to determine whether the future interest is valid under the common law version of the RAP. If so, the future interest is automatically valid under both of the modern approaches. If the future interest being test is *void* under the common law version of the RAP:

---

20. Remember that to RAP-vest, an EI must come into present possession; a CR or VRSO must only turn into a VR.

- in a wait-and-see jurisdiction, one waits to see when the future interest actually does RAP-vest within the perpetuities period.

- in a USRAP jurisdiction, one waits for 90 years to see if the future interest actually does RAP-vest within the 90–year period.

If the future interest has not RAP-vested within the perpetuities period, under these modern approaches the court will reform the grant language. In reforming the grant language (unlike the common law's striking approach), the court will consider the grantor's intent. To the extent possible, the court will rewrite the grant to RAP-vest the future interest while still approximating the grantor's intent for the disposition of the property.

RULE AGAINST PERPETUITIES
CHECKLIST

With the above Review in mind, the Rule Against Perpetuities Checklist is presented below.

A. CLASSIFY THE FUTURE INTERESTS AND DETERMINE WHETHER THE GRANTING INSTRUMENT CONTAINS A SAVINGS CLAUSE. Classify the future interests in the grant to determine if the grant contains an EI, a CR or a VRSO. If the grant contains any of these three types of future interests, note that the existence of a savings clause in the granting instrument eliminates the need to strike any future interest that is void under the RAP. Absent a savings clause, each of the three types of future interests must be tested for validity under the common law version of the RAP (even if the jurisdiction applies a modern approach).

Begin by identifying the perpetuities period and the relevant LIB according to Part B of the checklist. If the future interest being tested is an EI, proceed to Part C. If the future interest being tested is a CR, proceed to Part D. If the future interest being tested is a VRSO, proceed to Part E. If the jurisdiction applies the common law version of the RAP, proceed to Part F to strike a void future interest. If the jurisdiction applies a modern version of the RAP, proceed to Part G for further analysis of a future interest that is void under the common law version of the RAP.

B. **DETERMINE THE PERPETUITIES PERIOD AND THE RELEVANT LIVES IN BEING.** Identify the point in time when the perpetuities period begins and use this moment as your reference point to identify the relevant LIB.

   1. **Perpetuities Period Begins?** The perpetuities period begins when the future interests created by the language of the grant become effective.

      a. **Inter Vivos Grant.** The perpetuities period begins when the grant of the future interest becomes irrevocable.

      b. **Devise In A Will.** The perpetuities period begins when the testator who made the will containing the grant dies.

   2. **Relevant LIB?** List all individuals who are alive when the grant is made and whose actions during life or by their death can impact the future interest being tested.

      a. **LIB Expressly Named Or Described In Grant.** Consider all individuals who are either named or described as a class in the language of the grant as potential candidates for your list of relevant LIB.

      b. **LIB Implied From Grant Language.** Consider whether persons not identified or described in the language of the grant who nevertheless are relevant LIB (e.g., the parents of a class of grandchildren).

C. **TESTING AN EXECUTORY INTEREST.** An EI is RAP-vested once the EI comes into present possession. Look to the terms and conditions of the grant language to determine when, if ever, the EI is extinguished ("fails").

   1. **When Must The EI Turn Into A Present Interest?** Focus on your list of relevant LIB to determine when the

perpetuities period ends. If the EI could turn into a present interest beyond the lifetime of all of your relevant LIB (plus 21 years), then the EI is void. Proceed to Part F to strike the grant language that creates the EI.

2. **When Must The EI Be Extinguished?** Focus on your list of relevant LIB to determine when the perpetuities period ends. If the EI permanently could be extinguished beyond the lifetime of all relevant LIB (plus 21 years), then the EI is void. Proceed to Part F to strike the grant language that creates the EI.

3. **Is The EI Valid?** If the EI must, under all circumstances, either turn into a present interest or be forever extinguished within the perpetuities period (relevant LIB plus 21 years), then the EI is valid under the RAP.

D. **TESTING A CONTINGENT REMAINDER.** If the CR is held by an individual, proceed to Part D.1. If the CR is a class gift, proceed to Part D.2.

1. **CR Held By An Individual.** A CR held by an individual is RAP-vested when all preconditions are satisfied and the CR turns into a VR. The CR does not need to come into present possession within the perpetuities period. The RAP analysis depends on whether the jurisdiction applies the Doctrine of Destructability.

   a. **Doctrine of Destructibility Applies.** Focus on the moment of natural termination of the prior present interest.

      i. **Must the natural termination of the prior present interest (LE or TY) occur within the perpetuities period (relevant LIB plus 21 years)? If yes**, the CR is valid. The CR will either RAP-vest or be destroyed at the moment of natural termination of the prior present interest due to the Doctrine of Destructibility.

      ii. **Could the prior present interest (LE, TY or FT) naturally terminate**

after the perpetuities period ends (relevant LIB plus 21 years)? If yes, the CR is void, unless you can show that the ability to satisfy the precondition is held or controlled solely by persons who were alive at the time the grant was made. Remember that to satisfy the RAP, the CR does not need to come into present possession within the perpetuities period. The CR only must turn into a VR or be permanently extinguished because it becomes impossible for the precondition to be satisfied within the perpetuities period.

- **If only persons who are alive when the grant is made can determine whether the precondition is satisfied**, then the CR is valid if the precondition itself does not contain a time element exceeding 21 years.

- **If the precondition contains a time element that exceeds 21 years**, determine if the individual who holds the CR must either satisfy or fail the time element within the perpetuities period (LIB plus 21 years). If not, then the CR is void. Proceed to Part F to strike the void CR.

- **If a person who is not alive at the time the grant is made can affect whether the precondition is satisfied, or if a LIB cannot satisfy a time element in the precondition within 21 years**, then the

CR is void. Proceed to Part F to strike the void CR.

b. **Doctrine of Destructibility Abolished.** The CR will survive and turn into a springing EI if the precondition has not yet been satisfied at the natural termination of the prior present interest. Focus on who has the ability to determine whether the precondition will be satisfied, and determine if all such persons are alive at the time the grant is effective (LIB).

   i. **Can the precondition only be satisfied by the actions during life or due to the death of a LIB? If yes,** the CR is valid if the precondition does not contain a time element exceeding 21 years.

   ii. **If the precondition contains a time element that exceeds 21 years,** determine if the individual who holds the CR must be able to satisfy the time element within the perpetuities period (LIB plus 21 years). **If yes,** the CR is valid. **If no,** then the CR is void. Proceed to Part F to strike the void CR.

   iii. **Can the precondition be satisfied by the actions during life or due to the death of a person who was not alive at the time the grant was made? If yes,** the CR is void. Proceed to Part F to strike the void CR.

2. **CR Class Gift.** A CR held by a class is RAP-vested when the class closes and all internal preconditions imposed on the class members (if any) are satisfied by *all* class members. RAP-vesting occurs when the CR turns into a VR. The CR does not need to come into present possession within the perpetuities period. The RAP analysis

depends on whether the governing jurisdiction applies the Doctrine of Destructibility.

a. **Doctrine of Destructibility Applies.** Focus on the moment of natural termination of the prior present interest.

    i. **Must the natural termination of prior present interest (LE or TY) occur within the perpetuities period (LIB plus 21 years)? If yes,** the CR is valid. The CR will either RAP-vest or be destroyed at the moment of natural termination of the prior present interest due to the Doctrine of Destructibility.

    ii. **Could the prior present interest (LE, TY or FT) naturally terminate after the perpetuities period ends (LIB plus 21 years)? If yes,** the CR is void, unless you can show that the class will close and all internal preconditions (if any) imposed on the class members will, under all circumstances, be satisfied by *all* class members within the perpetuities period under the all-or-nothing rule for class gifts.

      • **If all parents who can give rise to class members are alive at the time the grant is made,** then the class will close within the perpetuities period because the parents are all relevant LIB. If there are no other internal preconditions, the CR is valid.

      • **If a parent to the class could be born after the grant is made,** then the afterborn parent can prevent the class from closing in time, and the CR class gift is void. Proceed to Part F to strike the void CR.

- **If the grant contains an internal precondition,** determine when all class members will satisfy the internal precondition. Under the all-or-nothing rule for class gifts, each and every member of the class must be able to satisfy an internal precondition (or as a group must all fail the precondition) within the perpetuities period. If the CR class gift is void, proceed to Part F to strike the void CR.

b. **Doctrine of Destructibility Abolished.** Under the exception to the Rule of Convenience, a CR held by a class will survive and turn into a springing EI if, at the moment of natural termination of the prior present estate, there are still no class members or no class members have satisfied an internal precondition. The CR class gift is void under the RAP unless the class will close and all internal preconditions imposed on the class members (if any) will be satisfied within the perpetuities period.

i. **When will the class close?** Are all parents who can give rise to class members alive at the time the grant is made? **If yes,** the class will close within the perpetuities period.

- **If there are no other internal preconditions,** the CR is valid.

- **If the grant contains internal preconditions,** determine when all class members will satisfy the internal precondition. Proceed to Part C.2.b.ii for further analysis.

- **If a parent to the class could be born after the grant is made,** then the afterborn parent can prevent the class from closing in time, and the CR class gift is void. Proceed to Part F to strike the void CR.

ii. **When will an internal precondition be satisfied by all class members?** Under the all-or-nothing rule for class gifts, each and every member of the class must be able to satisfy an internal precondition (or as a group must all fail the precondition) within the perpetuities period (relevant LIB plus 21 years).

- **If only persons who were alive when the grant was made will determine or influence whether the internal precondition is satisfied,** then the CR is valid so long as the precondition does not contain a time element exceeding 21 years.

- **If the precondition contains a time element that exceeds 21 years,** determine if each class member must satisfy the time element within the perpetuities period (LIB plus 21 years). **If yes**, the CR is valid. If no, then the CR is void. Proceed to Part F to strike the void CR.

- **If a person born after the grant is made can determine or influ-**

ence **whether the precondition is satisfied for a class member,** then the CR is void because the afterborn person can cause the precondition to be satisfied after the perpetuities period ends. Proceed to Part F to strike the void CR.

E. TESTING A VESTED REMAINDER SUBJECT TO OPEN. A VRSO does not need to come into present possession within the perpetuities period to satisfy the RAP. A VRSO satisfies the RAP if the VRSO turns into a VR within the perpetuities period (LIB plus 21 years).

A VRSO closes and turns into a VR at the earlier of: (1) the natural termination of the prior present interest; or (2) when it becomes impossible for any more class members to come into existence (typically, the class closes by death because a parent or parents have died, and no more children or grandchildren can be born).

1. Must The Class Close Within The Perpetuities Period? Determine when the VRSO will close under Parts E.1.a and E.1.b of the checklist.

a. Does The Class Close By Natural Termination Of The Prior Present Interest? Must the prior present interest (LE or TY) naturally terminate within the perpetuities period (LIB plus 21 years)?

i. If yes, then under the Rule of Convenience the VRSO will close within the perpetuities period.

- **If the grant does not contain an internal precondition,** the VRSO is valid.

- **If the grant contains an internal precondition,** proceed to Part E.2 for further analysis.

ii. If no, proceed to Part E.1.b to determine whether the class closes by death within the perpetuities period.

b. Does The Class Close By Death? Are the persons (typically, parents) who give rise to the class members all LIB at the time the grant is made?

    i. If yes, then the VRSO will close within the perpetuities period upon the death of the last to die of the LIB who give rise to the members of the class.

      • **If the grant does not contain an internal precondition,** the VRSO is valid.

      • **If the grant contains an internal precondition,** proceed to Part E.2 for further analysis.

    ii. If no, then the VRSO is void due to one or more persons who could be born after the grant is made, thereby preventing the class from closing within the perpetuities period. Proceed to Part F to strike the void VRSO.

2. Is An Internal Precondition Satisfied By All Class Members Within The Perpetuities Period? If the grant contains an internal precondition, under the all-or-nothing rule for class gifts each and every member of the class must be able to satisfy the internal precondition within the perpetuities period or else the VRSO is void for all class members, even for those members who have satisfied the internal precondition within the perpetuities period.

    a. Are Only Persons Who Were Alive When The Grant Was Made Able To Determine Or Influence Whether The Internal Precondition Is Satisfied?

> i. **If yes,** the VRSO is valid so long as the precondition does not contain a time element exceeding 21 years.
>
> ii. **If the precondition contains a time element that exceeds 21 years**, determine if each class member must satisfy the time element within the perpetuities period (LIB plus 21 years). **If yes**, the VRSO is valid. **If no**, then the VRSO is void. Proceed to Part F to strike the void VRSO.

    b. Could A Person Born After The Grant Is Made Determine Or Influence Whether The Precondition Is Satisfied For A Class Member? If yes, the VRSO is void because the afterborn person can cause the precondition to be satisfied for one of the class members after the perpetuities period ends. Under the all-or-nothing rule for class gifts, the VRSO is void, even for those class members who have satisfied the precondition within the perpetuities period. Proceed to Part F to strike the void VRSO.

F. UNDER THE COMMON LAW RAP, STRIKE ANY VOID FUTURE INTEREST AND RE–ANALYZE THE GRANT. If a future interest is void under the common law version of the RAP, proceed to Parts F.1 through F.3 below. If the jurisdiction applies a modern approach to the RAP, omit Part F and proceed directly to Part G of the checklist.

    1. Strike The Void Future Interest. Begin at the end of the granting clause that creates the void future interest and work backwards to "line out" the void language. Stop striking once you reach the end of the granting clause for the next prior interest that is valid.

    2. Reclassify The Interests Created By The Revised Grant. Read the revised grant language that remains and determine what present and future interests are created. Do not consider the original grantor's intent when reclassifying the remaining interests.

3. **Analyze The Facts Using The Revised Grant Language.**
Treat the revised grant language as if it were the original
language of the grant and apply the facts of the problem
accordingly. Do not consider the original grantor's intent
(it will likely be contradicted).

G. **MODERN RAP APPROACHES.** If the jurisdiction applies the
wait-and-see approach, proceed to Part G.1. If the jurisdiction
applies the USRAP approach, proceed to Part G.2.

1. **Wait–And–See Approach.** Is the future interest valid
under the common law version of the RAP?

   a. **If yes,** then the future interest is valid under
   the wait-and-see approach.

   b. **If no**, do not strike the future interest. Wait to
   see if the future interest RAP-vests within the
   common law perpetuities period (LIB plus 21
   years).

      i. **An EI** becomes RAP-vested when the
      interest comes into present posses-
      sion or is permanently extinguished.

      ii. **A CR or VRSO** becomes RAP-vested
      when the future interest turns into a
      VR or, for a CR, is permanently
      extinguished. Under the all-or-
      nothing rule for class gifts, any pre-
      conditions must be satisfied by all
      class members within the perpetu-
      ities period.

   c. **If the future interest has not RAP-vested by
   the end of the perpetuities period,** the court
   must reform the grant to RAP-vest the future
   interest in a manner that most closely approximates the original intent of the grantor.

2. **USRAP Approach.** Is the future interest valid under the
common law version of the RAP?

   a. **If yes,** then the future interest is valid under
   the USRAP.

b. **If no**, do not strike the future interest. Wait to see if the future interest RAP-vests within 90 years from the moment when the grant is made.

i. **An EI** becomes RAP-vested when the interest comes into present possession or is permanently extinguished.

ii. **A CR or VRSO** becomes RAP-vested when the future interest turns into a VR or, for a CR, is permanently extinguished. Under the all-or-nothing rule for class gifts, any pre-conditions must be satisfied by all class members within the perpetuities period.

c. **If the future interest has not RAP-vested by the end of the 90 year term,** the court must reform the grant to RAP-vest the future interest in a manner that most closely approximates the original intent of the grantor.

ILLUSTRATIVE PROBLEMS

Here are several problem sets that illustrate how the Checklist can be used to resolve Rule Against Perpetuities questions.

■ PROBLEM 4.1 ■

RAP Problems on Executory Interests

In Grants #1 through #7 below, assume that all individuals named in the grant are alive. What is the state of the title in a jurisdiction that applies the common law version of the RAP?

1. "To A and his heirs so long as the land is used as a farm, but if the premises ever cease to be used as a farm, then to B and his heirs."

2. Refer to Grant #1 above. If B is cooperative, is it possible to rewrite the grant to achieve O's intended result?

3. "To A and her heirs so long as A uses the land for a farm, but if A ever ceases to use the land as a farm while A is alive, then to B and her heirs."

4. "To ABC Corporation and its heirs, successors, and assigns, but if the Corporation ever ceases to use the land as a manufacturing facility, then to B and his heirs."

5. "To A and her heirs so long as the land is used for a farm, but if the premises cease to be used as a farm during A's lifetime or within 21 years of the date of A's death, then to B and his heirs."

6. "$50,000 to the first child of A who graduates from law school." Assume at the time the grant becomes effective, A is alive and has one daughter, Pam, who is a third-year law student at the State University College of Law.

7. "To my son Ben for life, then to the Red Cross and its heirs, successors and assigns, but if the Red Cross ever fails to respond in a timely manner to a tornado in my home State of Kansas, the property shall go to my Uncle Joseph and his heirs."

Analysis

RAP Problems on Executory Interests

1. **Testing:** A has a FSSEL; B has a shifting EI in FSA. The EI must be tested under the RAP. Note carefully that the grant does not say that the EI will turn into a present interest only if A (a LIB) ceases to use the land as a farm. Grant #1 is an "open-ended" EI with no definite person or time limit for when the shifting EI will come into present possession or be permanently extinguished. Therefore, the EI is void under the RAP. After the grant is made, 200 years later (more than 21 years after the

death of the last person who is alive at the time the grant is made) the current owner of the land could cease to use the land as a farm. At that point the EI could RAP-vest by coming into present possession. This possibility is shown by the diagram below.

Grant #1

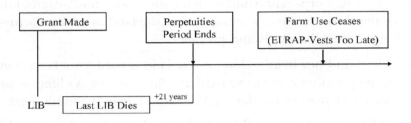

Note that the grant language "to A and his heirs" does not limit ownership of the land to A or A's intestate heirs. The "and his heirs" language merely indicates that A is receiving a FSA, not a LE.

Striking and Answer: Begin striking at the end of the word "heirs" and continue striking backwards through the word "but." The revised grant after striking is "to A and his heirs so long as the land is used as a farm." Your answer to the question presented ("What is the state of the title in a jurisdiction that applies the common law version of the RAP?") should be: A has a FSD; the grantor O has a PR.

2. Yes. A PR or a RE held by B would not be subject to the RAP. O could convey the property to B first in FSA, with the understanding that B would then convey a FSD (retaining a PR) or a FSSCS (retaining a RE) to A.

    Of course, if B refused to make the second conveyance to A, then O cannot revoke the grant of the FSA interest in the property to B.

3. **Testing:** A has a FSSEL; B has a shifting EI in FSA. The EI must be tested under the RAP. Compare this grant language to the

language in Grant #1. Here, the grant specifies that the triggering action (ceasing to use the land as a farm) that RAP-vests B's EI by making the EI come into present possession as a FSA must be taken by A, who is a LIB at the time the grant is made. If A never ceases to use the land as a farm during A's lifetime, then B's EI can never come into present possession—it would be permanently extinguished at A's death. The person A is the LIB who "tethers" or "anchors" B's EI by establishing A's lifetime as the period for when, if ever, the EI either will RAP-vest by coming into present possession or be forever extinguished. Using the parlance of the validating life method, A is the validating life for the EI, which is valid under the RAP.

Answer: The state of the title is: A has a FSSEL; B has a shifting EI in FSA.

4. **Testing:** In terms of RAP-testing, Grant #4 is very similar to Grant #1. ABC Corporation has a FSSEL; B has a shifting EI. The EI must be tested under the RAP. Note that the holder of the FSSEL, ABC Corporation, is an entity and therefore does not count as a LIB for purposes of RAP testing. Lives in being must be real living persons (corporations or animals do not count as LIB). Although a corporation must act ("ceases to use the land as a manufacturing facility") through living persons (its corporate officers and employees), the triggering event that defeases ABC Corporation is not tethered or anchored to the actions of a person who is living at the time the grant is made. Thus, Grant #4 is an "open-ended" EI with no definite person or time limit for when the shifting EI will RAP-vest by coming into present possession. The EI is void under the RAP because 200 years after the grant is made (more than 21 years after the death of the last LIB), the ABC Corporation could cease to use the land as a manufacturing facility, and only then (too late) the EI would RAP-vest by coming into present possession.

Striking and Answer: Begin striking at the end of the word "heirs" and continue striking backwards through the word "but." The revised grant after striking is "to ABC Corporation and its heirs, successors, and assigns." ABC Corporation has a FSA (despite the contradiction with the grantor O's intent).

In comparing revised Grant #4 with revised Grant #1, why did ABC Corporation in Grant #4 end up with a FSA, whereas A in Grant #1 ended up with a FSD? This result may seem arbitrary, and it is—it is purely a function of the punctuation used in the original grant language. This punctuation delineates the beginning and end of each granting clause. Standing alone, it makes no sense to leave in as part of Grant #4 the phrase "but if the Corporation ever ceases to use the land as a manufacturing facility," so this phrase is struck from the grant. As a result, the state of the title is: ABC Corporation holds a FSA.

5. **Testing:** A has a FSSEL; B has a shifting EI in FSA. The EI must be tested under the RAP. Compare this grant language to the language in Grant #1 and Grant #3 above. Here, the grant specifies that the triggering action (ceasing to use the land as a farm) that RAP-vests B's EI by making it come into present possession as a FSA must be taken by A (who is a LIB) or within 21 years after A's death. This language stretches the triggering event out to the maximum duration of the perpetuities period. If A never ceases to use the land as a farm during A's lifetime or within 21 years after A's death, then B's EI can never come into present possession—it would be extinguished at the very end of the perpetuities period, which is measured as A's lifetime plus 21 years. The person A is the LIB who tethers or anchors the EI by determining whether the EI will RAP-vest by coming into present possession or be forever extinguished. Using the parlance of the validating life method, A is the validating life for the EI, which is valid under the RAP.

Answer: The state of the title is: A has a FSSEL; B has a shifting EI in FSA.

6. **Testing:** This grant gives a springing EI to the first child of A who graduates from law school. It is at the point of graduation that the EI will RAP-vest by coming into present possession and the graduate will receive the $50,000. Although Pam is close to graduating, there is no guarantee of graduation. In our imaginary RAP world, Pam dies soon after the grant is made and never graduates.

Grant #6 introduces the most common scenario that makes a future interest void under the RAP—the *afterborn child problem*. A is alive and could have another child, X, born after the time the grant is made. The parent A dies, of course, shortly after X is born. In our imaginary RAP world, all other LIB at the time the grant is made quickly die too. Then, 50 years later the afterborn child X finally graduates from a law school and comes into present possession of the $50,000. At that point, however, the perpetuities period has long expired. The EI is void under the RAP. This scenario is illustrated by the diagram below.

Grant #6

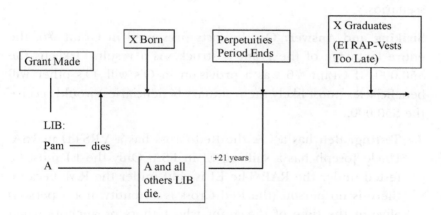

The diagram technique is very useful for analyzing afterborn child scenarios. In diagraming the possibility of an afterborn child, draw the birth of the afterborn child *above* the timeline. This way you know that the afterborn child "X" is not a LIB and cannot be used to satisfy the perpetuities period.

Using the other methods of RAP-testing, this grant is flawed because the springing EI lacks a tether or anchor person whose lifetime or death limits the universe of potential law school graduates to persons who are LIB at the time the grant is made. In the parlance of the validating life method, the EI is void because there is no validating life.

To sharpen your analytical skills, assume that Grant #6 is part of A's will, or that A is dead at the time O makes the grant. If A is dead at the time the grant becomes effective, then the springing EI would be valid under the RAP. Here's why. Due to A's death, the universe of potential law school graduates (A's children) would be a fixed group of LIB. A's death eliminates the problematic possibility of an afterborn child. If A is dead when Grant #6 is made, all of A's children would the tethers or validating lives for the springing EI. For the EI to be valid under the RAP, you do not need to know which one of A's children will be the first to graduate from college. You just need to show that whoever graduates first is guaranteed to be a LIB, and therefore the springing EI will come into present possession within the perpetuities period under all possible scenarios.

Striking and Answer: On the facts presented in Grant #6, the entire language of the grant is struck. As a result, O keeps the $50,000. If Grant #6 was a provision in O's will, O's other will beneficiaries (most likely the residuary beneficiaries) would receive the $50,000.

7. **Testing:** Ben has a LE; the Red Cross has a VRSTD in FSA; Uncle Joseph has a shifting EI in FSA. Only the EI must be tested under the RAP. The EI is void under the RAP because there is no person (the Red Cross is an entity, not a person) alive at the time of the grant who tethers or anchors when Uncle Joseph's EI either comes into present possession or is permanently extinguished. After Ben's death, 200 years later the Red Cross could fail to respond in a timely manner to a tornado in Kansas, and at that point (more than 21 years after all LIB are deceased) Uncle Joseph's EI would come into present possession as a FSA.

Grant #7 is another example of an "open-ended" EI with no definite time set for when the shifting EI is extinguished. The possibility that the EI could come into present possession too late is illustrated by the diagram on the following page.

Grant #7

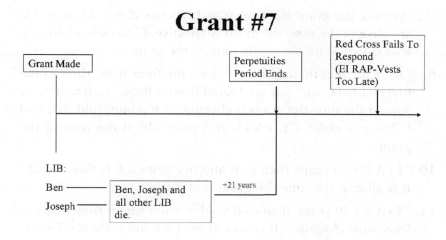

Note that Uncle Joseph is not a measuring life or validating life for his EI because (1) it is the actions of the Red Cross that determine when the EI comes into present possession; and (2) according to the language of the grant, Uncle Joseph does not have to be alive to take present possession of the property.

■ PROBLEM 4.2 ■

RAP Problems On Contingent Remainders Held By Individuals

In Grants #8 through #12 below, assume that: (1) all individuals named in the grant are alive, unless otherwise indicated; and (2) the modern rule presumption for conveyance of a FSA by the grantor O applies. In analyzing each grant, begin by assuming that the governing jurisdiction applies the common law Doctrine of Destructibility of Contingent Remainders and test the future interests that are subject to the RAP using Part D.1.a of the Checklist. Then assume that the governing jurisdiction has abolished the Doctrine of Destructibility and test the future interests that are subject to the RAP using Part D.1.b of the Checklist. For each grant, what is the state of the title in a jurisdiction that applies the common law version of the RAP?

8. "To A for life, then to B's children for their lives, then to the first child of C who has graduated from college." B is dead at

the time the grant is effective and has one child, B1. A and C are alive at the time the grant is effective. C has one child, C1, who is two years old at the time of the grant.

9. "To A for life, then to B's children for their lives, then to the first child of C who has graduated from college." A, B and C are alive at the time the grant is effective. B has one child, B1, and C has one child, C1, who is two years old at the time of the grant.

10. "To A for 50 years, then to B and her heirs if B is then living." B is alive at the time the grant is effective.

11. "To A for 50 years, then to B's oldest child who is then living in fee simple absolute." B is alive at the time the grant is effective, but B has no children.

12. "To A and the heirs of A's body, then to the oldest descendant of B who is then living." A and B are alive at the time the grant is effective. Each one has a child, A1 and B1.

Analysis

RAP Problems On Contingent Remainders Held By Individuals

8. Testing: A has a LE; B1 has a VR in LE (the class is closed because B is dead); C1 has a CR in FSA. The CR must be tested under the RAP.

Doctrine of Destructibility Applies

At the time the grant is made, A, B1, C and C1 are all LIB. The immediately preceding estate for the CR being tested is a LE that will expire naturally at either B1's death (if B1 survives A) or at A's death (A survives B1). Because both A and B1 are LIB at the time the grant is made, the CR held by C1 is valid. The CR will either turn into a VR (because the first child of C will graduate from college) before the last to die of A and B1, or the CR will be destroyed due to the Doctrine of Destructibility if the precondition has not been satisfied at the death of the last to die of A and B1. A and B1 are the "tethers" that anchor the CR. Using the parlance of the validating life method, A and B1 are both validating lives for the CR, which is valid under the RAP. (Note: there can be more than one validating life for a future interest. See the Appendix at the end of Chapter 4 for further explanation of the validating life method).

Answer: In a jurisdiction that applies the Doctrine of Destructibility, A has a LE, B1 has a VR in LE, and C1 has a CR.

Doctrine of Destructibility Abolished

In a jurisdiction that has abolished the Doctrine of Destructibility, the CR held by C1 is void under the RAP. To understand why, ask yourself: Is the precondition guaranteed to be satisfied by the actions during life or due to the death of a LIB? The answer is "no" because Grant #8 presents an afterborn child problem.

Recall that C is alive at the time the grant is made and could have more children. Satisfaction of the precondition in the CR—being the first child of C to graduate from college—is not limited solely to a LIB at the time the grant is made. C is alive and could have an afterborn child ("CX"). Shortly after CX is born, A, B, B1, C and C1 (and all other LIB) could die, and then more than 21 years later the afterborn CX could satisfy the precondition and graduate from college. Such a series of events would RAP-vest the CR after the perpetuities period expired, thereby making the CR void under the RAP. This situation is illustrated by the diagram on the following page.

Grant #8

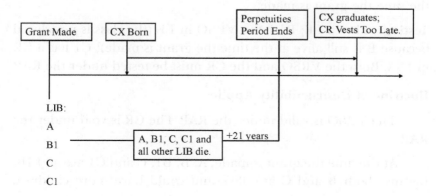

Using the other methods of RAP-testing, the CR is void because the CR lacks a tether or anchor that limits the universe of C's children (all potential college graduates) to persons who are LIB at the time the grant is made. Using the parlance of the validating life method, the CR is void because there is no validating life. Neither A nor B1 (nor anyone else) can be a validating life for the CR because (in a jurisdiction that has abolished the Doctrine of Destructibility) the CR would not be destroyed at the death of the last to die of A and B1. Rather, the CR would turn into a springing EI and ownership of the property would remain in "limbo." The CR-turned-EI would not RAP-vest by coming into present possession until a child of C—which could include the afterborn child of CX—graduates from college.

Striking and Answer: Begin striking at the end of the word "college" and continue backwards through the word "then." The revised grant after striking is "To A for life, then to B's children for their lives." After striking the void CR, the state of the title is: A has a LE; B1 has a VR in LE; and the grantor O holds a REV.

9.   Grant #9 introduces very important concepts that form the building blocks for more advanced analysis. Be sure you understand Grant #9 before moving on to the other problems.

Begin by noting how Grant #9 is different from Grant #8. The grant language is exactly the same. But in Grant #8, B was dead at the time the grant was made and therefore could not have any more children. In Grant #9, B is alive at the time of the grant, and therefore can have afterborn children who will not be LIB at the time the grant is made.

Testing: A has a LE; B1 has a VRSO in LE (the class is not closed because B is still alive at the time the grant is made); C1 has a CR in FSA. Both the VRSO and the CR must be tested under the RAP.

Doctrine of Destructibility Applies

The VRSO is valid under the RAP. The CR is void under the RAP.

At the time the grant is made, A, B, B1, C and C1 are all LIB. Because both B and C are alive and could have more children,

Grant #9 presents a *double afterborn child scenario*. Double afterborn child scenarios require imagination to conjure up, which is why this particular pattern tends to appear on an exam. From the professor's perspective, a double afterborn child problem is an easy way to separate the "A" students from the rest of the class.

Begin by testing the VRSO. Ask yourself: When must the class of B's children close and turn into a VR, and will the class close within the perpetuities period? The class of B's children will close at the natural termination of A's life estate, which satisfies the perpetuities period because A is a LIB. The class also could close earlier at B's death, which also satisfies the perpetuities period because B is a LIB. Either way, the VRSO closes and turns into a VR within the perpetuities period. Therefore, the VRSO is valid under the RAP.

Now test the CR. The immediately preceding estate for the CR being tested is a LE that could expire naturally at A's death (if A outlives all of B's children). If that happens, the preceding LE will terminate within the perpetuities period because A is a LIB.

But suppose that A dies and at least one of B's children is alive. Then the immediately preceding LE will terminate not at A's death, but rather at the death of the last to die of B's children. Because B is alive at the time the grant is made, B could have an afterborn child, BX. The possibility of the afterborn BX (who is not a LIB at the time the grant is made) extends the natural termination of the preceding LE beyond the perpetuities period. The CR is void, unless you can show that only a person who is alive at the time the grant is made (a LIB) will control whether the precondition is satisfied. Do only persons who are LIB control when the first child of C graduates from college? No, because C is alive and can have an afterborn child, CX. CX, who is not a LIB, could satisfy the precondition of being the first child of C to graduate from college. Here's how this double afterborn child scenario could unfold.

Assume that BX and CX are born after the grant is made. Next, all of our LIB (A, B, B1, C and C1) die, and 21 years pass. The perpetuities period has expired. BX is still alive, and CX is still alive, but CX has not yet graduated from college. The CR is void under the RAP because it is in "limbo." We cannot tell if the CR will turn into a VR or be permanently extinguished due to the Doctrine of Destructibility by the end of the perpetuities period.

This scenario is illustrated by the diagram below. Note that by diagraming afterborn children above the timeline, and keeping LIB (who all unfortunately die in our bizarre RAP world) below the timeline you can literally see the "problem."

Grant #9

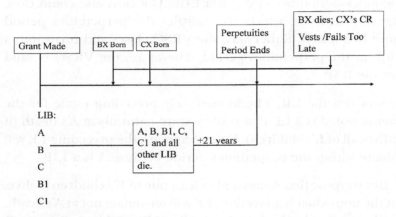

Striking and Answer: Begin striking at the end of the word "college" and continue backwards through the word "then." The revised grant after striking is "To A for life, then to B's children for their lives." The state of the title is: A has a LE; B1 has a VRSO in LE; and the grantor O holds a REV.

To sharpen your analytical skills, assume that C was dead at the time the grant was made. Would the CR still be void? No, because all of C's children (here, just C1) would be LIB, and as LIB C's children would control whether or not the precondition of graduating from college is satisfied. Whenever the immediately preceding LE terminates, a LIB (here, C1) will either have previously graduated from college (the CR turned into a VR and RAP-vested within C1's life), or C1 will not have graduated from college (and the CR would be destroyed by the Doctrine of Destructibility). Either way, it all happens during C1's lifetime or at

C1's death. The CR held by C1 (based on our changed factual assumption that C is dead at the time the grant is made) would be valid.

Doctrine of Destructibility Abolished

The Doctrine of Destructibility in Grant #9 did not "save" the CR because of the possibility that the natural termination of the immediately preceding LE could be extended by the afterborn child (BX) beyond the perpetuities period. Therefore, the analysis is exactly the same in a jurisdiction that has abolished the Doctrine of Destructibility. The CR is void and is struck from the grant. The state of the title is: A has a LE; B1 has a VRSO in LE; and the grantor O holds a REV.

10. Testing: A has a TY; B has a CR in FSA; O holds a REV (because B's CR may be extinguished). The CR must be tested under the RAP.

Doctrine of Destructibility Applies

In a jurisdiction that applies the Doctrine of Destructibility, the focal point of analysis for the CR is whether the prior present estate must terminate naturally within the perpetuities period. Here, A's TY for 50 years can naturally terminate after the perpetuities period ends. A could die immediately and 21 years could pass. (Note: At A's death, the TY is not extinguished, but instead passes to A's estate.) The CR held by B is void, unless you can show that only a person who is alive at the time the grant is made (a LIB) will control whether the precondition is satisfied.

Does only a LIB control whether B is living at the natural termination of the prior TY? Yes, because B is a LIB at the time the grant is made. B will determine whether or not B is alive (the CR turns into a VR and thereby RAP-vests) or is dead (the CR is permanently extinguished) at the time the TY naturally terminates. The CR is valid under the RAP in a jurisdiction that applies the Doctrine of Destructibility. B is a LIB who "tethers" the CR. Using the parlance of the validating life method, B is his own validating life for B's CR.

Answer: The state of the title is: A has a TY; B has a CR in FSA; O holds a REV.

Doctrine of Destructibility Abolished

In a jurisdiction that has abolished the Doctrine of Destructibility, the focal point of analysis for the CR is whether the precondition can only be satisfied by the actions during life or due to the death of a LIB at the time the grant becomes effective. In Grant #10, the precondition is survivorship by B for a term of 50 years. This precondition can only be satisfied by B, who is a LIB at the time the grant is made. Therefore, B's CR is valid under the RAP in a jurisdiction that has abolished the Doctrine of Destructibility.

Answer: The state of the title is: A has a TY; B has a CR in FSA; O holds a REV.

11. Testing: A has a TY; B's (unborn) child has a CR in FSA; O holds a REV. The CR must be tested under the RAP.

Begin by noticing that B is alive but has no children at the time the grant is made. Consequently, the "oldest child of B" necessarily will be an afterborn child.

Doctrine of Destructibility Applies

In a jurisdiction that applies the Doctrine of Destructibility, the focal point of analysis for the CR is whether the prior present estate must terminate naturally within the perpetuities period. Here, A's TY for 50 years can naturally terminate after the perpetuities period ends. A could die immediately and 21 years could pass. (Note: At A's death, the TY is not extinguished, but instead passes to A's estate.) The CR held by B's (unborn) oldest child is void, unless you can show that only a person who is alive at the time the grant is made (a LIB) will control whether the precondition (being the oldest child of B and surviving until the end of the TY) is satisfied.

Does only a LIB control this precondition? No, because the oldest child of B necessarily must be an afterborn child and therefore is not a LIB at the time of the grant. Consider the following scenario, which would make the CR void under the RAP.

Assume that B's first child, BX, is born shortly after the time of the grant. Next, A dies (but the TY continues). B dies, and then all other LIB at the time the grant is made die. Next, 21 years pass and the perpetuities period ends. But there are still approximately 29 more years to go until the prior TY naturally terminates and we will know whether BX will survive and satisfy the precondition (the CR turns into a VR and thereby RAP-vests) or BX fails to survive (the CR is permanently extinguished). The CR is void under the RAP because it is still in "limbo" (we cannot tell if it will turn into a VR or be permanently extinguished) at the end of the perpetuities period. This scenario is illustrated by the diagram below.

Grant #11

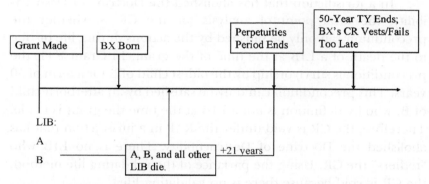

Striking and Answer: Begin striking at the end of the word "living" and continue backwards through the word "then." The revised grant after striking is "To A for 50 years." The state of the title is: A has a TY; O holds a REV.

To sharpen your analytical skills, assume instead that B had one child, Brad, who was alive at the time the grant was made. Would the CR still be void? Yes. Although Brad would be a LIB at the time the grant is made, Brad could die shortly afterwards, and the same afterborn child scenario described above would render the CR void.

Now, assume instead that the A's TY is for any period of time that is less than or equal to 21 years, not for 50 years. Would the CR still be void? Again, the focal point for analysis of the CR is whether the prior present estate must terminate naturally within the perpetuities period. Here, A's TY for up to 21 years must naturally terminate by the end of the perpetuities period because the perpetuities period always includes a fixed 21 year block of time. When the TY expires, in a jurisdiction that applies the Doctrine of Destructibility the CR must either RAP-vest (because B has an oldest child who is alive) or be permanently extinguished (destroyed because B has no child who is alive to take present possession of the property). In this variation, the CR is valid under the RAP in a jurisdiction that applies the Doctrine of Destructibility because the TY is limited in duration to 21 years.

Doctrine of Destructibility Abolished

In a jurisdiction that has abolished the Doctrine of Destructibility, the focal point of analysis for the CR is whether the precondition can only be satisfied by the actions during life or due to the death of a LIB at the time of the grant. In Grant #11, the precondition is survivorship by the oldest child of B for a term of 50 years. This precondition can only be satisfied by an afterborn child of B, who by definition is not a LIB at the time the grant is made. Therefore, the CR is void under the RAP in a jurisdiction that has abolished the Doctrine of Destructibility. There is no LIB who "tethers" the CR. Using the parlance of the validating life method, the CR is void because there is no validating life.

Striking and Answer: Begin striking at the end of the word "living" and continue backwards through the word "then." The revised grant after striking is "To A for 50 years." The state of the title is: A has a TY; O holds a REV.

12. Testing: A has a FT; B's (unascertainable) oldest descendant has a CR in FSA; O holds a REV. The CR must be tested under the RAP.

Begin by noticing that Grant #12 presents a double afterborn child scenario. The afterborn child of A, A2, can extend the termination point of A's FT out into the future. The afterborn child of B, B2, can be the oldest living descendant of B when the afterborn child A2 finally dies and the FT naturally terminates. The possibility of two afterborn children is a signal that the CR is likely to be void under the RAP.

Doctrine of Destructibility Applies

In a jurisdiction that applies the Doctrine of Destructibility, the focal point of analysis for the CR is whether the prior present estate must terminate naturally within the perpetuities period. Here, the natural termination of A's FT can be extended indefinitely by A's afterborn descendants. The FT will naturally terminate at the death of A's last living descendant. A could have an afterborn child, A2, shortly before A dies. Next, A and A1 die. Then, B has an afterborn child, B2, shortly before B, B1 and all other LIB at the time of the grant die. But the afterborn child A2 lives on for far longer than 21 years after the last LIB dies. Finally, A2 dies and the FT naturally terminates, but this occurs long after the perpetuities period ends.

The CR held by B's oldest living descendant is void, unless you can show that only a person who is alive at the time the grant is made (a LIB) will control whether the precondition (being the oldest descendant of B who survives until the FT terminates). Does only a LIB control this precondition? No, because the oldest living descendant of B when the FT terminates at A2's death could be the afterborn child of B, B2, who is not a LIB at the time of the grant. This double afterborn child scenario, illustrated by the diagram below, makes the CR void.

Grant #12

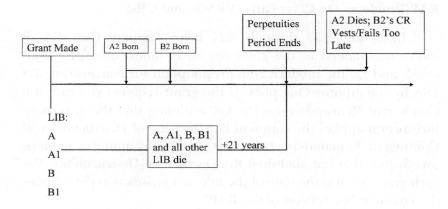

Striking and Answer: Begin striking at the end of the word "living" and continue backwards through the word "then." The revised grant after striking is "To A and the heirs of A's body." The state of the title is: A has a FT; O holds a REV.

Doctrine of Destructibility Abolished

In a jurisdiction that has abolished the Doctrine of Destructibility, the focal point of analysis for the CR is whether the precondition can only be satisfied by the actions during life or due to the death of a LIB at the time the grant is made. In Grant #12, the precondition is survivorship by the oldest descendant of B until A's FT terminates. This precondition could be satisfied by the afterborn child of B, B2, as shown in the diagram. Therefore, the CR is void under the RAP in a jurisdiction that has abolished the Doctrine of Destructibility. There is no LIB who "tethers" the CR. Using the parlance of the validating life method, the CR is void because there is no validating life.

Striking and Answer: Begin striking at the end of the word "living" and continue backwards through the word "then." The revised grant after striking is "To A and the heirs of A's body." The state of the title is: A has a FT; O holds a REV.

■ **PROBLEM 4.3** ■

RAP Problems On Class Gifts (VRSOs and CRs)

In Grants #13 through #21 below, assume that: (1) all individuals named in the grant are alive, unless otherwise indicated; and (2) the modern rule presumption for conveyance of a FSA by the grantor O applies. If the grant requires you to test a Contingent Remainder, test the CR assuming that the governing jurisdiction applies the common law Doctrine of Destructibility of Contingent Remainders. Next, test the CR assuming a modern jurisdiction that has abolished the Doctrine of Destructibility. For each grant, what is the state of the title in a jurisdiction that applies the common law version of the RAP?

13. O conveys Blackacre "to A for life, then to A's children for their lives, then upon the death of the last to die of A and A's children, to B if A dies without any surviving children." Assume that A and B are alive at the time the grant becomes effective. A has one child, A1.

14. O conveys Blackacre "to A for life, and on A's death to A's children for their lives, and upon the death of the last to die of A and A's children, to B if A has no descendants who survive the children of A." Assume A and B are alive at the time the grant becomes effective. A has three children, A1, A2 and A3.

15. O conveys Blackacre "to A for life, and on A's death to A's children for their lives, and upon the death of the last to die of A and A's children, to B's children." Assume that A and B are alive at the time the grant becomes effective. B has one child, B1. A has no children.

16. O conveys Blackacre "to A for life, and on A's death to A's children for their lives, and upon the death of the last to die of A and A's children, to B's living children." Assume that A and B are alive at the time the grant becomes effective. B has one child, B1. A has no children.

17. O conveys Blackacre "to A for life, and on A's death to A's children for their lives, and upon the death of the last to die of A and A's children, to A's grandchildren." Assume that A is alive at the time the grant becomes effective. A has one child, A1, and one grandchild, GA1.

18. O's will devises Blackacre "to A for life, and on A's death to A's children for their lives, and upon the death of the last to die of A and A's children, to O's grandchildren." Assume A is alive at the time the grant becomes effective. A has one child, A1. O has one child, O1, and one grandchild, GO1.

19. O conveys Blackacre "to A for life, and on A's death to A's children for their lives, and upon the death of the last to die of A and A's children, to O's grandchildren." Assume A is alive at the time the grant becomes effective. A has one child, A1. O has one child, O1, and one grandchild, GO1.

20. O conveys Blackacre "to A for life, then to A's widow, if any, for life, then to A's children who survive A's widow." Assume that A is alive and married to W1 at the time the grant becomes effective. A has one child, A1.

21. O conveys Blackacre "to A for life, then to A's children who reach age 30." Assume that A is alive and has one child, A1, who is age 35 at the time the grant becomes effective.

Analysis

13. Testing: A has a LE; A1 has a VRSO in LE; B has a CR in FSA (because the modern presumption applies); O holds a REV. Both the VRSO and the CR must be tested under the RAP.

VRSO in LE: Applying Part E of the Checklist, this is a VRSO with no internal preconditions. The VRSO will close at the natural termination of A's prior LE. Because A is a LIB, A's LE terminates within the perpetuities period, thereby making A1's VRSO valid under the RAP. A is the "tether" or validating life for the VRSO in LE. This analysis is illustrated in the diagram on page 167.

CR in FSA: First, notice that this grant presents a potential afterborn child scenario. The prior present estate that comes before B's CR could be a LE held by one of A's afterborn children because A is alive at the time of the grant and could have another child, A2. The possibility of the afterborn child A2 could extend the LE held by A's children so that the LE could naturally terminate after the perpetuities period ends (i.e., A2 may not die until more than 21 years after all LIB at the time of the grant are dead). This afterborn child scenario is illustrated by the diagram on the following page.

Second, notice that B does not need to be alive for B's CR to turn into a VR (if A dies without surviving children) or be extinguished (if A dies with surviving children). If B dies before A, B's CR simply passes to B's estate.

Third, remember that in order to RAP-vest, B's CR does not need to come into present possession. B's CR only must turn into a VR within the perpetuities period. This point is important because B's CR will not come into present possession until the last child of A dies and the prior LE naturally terminates. Due to the possibility of an afterborn child of A, B's CR may not come into present possession until more than 21 years after the last LIB dies. All that matters for RAP-testing, however, is whether B's CR turns into a VR or is permanently extinguished within the perpetuities period (LIB plus 21 years).

After digesting these important introductory points, let's analyze the CR in FSA. B holds an individual CR, so we will apply Part D.1 of the Checklist.

In a jurisdiction that applies the Doctrine of Destructibility, the prior present estate (the VRSO in LE held by A's children) could naturally terminate after the perpetuities period ends due to the possibility of the afterborn child, A2. Nevertheless, B's CR is valid under the RAP because the ability to satisfy the precondition is held solely by a LIB (here, A). A is the "tether" or validating life for the CR in FSA.

In a jurisdiction that has abolished the Doctrine of Destructibility, B's CR is valid under the RAP because the precondition can only be satisfied solely by A, who is a LIB. Either A will die with surviving children, or A will not. A is the "tether" or validating life for the CR in FSA.

Grant #13

Why A is the tether/validating life for both A1's VRSO and B's CR

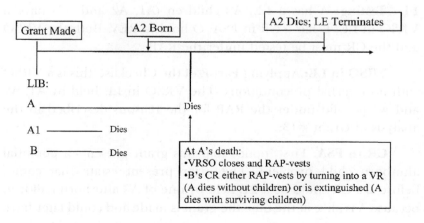

Note carefully that in this particular grant B is not a "tether" or validating life for B's CR. Why is that? Here, B's life or death has no impact on whether the precondition will be satisfied or not. B can die before A or B can die after A—it matters not. The only person who matters in terms of the precondition for B's CR is A. This analysis is illustrated by the diagram below. Note the "gap" between 21 years after B's death and when B's CR either vests or fails. This "gap" shows you why B is not a tether or validating life for B's CR.

Grant #13
Why B is not a tether/validating life for B's CR

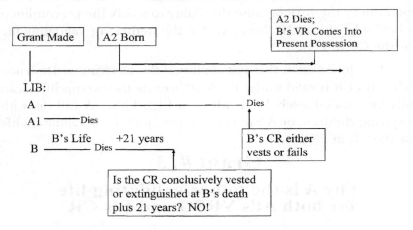

14. Testing: A has a LE; A's children (A1, A2 and A3) have a VRSO in LE; B has a CR in FSA; O holds a REV. Both the VRSO and the CR must be tested under the RAP.

VRSO in LE: Applying Part E of the Checklist, this is a VRSO with no internal preconditions. The VRSO in LE held by A1, A2 and A3 is valid under the RAP for the reasons described in the analysis of Grant #13.

CR in FSA: First, notice that this grant presents a potential afterborn child problem. The prior present estate that comes before B's CR could be a LE held by one of A's afterborn children because A is alive at the time the grant is made and could later have another child, A4. A's children who are LIB (A1, A2 and A3) could all die shortly after the grant is made. The possibility of the afterborn A4 could extend the LE held by A's children so that the LE could naturally terminate after the perpetuities period ends (i.e., A4 may not die until more than 21 years after all LIB at the time of the grant are dead). This afterborn child scenario is illustrated by the diagram on the following page.

Second, notice that B is not a "tether" or validating life for B's CR for reasons similar to those described in the analysis of Grant #13 above. A and A's children, not B, will determine whether the precondition for B's CR (whether A has surviving descendants when the last child of A dies) will be satisfied.

B holds an individual CR, so we will apply Part D.1 of the Checklist. In a jurisdiction that applies the Doctrine of Destructibility, the prior present estate (the VRSO in LE held by A's children) could naturally terminate after the perpetuities period ends due to the possibility of the afterborn child, A4. Unlike the situation in Grant #13, however, in Grant #14 the ability to satisfy the precondition is not held solely by a LIB. Therefore, B's CR is void under the RAP. The death of the afterborn child A4 will determine whether or not the precondition is satisfied. At A4's death, we will know whether or not A has surviving descendants. Until A4's death, however, B's CR is in "limbo"—we do not know whether the CR will turn into a VR or be permanently extinguished. A4's death could occur more than 21 years after the last LIB dies and the perpetuities period has ended. This scenario is illustrated by the diagram below.

In a jurisdiction that has abolished the Doctrine of Destructibility, B's CR is void for the same reason. The ability to satisfy the precondition is not held solely by a LIB, but rather can be determined by the life and death of the afterborn child, A4. This scenario is illustrated by the diagram on the following page.

Grant #14
Testing B's CR

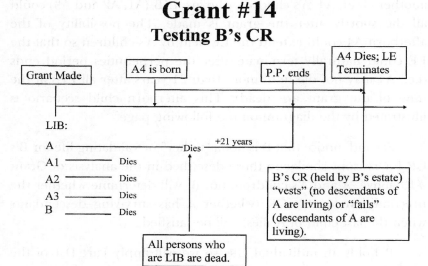

Grant Made | A4 is born | P.P. ends | A4 Dies; LE Terminates

LIB:

A ———————————— Dies ——+21 years——

A1 ———— Dies
A2 ———— Dies
A3 ———— Dies
B ———— Dies

All persons who are LIB are dead.

B's CR (held by B's estate) "vests" (no descendants of A are living) or "fails" (descendants of A are living).

Striking and Answer: Begin striking at the end of the word "descendants" and continue backwards through the comma after the word "lives." The revised grant after striking is "to A for life, and on A's death to A's children for their lives." The state of the title is: A has a LE; A1, A2 and A3 have a VRSO in LE; O holds a REV.

15. Testing: A has a LE; A's (unborn) children have a CR in LE; B1 has a VRSO in FSA. Both the CR and the VRSO must be tested under the RAP.

CR in LE: A's (unborn) children hold a CR class gift, so we will apply Part D.2 of the Checklist. In a jurisdiction that applies the Doctrine of Destructibility, the prior LE will naturally terminate at A's death. Because A is a LIB, the prior LE terminates within the perpetuities period, thereby making the CR in LE valid under the RAP. A is the "tether" or validating life for the CR.

In a jurisdiction that has abolished the Doctrine of Destructibility, the CR held by A's (unborn) children is valid under the RAP because the precondition can be satisfied solely by A, who is a LIB. Either A will die with surviving children, or A will not. A is the "tether" or validating life for the CR in LE.

VRSO in FSA: Begin by noting that Grant #15 presents a possible afterborn child scenario because A is alive and could have a child after the grant becomes effective. The possibility of an afterborn child of A means that the prior CR in LE could naturally terminate after the perpetuities period ends (i.e., A's afterborn child may not die until more than 21 years after all LIB at the time of the grant are dead).

Does the possibility of an afterborn child in Grant #15 make the VRSO in FSA void under the RAP? The VRSO, which contains no internal preconditions, is analyzed using Part E of the Checklist.

B1's VRSO in FSA is valid under the RAP because the class of B's children will close at the death of B, who is a LIB at the time the grant is made. (Remember: a VRSO becomes RAP-vested when the class closes and the VRSO turns into a VR; it is not necessary for the VRSO to come into present possession within the perpetuities period.) B is the "tether" or validating life for the VRSO in FSA.

16.   Testing: A has a LE; A's (unborn) children have a CR in LE; B1 has a CR in FSA; O holds a REV. Both CRs must be tested under the RAP.

CR in LE: A's (unborn) children hold a CR class gift, so we will apply Part D.2 of the Checklist. The CR in LE held by A's unborn children is valid under the RAP for the reasons described in the analysis of Grant #15.

CR in FSA: First, notice that Grant #16 presents a possible double afterborn child scenario. A is alive and could have another child, A1, who is born after the grant is made. A1's lifetime could extend the natural termination point of the prior LE held by A's children to beyond the end of the perpetuities period. A1 could die more than 21 years after the last LIB at the time of the grant is dead. B is alive at the time of the grant and could have an afterborn child, B2. The potential double afterborn child scenario in Grant #16 is illustrated in the diagram on the following page.

Second, notice how the CR held by B's children in Grant #16 is different from the VRSO held by B's children in Grant #15. In Grant #15, there were no internal preconditions. In Grant #16, B's death still leaves the CR held by B's children in "limbo." The internal precondition of the CR requires that B's children must be living at the death of the last child of A (which could include the afterborn child, A1). It is only at the death of the last child of A that we will know conclusively whether the CR turns into a VR (B has surviving children) or is extinguished (B has no surviving children).

B1 holds a CR class gift with an internal precondition, so we will apply Part D.2 of the Checklist. In a jurisdiction that applies the Doctrine of Destructibility, the natural termination of the prior LE held by A's children could be extended bythe lifetime of the afterborn A1 so that termination occurs after the perpetuities period ends. Although the parent B is a LIB and the class of B's children closes at B's death, the CR contains an internal precondition, namely survivorship by B's children until the last child of A dies. This precondition is not *solely* controlled by a LIB because an afterborn child, A1, could be the last child of A to die, and an afterborn child of B, B2, could be the surviving child of B. This scenario, which makes the CR in FSA void under the RAP, is illustrated by the diagram below.

In a jurisdiction that has abolished the Doctrine of Destruct-ibility, although the parent B is a LIB and the class of B's children closes at B's death, the CR contains an internal precondition, namely survivorship by B's children until the last child of A dies. This precondition is not solely controlled by a LIB because an afterborn child, A1, could be the last child of A to die, and an afterborn child of B, B2, could be the surviving child of B. This scenario, which makes the CR in FSA void under the RAP, is illustrated by the diagram on the following page.

Grant #16
Testing The CR

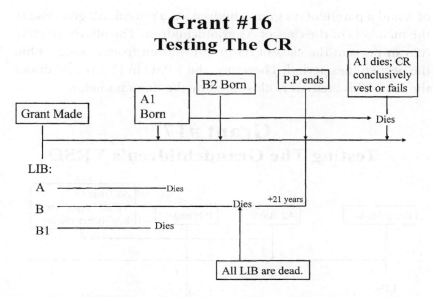

Striking and Answer: Begin striking at the end of the phrase "B's living children" and continue backwards through the comma after the word "lives." The revised grant after striking is "to A for life, and on A's death to A's children for their lives." The state of the title is: A has a LE; A's unborn children have a CR in LE; O holds a REV.

17. Testing: A has a LE; A1 has a VRSO in LE; GA1 has a VRSO in FSA. Both VRSOs must be tested under the RAP.

VRSO in LE: Applying Part E of the Checklist, this is a VRSO with no internal preconditions. The VRSO in LE held by A1 is valid under the RAP for the reasons described in the analysis of Grant #13.

VRSO in FSA: Begin by noticing that Grant #17 presents a potential afterborn child scenario. A is alive and could have another child, A2, who is born after the grant is made. Applying Part E of the Checklist, the potential afterborn child A2 impacts the VRSO in two ways. First, A2's lifetime could extend the natural termination of the prior LE held by A's children to beyond the end of the perpetuities period. A2 may die more than 21 years after the last LIB at the time the grant was made dies. Second, A2 is both a child of A and a parent of A's grandchildren. As a parent, A2 gives rise to the members of the class of A's grandchildren. The afterborn child A2 can prevent the class of A's grandchildren from closing within the perpetuities period. Therefore, the VRSO in FSA is void under the RAP. This analysis is illustrated by the diagram below.

Grant #17
Testing The Grandchildren's VRSO

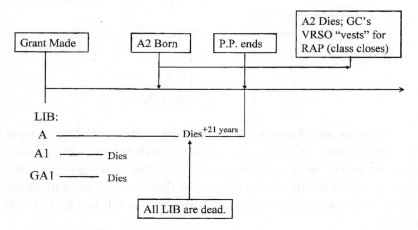

Striking and Answer: Begin striking at the end of the phrase "A's grandchildren" and continue backwards through the comma after the word "lives." The revised grant after striking is "to A for life, and on A's death to A's children for their lives." The state of the title is: A has a LE; A1 has a VRSO in LE; O holds a REV.

18. Testing: A has a LE; A1 has a VRSO in LE; GO1 has a VRSO in FSA. Both VRSOs must be tested under the RAP.

VRSO in LE: Applying Part E of the Checklist, this is a VRSO with no preconditions. The VRSO in LE held by A1 is valid under the RAP for the reasons described in the analysis of Grant #13.

VRSO in FSA: Begin by noticing that this grant is part of a devise in O's will. Thus, at the time this grant is made, O is dead. O's death eliminates the possibility of an afterborn child problem regarding the VRSO held by O's grandchildren. As in Grant #17, a potential afterborn child of A could extend the natural termination of the prior LE held by A's children to beyond the end of the perpetuities period. A2 may die more than 21 years after the last LIB at the time the grant was made dies. Unlike Grant #17, however, the only person who can give rise to the members of the class of O's grandchildren is the parent, O1, who is a LIB at the time the grant is made at O's death. Therefore, the VRSO in FSA is valid under the RAP. O1 is the "tether" or validating life for the VRSO held by GO1. This analysis is illustrated by the diagram below.

Grant #18
Testing The Grandchildren's VRSO

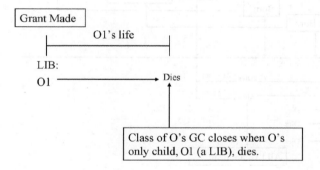

19.   Testing: A has a LE; A1 has a VRSO in LE; GO1 has a VRSO in FSA. Both VRSOs must be tested under the RAP.

VRSO in LE: Applying Part E of the Checklist, this is a VRSO with no preconditions. The VRSO in LE held by A1 is valid under the RAP for the reasons described in the analysis of Grant #13.

VRSO in FSA: Notice that one significant fact has changed in Grant #19 as compared with Grant #18. In Grant #19, O is making a lifetime conveyance, not a devise under a will. Thus, at the time this grant is made, O is alive and A is alive, creating a potential double afterborn child scenario.

Applying Part E of the Checklist, as in Grant #17 a potential afterborn child of A, A2, could extend the natural termination of the prior LE held by A's children to beyond the end of the perpetuities period. A2 may die more than 21 years after the last LIB at the time the grant was made dies. O is alive at the time of the grant and could have an afterborn child, O2. As a parent, O2 gives rise to the members of the class of O's grandchildren. The afterborn child O2 can prevent the class of O's grandchildren from closing within the perpetuities period. Therefore, the VRSO in FSA is void under the RAP. This analysis is illustrated by the diagram below.

Grant #19
An Inter Vivos Transfer By O

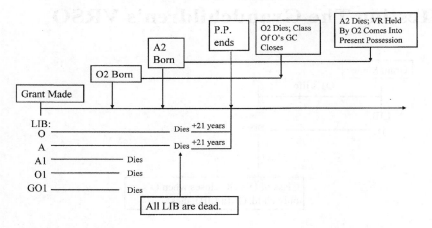

Striking and Answer: Begin striking at the end of the phrase "O's grandchildren" and continue backwards through the comma after the word "lives." The revised grant after striking is "to A for life, and on A's death to A's children for their lives." The state of the title is: A has a LE, A1 has a VRSO in LE; O holds a REV.

20.   Testing: A has a LE; W1 has a CR in LE (because A's "widow" is unascertainable until A's death); A1 has a CR in FSA; O holds a REV. Both CRs must be tested under the RAP.

The key to analyzing Grant #20 is to recognize that A's current wife, W1, may not be A's "widow" at the time of A's death. Another woman born after the time the grant is made (W2), could be A's wife at A's death. For this reason, Grant #20 is known as the "case of the unborn widow." The afterborn widow (W2) creates the same RAP problems as an afterborn child. In addition, A is alive at the time the grant is made and could have an afterborn child. Thus, Grant #20 presents a double afterborn person scenario—one afterborn widow and one afterborn child.

CR in LE: The CR in LE is held by an individual, so we apply Part D.1 of the Checklist. In a jurisdiction that applies the Doctrine of Destructibility, the moment of natural termination of the prior LE held by A must occur within the perpetuities period because A is a LIB at the time the grant is made. At A's death, A's widow will be ascertainable. Therefore, the CR in LE held by A's widow is valid under the RAP. A is the "tether" or validating life for the CR.

In a jurisdiction that has abolished the Doctrine of Destructibility, the precondition (being A's widow) can only be satisfied at A's death. Because A is a LIB at the time the grant is made, the CR in LE held by A's widow is valid under the RAP. A is the "tether" or validating life for the CR.

CR in FSA: Begin by noticing that W1 could die immediately after the grant is made. A could (imagine all possibilities) later marry W2, who was not yet born when the grant was made and therefore is not a LIB. A and W2 could have an afterborn child, A2, who is a member of the class of A's children. This scenario is illustrated by the diagram on page 178.

The CR in FSA is a CR class gift with an internal precondition, so we apply Part D.2 of the Checklist. In a jurisdiction that applies the Doctrine of Destructibility, the natural termination of the prior LE held by A's "widow" (here, the afterborn W2) could naturally terminate after the perpetuities period ends because W2 is not a LIB. W2 could die more than 21 years after the last LIB at the time the grant was made is dead. Although the parent A (who gives rise to A's children) is a LIB, the class gift to A's children contains an internal precondition, namely survivorship of A's widow. Due to the afterborn child A2, this precondition could be satisfied by A2 after the perpetuities period ends. (Remember, under the all-or-nothing rule for class gifts, every potential class member must satisfy the precondition within the perpetuities period or else the class gift is void for every class member, even those class members who are assured of satisfying the internal precondition within the perpetuities period.) Therefore, the CR in FSA is void under the RAP. This analysis is illustrated by the diagram below.

In a jurisdiction that has abolished the Doctrine of Destructibility, the class of A's children will close at A's death. Because A is a LIB, the class of A's children will close within the perpetuities period. But there is also a precondition, survivorship of A's widow, that must be satisfied before the CR in FSA turns into a VR. Due to the afterborn child A2, this precondition could be satisfied by one member of the class, A2, after the perpetuities period ends. Under the all-or-nothing rule for class gifts, every potential class member must satisfy the precondition within the perpetuities period or else the class gift is void. Therefore, the CR in FSA is void under the RAP. This analysis is illustrated by the diagram below.

Grant #20
The Unborn Widow

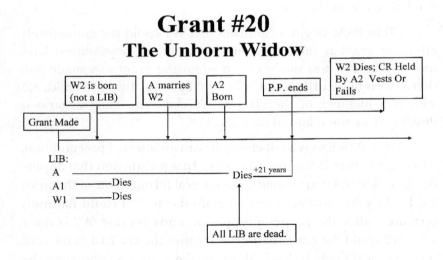

Striking and Answer: Begin striking at the end of the phrase, "who survive A's widow" and continue striking backwards through the comma before the phrase, "if any, for life." The revised grant after striking is "to A for life, then to A's widow, if any, for life." The state of the title is: A has a LE; A's widow has a CR in LE; O holds a REV.

21. Testing: A has a LE; A1 has a VRSO in FSA. The VRSO in FSA must be tested under the RAP.

VRSO in FSA: Begin by noticing that Grant #21 presents an afterborn child problem. A is alive and could have an afterborn child, A2, who would be a member of the class of A's children. Applying Part E of the Checklist, the class of A's children closes at the death of A, who is a LIB at the time the grant is made. But the VRSO contains an internal precondition. Although A1 has satisfied the precondition of attaining age 30, under the all-or-nothing rule for class gifts every member of the class of A's children, including the afterborn child A2, must satisfy the age precondition within the perpetuities period. Here, the precondition contains a time element that exceeds 21 years (the "fixed" part of the perpetuities period). This precondition may not be satisfied if A2 is born shortly before A dies (and all other LIB, including A1, are dead). This scenario is illustrated by the diagram below.

Grant #21
Precondition At Age 30

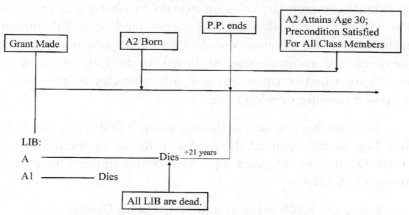

The fundamental problem with Grant #21 is that, although the class of A's children must close at A's death (remember, A is a LIB), the precondition has a time element that exceeds 21 years. If the precondition were set at attaining age 21, then even an afterborn child A2 must either satisfy or conclusively fail to satisfy the precondition within the perpetuities period. Taking the afterborn child analysis out to its most extreme limit, assume that the afterborn child A2 is born one minute before A dies. A2 will either die before attaining age 21, or will turn age 21 one minute before the perpetuities period ends (21 years following A's death).[21] The VRSO in FSA would be valid under the RAP. A would be the "tether" or validating life for the VRSO held by A's children. As written, however, the VRSO in FSA is void under the RAP due to application of the all-or-nothing rule for class gifts.

Striking and Answer: Begin striking at the end of the phrase, "who reach age 30" and continue striking backwards through the comma before the word "life." The revised grant after striking is "to A for life." The state of the title is: A has a LE; O holds a REV.

■ PROBLEM 4.4 ■

Your client is a private developer who would like to buy 1,200 acres of vacant land from the current owner, Tom Smith. The land is located in the State of Bliss. The State of Bliss has adopted the traditional common law rules on matters involving real property. The client plans to develop the vacant land as a $20 million exclusive housing development. You have been retained to advise the client concerning the state of the title to the 1,200 acres and to investigate whether there are any title obstacles to the client's proposed housing development.

In reviewing the state of the title to the 1,200 acres, you learn that Tom Smith acquired the land as a devise under the will of Omar Ollad over 30 years ago. The devise under Omar's will provided as follows:

I give my 1,200 acres of land, located on County Road #6, in Bee County in the State of Bliss, to my friend Tom Smith for him to preserve in its natural state as a

---

21. To be even more extreme, remember that if A is a male, the perpetuities period is extended to 21 years and 10 months.

**wildlife sanctuary, but if the land ever ceases to be used
as a wildlife sanctuary, then it shall go to my surviving
brothers and sisters and their heirs, in equal shares.**

Assume that the 1,200 acres have been maintained as a wildlife
sanctuary since Omar's death. As part of your investigation, you
discover that Omar had one surviving brother, Brian Ollad, and
one surviving sister, Sanguine Ollad, at Omar's death. Other than
the above devise, Omar's will left all of his real and personal
property to Brian and Sanguine. If Omar had died without a will,
Brian and Sanguine would have been Omar's intestate heirs.

Based on these facts, what legal advice will you give to your
client?

Analysis

Preliminary Points: Before engaging in your analysis, pause
and note carefully the role the problem asks you to assume. You are
not being asked to assume the role of a judge who is deciding a
case. You are not being asked to serve as an advocate for one of the
parties in a litigation setting. You are to assume a counseling role
for a client who is about to make a $20 million investment. This role
requires you to analyze the problem and discuss all potential
outcomes with your client. If you can provide a solution to every
outcome, so much the better. If not, at least if the most unlikely
outcome becomes reality, your client cannot come back and com-
plain, "Why didn't you tell me this could happen?"

Responding to a RAP essay exam question such as this one
requires several analytical steps. First, classify the present and
future interests created by the grant and identify any future
interests that must be tested under the RAP. Second, test any future
interests that are subject to the RAP. Third, if a future interest is
void under the RAP, strike the void future interest and reclassify the
present and future interests under the language of the revised
grant. Fourth, answer the question based on the revised grant
language. If it is unclear whether a court will interpret the original

grant language as a violation of the RAP, answer the question assuming all possible judicial interpretations of the original grant language.

Answer: Omar's will appears to grant Tom Smith a FSSEL in the 1,200 acres, and a shifting EI in FSA to Brian and Sanguine as Omar's surviving brother and sister. The shifting EI in FSA must be tested for compliance with the common law version of the RAP, which has been adopted by the State of Bliss. The RAP provides that "no future interest is valid unless it either vests or fails to vest within a life or lives in being plus twenty-one years."

There are two possible interpretations of the language in Omar's will. On the one hand, the devise language could be interpreted as requiring the land to be used as a wildlife sanctuary only for the life of Tom Smith (*"for him* to preserve"). If a court adopts this interpretation ("Interpretation One"), the shifting EI in FSA would be valid under the RAP. Tom Smith is a LIB at Omar's death when the devise was made; therefore, the defeasing event will either occur during Tom's life, or the restriction will be permanently extinguished at Tom's death. Under Interpretation One, the state of the title to the 1,200 acres would be that Tom Smith holds a FSSEL and Brian and Sanguine hold a shifting EI in FSA.

On the other hand, the devise language could be interpreted as requiring the land to be used as a wildlife sanctuary forever ("if the land *ever* ceases to be used"). Under this interpretation, the shifting EI in FSA would be void under the RAP because a million years hence, after all LIB at the time of the grant are deceased, the land could cease to be used for the stated purpose. At that moment, the shifting EI in FSA would come into present possession (it would "vest" for purposes of the RAP) too late. If a court adopts this interpretation of the devise language ("Interpretation Two"), then under the common law RAP the court would strike the devise in the will back to the phrase "to preserve in its natural state as a wildlife sanctuary." After this judicial striking occurs, the state of the title would be that Tom Smith holds a FSD, and Omar's estate holds a

PR. Under the traditional common law rules, a PR is not devisable, so the PR today would be held by Omar's intestate heirs, Brian and Sanguine.

Given that the language of the devise is ambiguous, the client should (before investing $20 million) require Tom Smith to bring (and pay for) a quiet title action so that a court can decide the state of the title to the 1,200 acres. Once a court conclusively determines the state of the title to the 1,200 acres, then the client will have a defined set of future interest holders to negotiate with for the purchase of FSA title to the 1,200 acres.

If the court adopts Interpretation One, the client can acquire FSA title to the 1,200 acres (free of the wildlife sanctuary restriction) by purchasing the FSSEL from Tom Smith and the shifting EI in FSA from Brian and Sanguine.

If the court adopts Interpretation Two, the client may want to consider looking for another tract of land for the proposed housing development. Although the client could purchase the FSD from Tom Smith, the client would be unable to purchase the PR from Brian and Sanguine because a PR is only inheritable, not alienable, under the traditional common law rules. Therefore, the client would not be able to acquire FSA title to the 1,200 acres, and there is a risk that development of the land would trigger the defeasing event (ceasing to be used as a wildlife sanctuary). Under Interpretation Two, if the defeasing event is triggered, then Brian and Sanguine as the holders of the PR would automatically acquire FSA title to the 1,200 acres.

There are two possible options that the client could pursue to acquire FSA title to the 1,200 acres if the court adopts Interpretation Two of the devise language. Neither option appears very attractive. First, the client could require Tom Smith to bring a second quiet title action and ask the court to strike the wildlife sanctuary use restriction on the 1,200 acres as an invalid restraint on the alienation of the land. This action may or may not be successful, depending on the number of potential buyers who would be willing to purchase the 1,200 acres and maintain the land as a wildlife sanctuary.

Second, in conjunction with the purchase of the FSD title from Tom Smith, the client also could negotiate a legally binding agreement with Brian and Sanguine. Under this legally binding agreement, Brian and Sanguine would agree that, once the client broke ground on the development and triggered the defeasing event (failure to maintain the land as a wildlife sanctuary), Brian and Sanguine would convey their FSA title (acquired automatically by operation of law via the PR interest) immediately to the client. The legally binding agreement for Brian and Sanguine to sell the land to the client may not be acceptable to the client. Brian and Sanguine may charge a premium price as consideration for the agreement to convey their FSA title after the defeasing event is triggered by the client's development of the land.

Concluding Points: Once you have studied the real estate transactions part of your Property course, come back to Problem 4.4 and let your imagination run wild. After studying the rules unique to real property transactions, you will understand how the sections of your Property course on present and future interests and the RAP intersect with the rules for buying and selling real property, the concept of marketable title and deed warranties, and the concept of a recorded chain of title to the real estate. Problem 4.4 presents a basic fact pattern that you can use to add layers of additional imaginary facts, and then expand your analysis to practice applying the unique rules for real property transactions.

■ PROBLEM 4.5 ■

Do you want more practice? Review the grants in Problem 3.1 at the end of Chapter 3 and see if you can find any future interests that are void under the RAP.

Analysis

All of the future interests in the Problems at the end of Chapter 3 are valid under the RAP. If you can explain why, you have mastered the RAP.

POINTS TO REMEMBER

- The RAP ignores subsequent events that occur after the future interest is created. You, too, must ignore subsequent events until *after* you have first determined that all EIs, CRs and VRSOs are valid under the RAP.

- The RAP ignores the grantor's intent. If a future interest violates the RAP, then whatever the grant language becomes after striking the void future interest is treated as the original grant language, even if the result is clearly contrary to the grantor's intent.

- The RAP gives every future interest (EI, CR and VRSO) a fixed 21 years to become RAP-vested or be destroyed. Whether the future interest has *more* time than 21 years depends on how the grant is structured to link the future interest to the life or death of persons who are alive at the time the grant is made.

- It is the possibility of an afterborn person or persons that often makes a future interest void under the RAP. Be wary of class gifts that could include an afterborn person as a member of the class.

APPENDIX

THE VALIDATING LIFE METHOD

The Two–Step Process For The Validating Life Method

The validating life method generally is taught as a two-step process. These two steps introduce terminology that many students find confusing. As you read the description of the two-step process below, think of the "measuring lives" as a *pool of potential solutions* to the RAP problem you are analyzing. A validating life is *the solution* to your RAP problem. If you find a validating life (a "solution"), the future interest you are testing under the RAP is valid. If you exhaust your pool of possibilities (the measuring lives) and yet you cannot find a validating life, then the future interest you are testing is void under the RAP.

Step One: Identify Measuring Lives. The first step under the validating life method is to identify the measuring lives who form your pool of possible solutions. This step is illustrated by the chart below.

Finding Measuring Lives

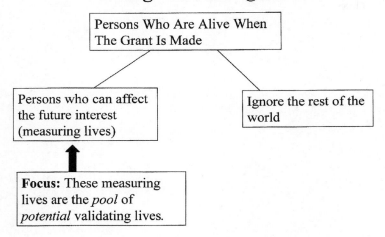

Measuring lives must be people who are alive at the time the grant is made and the perpetuities period begins. Measuring lives also must be relevant to the future interests in the grant. Ignore the rest of the world. In our imaginary RAP world, the rest of the world always dies soon after the grant is made.

If there are multiple future interests that must be tested under the RAP, each future interest can use a different person as a potential measuring life. There does *not* have to be a single measuring life for *all* of the future interests being tested.

Step Two: Determine If There Is A Validating Life.

The second step under the validating life method is to scrutinize your pool of measuring lives, one by one, to determine if at least one measuring life is a validating life. A validating life is any person who is alive at the time the grant is made whose life or death proves conclusively that the future interest being tested under the RAP must, under all circumstances, either RAP-vest or be extinguished forever within the perpetuities period. This step is illustrated by the chart below.

Finding A Validating Life

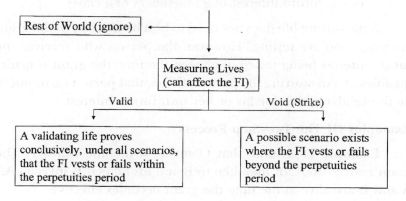

In step two, ask yourself whether you will know, with absolute certainty, under all imaginable circumstances (remember those fertile octogenarians who have afterborn children) that the future interest being tested conclusively will either RAP-vest or be permanently extinguished within 21 years after the death of the measuring life person you are examining. If you can answer "yes" to this question, then the measuring life person is a validating life who conclusively proves that the future interest being tested satisfies the

RAP. If you examine each of the measuring lives and discover that not one of them is a validating life, then the future interest being tested is void under the RAP.

Tips For Identifying The Pool Of Measuring Lives

A measuring life person is any human being who is alive at the time the perpetuities period begins and who has the ability to affect the vesting or failing of the future interest. To be confident in your RAP analysis using the validating life method, you must be confident in your ability to define the pool of measuring lives. To define the pool of measuring lives accurately and completely, look for:

- A person whose life or death affects when the future interest vests or fails.

- A person whose life or death affects the term or nature of the future interest.

- A person who affects the identity or number of beneficiaries of the future interest (e.g., members of a class).

A measuring life does not need to be a beneficiary of the grant language you are testing. However, the person who receives the future interest being tested, if alive at the time the grant is made, qualifies as a measuring life person. Often, that person turns out to be the validating life for his or her own future interest.

Examples Of The Two–Step Process

Example 1: Assume that O makes a lifetime transfer. The grant reads: "To A for life, then to B and his heirs if B survives A." A and B are alive at the time the grant becomes effective.

B has a CR that must be tested under the RAP. A and B are both potential measuring lives to examine for a solution. A is a validating life for B's CR interest because at A's death B will either be alive (the CR will turn into a VR and come into present possession) or B will be dead (the CR will be extinguished at B's death). B also is a validating life for B's own CR interest. During B's life, A will either die (B's CR will turn into a VR and come into present possession) or B will die before A (thereby extinguishing B's CR).

Note that in Example 1 these are two validating lives for the CR. Generally, you do not need to identify all of the validating lives for a future interest that is subject to the RAP. Your professor will be pleased if you can merely identify one!

Example 2: Assume that O makes a lifetime transfer. The grant reads: "To A and his heirs, but if A ever remarries, then to B and his heirs." A and B are alive at the time the grant becomes effective.

B has a shifting EI that must be tested under the RAP. A is a potential measuring life for B's EI because A's conduct during A's life (remarriage) will determine if B's shifting EI will RAP-vest by coming into present possession (A remarries) or be permanently extinguished (A dies having failed to remarry). Note carefully that, although named in the grant as the holder of the EI, B is not a potential measuring life for the EI. Why? Because it is not B's conduct that affects the triggering event; A's conduct (remarriage or not) controls. If B dies first, then A later remarries, B's estate would own the property. In Example 2, A (and only A) is the validating life for B's shifting EI, which is valid under the RAP.

Example 3: Assume that O makes a lifetime transfer. The grant reads: "To A for life, then to B if B attains the age of 30." A and B are alive at the time the grant becomes effective. B is five years old.

B has a CR that must be tested under the RAP. B is the validating life for his own CR interest. The length of B's life will determine if his CR will vest (B lives until the age of 30) or fail to vest (B dies before reaching the age of 30).[22]

---

22. In a jurisdiction that continues to follow the common law Doctrine of Destructibility of Contingent Remainders, A also would be a validating life for B's interest. If the jurisdiction has abolished the Doctrine of Destructibility, A cannot be a validating life for B's future interest. Recall that if the jurisdiction has abolished the Doctrine of Destructibility, B's CR is not destroyed at A's death if B has not yet satisfied the precondition of attaining age 30. If A dies when B is age 6, B will still only be age 27 (not age 30) 21 years after A's death.

Example 4: Assume that O makes a lifetime transfer. The grant reads: "To my wife W for life, then to my children in equal shares." O has one child, O1, at the time the grant becomes effective.

O's child O1 has a VRSO that must be tested under the RAP. O is a potential measuring life because O will affect the number of class members ("O's children"). O is a validating life for the VRSO because at O's death the class closes and the VRSO held by O's children becomes a VR.

One Final Thought

Despite this Appendix, you still may not feel you understand how the validating life method works. Rather than continuing to struggle, work the Problems at the end of Chapter 4 and focus on the tether method and the timeline/diagram method. All methods, if properly applied, will lead you to the correct answer.

CHAPTER 5

Co-Ownership

T here is no overarching grand theme to the rules for property held in co-ownership. Rather, there are simply lots of rules to master. These rules consist of the attributes of the forms of co-ownership under the common law—how co-ownership is created, the survivorship rights among co-owners (if any), and how co-ownership interests are transferred or changed in form (if at all). Situations that trigger special rules involve disputes between co-owners, the rights of creditors of a co-owner, and rights of married couples. Finally, property co-owned as community property (as opposed to the common law forms of co-ownership) has its own set of unique rules.

CO–OWNERSHIP REVIEW

Creation Of The Common Law Forms Of Co–Ownership

Co-ownership involves the concurrent or simultaneous ownership of a piece of property by more than one person. The common law recognized three types of co-ownership: (1) the tenancy in common ("TIC"); (2) the joint tenancy with right of survivorship ("JTWROS"); and (3) for a husband and wife only, the tenancy by the entirety ("TBE").

Today, the default form of common law co-ownership is the TIC. Thus a conveyance "to A and B" is presumed to create a TIC if A and B are not married to each other.

Under the common law, the creation of a JTWROS requires both:

- The appropriate magic words—a phrase in the conveyance indicating that the co-owners have a right of survivorship; and

- The existence of the "four unities" at the time of the transfer—time, title, interest and possession.

The creation of a TBE under the common law requires the existence of the fifth unity of marriage between a husband and wife. To create a TBE, the parties must already be married at the time the property is acquired. If the parties jointly acquire the property before marriage and then marry afterwards, a TIC is created, or, if a right of survivorship is explicit, a JTWROS results.

Modern rule jurisdictions may not strictly enforce the common law requirements of the four unities and may prefer to focus instead on the intent of the grantor. In a modern rule jurisdiction, A's conveyance of the property from sole ownership by A "to A and B, as joint tenants with right of survivorship" creates a JTWROS. At common law, such a conveyance would fail to create a JTWROS because it would fail the unities of time and title. The common law would view the grantor A as acquiring his original interest in the property at an earlier time and through a different instrument than B did. The common law would not permit the owner of property (here, A) to be both the grantor and a grantee of the same property. Because A already owned the property, the common law treated this conveyance as a transfer of a one-half TIC share from A to B.

Key Attributes: The TIC

Each grantee of a TIC receives an undivided share of the property. The concept of an undivided share is a difficult idea to grasp because each co-owner physically can possess (i.e., can trample over) the entire property when the shares of the co-owners are undivided. The co-owners are not "sharing" anything in terms of dividing up the property. Rather, every co-owner who holds an undivided share is entitled to use all of the property.

Unless otherwise specified in the language of the grant, the shares of the co-owners are equal. For example, in a conveyance "to A, B and C," each of the grantees receives an undivided one-third share as a TIC.

Each co-owner may transfer a TIC interest during life by a sale or by a gift, and at death by will or by intestate succession. The recipient of the co-owner's TIC interest likewise becomes a TIC with the other co-owners of the property.

A TIC interest may be given as collateral to secure the individual debt of that co-owner. A TIC interest is reachable by the creditors of a TIC through the mechanism of attachment and foreclosure of a judgment lien.[1]

Key Attributes: The JTWROS

Each grantee of a JTWROS interest receives an undivided share of the property. Unless otherwise specified in the language of the grant, the shares are of equal size. For example, in the conveyance "to A, B and C as joint tenants with right of survivorship," the grantees each receive an undivided one-third share in the property as JTWROS.

Each grantee's JTWROS interest may be conveyed during life by sale or by gift. Once a JTWROS interest is conveyed to another person, at least two of the four unities (time and title) have been destroyed. Therefore, the recipient becomes a tenant in common with the remaining joint tenants. For example, if the grantee A in the conveyance above conveyed his interest to D, D would own a one-third share in the property as a TIC with B and C. B and C, however, would remain joint tenants as between each other.[2]

---

1. *See* discussion *infra* Background On How Judgment Liens Work.

2. This common law attribute modernly has been modified in many jurisdictions so that a conveyance does not constitute a severance of the JTWROS unless the intent to sever is evident from the language of the conveying instrument. Professors tend to test students over the common law rule, however, so do not apply this modern law rule unless your professor has stressed that a modern statute may override the common law rule in this situation.

No joint tenant's interest may be conveyed by will or pass by intestate succession so long as the JTWROS exists. To illustrate using the example above, if B died survived by C and D, C would receive B's undivided one-third share as the survivor of B and C. C and D would then own the property as a TIC. C would own an undivided two-thirds share in the property, and D would own an undivided one-third share.

Judgment creditors of a joint tenant may reach a JTWROS interest through the mechanism of attachment and foreclosure of a judgment lien. The purchaser at a foreclosure sale acquires the joint tenant's interest in the property as a TIC.

To illustrate the judgment lien scenario, assume that the grantor O conveys property "to A, B and C as joint tenants with right of survivorship." After this conveyance X, a creditor of A, obtains a judgment lien on A's interest and forecloses. The purchaser of A's undivided one-third share at the foreclosure sale would acquire A's one-third share as a TIC with the remaining co-owners, B and C. B and C would continue to each own an undivided one-third share in the property as a JTWROS as between each other.

Methods For Severing A JTWROS

Foreclosure of a judgment lien is just one of four universally recognized methods to sever a JTWROS and thereby transform the severed share into a TIC interest. These four universally recognized methods of severing a JTWROS are explained below.

A fifth possible method—the granting of a mortgage by a joint tenant—only severs a JTWROS in a minority jurisdiction that follows the **title theory of mortgages.** Under the title theory of mortgages, granting a mortgage is treated as an actual transfer of title from the mortgagor (here, a joint tenant) to the mortgagee, thereby destroying the unity of title necessary for a JTWROS. Most jurisdictions follow the **lien theory of mortgages**. In a lien theory jurisdiction, the granting of a mortgage by a joint tenant does not sever the share of the joint tenant. The mortgagee in a lien theory jurisdiction holds only a lien on, not actual title to, the joint tenant's share of the property.

Before discussing in detail the methods for severing a JT-WROS, a few introductory caveats are necessary. Note carefully that the first method listed below, a voluntary transfer by a joint tenant to a third party, can be done secretly and is effective even if it is done without the knowledge or consent of the remaining joint tenants.[3] Further note that merely executing a will that attempts to leave the testator's JTWROS interest in property to someone else does not sever the testator's JTWROS interest. Unless the testator's JTWROS is severed and changed into a TIC interest *before* the testator's death, the will's purported devise of the JTWROS share is void. If the testator holds a JTWROS share at death and fails to survive the other joint tenant(s), the JTWROS interest is extinguished at the testator's death, leaving nothing in the estate for the will to devise.

With these caveats, the methods by which a JTWROS share is severed and transformed into a TIC share are:

- **the voluntary lifetime transfer to a third party** by gift or sale (no knowledge or consent of the other joint tenants is required).

- **the mutual agreement of the joint tenants** to sever their JTWROS and convert the shares to TIC interests.

- **a judicial partition action.**[4]

---

3. More controversial is the attempted "secret" severance where one joint tenant attempts to sever by conveying her JTWROS interest to herself as a TIC interest. A few courts have permitted such a "to self" secret severance. *See, e.g.,* Riddle v. Harmon, 102 Cal.App.3d 524, 162 Cal.Rptr. 530 (1980). Permitting a "to self" secret severance violates the common law rule that an owner of property cannot convey that property to himself as both grantor and grantee. To avoid the common law prohibition on "to self" conveyances, the grantor can convey the grantor's share to a straw man, who then reconveys back to the grantor, or the grantor

can convey the property to a trust having the grantor as the trustee. In either case, the interest transferred will be severed from the JTWROS and converted into a TIC share.

4. The usual method of judicial relief in a judicial partition action is to order the property sold and the proceeds divided proportionately according to each co-owner's share. It is usually not feasible or in the best interests of the co-owners for the court to order a physical partition of the property. Note that unless it is limited in time to a reasonable duration, an agreement among co-owners not to seek a judicial partition of the property is void as a restraint on alienation.

- **a foreclosure sale** of a joint tenant's interest by a judgment creditor who attached a judgment lien to the joint tenant's interest in the property.

- **(in a title theory of mortgages jurisdiction only), by granting a mortgage** on the property where less than all the joint tenants are the mortgagors.

Background On How Judgment Liens Work

The third and fourth methods of severing a JTWROS listed above require a background understanding of judgment liens and the recording system for real estate titles. Judgment liens and the recording system are key points of intersection that may not be discussed until much later in your Property course.[5] Issues involving judgment liens also arise in the context of property owned as a TBE.[6] For these reasons, it is helpful to pause and review how judgment liens work so that you can understand how judgment liens intersect with co-ownership interests in real estate.

When a creditor obtains a verdict and judgment for the award of money[7] against a debtor, the creditor normally records the court's order of judgment in the land title records system for every county in which the creditor thinks the debtor may own an interest (including a co-ownership interest) in real estate. Once the judgment is recorded, a lien for the amount of the judgment automatically (by operation of law) attaches to all real estate in that county owned by the debtor, including property co-owned by the debtor as a TIC or a JTWROS.[8] Moreover, the recorded judgment lien also attaches automatically to any property later acquired by the debtor in the county where the judgment lien has been recorded.

If the debtor attempts to sell any real estate that is subject to the judgment lien, the prospective buyer will have notice of the

---

5. *See infra*, Chapter 8, Recording Acts and Adverse Possession.

6. *See infra* Key Attributes: The TBE.

7. The judgment could be an award of tort damages or for money the debtor owes to a commercial creditor.

8. Whether the judgment lien attaches to real estate held by the debtor as a TBE depends on the rule the jurisdiction follows. *See* discussion *infra* Key Attributes: The TBE.

recorded judgment lien. Normally, the debtor/seller will pay off the judgment lien to the judgment creditor using part of the proceeds from the sale of the property so that the buyer will acquire "clean" title to the real estate (i.e., title that is free of the creditor's judgment lien). If the debtor/seller does not pay off the judgment lien at the closing, the prospective buyer will purchase the real estate subject to the obligation to pay off the creditor's judgment lien.

Rather than waiting for a sale of the real estate in order to be paid, the judgment creditor may decide instead to "force" payment by bringing a judicial foreclosure action. Note that the owner of the real estate being foreclosed upon could be the original judgment debtor, or it could be a subsequent owner who agreed (foolishly) to take the real estate from the original judgment debtor subject to the creditor's judgment lien.[9] In a foreclosure action, the court orders the real estate that is subject to the judgment lien to be sold at public auction, with the sale proceeds going first to pay off the creditor who holds the judgment lien.

What happens if the real estate that is being foreclosed upon is co-owned, and only one of the co-owners is the debtor of the creditor who is bringing the foreclosure action? The court will order a foreclosure sale of the debtor's partial co-ownership interest in the real estate. The sale proceeds will be paid first to the foreclosing creditor to pay off the judgment lien. Any remaining money after the judgment lien is paid goes to the debtor/co-owner.

If the debtor's co-ownership interest in the property fore-closed was held as a JTWROS, the foreclosure sale severs the debtor's joint tenancy interest. The purchaser at the foreclosure sale acquires the debtor's share as a TIC interest.

Of course, the purchaser at the foreclosure sale may not want to remain as a co-owner of the property. As a co-owner, the purchaser can bring a judicial partition action and ask the court to partition the property. A successful claim for partition of the

---

9. This subsequent owner may be either a purchaser or a donee.

property usually results in a partition by public sale rather than a physical judicial partition of the real estate. The public sale provides the foreclosure sale purchaser with the opportunity to either buy the remaining shares in the property, or to "cash out" by selling the share that was purchased at the foreclosure sale. The mere threat of bringing a judicial partition action also provides the foreclosure sale purchaser with significant negotiation leverage vis-a-vis the other remaining co-owners of the property. Rather than risk losing the real estate to a higher bidder at the judicial partition sale, the remaining co-owners may be persuaded voluntarily to buy (perhaps at a premium price) the foreclosure sale purchaser's co-ownership interest in the property simply to avoid a threatened partition judicial action.

Key Attributes: The TBE

In a TBE, the spouses must convey the TBE property jointly (i.e., together) while both spouses are alive. A TBE can be severed only by a divorce decree. After a severance by divorce, the property is held by the ex-spouses as a TIC. If the TBE is not severed during life through divorce, at the death of one spouse the surviving spouse becomes the sole owner of the entire property.

Jurisdictions that recognize the TBE are fractured concerning the rights of creditors to TBE property. The **majority rule** is that the creditor of only one spouse cannot acquire TBE property to satisfy the debts of that spouse so long as the other spouse remains alive.[10] Under the majority rule, a creditor's recorded judgment lien against only one spouse does not attach to TBE property unless and until the other spouse dies first, thereby leaving the debtor-spouse with sole ownership of the property. Thus, in a majority rule jurisdiction, the spouses jointly may convey the TBE property free of any recorded judgment lien against one spouse or the other to

---

10. *E.g.*, Sawada v. Endo, 57 Haw. 608, 561 P.2d 1291 (1977). The majority rule interprets the effect of the Married Women's Property Act as prohibiting one spouse from voluntarily assigning that spouse's share of the TBE property to someone else. Based on this interpretation, it follows that a creditor of the debtor-spouse cannot involuntarily alienate the debtor-spouse's share of TBE property through attachment of a judgment lien and foreclosure while the other spouse is alive.

a third party while both spouses are alive. Of course, if the creditor has obtained a judgment lien against both spouses (e.g., an unsecured loan or credit card obligation that was jointly undertaken by both spouses), then the judgment lien will attach to the TBE property while both spouses are alive.

Rights Among Co–Owners

The concept that co-owners each hold an undivided share in the property means that each co-owner has the right to physical possession of the property as a whole. This concept inherently presents the potential for conflicts among co-owners. In the absence of a written agreement describing and defining the rights among co-owners, Property law resolves disputes among co-owners by using default rules. The most commonly studied default rules in the first-year Property course involve: (1) occupying co-owners; (2) the leasing of the property by less than all of the co-owners to a third party; (3) adverse possession claims by one co-owner; and (4) the allocation of the income and expenses of the property among the co-owners. These default rules are reviewed below.

The Occupying Co–Owner

Under the **majority rule**, absent an agreement to the contrary each co-owner is entitled to use and possess the entire property and is not liable to pay rent to the other co-owners for such use. A co-owner in possession cannot, however, oust another co-owner, who has an equal right to use and possess the property in its entirety. An **ouster** occurs if the occupying co-owner refuses a demand by another co-owner to be allowed to use and possess the property.[11] If an ouster occurs, the occupying co-owner must pay fair market value rent to the ousted co-owner.

The **minority rule** is that if the occupying co-owner is in exclusive use and possession of the property, the occupying co-

---

11. Courts vary on the nature of the demand required to trigger an ouster. Some courts require the equivalent of a physical or constructive eviction (a "lockout") of the requesting co-owner by the occupying co-owner. Other courts find that a demand for equal use that is rejected by the occupying co-owner is sufficient to trigger an ouster and with it the obligation to pay rent to the ousted co-owner.

owner automatically owes fair market value rent to the other
co-owner. No ouster (i.e., a demand and denied access) of a
co-owner is necessary under the minority rule to trigger the
occupying co-owner's obligation to pay fair market value rent for
the use of the property.

Leasing Co–Owned Property To Third Parties

If one co-owner unilaterally leases a portion of the property to
a third party, the lease itself is not void if the other co-owner(s)
refuse to consent to the lease and later object to it.[12] Nor does the
lease sever the JTWROS. Two important implications for the tenant
of the lease flow from this lack of severance. First, if the co-owner
who leased the property dies, the lease itself is extinguished along
with the leasing co-owner's JTWROS interest at death. Second, any
co-owner of the property who is not a party to the lease is still
entitled to use and possess the entire property, including the leased
premises. If a nonleasing co-owner demands and is denied access to
the leased premises by the tenant, under the majority rule described above an ouster occurs. Depending on the terms of the
lease agreement, the tenant also may have to pay (in addition to the
lease agreement rent) a proportionate share of fair market value
rent to the ousted co-owner.

Adverse Possession Claims

Absent an agreement to the contrary, each co-owner of the
property has an equal right to use and occupy the entire property.
A co-owner is not required, however, to exercise this right. Therefore, the fact that one co-owner is in exclusive possession of the
property is not sufficient to provide the notice necessary to
establish an adverse possession claim against another co-owner who
chooses not to use or occupy the property.[13]

Allocating Income, Taxes, and Mortgage Liability

Rents and profits received from third parties, taxes and
mortgage payments are allocated among co-owners according to

---

12. *See* Swartzbaugh v. Sampson, 11 Cal.-
App.2d 451, 54 P.2d 73 (1936).

13. For a discussion of the elements necessary to perfect title to real estate by adverse
possession, see Chapter 8, Recording Acts
and Adverse Possession.

their proportionate interests in the property. If one co-owner pays more than his or her proportionate share of taxes or mortgage liability, then that co-owner may seek reimbursement from the other co-owners by bringing a contribution action against them.

Repairs and Improvements

The co-owner who pays the entire cost of repairs or improvements to the property cannot claim reimbursement from the other co-owners by bringing a contribution action. The co-owner who paid for repairs may, however, bring an accounting or partition action and will receive credit for the cost of the repairs. The co-owner who pays for improvements may attempt to bring a partition action. In a physical partition, the court may award the improved portion of the property to the co-owner who paid for the improvements *if* the property physically can be divided fairly.

To physically divide the property fairly, the court must determine whether the co-owner who paid for the improvements can receive the improved portion of the property without decreasing the value of the other co-owner's share of the property below what it would have been worth before the improvements. This balancing of interests, values, and physical shares of real estate is, as a practical matter, virtually impossible to achieve. For this reason, courts strongly favor a sale of the property instead of a physical partition. In a partition sale, the co-owner who paid for the improvements will receive as an additional share of the sale proceeds the increased value of the property that is attributable to the improvements that were made.

Community Property

Teaching and testing community property presents a dilemma for the first-year Property professor. Some professors choose to teach hardly anything at all, and leave the details to a separate course on community property. Other professors choose to cover just enough of the basics so that students can muddle through on the bar exam. If your law school is located in one of the ten states[14] that recognize community property as a form of co-ownership, most likely your professor will choose the first option. If your law school is located in a common law state, most likely your professor will choose the second option. Take your cue from your professor in deciding how much time to spend on learning the rules of community property. The Review below focuses on the fundamental principles of community property, and omits jurisdiction-specific nuances.

Community property ownership is the presumed (default) form of ownership of any property that is acquired while a couple is married and domiciled in a community property jurisdiction using the earnings[15] of either spouse. Even if the property being acquired is legally titled in the name of one spouse alone, the other spouse is presumed to own an undivided one-half interest in the property as community property (notwithstanding what the deed or other document of legal title indicates). Couples who bring their separate property into the marriage, or who acquire separate property during the marriage by gift, devise or inheritance, can agree to hold their separate property as community property.

In classifying property as community property, one point often misunderstood by students is that community property can include real estate that is located in a non-community property state. For example, if a married couple is domiciled in California, and uses their earnings to acquire real estate in Colorado, the Colorado real estate is presumed to be held as community property.

Another point of misunderstanding is the enduring nature of community property. Once an asset is acquired as community property, its character does not change if the married couple later changes their domicile to a non-community property state. For

---

14. Arizona, California, Idaho, Louisiana, Nevada, New Mexico, Texas, and Washington have always recognized community property. Wisconsin has effectively adopted community property by state statute, and Alaska by statute permits married spouses to elect to treat their property as community property.

15. Note carefully what is being excluded by limiting community property to property that is acquired using *earnings*. Property that is acquired by one spouse during the marriage as a gift, devise, or an inheritance is not community property. It is presumed to be the separate property of the spouse who received the gift, devise, or inheritance.

example, if the married couple described above later relocates their domicile to Colorado, the Colorado real estate is presumed to remain as community property.

Finally, community property involves a "tracing" principle. If community property is sold, the sale proceeds (and whatever the sale proceeds may be invested in) are presumed to be community property. Thus, in the above example, if the married couple sells the Colorado real estate (either before or after relocating their domicile to Colorado) and uses the proceeds to purchase a house in Maine, the house in Maine is presumed to be held as community property pursuant to this tracing principle.

Transforming ("Transmuting") Community Property

How is community property transformed ("transmuted") into another form of property ownership? Couples who acquire community property can agree to hold their community property as the separate property of one spouse alone, or agree to hold the property as a TIC or as a JTWROS. Community property cannot, however, be changed by mutual agreement of the couple into TBE property so long as the couple is domiciled in a community property state. No community property jurisdiction recognizes the TBE form of co-ownership. Absent an agreement to transmute, the strong presumption of community property ownership prevails and applies to any property that meets the three-part definition (married, domiciled, earnings) of community property.

Conveying Community Property

Unlike property held as a TIC or as a JRWROS, as a general rule community property cannot be severed unilaterally through a conveyance to a third party by one spouse alone.[16] Both spouses jointly must agree to convey their interests in the community

---

16. The spouses mutually may accomplish a severance and conveyance of community property by engaging in the following two-step transmute process. First, the spouses agree to hold the community property as a TIC or as a JTWROS. Second, once the community property has been transmuted by mutual agreement into a TIC or a JTWROS, one spouse may unilaterally convey his or her TIC or JTWROS interest in the property to a third party.

property together as an undivided whole. For a valid conveyance of real estate held as community property, both spouses must sign the deed that transfers title to the real estate. This principle applies even if the original deed by which the real estate was acquired is titled in one spouse's name alone.

There are two exceptions to the general principle that both spouses must agree jointly to convey community property. First, one spouse acting alone can always voluntarily convey that spouse's undivided one-half community property interest to the other spouse, thereby transforming the community property conveyed into the separate property of the receiving spouse. Second, for community property other than real estate, the ability to manage community property (e.g., to sell it) generally follows how legal title to the property is held. Thus, shares of stock that are titled in the name of one spouse alone but are community property can be sold by the record holder spouse alone but are community property as the fiduciary manager of the community property on behalf of both spouses.

Rights Of Creditors To Community Property

What are the rights of creditors of a spouse to community property? The general rule is that the rights of creditors follow the management rights to community property. Thus, if the debtor-spouse has the right to manage the item of community property, creditors of the manager-debtor-spouse can reach that item of community property.

Death Of A Spouse

What are the rights of the surviving spouse to community property when the other spouse dies? Upon the death of one spouse, community property functions like TIC property. The deceased spouse's one-half interest in the community property becomes part of the deceased spouse's estate, and passes according to the terms of the deceased spouse's will, or by intestate succession if the deceased spouse died without a will.

Migrating Couples And Property Rights Of A Surviving Spouse

Although the problem of migrating couples is studied in depth in advanced courses on decedent's estates, the subject is often introduced in the first-year Property course. Your objective should be to grasp the ultimate outcome, namely that a surviving spouse receives a potential windfall if the migrating couple were longtime residents in a community property state and later changed their domicile to a common law state. Conversely, a surviving spouse can be left impoverished if the couple were longtime residents of a common law state and later changed their domicile to a community property state.

Several technical points contribute to the ultimate outcome for the surviving spouse. First, the state of domicile at death determines the property rights of the surviving spouse to the deceased spouse's estate. Common law states protect the property rights of a surviving spouse by the statutory elective share, which effectively restricts the ability of the deceased spouse to disinherit a surviving spouse by leaving all of the decedent's property to someone else under the terms of the decedent's will. Under an elective share statute, the surviving spouse is entitled to choose between: (1) taking the property left to the surviving spouse under the terms of the deceased spouse's will; or (2) "electing" against the will and choosing instead to take a percentage share (as determined by state law) of the deceased spouse's estate.[17] In addition, the surviving spouse in a common law state keeps any other property owned by the surviving spouse, which would include a one-half share in any community property acquired while the couple previously was domiciled in a community property state.

The potential for a windfall to the surviving spouse arises because longtime community property state residents who later change their domicile to a common law state are likely to have accumulated significant wealth as community property. Merely changing the state of domicile from a community property state to

---

17. State elective share statutes vary tremendously in the percentage of the surviving spouse's share of the deceased spouse's estate and in what property is included as part of the deceased spouse's estate in calculating the elective share. For example, under the 1990 version of the Uniform Probate Code the percentage share is determined on a sliding scale based on the length of the marriage and the decedent's estate is "augmented" to include lifetime transfers of property made by each spouse. See Unif. Prob. Code. §§ 2–203–2–209 (1990).

a common law state does *not* change the presumed ownership of
these assets as community property. Absent an agreement by the
couple to transmute, these assets retain their character as community property even though the domicile of the couple has changed
to a common law state.

Thus, at the death of one spouse, the surviving spouse owns
one-half of all community property assets. In addition, the surviving spouse has the choice of taking any assets left to the surviving
spouse under the terms of the deceased spouse's will or electing
against the will and choosing instead to take the statutory elective
share of the deceased spouse's estate. This is where the potential
windfall to the surviving spouse results. Recall that the deceased
spouse's estate necessarily would include the deceased spouse's
one-half interest in any community property assets. Consequently,
if most of the couple's wealth was accumulated as community
property, the surviving spouse would keep one-half of all community property, *and* could take the elective share percentage of the
deceased spouse's one-half interest in the community property
(and any other separate property owned by the deceased spouse at
death that is also part of the deceased spouse's estate).

In contrast, when longtime common law state residents
change their domicile to a community property state, the surviving
spouse is at an increased risk of being left impoverished if the
deceased spouse decides to disinherit the surviving spouse. Longtime common law state residents who change their domicile to a
community property state (typically, to retire) are unlikely to
accumulate significant wealth as community property. In the
retirement years, individuals typically lack significant earnings (a
prerequisite to acquiring community property) because they are
either not working or only work part-time.[18] If the couple is
domiciled in a community property state at the death of one

---

18. In some community property states,
investment earnings from non-community
property assets accumulated while the couple
resides in the community property state
would be treated as community property.

This is the type of jurisdiction-specific nu-
ance that you are likely to encounter on an
exam only if your professor emphasizes the
point during class.

spouse, the surviving spouse's primary financial protection is entitlement to one-half of any community property. Unfortunately for the surviving spouse, one-half of "zero" (little, if any, community property) is still zero. The terms of the deceased spouse's will may leave little or nothing to the surviving spouse. Thus, with little or no accumulated community property, the surviving spouse who does not own property in his or her own name can be left impoverished by the terms of the deceased spouse's will.

Divorce And The Division Of Marital Property

Upon divorce, marital property is divided between the spouses. Courts use the principle of equitable distribution to divide marital property between the divorcing parties. Many jurisdictions presume that marital property should be divided equally between the parties, unless the circumstances indicate that a less than equal division is more equitable.

Disputes in divorce property settlements arise because it can be difficult to determine what is marital property. Some jurisdictions define marital property broadly as all property acquired during the marriage. Other jurisdictions limit marital property to property acquired using earnings during marriage and exclude property acquired before marriage or property acquired during marriage by gift, devise or inheritance.

A dispute may arise when one of the spouses works during the marriage and supports the other spouse's efforts to obtain an educational degree. In this situation (other than in New York[19]) the courts generally rule that the future economic value—earnings anticipated to be earned in the future—of an educational degree is not marital property.[20] In jurisdictions that do not recognize an educational degree as marital property, a court may award the

---

19. *See* O'Brien v. O'Brien, 66 N.Y.2d 576, 498 N.Y.S.2d 743, 489 N.E.2d 712 (1985) (medical license is marital property). In New York, the future economic value of celebrity status that was enhanced during the mar- riage also is treated as marital property. *See* Elkus v. Elkus, 572 N.Y.S.2d 901 (1991).

20. *See, e.g.*, In re Marriage of Graham, 194 Colo. 429, 574 P.2d 75 (1978).

contributions of one spouse to the other spouse's support while obtaining the educational degree or professional license as reimbursement alimony.[21]

Marriage And Related State Property Rights Of Same–Sex Couples

The leading case on same-sex marriage and the related state property rights of same-sex couples is *Goodridge v. Department of Public Health.*[22] In *Goodridge*, the Massachusetts Supreme Court held that under state law civil marriage was available to same-sex couples. For purposes of federal law, the Defense of Marriage Act of 1996[23] ("DOMA") defines marriage as limited to a legal union between one man and one woman as husband and wife.

The topic of same-sex marriage generates a lively classroom debate. General themes to consider in answering an exam question on this topic include the following:

- Is same-sex marriage analogous to the civil rights struggles of minority groups?

- Should federal law (federalism) trump the power of individual states (states' rights) to determine the civil and property rights of their citizens?

- Should elected legislative officials or unelected judges decide what constitutes "marriage"?

You should add to this exam preparation list additional themes that emerge as part of your own classroom discussion.

CO–OWNERSHIP CHECKLIST

With the above Review in mind, the Co–Ownership Checklist is presented below.

---

21. *See, e.g.*, Mahoney v. Mahoney, 91 N.J. 488, 453 A.2d 527 (1982).

22. 440 Mass. 309, 798 N.E.2d 941 (2003).

23. 28 U.S.C. § 1738C.

A. **DETERMINE THE TYPE OF CO–OWNERSHIP.** Determine if the property is held as community property or in a common law form of co-ownership using Part A.1 of the checklist below. If the property is not community property, proceed to Part A.2 of the checklist to determine the specific type of common law co-ownership, and to Part B to analyze how subsequent events may affect title to the property. If the property is community property, proceed to Part C to analyze how subsequent events may affect title to the property.

    1. **Community Property.** The property is presumed to be owned as community property if the owners were married at the time the property was acquired, domiciled in a community property state and the property was acquired using earnings of either spouse.

        a. **Domiciled In A Community Property State.** When the married couple acquired the property, were they domiciled in one of the following states: Arizona; California; Idaho; Louisiana; Nevada; New Mexico; Texas; Washington; or Wisconsin?[24]

            i. **Separate Property.** Property acquired by one spouse alone, either before marriage or while the couple is domiciled in a non-community property state, is the separate property of the acquiring spouse.

            ii. **Common Law Form Of Ownership.** Property acquired by the couple jointly before marriage, or property acquired by the couple jointly after marriage while domiciled in a non-community property state, is held in a common law form of co-ownership.

---

24. If domiciled in Alaska, the couple can elect to treat their property as community property.

Proceed to Part A.2 to determine the type of common law co-ownership.

   iii. Community Property By Agreement. Once domiciled in a community property state, a married couple can agree to hold property acquired while previously domiciled in a common law state as community property.

b. Using Money Earned While Married. Was the property acquired using money that was earned by either spouse while married?

   i. Separate Property. Property acquired by one spouse alone during marriage using money earned prior to the marriage, or property acquired by one spouse alone by gift, devise or inheritance is the separate property of the acquiring spouse.

   ii. Common Law Form. Property acquired jointly by the couple using money earned prior to marriage, or property acquired jointly by gift or devise after marriage is held in a common law form of co-ownership. Proceed to Part A.2 to determine the type of common law co-ownership.

   iii. Community Property By Mutual Agreement. Once domiciled in a community property state, a married couple can agree to hold property that is not acquired using earnings as community property.

2. Common Law Form Of Co—Ownership. Determine if property originally titled in the name of more than one person is initially held as a JTWROS, as a TBE, or as a

TIC using Part A.2 of the checklist below. Next, proceed to Part B to analyze how subsequent events may affect title to the property.

    a.   **JTWROS.** Determine if the jurisdiction applies the common law rule or the modern rule for creation of a JTWROS.

        i.   **Common Law Rule.** The property must be titled as held in JTWROS, and the four unities below must be satisfied.

- **Time.** Did the co-owners acquire their interests at the same time?

- **Title.** Did one and the same written instrument convey title to all the co-owners? Property jointly acquired through intestate succession fails the title requirement and thus is always held as a TIC.

- **Interest.** Are all the interests of the co-owners equal and of the same type and duration?

- **Possession.** Is each co-owner entitled to possess the entire property?

- **Common Law Rule On "Grantor As Grantee" Transfers.** If the same person is both grantor and grantee (e.g., the grantor A conveys his property "to A and B as JTWROS"), the unities of time and title fail and the property is held as a TIC.

        ii.   **Modern Rule.** Did the grantor expressly intend to create a JTWROS? Look to the language of the deed or will conveying the property as the

best evidence of intent. The four
unities are not required.

- **Modern Rule On "Grantor As Grantee" Transfers.** If the same person is both grantor and grantee (e.g., the grantor A conveys his property "to A and B as JTWROS"), under the modern rule the property is held as JTWROS based on the grantor's intent.

b. **TBE.** To be held as a TBE, the jurisdiction must: (1) recognize the TBE form of co-ownership (the common law recognized the TBE, but many modern common law jurisdictions do not, and no community property jurisdiction recognizes the TBE); (2) satisfy the four unities for a JTWROS described in Part A.2.a.i of the checklist above; and (3) the property must have been acquired while the co-owners were husband and wife.

   i. **Common Law Rule Presumption Of TBE.** If the jurisdiction recognizes the TBE, property conveyed "to A and B" while A and B are husband and wife is presumed to be held as a TBE.

c. **TIC.** If jointly owned property does not satisfy the requirements for property held as a JTWROS or as a TBE, then the property is held as a TIC as the default form of co-ownership.

B. **ATTRIBUTES OF COMMON LAW CO–OWNERSHIP (SUBSEQUENT EVENTS ANALYSIS).** Use the checklist below to determine the effect of subsequent events on ownership of the property. For disputes involving an attempted voluntary transfer or severance of a co-ownership interest, proceed to Part B.1 of the checklist. For the death of a co-owner, proceed to Part B.2. For disputes among co-owners, proceed to Part B.3. For disputes involving creditors, proceed to Part B.4. If the dispute involves the property rights of a surviving spouse, or a divorce and the related division of marital property, proceed to Part D.

1. **Voluntary Transfer Or Severance Of Co–Ownership Interests.**

   a. **Transfer Of JTWROS Interest.** Did a joint tenant transfer the joint tenant's interest to a third party? **If yes**, the transferred interest is severed and becomes a TIC. Any remaining JTWROS interests remain unchanged.

      i. **Knowledge And Consent Not Required.** A severance by voluntary transfer to a third party is effective without the knowledge or consent of the other joint tenants.

      ii. **Secret "Self" Severance.** An attempted severance by transferring the property to oneself as a TIC is void under the common law rule. Modernly, a few jurisdictions (e.g., California) permit such a secret "self" severance.

      iii. **Attempted Transfer At Death Via Will.** To transfer a JTWROS interest at death via a devise under a will, the testator must validly sever the JT-WROS interest and thereby change it to a TIC interest prior to death. If the JTWROS is not severed prior to death, the attempted devise under the will is not effective because the JTWROS interest of the decedent was extinguished at death and therefore is not part of the decedent's estate.

   b. **Mutual Agreement To Sever JTWROS Interests.** Did all the joint tenants mutually agree to sever their JTWROS interests? **If yes**, they own the property as a TIC.

    c.   **Transfer Of TBE Property.** Did both husband and wife agree together to convey the property? **If yes**, the transfer is valid. **If no**, the attempted transfer is invalid. TBE property cannot be severed by a unilateral attempted conveyance by one of the spouses.

2.   **Death Of A Co—Owner.** Apply the appropriate rule below based on the form of co-ownership held by the deceased co-owner at death.

    a.   **JTWROS Property.** The deceased co-owner's share is allocated to the surviving joint tenant(s). Do not allocate to any person who owns a TIC or TBE share in the same property.

    b.   **TBE Property.** The deceased spouse's share goes to the surviving spouse.

    c.   **TIC Property.** The deceased co-owner's share passes to the deceased co-owner's estate. Subsequent ownership is determined by the terms of the deceased co-owner's will, or by state intestate succession law if the co-owner died without a valid will.

3.   **Disputes Among Co—Owners.** Identify the nature of the dispute and apply the appropriate rule.

    a.   **Disputes Concerning Occupancy By A Co—Owner.** Is one of the co-owners occupying or otherwise using the property?

        i.   **Majority Rule.** Absent a contrary agreement, any co-owner is entitled to occupy and use the entire property rent-free.

           •   **Ouster Occurs.** Under the majority rule, a co-owner in possession must pay fair market value rent to any other co-owner who has been ousted by the co-owner in possession.

- **Definition Of Ouster.** Ouster occurs in all jurisdictions if the other co-owner demands to use the property and is physically prevented from doing so by the co-owner in possession. Some jurisdictions recognize ouster if a demand for shared use is made and the co-owner in possession rejects the demand.

  ii. **Minority Rule.** Absent a contrary agreement, an occupying co-owner must pay fair market value rent to the other co-owner(s) for use of the property.

b. **Disputes Over A Lease Authorized By Less Than All Co—Owners.** Did one co-owner lease a portion of the property to a third party without the consent of the other co-owner(s)?

  i. **Lease Is Valid.** The lease is valid even if the other co-owner(s) did not know of or refused to consent to the lease to the third party.

  ii. **Lease Not A Severance Of JTWROS.** A lease of part of the property by one co-owner does not sever a JTWROS.

  iii. **Effect If Leasing Joint Tenant Dies.** If the co-owner who leased the property dies, the lease is extinguished if the leasing co-owner's interest was part of a JTWROS. If the leasing co-owner's interest was held as a TIC, the lease remains intact.

  iv. **Ouster May Trigger Additional FMV Rent.** If another co-owner who did not consent to the lease is ousted from the leased premises by the tenant, the tenant may also owe fair market value rent to the ousted co-owner under the majority rule for an ousted co-owner described in Part B.3.a.i of the checklist above.

c. **Disputes Over Mortgaging Co-Owned Property.** Use the checklist below to determine whether the mortgage severs the share of the mortgagor and analyze the effect of subsequent events after the mortgage is granted.

     i. **JTWROS Property: Does The Mortgage Sever?** In alien theory (majority) jurisdiction, a JTWROS is not severed if one joint tenant grants a mortgage on the joint tenant's interest in the property. In a title theory (minority) jurisdiction, the mortgaging joint tenant's interest is severed and becomes a TIC interest.

         • **TIC Property.** Any tenant in common can mortgage his or her TIC interest in the property. The mortgage is limited to the TIC share of the property.

         • **TBE Property.** Both husband and wife must mortgage the property together in order for the mortgage to attach to the real estate.

     ii. **JTWROS Property: Effect Of Death On The Mortgage?** Determine if the jurisdiction applies the lien theory or title theory of mortgages and apply the appropriate rule below.

         • **Lien Theory (Majority) Jurisdiction.** The extent of the mortgage co-exists with the mortgaging joint tenant's undivided interest in the property. If the mortgaging joint tenant fails to survive, the mortgage is extinguished by the death of the mortgaging joint tenant. If the mortgaging joint tenant is the survivor, the mortgage extends to the entirety of the property. If the mortgaging joint tenant owns 100% of the property as the survivor, the mortgagee can collect the debt owed from 100% of the proceeds at a foreclose sale.

- **Title Theory (Minority) Jurisdiction.** The original grant of the mortgage severs the mortgaging joint tenant's interest and turns it into a TIC interest. Therefore, death of either the mortgagor or the other co-owners of the property has no impact on the mortgage, which remains as an encumbrance on the mortgagor's TIC share.

iii. **JTWROS Property: Effect Of Foreclosure?** Determine if the jurisdiction applies the lien theory or title theory of mortgages and apply the appropriate rule below.

- **Lien Theory (Majority) Jurisdiction.** Foreclosure of the mortgaging joint tenant's interest severs the JTWROS and converts the mortgagor's interest into a TIC. The foreclosing mortgagee is entitled only to the sale proceeds from the TIC interest. If there are two or more other joint tenants besides the mortgagor, their JTWROS interests are not affected by the foreclosure sale. The foreclosure sale purchaser holds a TIC share in the property.

- **Title Theory (Minority) Jurisdiction.** The foreclosing mortgagee is entitled only to the sale proceeds from the severed TIC interest held by the mortgagor. If there are two or more other joint tenants besides the mortgagor, their JTWROS interests are not affected by the foreclosure sale. The foreclosure sale purchaser holds a TIC share in the property.

d. **Disputes Over Other Money Issues.** Identify the nature of the dispute and apply the appropriate rule.

    i. **Income, Taxes And Mortgage Liability.** Absent an agreement among the co-owners, income from the property, taxes owed, and mortgage liability are allocated pro rata among the co-owners based on their proportionate shares in the property.

    ii. **Repairs.** The co-owner who pays for repairs is not entitled to reimbursement from the other co-owners and can only recover the costs of the repairs in the form of a credit as part of an accounting action or a partition sale.

    iii. **Improvements.** The co-owner who

pays for improvements is not entitled to reimbursement from the other co-owners. The improving co-owner can only recover the costs of the improvements through a partition sale, where the improving co-owner receives from the sale proceeds the increase in value of the property attributable to the improvements. In a physical partition, the improving co-owner may receive the improved portion of the property in the rare circumstance where this can be done in a manner that is fair to the other co-owners.

4. **Disputes Involving Creditors Of A Co–Owner**. Creditors of a co-owner can reach any real property (including a JTWROS or TIC interest) owned by the co-owner to the same extent that the debtor could voluntarily transfer the JTWROS or TIC interest in the property. For TBE property, under the majority rule creditors of one spouse alone cannot reach TBE property while the other spouse is alive. A creditor of both spouses can reach TBE property.

   a. **Mechanics Of A Creditor's Judgment Lien.** Once recorded, the creditor's judgment lien attaches automatically by operation of law to any real property (or a partial TIC or JTWROS interest therein) owned by the debtor in the county where the lien is filed. The judgment lien also attaches to the debtor's after acquired real property (or a partial TIC or JTWROS interest therein). Once the lien attaches, the lien continues to encumber the property if the property is later transferred. Once the judgment lien has attached, the creditor may bring a foreclosure action, where the court will order the real property (or partial interest therein) encumbered by the judgment lien to be sold at public auction. The sale proceeds are used first to repay in full the debt owed to the foreclosing creditor, with any remaining balance going to the owner of the property interest that was foreclosed.

b. **Debtor's Interest Is TIC Or JTWROS.** A creditor can always reach (via foreclosure of an attached judgment lien) any partial property interest held by the debtor as a TIC or a JTWROS. Foreclosure of the attached judgment lien severs the debtor's JTWROS interest and converts it to a TIC interest. The foreclosing creditor is entitled only to the sale proceeds from the TIC interest. If there are two or more other joint tenants besides the debtor, their JTWROS interests are not affected by the foreclosure sale.

c. **Debtor's Interest Is TBE.** The majority rule is that while both spouses are alive, the judgment lien of a creditor of only one spouse does not attach to TBE property (based on the Married Women's Property Act).

   i. **Lifetime Transfers Of TBE Property.** Under the majority rule, both spouses can convey the TBE property together to a third party unencumbered by (free of) the creditor's judgment lien.

   ii. **Effect Of Death.** If the TBE property is held by both spouses and the debtor-spouse dies first, the creditor's judgment lien cannot attach to the property. If the non-debtor-spouse dies first, then the creditor's judgment lien attaches to the entirety of the property and can be foreclosed

by the creditor, who would be entitled to repayment from 100% of the
sale proceeds.

iii. Exception Where Both Spouses Are Joint Debtors. If both spouses are joint debtors of the creditor, the policy underlying the Married Women's Property Act is not implicated. The creditor's judgment lien attaches to the entirety of the TBE property and can be foreclosed.

C. ATTRIBUTES OF COMMUNITY PROPERTY OWNERSHIP (SUBSEQUENT EVENTS ANALYSIS). Determine the effect of subsequent events on the ownership of community property. If the dispute involves the community property rights of a surviving spouse, proceed to Part D.

1. Transfers and Transmuting Issues. Identify the nature of the dispute and apply the appropriate rule.

a. Attempted Unilateral Transfers Of Community Real Property. For real property held by the spouses as community property, irrespective of how legal title to the real estate is held, both spouses must agree to convey and both must sign the deed that transfers title to the real estate.

i. Exception For Transfer To Spouse. One spouse always may unilaterally convey that spouse's interest in community property to the other spouse, who then holds the property as separate property.

ii. Exception For Management Rights To Personal Property. For personal property, the spouse with management rights unilaterally may transfer the community property.

b. Transmuting Community Property Into Another Form Of Ownership By Mutual

Agreement. Spouses can agree to hold community property as the separate property of one spouse alone, or in another form of co-ownership recognized by the jurisdiction of domicile. No community property state recognizes the TBE form of co-ownership.

    c. **Changing Another Form Of Ownership To Community Property By Mutual Agreement.** Spouses who are domiciled in a community property state can mutually agree to hold any separate property of one spouse, or property held in another form of co-ownership, as community property.

  2. **Rights Of Creditors.** Creditor's rights generally are co-terminous with the debtor's management rights to community property.

  3. **Death Of A Spouse**. There are no survivorship rights for community property. The deceased spouse's one-half interest in community property passes to the deceased spouse's estate. New ownership of the deceased spouse's one-half interest in community property is determined by the deceased spouse's will, or by a statute of intestate succession if the deceased spouse died without a will.

D. **DEATH AND DIVORCE.** Identify the nature of the dispute using the list below and apply the appropriate rule.

  1. **Death: Property Rights Of The Surviving Spouse.** Identify the state of domicile at death to determine the property rights of the surviving spouse.

    a. **Domicile At Death In Common Law State.** The surviving spouse is entitled to choose between: (1) taking the property left to the surviving spouse under the terms of the deceased spouse's will; or (2) electing against the will and choosing instead to take the statutory elective share of the deceased spouse's estate.

      • **In addition**, the surviving spouse keeps any other property owned by the surviving spouse (including a one-half share of any previously acquired community property).

b. **Domicile At Death In Community Property State.** The surviving spouse owns one-half of any community property, plus any property owned by the deceased spouse that is left to the surviving spouse under the terms of the deceased spouse's will or as an intestate heir.

c. **Rule For Migrating Couples.** As a general rule, the surviving spouse receives a potential windfall if the couple were longtime community property state residents and later changed domicile to a common law state. The surviving spouse can be left impoverished (disinherited under the deceased spouse's will) if the couple were longtime common law state residents and later changed domicile to a community property state.

   i. **Community Property State Residents Who Change Domicile To A Common Law State.** The couple is likely to have accumulated significant assets as community property. At the death of one spouse, the surviving spouse owns one-half of all community property. In addition, the surviving spouse has the choice of: (1) taking any assets left to the surviving spouse under the terms of the deceased spouse's will; or (2) electing against the will and choosing instead to take the statutory elective share of the deceased spouse's estate (which includes the deceased spouse's one-half interest in previously acquired community property).

      ii. **Common Law State Residents Who Change Domicile To Community Property State.** The couple is unlikely to have accumulated significant assets as community property using earnings while married and domiciled in a community property state. At the death of one spouse, the surviving spouse is entitled to one-half of all community property (if any has been acquired), plus any property owned by the deceased spouse that is left to the surviving spouse under the terms of the deceased spouse's will (which may be nothing) or as an intestate heir.

   2. **Divorce: Marital Property Rights.** Determine the couple's marital property and divide it using the principle of equitable distribution.

      a. **Determining Marital Property.** Determine what property is marital property using the jurisdiction's definition. Some jurisdictions by statute or case law define marital property broadly as all property acquired during the marriage. Other jurisdictions define marital property as property acquired using earnings during marriage, and exclude property acquired before marriage or property acquired during marriage by gift, devise or inheritance.

         i. **Educational Degrees Or Professional Licenses.** The future economic value (estimated future earnings) of an educational degree or a professional license is not marital property (except in New York).

        ii. **Reimbursement Alimony.** In jurisdictions that do not recognize an educational degree or a professional license as marital property, a court may award the financial contributions of one spouse to the other spouse's support while obtaining an educational degree or professional license as reimbursement alimony.

b. **Equitable Distribution Of Marital Property.** Courts use the principle of equitable distribution to divide marital property between the divorcing parties. Many jurisdictions presume that marital property should be divided equally between the parties.

ILLUSTRATIVE PROBLEMS

Here are three problems that illustrate how the Checklist can be used to resolve co-ownership questions.

■ PROBLEM 5.1 ■

In Year 1, Oscar, who was the sole owner of Greenacre, validly conveyed Greenacre to his four children using a deed that read in relevant part as follows:

"To my children, A, B, C and D, in fee simple absolute, as joint tenants with full rights of survivorship as at common law."

In Year 2, A married R.

In Year 3, B conveyed his interest in Greenacre to his son, S, and his daughter-in-law, T, as TBE.

In Year 4, C wrote a will leaving her interest in Greenacre to her daughter, U.

In Year 5, D died, survived by A, R, B, S, T, C and U.

In Year 6, S died, survived by A, R, B, T, C and U.

In Year 7, C died, without having changed her will written in Year 4. A, R, B, T and U survived.

What is the state of the title to Greenacre after C's death?

Analysis

Oscar's conveyance created a JTWROS among his four children. Under both the common law rule and the modern intent test for creation of a JTWROS, each child owned an undivided one-fourth interest in Greenacre as a JTWROS. Under the common law rule, the deed indicated that a JTWROS was being created, and the four unities of time, title, interest and possession are satisfied. All four children received their interest at the same time as part of the same deed. Each child is entitled to immediate possession because each child owned the same interest—a fee simple absolute—in the property. Under the modern rule, the deed language is the best evidence of Oscar's intent to convey a one-fourth JTWROS interest in Greenacre to each child.

A's marriage to R in Year 2 had no effect on the title to Greenacre. Even if A and R are domiciled in a community property jurisdiction, property acquired by A prior to the marriage remains A's separate property.

B's conveyance to S and T in Year 3 severed B's one-fourth JTROS interest. S and T received B's one-fourth interest as a TBE as between themselves and as a TIC with A, C and D. A, C and D continue to each own their one-fourth interests in Greenacre as JTWROS as among each other.

C's will leaving C's interest in Blackacre to U in Year 4 had no effect on the title to Greenacre. Merely executing the will did not sever C's JTWROS interest.

When D died, his one-fourth JTWROS interest passed by right of survivorship to C and A. They each received a one-eighth share. After D's death, C and A each held a three-eighths interest in Greenacre as JTWROS as between each other. Because B's conveyance severed B's interest, S and T did not receive any of D's interest when D died.

When S died, T becomes the sole owner of the one-fourth interest as the surviving tenant by the entirety.

When C died, C's three-eighths JTWROS interest in Greenacre was extinguished and passed to A as the surviving joint tenant. Because C never severed C's JTWROS interest while C was alive, C's attempted devise of C's interest to U via the will was void.

The final state of the title to Greenacre is that, after C's death, A owns an undivided three-quarters interest and T owns an undivided one-quarter interest. A and T own their respective shares in Greenacre as TIC.

■ **PROBLEM 5.2** ■

Refer to the facts of Problem 5.1 above. Assume that in Year 3, B was the driver of a vehicle that was involved in a car accident and negligently injured X. X brought a tort action against B and obtained a judgment of $10,000 against B. X validly recorded the judgment lien in the county where Greenacre is located before B conveyed his interest in Greenacre to S and T as TBE.

If B refuses to pay the $10,000 judgment to X, what may X do to recover the $10,000 judgment? Explain briefly.

Analysis

X can recover by bringing a foreclosure action based on X's recorded judgment lien. When the judgment lien was recorded, B owned a one-fourth JTWROS interest in Greenacre. Once the judgment lien was recorded, the lien attached to B's one-fourth JTWROS interest. The lien remained attached and continued to encumber the one-fourth property interest in Greenacre when B severed B's interest and conveyed it to S and T as TBE. (Note: The status of S and T as TBE does not protect them from *prior* liens that have *already attached* to the property.)

X may bring a foreclosure action and ask the court to auction the one-fourth interest in Greenacre that is encumbered by the judgment lien. The court will order S and T's one-fourth interest to be sold, and the sale proceeds will be used first to pay X's $10,000 judgment. Any sale proceeds remaining after X is repaid in full will belong to S and T as the current owners of the interest in real property that was foreclosed. If the foreclosure sale brings less than $10,000, X will receive only the amount of the sale proceeds.

■ PROBLEM 5.3 ■

Husband ("H") and Wife ("W") are married and domiciled in Seattle, Washington. While married to H, W used her earnings to purchase 100 shares of stock in a local company. The stock was titled in W's name alone on the stock certificate of ownership.

H and W later retired and moved to Colorado. W died, leaving the 100 shares of company stock in her will to her sister, Alice. (Assume that W left $10 million in other property under the will to her surviving spouse, H. H decided not to take a statutory elective share of W's estate).

Who owns the 100 shares of company stock after W's death?

Analysis

H and W were married and domiciled in Washington, which is a community property state. The 100 shares of company stock was purchased with W's earnings while H and W were married and domiciled in Washington. Therefore, the shares of company stock are presumed to be held by H and W as community property. W's sole ownership title as indicated on the stock certificate of ownership does not rebut this strong presumption. Moreover, there is no indication of a mutual agreement by H and W that the stock is being held as the separate property of W.

The company stock remained community property when H and W changed their state of domicile to Colorado, which is a common law state. The characterization of an asset originally acquired as community property does not change with a change of domicile.

When W died, her one-half community property interest in the 100 shares of company stock passed through W's estate and to Alice pursuant to the terms of W's will. H's one-half community property interest in the stock was retained by H. At W's death, Alice and H each own 50 shares of the company stock.

POINTS TO REMEMBER

- Whenever a married couple acquires property, focus closely on their state of domicile to determine if the property is presumed to be held as community property. Beware of the less obvious community property jurisdictions, such as Washington and Idaho. Remember that if the three-part acquisition test for community property (married, earnings, domicile) is satisfied, the strong presumption of community property will override the fact that the property acquired may have been titled in one spouse's name alone on a document or instrument of ownership.

- Under the common law rule, property expressly titled as held in JTWROS nevertheless is treated as a TIC if the four unities of time, title, interest and possession are not satisfied on the facts. Analyze the facts closely and be watchful for a failure of one of these four unities. The analysis could in fact turn on whether the jurisdiction strictly follows the common law rule or the modern intent test for creation of a JTWROS. When in doubt (either as to the facts, or as to what rule the jurisdiction will apply), try to analyze subsequent events under both possible scenarios (if the property is held as JTWROS, and if the property is held as TIC).

- A judgment lien, once filed, attaches to any real property owned by the debtor in the county where the judgment lien is filed, and also attaches to any property acquired afterwards by the debtor in that county. Once a recorded judgment lien attaches to real property, the lien "sticks" and continues to encumber the real estate even if the debtor later transfers the real estate to someone else. Under the majority rule in a jurisdiction that recognizes the TBE, a judgment lien against only one debtor-spouse does not attach to TBE property owned or after acquired while both spouses are alive.

- If real property is acquired as community property, both spouses must execute the deed that subsequently conveys title to the real estate to validly convey the real estate.

- Merely changing domicile from a community property state to a common law state does not change the ownership of assets originally acquired as community property. Absent an agreement by the couple to transmute, the assets retain their character as community property, and any assets acquired in exchange for community property are presumed to be community property.

CHAPTER 6

Landlord and Tenant

L earning the individual rules that govern the landlord-tenant relationship is not difficult. Organizing these rules, however, can be challenging. The major Property casebooks tend to present landlord and tenant law in a haphazard manner, leaving it up to the student to reorder the rules in a logical sequence that facilitates problem solving.

Chapter 6 presents the rules of landlord and tenant law in the order you typically would apply them to resolve a dispute. The primary issues in almost all landlord and tenant disputes center around the landlord's claim for rent or to evict a nonpaying tenant and the tenant's myriad defenses. Understanding how the landlord's claims and the tenant's defenses fit together is the key to mastering landlord and tenant law.

There are, of course, disputes that do not center around the payment of rent or eviction of the tenant. But these disputes involve easily recognized situations, such as tenant claims of housing discrimination or tort liability, or additional claims by the landlord against a subtenant where the lease has been assigned or sublet by the original tenant.

Given that organization often is what students need most, this Review focuses on how the concepts and theories of landlord and tenant law fit together when the landlord seeks to collect rent or evict a nonpaying tenant. The Review also explains assignments and subleases in detail. The Checklist at the end of Chapter 6 organizes these rules and further summarizes the rules for resolving housing discrimination and tort liability issues.

LANDLORD AND TENANT REVIEW

Determining The Types And Duration Of The Tenancy

The starting point for resolving a dispute is to determine whether the parties have a lease arrangement. If the parties' arrangement is not a lease, then other legal rules will govern their rights and duties. Beware of a private land use arrangement that may be called a "lease" by the parties, but that is really a license, easement, or profit right.[1]

Assuming the parties are in a true lease arrangement, determining the type of tenancy created (term of years, periodic, or at will[2]) is important because the tenant owes rent to the landlord until the lease terminates. The type of tenancy determines the duration of the lease term for which rent is due, and also determines when and how the lease terminates. You must know this information to estimate how much lost rent potentially is owed to the landlord as damages.

Holdover Tenants

A tenant who overstays the termination date of the lease gives rise to a unique issue—the problem of the **holdover tenant**.[3] The landlord must elect between two options in dealing with a holdover

---

1. For a discussion of licenses, easements and profits, see Chapter 9, Easements, Profits, Real Covenants and Equitable Servitudes.

2. If the parties agree that one party alone (either the landlord or the tenant) has the unilateral power to terminate the tenancy, then we say that the tenancy is *determinable*. If the duration of the tenancy is unspecified and only the tenant has a unilateral power of termination, the jurisdiction will either imply

a power of termination in the landlord and treat the arrangement as a tenancy at will, or rule that only the tenant may terminate the lease, effectively creating a determinable life estate. *E.g.,* Garner v. Gerrish, 63 N.Y.2d 575, 483 N.Y.S.2d 973, 473 N.E.2d 223 (1984).

3. A holdover tenant situation is also known as the tenancy at sufferance.

tenant. The landlord may evict the holdover tenant, or the land-lord may elect to renew the holdover tenant's lease. In a jurisdiction that follows the **American Rule** concerning a tenant's right to actual physical possession of the leased property, the landlord may lease the property to a new tenant even though a holdover tenant remains in possession of the leased premises. In an American Rule jurisdiction, it is the new tenant who is responsible for evicting a holdover tenant, while still having to pay rent to the landlord.

In a jurisdiction that follows the **English Rule**, the landlord must evict a holdover tenant. The new tenant is excused from paying rent until the landlord successfully evicts the holdover tenant. Even in an English Rule jurisdiction, the landlord only must make the leased property physically available for the tenant to occupy on the first day of the lease term. Thereafter, it is the tenant's responsibility to ward off trespassers and defend the tenant's legal right to possession and use of the leased premises.

Disputes To Evict A Nonpaying Tenant And Collect Rent

The primary dispute in landlord and tenant law centers around the tenant's obligation to pay rent due under the terms of the lease. Under the common law, the tenant's duty to pay rent due to the landlord was independent of any obligations of the landlord under the terms of the lease. Modernly, at least some of the landlord's lease covenants are dependent so that the landlord's breach of certain terms in the lease may excuse the tenant from her obligation to pay the rent due under the lease. Under the modern approach, the two most important dependent lease covenants that bind the landlord are the **covenant of quiet enjoyment** and, for residential properties only, the **implied warranty of habitability**. The covenant of quiet enjoyment ("CQE") and the implied warranty of habitability ("IWH") are discussed later in Chapter 6.

Landlord's Options Depend On Nonpaying Tenant's Possession Or Abandonment

When a tenant fails to pay rent, the starting point for analyzing the range of options available to the landlord is to determine whether the tenant remains in possession of the property, or has abandoned the leased premises.

Eviction Of A Tenant In Possession

If the tenant remains in possession but fails to pay rent, the landlord may attempt to evict the tenant (with the ultimate objective of replacing that tenant with another one who will pay rent). Eviction terminates the lease, and thereby extinguishes the nonpaying tenant's obligation to pay rent after the eviction is completed. The evicted tenant will still owe rent due for the time the tenant remained in possession, but will not owe rent after being evicted.

Tenant's Responses To "Self–Help" Landlord Eviction

Eviction is fraught with potential traps and pitfalls for the landlord. The landlord who attempts to lock out the tenant and retake possession without using the judicial process (a "self-help" eviction) may pay damages to the tenant instead if a court later finds that the landlord's self-help eviction was wrongful. A **wrongful eviction claim** by the displaced tenant may arise for a number of reasons. A court may find that: (1) the landlord lacked authority under the terms of the lease[4] to retake possession; (2) the means used by the landlord to self-evict the tenant were not "peaceable"; or (3) the jurisdiction prohibits self-help eviction (even a peaceable one) and instead requires the landlord to use the judicial process[5] to evict a tenant.

For a residential tenancy, the landlord's eviction of the nonpaying tenant may be wrongful if the landlord has violated the

---

4. In addition to empowering the landlord to retake possession if the tenant fails to pay rent, the lease also may give the landlord the right to terminate the lease and retake possession if the tenant breaches other enumerated tenant covenants in the lease. For example, in a commercial lease the tenant may covenant to operate its business in a lawful manner in compliance with all federal and state laws and regulations. The lease may give the landlord the power to terminate the lease and retake possession if such a covenant is breached by the tenant.

5. At common law, the landlord would bring a claim for ejectment to evict a nonpaying tenant. Ejectment actions are garden-variety civil litigation, and therefore are costly and time-consuming. Modernly, all states have statutes that authorize summary eviction actions. A summary eviction action expedites the eviction litigation by eliminating discovery and limiting the types of defenses the tenant may assert. For this reason, today's landlords generally use summary eviction and not ejectment to evict a nonpaying tenant.

IWH. The landlord's breach of the IWH can make the tenant's nonpayment of rent to the landlord *lawful*,[6] thereby making the landlord's self-help eviction *unlawful*. If the tenant being evicted has given the landlord repeated notice of needed repairs to the property (without a response from the landlord), a court may find that the landlord has engaged in a prohibited **retaliatory eviction**. Finally, a court may find that a landlord who selectively exercises the power under the lease to engage in a self-help eviction and retake possession of the property in a discriminatory manner has engaged in **prohibited housing discrimination** under the federal Fair Housing Act[7] ("FHA").

Summary Eviction Actions

Given these possible outcomes, the landlord may prefer to bring a summary eviction action in court rather than engage in a self-help eviction.[8] Today, the tenant may assert the above-described claims (wrongful eviction, breach of IWH, retaliatory eviction, and prohibited housing discrimination under the FHA) as potential defenses to the landlord's claim for summary eviction. If the tenant ultimately loses and is evicted, the tenant will owe rent until the eviction occurs, but not for the remaining lease term. Eviction terminates the lease, and with it the tenant's obligation to pay rent.

Landlord's Options When Tenant Abandons

If the tenant vacates the leased premises with no intention of returning and has ceased paying rent, the tenant has abandoned

---

6. Under the IWH, the tenant cannot lawfully stop paying rent to the landlord until *after* the tenant has given the landlord notice that the IWH has been breached and that repairs to the leased premises are needed. The tenant is not excused from paying rent, but can withhold payment of rent to the landlord until the repairs are completed. If breach of the IWH is asserted as a tenant defense in a summary eviction action, the court may require that rent be paid into an escrow account. *E.g.,* Javins v. First National Realty Corp., 428 F.2d 1071 (D.C. Cir. 1970).

7. *See* 42 U.S.C. § 3604(b) (prohibiting discrimination in the terms and conditions of the lease).

8. Of course, if the jurisdiction prohibits self-help eviction by landlords, then the landlord can only evict a nonpaying tenant in possession by using the judicial process.

the property. The landlord has a different set of options to deal with the tenant who has abandoned the leased property without paying all of the rent due under the terms of the lease.

First, the landlord may choose to treat the tenant's abandonment as an implied offer of surrender,[9] and accept the tenant's surrender. If the landlord accepts the tenant's offer of surrender, the lease is terminated, and the abandoning tenant is not liable for the remaining rent due under the terms of the lease.[10]

Second, the landlord may refuse to accept the tenant's surrender, but attempt to relet the premises to mitigate the abandoning tenant's damages. In a **majority rule jurisdiction**, the landlord has an affirmative duty to mitigate the tenant's damages (rent due for the rest of the lease term) by making a reasonable effort to relet the leased premises. In a **minority rule jurisdiction**, the landlord may allow the property to sit vacant until the abandoning tenant's lease term expires, and then sue the abandoning tenant for all of the rent due under the terms of the lease.[11]

Anticipatory Repudiation Damages

An offer of surrender by an abandoning tenant that is accepted by the landlord normally cuts off the tenant's liability for future rent due under the remaining term of the lease. If the tenant clearly repudiates the lease, a few courts have applied the contract-based **doctrine of anticipatory repudiation** and permitted the landlord to collect damages for the tenant's repudiation of the lease prior to the expiration of the lease term.[12] Permitting the

---

9. The tenant's offer of surrender may be made express (rather than implied) through words or a writing.

10. The tenant may, however, be liable for anticipatory repudiation damages. *See infra*, Anticipatory Repudiation Damages.

11. Under traditional landlord and tenant law, rent is owed only as it is due to be paid under the terms of the lease. Therefore, to collect all of the rent lost under the abandoning tenant's lease as damages, the landlord

must wait until after the term of the lease expires. To bring a claim for lost rent *before* the lease term expires, the landlord's claim must be based on the contract doctrine of anticipatory repudiation.

12. Under the doctrine of anticipatory repudiation, the measure of the landlord's damages is the difference between the lease rental rate and the (lower) fair market rent for the remainder of the lease term. The landlord usually seeks anticipatory repudia-

landlord to recover anticipatory repudiation damages is an exception to the rule of landlord-tenant law that rent is owed only as it becomes due under the terms of the lease.[13]

Exam Tip: Analyzing Ambiguous Landlord Conduct

Although the landlord may expressly accept a tenant's offer of surrender in writing, more often the landlord's statements and conduct after a tenant has vacated the leased premises are ambiguous. The tenant has every incentive to characterize the landlord's ambiguous conduct as an implied acceptance of the tenant's offer of surrender, thereby terminating the lease and extinguishing the tenant's ongoing obligation to pay rent. From the landlord's perspective, the landlord's ambiguous conduct may be purposefully strategic. The landlord may want to wait and see what happens before deciding to accept an offer of surrender by the tenant.

Once the current tenant has vacated the property, the landlord may quickly find another tenant who will pay an even higher rent. In this situation, the landlord will accept the tenant's offer of surrender and terminate the abandoning tenant's lease. By terminating the abandoning tenant's lease, the landlord clearly is entitled to keep the higher rent from the new tenant.

Alternatively, the landlord may be unable to relet the premises immediately, or the landlord eventually may relet the premises to a new tenant at a lower rent. Here, the landlord will not want to accept the abandoning tenant's offer of surrender. The landlord will characterize his efforts to relet the premises as merely an attempt to mitigate the abandoning tenant's damages. Ultimately, the landlord will seek to recover from the abandoning tenant the net amount of the rent lost by the landlord for the remainder of the lease term.

The landlord's argument that efforts at reletting were merely an attempt to mitigate the abandoning tenant's damages is more

---

tion damages immediately rather than waiting until the expiration of the lease term. If the landlord recovers anticipatory repudiation, the amount of future lost rent awarded as damages will be discounted to a present value and paid as a lump sum.

13. *See supra* note 11.

compelling in a jurisdiction that requires the landlord to mitigate an abandoning tenant's damages. In a majority rule jurisdiction, the landlord has a duty to mitigate the damages owed by the abandoning tenant by making reasonable efforts to relet the property. If the jurisdiction follows the minority rule, the landlord has no duty to mitigate. In a minority rule jurisdiction, the landlord can do nothing, let the leased property sit vacant, wait until the abandoning tenant's lease expires, and then sue the abandoning tenant for all of the rent due under the terms of the lease. Of course, the landlord in a minority rule jurisdiction voluntarily may attempt to relet the vacant premises, but the point is that the landlord has no legal duty to do so.

Abandoning Tenant's Defenses

The tenant who abandons the leased premises has multiple defenses to the landlord's claim for lost rent due under the terms of the lease. Both commercial and residential tenants may assert a **breach of the CQE** by the landlord. To assert a breach of the CQE, the tenant must prove that the landlord's wrongful conduct caused substantial interference with the tenant's use and enjoyment of the leased premises. The tenant must give notice to the landlord of the interference and a reasonable opportunity for the landlord to cure the problem. If the landlord fails to cure the problem, to assert a breach of the CQE the tenant must vacate the leased premises[14] within a reasonable time after giving notice to the landlord.

Breach of the CQE is tantamount to a constructive eviction by the landlord that relieves the tenant of the obligation to pay further rent to the landlord. The most difficult hurdle for the tenant to overcome in asserting a breach of the CQE usually is showing that the landlord has engaged in wrongful conduct that caused the problem leading to the constructive eviction. Prove of wrongful landlord conduct may be established by showing that the landlord

---

14. If the tenant vacates only part of the premises due to a breach of the CQE, the tenant cannot prorate his rent and must continue to pay the entire rent due under the terms of the lease. Only an actual (as opposed to a constructive) eviction of the tenant by the landlord from part of the premises will excuse the tenant's obligation to pay rent.

violated one of the landlord's express covenants (promises by the landlord) in the written lease agreement, or that the landlord violated one of the common law duties imposed on landlords by Property law. The common law duties imposed on landlords are:

- the duty to maintain common areas;

- the duty to disclose latent defects;

- the duty to make promised repairs non-negligently;

- the duty not to make affirmative misrepresentations concerning the condition of the leased premises;

- the duty to provide habitable premises for the short-term lease of a furnished dwelling; and

- the duty to abate immoral or nuisance conduct by other tenants on the landlord's property.

In addition to asserting a breach of the CQE, a residential tenant may assert a **breach of the IWH**. The residential tenant is much more likely to prevail using a IWH theory than a CQE theory because the IWH defense does *not* require the tenant to prove that the landlord engaged in wrongful conduct. To assert a breach of the IWH, the tenant must show that condition of the leased premises is unsafe and unfit for human habitation. Under the IWH, the cause of the problem does not have to be the landlord's wrongful conduct. If the landlord is not aware of the condition of the leased premises, then the tenant is required to give the landlord notice and an opportunity to repair the condition. Unlike the CQE, the residential tenant does *not* need to vacate the leased premises to assert the breach of the IWH as a defense to the landlord's claim for nonpayment of rent. The residential tenant has the option of: (1) vacating the leased premises, ceasing rent payments, and suing the landlord for damages; or (2) remaining in possession of the leased premises and either withholding all rent due until the landlord remedies the condition or deducting a reasonable amount from the rent due and using the money for necessary repairs.

If the tenant can prove that the landlord knew the leased premises were unsafe at the time the tenant entered into the lease, a commercial or a residential tenant may argue that the lease was **illegal**.[15] Although the tenant is excused from paying the rent due under the terms of an illegal lease, a court may order the tenant to pay the market value rent of the property in its "as is" condition (which may be zero if the conditions are bad enough). An illegal lease creates a tenancy at will. If the court rules the lease is illegal, the landlord can terminate immediately, so an illegal lease theory works best as a defense to nonpayment of rent by a tenant who has already vacated the leased premises.

Other Abandoning Tenant Defenses

Other defenses asserted by an abandoning tenant generally cluster around the tenant's legal or physical right to possess and use the leased premises. These defenses arise in the context of unique (and therefore easily recognizable) circumstances.

Occasionally, a tenant in possession of the property (the "occupying tenant") discovers that another tenant (the "competing tenant") claims to have a superior legal right to possession of the leased premises. For example, the competing tenant may claim that the landlord leased the premises to the competing tenant before executing the lease with the occupying tenant, and therefore the competing tenant has the superior legal right to possession of the premises under the common law rule of first in time, first in right.

In this situation, the competing tenant's mere assertion of a superior legal right to the leased premises does not excuse the occupying tenant from paying rent. The occupying tenant must continue to pay rent to the landlord unless and until a court ousts the occupying tenant by ruling that the competing tenant does, in fact, have the superior legal right to possession of the leased premises. Until ousted by a judicial ruling, the occupying tenant is using the landlord's property and must continue to pay the landlord rent for that use.

Other possible defenses to a claim for nonpayment of rent for a tenant who has abandoned the leased property arise if circum-

---

15. *E.g.,* Brown v. Southall Realty Co., 237 A.2d 834 (D.C. 1968).

stances change significantly after the tenant executes the lease. A drastic change in circumstances may make it illegal or impossible to perform under the lease, thereby terminating the lease. For example, there may be a change in the law so that the tenant's use of the property becomes illegal.[16] Or, the property itself may be destroyed, thus making it impossible for the tenant to occupy the leased premises.[17]

For commercial tenants only, a closely related (but not identical) tenant defense is that changed circumstances have so frustrated the fundamental purposes of the lease that the lease should be treated as terminated. The frustration defense is asserted when a commercial tenant's use remains legal and it is not impossible for the commercial tenant to perform under the lease, but it has become a hardship for the tenant to continue to perform due to the changed circumstances. Financial difficulty in paying the rent owed under the lease is not, however, considered a "hardship" that entitles a commercial tenant to terminate the lease.

Disputes Other Than For The Payment Of Rent

In addition to bringing a claim for nonpayment of rent or to evict a nonpaying tenant, the landlord may bring other claims against the tenant for damages. For example, the landlord may sue the tenant for damages incurred by the landlord that reasonably result from the tenant's breach of a specific covenant[18] in the lease. For a commercial tenant, deterioration in the physical condition of the leased premises caused by the tenant's failure to make repairs necessary to maintain the condition of the leased premises[19] (known

---

16. If the tenant must obtain a permit to operate and fails to do so, the tenant later cannot claim that the lease is terminated due to the illegality of the tenant's use. The tenant bears the risk of obtaining any permit necessary to make the tenant's use legal.

17. Under the common law, a tenant was still liable for rent due under the terms of the lease if the leased property was destroyed. Today, the vast majority of states provide that, absent express language in the lease to

the contrary, the lease is terminated if the leased premises are destroyed. The lease is not terminated, however, if the destruction of the property is due to the tenant's own negligence.

18. For example, the lease may require the tenant to install or remove fixtures, provide services such as lawn care for the entire property in exchange for reduced rent, etc.

19. For a residential tenant, this common law duty of the tenant is eliminated by the

as involuntary or permissive waste) may cause the landlord to bring a damages claim. The landlord also may bring a damages claim for affirmative waste if the tenant changed the physical condition of the leased premises.

The tenant, too, may have other types of claims against the landlord. Although usually asserted as a defense to a claim for nonpayment of rent, a commercial or a residential tenant may bring a claim against the landlord for damages resulting from the landlord's breach of the CQE that has resulted in the constructive eviction of the tenant. A residential tenant also may bring a direct claim for damages against the landlord for a breach of the IWH. A tenant who has been evicted may bring a direct claim for damages against the landlord for wrongful eviction or retaliatory eviction. A residential tenant also may bring a claim for prohibited housing discrimination under the federal FHA.[20] Both commercial and residential tenants may bring a claim for racial discrimination under the Civil Rights Act of 1866 ("CRA").[21] Finally, any tenant (or the tenant's guests) may assert a tort claim against the landlord for personal injuries that result from a negligent breach of one of the landlord's (limited) common law duties or an express duty of the landlord that is contained in the lease.

Disputes Involving A Subtenant (Assignment And Sublease Arrangements)

Some students struggle so much with the archaic vocabulary of assignments and subleases that they never grasp the fundamental implications of characterizing the arrangement as an assignment or a sublease. Below is a summary of the major points of distinction from the perspective of the landlord.

---

landlord's duty to make repairs under the IWH.

20.   42 U.S.C. §§ 3601 et seq.

21.   42 U.S.C. § 1982. Unlike the FHA, the CRA only prohibits discrimination on the basis of "race" in refusing to rent property. "Race" under the CRA is based on identifiable ancestry or ethnic characteristics. *See* Saint Francis College v. Al–Khazraji, 481 U.S. 604 (1987). Unlike the FHA, the CRA also does not prohibit the landlord from racial discrimination against tenants by having different terms and conditions for renting the property, such as charging a higher monthly rent, restricting the tenant's other privileges, or requiring a higher damages deposit. The CRA applies to the rental of all types of property, not just residential housing.

- A sublessee who does not assume the terms of the original lease cannot be sued for money.[22] The landlord's only option is to evict a sublessee who is in possession without paying rent.

- An assignee can be sued for rent due, but only for the period beginning when the assignment occurred until the end of the lease term. This result occurs because an assignee is in privity of estate with the landlord.

- An assignee of commercial property can be sued for failure to make repairs necessary to maintain the condition of the leased premises (known as the covenant of good repair). The covenant of good repair is implied by law whenever two parties are in privity of estate.

- For an assignee of residential property, the covenant of good repair is eliminated by the IWH, which requires the landlord to make necessary repairs.

The landlord has more options if the subtenant (either a sublessee or an assignee) agrees to assume the obligations of the tenant under the terms of the original lease. The subtenant's agreement to assume the original lease terms can be made directly with the landlord, but more often the agreement is made with the original tenant or a subtenant. Even if the landlord is not a party to the assumption agreement, the landlord can sue to enforce the terms of the original lease against the assuming subtenant as a third party beneficiary of the assumption agreement. An assumption agreement allows the landlord to sue the assignee or sublessee who assumes the terms of the original lease for: (1) failure to pay rent due under the terms of the original lease; and (2) any other breach of the contractual terms of the original lease.

A sublessee who assumes the original lease is foolish because now the landlord can sue the sublessee for damages for failing to pay rent or failing to perform any other tenant covenants under

---

22. This result occurs because neither privity of contract nor privity of estate exists between the landlord and a sublessee.

the terms of the original lease. The landlord's claim for damages for these items is based on privity of contract, which exists (where none existed before) by virtue of the sublessee's agreement to assume the tenant obligations under the terms of the original lease.

An assumption by an assignee gives the landlord two theories—privity of contract and privity of estate—to rely upon in making a claim for rent due against an assignee. The assumption agreement expands the scope of the assignee's potential liability by making the assignee liable for performing any additional original tenant covenants in the lease.

After an assignment or a sublease has occurred, what is the potential liability of the original tenant? As a general rule, the original tenant is not excused from performing the tenant covenants (rent and anything else the tenant promised to do) in the original lease. Note carefully that the landlord's mere consent to the original tenant's assignment or sublease of the property does not relieve the original tenant of her obligations under the lease.

Normally, the original tenant is liable for any breach of the terms of the original lease (including a breach by an assignee or a sublessee). The only exception to this general rule occurs when the landlord grants a **novation**. A novation is granted where the landlord expressly agrees to release the original tenant from her obligations under the original lease. A novation always is express; a novation is never implied merely because the landlord has consented to the assignment or sublease of the property. Bottom line, the landlord's mere consent to the assignment or the sublease *never* lets the original tenant off the hook for liability under the terms of the original lease.

Analyzing Assignment And Sublease Arrangements

Jurisdictions use either the common law test or the modern test for determining whether an arrangement with a subtenant is an assignment or a sublease. On the exam, the arrangement may be ambiguous. Your goal is to show your professor that you know the rules for *both* an assignment and a sublease. In other words, your best strategy if the arrangement on the exam is ambiguous is to analyze all possibilities. Below is a summary of the rules to apply if the arrangement is ambiguous.

- The original tenant is liable to the landlord for any breach of the terms of the original lease, whether that breach is caused by the original tenant or by a subsequent assignee or sublessee (unless the landlord has expressly granted a novation—but remember—the landlord's permission to assign or sublease is *not* a novation).

- If the arrangement is a sublease, the landlord can only evict the sublessee for nonpayment of rent.

- If the arrangement is an assignment, the landlord can sue the assignee for rent and, for a commercial property only, for breach of the implied covenant of good repair. (The IWH supercedes the implied covenant of good repair for a residential property.)

- If the subtenant (whether a sublessee or an assignee) assumed the terms of the original lease, the landlord can sue the subtenant for any breach of the tenant covenants in the original lease. If the assumption agreement is between two tenants, the landlord may still enforce it as a third party beneficiary of the assumption agreement.

The subtenant may, of course, assert the same types of defenses as the original tenant to ward off eviction or a claim for nonpayment of rent. Problem 6.1 at the end of Chapter 6 illustrates this situation.

Analyzing Claims Against Intermediate Subtenants

Claims against intermediate subtenants arise if there is a series of assignments or subleases to successive subtenants. Often the last subtenant in the chain is either bankrupt, absconded, or was a sublessee who did not assume the original lease covenants and therefore cannot be sued by the landlord for lost rent or damages to the property. Who else in the chain of subtenants can the landlord sue? Below is a summary of the rules for an intermediate subtenant analysis.

- ■ The landlord cannot sue any intermediate subtenant who is a sublessee for rent or damages. A sublessee cannot be sued for rent or damages because a sublessee is not in privity of contract or privity of estate with the landlord. A sublessee in possession can only be evicted.

- ■ Any intermediate assignee who later subleases the property remains liable for rent and damages for the sublessee's failure to keep the premises in good repair. This result occurs because the intermediate assignee who subleases remains in privity of estate with the landlord.

- ■ Any intermediate assignee who later assigns the property is liable for rent due and damages for failure to keep the property in good repair while the intermediate assignee was in legal possession of the property. This result occurs because the intermediate assignee is liable only for the period when the intermediate assignee is in privity of estate with the landlord. The intermediate assignee who later assigns is not liable for rent that accrued or damages incurred after the intermediate assignee assigned the property because privity of estate terminates with the assignment.

- ■ Absent a novation by the landlord, an intermediate subtenant (either an assignee or sublessee) who assumed the original lease terms is liable for all rent and all damages resulting from any breach of the original tenant covenants in the lease from the moment of the assumption until the termination of the lease. The landlord may sue the subtenant as a third party beneficiary of the assumption agreement.

 LANDLORD AND TENANT CHECKLIST

With the above Review in mind, the Landlord and Tenant Checklist is presented below.

A. **DETERMINE THE TYPE OF LEASE ARRANGEMENT.** Does a lease arrangement exist? If so, what type of tenancy is created between the landlord and tenant? Or, has some other type of private land use arrangement been created instead?

1. **Types Of Lease Arrangements.** Analyze the agreement between the parties to determine if a lease exists.

 a. **Term Of Years Tenancy.** A term of years lasts for a fixed period of time. The beginning and ending date are stated or can be ascertained.

 i. **Notice To Terminate?** No notice is required to terminate a term of years lease. The lease expires automatically at the end of the term.

 ii. **Effect Of Death?** Death of the landlord or the tenant has no effect on a term of years lease. The deceased tenant's estate is responsible for rent and other lease obligations for the duration of the term.

 iii. **Only One Party Can Terminate Prior To End Of Lease Term? If yes**, the arrangement is a determinable term of years.

 b. **Periodic Tenancy.** A periodic tenancy lasts for a fixed period that automatically renews until terminated by giving notice. No final termination date is stated in the lease, which can be renewed indefinitely.

 i. **Notice To Terminate?** The terminating party must give notice to terminate a periodic tenancy.

 • **Termination Date Must Be Specified In Notice.** The notice of termination must specify that the lease will be terminated on the last day of the period. If the notice does not specify the last day of the period as the termination date, the court will either treat the notice as effective as of the end of the next period, or treat the notice as ineffective to terminate the lease at all.

- **Advance Notice To Terminate Year–To–Year Tenancy.** Six months advance notice of termination is required.

- **Advance Notice To Terminate Month–To–Month Tenancy.** One month's advance notice of termination is required.

- **Advance Notice To Terminate Other Periodic Tenancies.** Advance notice of termination equal to the length of the period is required, but no longer than six months.

 ii. **Effect Of Death?** Death of the landlord or the tenant has no effect on a periodic tenancy. Unless the deceased tenant's estate wants to maintain the lease, the personal representative must give the notice to terminate.

 iii. **Only One Party Can Terminate? If yes**, the arrangement is a determinable periodic tenancy.

 c. **Tenancy At Will.** A tenancy at will lasts so long as both landlord and tenant mutually agree. The key characteristic of a tenancy at will is that the lease has no fixed duration or period. Both parties must have the right to terminate the lease for a tenancy at will to exist.

  i. **Notice To Terminate?** In a true tenancy at will, the landlord or the tenant can terminate the tenancy effective immediately without providing advance notice of the termination.

    ii. **Effect Of Death?** Death of the landlord or the tenant automatically terminates a tenancy at will.

    iii. **Only The Tenant Can Terminate?** If the duration of the lease is unspecified and the court rules that only the tenant may terminate, the tenant has a determinable life estate.

d. **Tenancy At Sufferance (Holdover Tenant).** A tenancy at sufferance arises when the tenant remains in possession after the lease term expires.

    i. **Landlord's Election Of Remedies Is Irrevocable.** The landlord must irrevocably elect to either evict the tenant or renew the original lease.

    ii. **Eviction Option.** The landlord evicts the holdover tenant and sues for damages for lost rent. Proceed to Part B.1 of the checklist for the landlord's method of eviction.

    iii. **Renewal Option.** The landlord treats the original lease as renewed. The terms and conditions of the original lease govern during the renewal period.

        • **Periodic Or Term Of Years For Renewed Lease?** The majority rule treats the renewed lease as a periodic tenancy (notice must be given later to terminate). The minority rule treats the renewed lease as a term of years (no notice required to terminate at the end of the renewed term).

- **Length Of Renewal?** The renewal period is determined either by how rent is paid in the original lease, or the length of the original term. Under either approach, the maximum renewal period is for one year.

2. **Other Property Arrangements.** Language that appears to create a lease may instead create a different type of property arrangement between the two parties. The numerous clausus principle supports characterizing the parties's arrangement as a standardized form of property rights to minimize transaction costs.

   a. **Determinable Life Estate.** In a determinable life estate, the owner grants another person the right to occupy the property for life or until that person decides to vacate.

   b. **License.** In a license, the owner grants another person permission to enter and/or use the owner's land. A license is revocable by the owner and is not transferable by the licensee to another person without the permission of the owner. See the Checklist at the end of Chapter 9 for further analysis.

   c. **Easement.** In an easement, the owner grants another person the right to ingress and egress across the owner's land. See the Checklist at the end of Chapter 9 for further analysis.

   d. **Profit.** In a profit, the owner grants another person the right to enter the owner's land and remove a natural resource (water, timber, coal, fish, wild game, etc.). See the Checklist at the end of Chapter 9 for further analysis.

3. **Statute Of Frauds.** The Statute of Frauds requires that certain types of private land use arrangements must be in the form of a writing, signed by the party to be bound, in order to be enforceable. A term of years lease for a term

of more than one year must be in the form of a writing that satisfies the Statute of Frauds. A periodic tenancy with a period that is less than or equal to one year does *not* need to satisfy the Statute of Frauds to be enforceable (even if the period renews so that the duration of the tenancy exceeds one year).

B. **LANDLORD CLAIMS AGAINST A NONPAYING TENANT (AND TENANT DEFENSES/COUNTERCLAIMS).** If the nonpaying tenant remains in possession of the leased property, proceed to Part B.1. If the nonpaying tenant is no longer in possession, proceed to Part B.2. Conclude your analysis by examining other potential landlord claims against the tenant under Part B.3.

1. **Tenant Remains In Possession.** The landlord may evict a nonpaying tenant who remains in possession prior to expiration of the lease. Eviction terminates the lease and with it the evicted tenant's obligation to pay rent for the remaining term of the lease.

a. **Self–Help Eviction Permitted?** At common law, self-help eviction is permitted if requirements i through iii below are satisfied. The modern trend is to prohibit self-help eviction and require the landlord to evict the nonpaying tenant in possession through the judicial process.

i. **Based On Tenant's Failure To Pay Rent?** A landlord can always evict a tenant for nonpayment of rent, provided that the landlord first gives the tenant notice and an opportunity to pay. It is not necessary for the landlord to have the express power to retake possession in the lease to engage in a self-help eviction based on the tenant's failure to pay rent.

ii. **Based On The Power To Retake Possession?** Did the tenant violate a term in the lease that triggers the landlord's express right under the lease to retake possession upon the tenant's default? **If no**, then the landlord cannot use self-help eviction. **If yes**, determine whether the landlord's means of self-help eviction were peaceable under iii below.

iii. **Peaceable Means?** Even if the landlord has the legal right to retake possession upon the tenant's default, the landlord's self-help eviction is a wrongful eviction if the means used to accomplish it are not peaceable. Look for circumstances that could lead to confrontation or violence between the landlord and the tenant to determine if the landlord's means of self-help eviction are peaceable.

b. **Tenant's Responses (Defenses And Counterclaims To An Eviction).** Determine the tenant's potential defenses and counterclaims using Parts B.1.b.i through b.iv.

i. **Wrongful Eviction Claim?** Was the landlord's self-help eviction wrongful? **If yes**, the tenant is entitled to damages for wrongful eviction and is not liable for rent after the eviction. The landlord's eviction is wrongful if: (1) the jurisdiction prohibits self-help eviction; (2) the landlord lacked the necessary authority under the lease to retake possession; or (3) the means used by the landlord to evict the tenant were not peaceable.

ii. **(Residential Property Only) Breach of IWH?** The tenant may lawfully withhold rent and remain in possession if: (1) the premises are so defective as to not be habitable; (2) the tenant has given notice to the landlord of the defective(s) that need to be repaired before ceasing to pay rent to the landlord; and (3) the landlord has failed to act to make the premises habitable. The landlord's eviction of the tenant for nonpayment of rent is not wrongful if the tenant stops paying rent first, and then afterwards provides notice to the landlord of repairs needed to make the premises habitable. Proceed to Part D for further analysis of a breach of the IWH.

iii. **(Residential Property Only) Retaliatory Eviction Claim?** Is the landlord's motive in evicting the tenant retaliation for tenant complaints about repairs that are needed to the property? **If yes**, the tenant may recover damages for a retaliatory eviction. Look to the timing and circumstances surrounding the tenant's complaint and the eviction by the landlord. State statutes may create a rebuttable presumption of retaliatory eviction if the eviction occurs within a certain number of months of the tenant's complaint.

iv. **(Residential Property Only) Claim Of Discrimination Under FHA § 3604(b)?** A landlord who selectively exercises a power under the lease to retake possession if the tenant defaults based on a FHA-protected category engages in discrimination in the terms and conditions of the lease. Proceed to Part G for further analysis of a tenant claim of prohibited housing discrimination under the FHA.

2. **Tenant Has Abandoned Possession.** Abandonment occurs if the tenant has vacated the leased premises with no intent of returning to occupy the premises and has ceased to pay rent due under the terms of the lease.

   a. **Landlord Accepts Offer Of Surrender.** Abandonment is an implied offer of surrender by the tenant to the landlord. The tenant also may expressly offer to surrender the leased premises to the landlord.

      i. **Acceptance Terminates The Lease.** The landlord's acceptance of an express or implied offer of surrender cuts off the tenant's obligation to pay further rent as of the moment of the landlord's acceptance. The tenant is still liable for rent that accrued up to the point of acceptance.

      • **Just Mitigating?** If the landlord relets the leased property, determine if the landlord's conduct is consistent with the provisions of the original lease (mitigating) or inconsistent (acceptance of surrender).

      • **Factors To Consider.** When analyzing the landlord's conduct as a potential acceptance of an offer of surrender, compare the rent, terms and conditions of the abandoning tenant's lease with the new lease. Any extension of duration or other changes in the terms suggest acceptance of the abandoning tenant's offer of surrender and termination of the old lease. Any alterations to the relet premises necessary for the new tenant suggest acceptance of the tenant's offer of surrender and termination of the old lease.

ii. **Are Anticipatory Repudiation Damages Available?** An abandoning tenant who clearly and unequivocally repudiates the lease may be liable for anticipatory damages to the landlord.

- **Measure Of Damages For Anticipatory Repudiation.** Damages for anticipatory repudiation are the difference between the lease rental rate and the (lower) fair market rent for the remainder of the lease term.

- **Landlord's Strategy.** The advantage of suing for anticipatory repudiation damages is that the landlord can sue the tenant for rent for the remaining balance of the lease term rather than waiting for the lease term to expire. The disadvantage is that the landlord must prove what the fair market rent will be for the remainder of the lease term. If awarded, anticipatory damages are paid as a discounted present value lump sum.

b. **Landlord Does Not Accept Offer of Surrender.** If the landlord does not accept the tenant's offer of surrender, the tenant remains liable for rent due under the terms of the lease. Under the common law rule, rent is due only as it accrues under the terms of the lease and cannot be accelerated (unless the court allows a contract claim for damages for anticipatory repudiation of the lease). Depending on the jurisdiction, the landlord may have a duty to mitigate the tenant's damages by making reasonable efforts to relet the leased premises.

i. **Did Landlord Have A Duty To Mitigate Damages?** The majority rule is that the landlord has a duty to make reasonable efforts to relet the premises to mitigate the abandoning tenant's damages for lost rent. The minority rule is that the landlord has no duty to mitigate the abandoning tenant's damages.

ii. **Vacant Stock?** In a majority rule jurisdiction, if the landlord has other units for rent, the landlord must treat the abandoned property as part of the landlord's vacant stock. The landlord must show the property to prospective tenants on the same basis as the landlord's other vacant units.

iii. **Effect Of Failure To Mitigate In Majority Jurisdiction?** Majority jurisdictions are divided concerning the consequences for a landlord who fails to mitigate. Some majority jurisdictions rule that the tenant owes no rent to the landlord at all. Other jurisdictions rule that the tenant owes only the difference between the lease rent rate and the rent the landlord would have received if the landlord had made reasonable efforts to relet the property.

c. Tenant's Responses (Defenses And Counter-claims To A Damages Claim For Rent). Determine the tenant's potential defenses and counterclaims using Parts B.2.c.i through c.iv.

        i. (All Properties) Constructive Eviction Claim (Breach Of CQE Defense). To assert a breach of the CQE, the tenant must give notice to the landlord of the situation giving rise to the breach and then vacate the leased premises within a reasonable time after giving the notice. Proceed to Part C for further analysis of a constructive eviction claim/breach of the CQE defense by the tenant.

        ii. (Residential Property Only) Breach of IWH. A breach of the IWH entitles the residential tenant to vacate the property and terminates the lease so that no more rent is owed to the landlord. The residential tenant must first give notice to the landlord of the condition making the premises uninhabitable and give the landlord a reasonable opportunity to make repairs before vacating to assert a breach of the IWH as a defense to the landlord's claim for nonpayment of rent. Proceed to Part D for further analysis of breach of the IWH.

        iii. (All Properties) Illegal Lease. Did the landlord know that the leased premises were uninhabitable or unsafe at the time the tenant entered into the lease? **If yes,** proceed to Part C.3 for further analysis of a potentially illegal lease.

        iv. Interference With Tenant's Legal Or

Physical Right To Possession (Illegality, Impossibility, And Frustration). These defenses, if applicable, will permit the tenant to vacate and terminate the lease, thereby cutting off the tenant's obligation to pay rent. Proceed to Part E for further analysis of these defenses.

3. **Other Landlord Damages Claims Based On Lease Terms Or Physical Harm To The Premises.** Determine if the landlord may have other damages claims against the tenant by using Parts B.3.a through 3.c.

    a. **Breach Of Contract Claim Based On Lease Terms.** Did the landlord incur damages because the tenant failed to perform any tenant promises under the terms of the lease?

    b. **(Commercial Property Only) Permissive Or Involuntary Waste.** Did the tenant fail to maintain the condition of the premises (normal wear and tear excluded)?

    c. **Affirmative Waste.** Did the tenant damage the leased property or change its physical condition? Under the common law rule, the landlord can recover damages for any change to the condition of the leased premises by the tenant (even a change that enhanced the property's value) as waste. The modern rule is that the tenant does not owe damages to the landlord for changes to the premises that enhance the value of the property (ameliorating waste).

C. **(ALL PROPERTIES) THE COVENANT OF QUIET ENJOYMENT, PARTIAL EVICTION AND THE ILLEGAL LEASE.** The CQE is implied in every lease. Proceed to Part C.1 for an analysis of breach of the CQE. A substantial breach of the CQE is tantamount to constructive eviction of the tenant from the entire premises by the landlord. For a partial eviction situation (actual or constructive), proceed to Part C.2. If the premises were defective at the commencement of the lease, proceed to Part C.3 to determine if the lease is illegal.

1. **Elements For Breach Of CQE.** A breach of the CQE occurs if the landlord's wrongful conduct causes a substantial interference with the tenant's use and enjoyment of the leased property.

   a. **Landlord's Wrongful Conduct.** Wrongful conduct by the landlord is established by a breach of an express covenant in the lease (e.g., a promise that the landlord will maintain heating/cooling/utilities service or provide needed repairs) or a breach of the common law duties of a landlord. These duties are the: (1) duty to maintain common areas; (2) duty to disclose latent defects; (3) duty to make promised repairs non-negligently; (4) duty not to make affirmative misrepresentations concerning the condition of the leased premises; (5) duty to provide habitable premises for the short-term lease of a furnished dwelling; and (6) duty to abate immoral or nuisance conduct by other tenants on the landlord's property.

      i. **Tort Liability?** The landlord also may be liable in tort for personal injuries that occur on the leased premises. For further analysis of potential tort liability claims, proceed to Part G.

      ii. **Failure To Act?** The landlord's wrongful conduct may consist of failing to act to stop conduct by third parties that substantially interferes with the tenant's use and enjoyment of the property. Examples include failing to stop nuisances or control activities in common areas that the landlord has a duty to maintain for the use of all tenants.

b. **Caused Substantial Interference.** Is the wrongful conduct by the landlord the cause of substantial interference with the tenant's use and enjoyment of the leased premises?

   i. **Objective Standard For Substantial Interference.** Would a reasonable person find the interference renders the premises unsuitable for the tenant's bargained-for use and enjoyment?

   ii. **Factors For Determining Substantial Interference.** Consider the following factors when discussing whether the interference is substantial. Is the interference with the tenant's use and enjoyment of the leased premises: (1) foreseeable by the tenant; (2) particularly severe or harmful in degree; (3) permanent or intermittent in nature; or (4) capable of being abated by the tenant?

   iii. **Partial Physical Interference.** If the interference affects only part of the leased premises, proceed to Part C.2 for further analysis.

c. **Tenant Gave Notice And Opportunity To Cure.** Did the tenant give notice to the landlord of the defect(s) or interference and a reasonable time for the landlord to cure the problem? **If no**, the tenant cannot asset a breach of the CQE.

d. **Tenant Vacated Within A Reasonable Time.** Did the tenant vacate the premises within a reasonable time after the interference occurred and notice had been given to the landlord?

i. **Traditional (Majority) View. If yes**, the tenant may terminate the lease, cease paying rent, and sue the landlord for damages resulting from the dislocation. **If no**, the tenant must continue to pay rent to the landlord, but can sue for damages.

ii. **Modern (Minority) View.** The tenant may remain in possession, abate rent, and sue for damages for breach of the CQE without vacating the property.

2. **(All Properties) Partial Eviction Claims.**

a. **Actual Eviction By Landlord From Part Of Premises.** The traditional view is that any actual eviction of the tenant by the landlord from all or part of the leased premises terminates the lease and relieves the tenant from paying all rent. The modern view is that the tenant may only partially abate the rent for a partial actual eviction by the landlord.

b. **Partial Constructive Eviction.** If the landlord's wrongful conduct causes a substantial interference with only part of the tenant's use and enjoyment of the premises, the tenant must continue to pay all rent due under the lease terms, but may sue the landlord for damages.

3. **Illegal Lease.** At the inception of the lease, did the landlord know that the leased premises were in substantial violation of the housing code or otherwise so unsafe as to be uninhabitable? **If yes**, the tenant is not liable for rent due under the terms of the lease.

D. **RESIDENTIAL LEASES: IMPLIED WARRANTY OF HABITABILITY (IWH).** The IWH applies only to leases of residential property. The common law rule is that the landlord has no duty to offer or maintain habitable leased premises. The modern rule is that residential leases contain an implied warranty (the IWH) that the landlord will offer and maintain residential premises for the duration of the lease that are fit for human habitation.

1. **Standard For IWH.** The touchstone standard for the IWH is whether the premises are safe and fit for human habitation. A substantial violation of the local housing code can establish a breach of the IWH, but a housing code violation is not necessary to establish a breach of the IWH.

   a. **Waiver By Tenant At Inception Of Lease.** The IWH is based on public health and safety and effective enforcement of housing codes. Any purported waiver of the IWH by the tenant is void.

   b. **Notice Of Needed Repairs.** If the landlord is not aware of the condition, the tenant is required to give notice to the landlord and a reasonable opportunity to repair before a breach of the IWH occurs.

2. **Tenant's Remedies For Breach Of IWH.** If the landlord fails to repair the condition that makes the leased premises uninhabitable, a breach of the IWH occurs that gives rise to the following tenant remedies.

   a. **Vacate, Cease Rent And Sue For Damages.** The tenant may terminate the lease, cease paying further rent, and sue for damages related to relocation (e.g., moving costs and higher rent for a replacement property).

   b. **Remain In Possession.** If tenant elects to remain in possession, the tenant may, after notice to and failure to respond by the landlord, either: (1) withhold the rent due until the landlord remedies the condition; or (2) deduct a reasonable amount from the rent due and use the money for necessary repairs.

   c. **Punitive Damages.** The court may award punitive damages to the tenant if the landlord knowingly and willfully refused to address conditions that are a significant health and safety danger.

3. **Retaliatory Eviction**. The landlord may not retaliate by evicting a tenant who makes a good faith request for needed repairs and who withholds rent until the repairs are made.

    a.   **Proof Of Retaliatory Motive.** To assert a claim of retaliatory eviction, the tenant must prove that the landlord's motive in evicting was to retaliate against the tenant for requesting repairs based on the landlord's duty under the IWH. A rebuttable presumption of retaliatory motive may arise under a state statute if the landlord's actions occur within a specified time (e.g., 3–6 months) after the tenant's notice that repairs are needed.

    b.   **Tenant Must Not Be In Prior Default On Rent.** To successfully assert a retaliatory eviction claim, the tenant cannot be in default on rent payments before providing notice of needed repairs to the landlord and withholding rent.

E. **TENANT'S DEFENSES TO NONPAYMENT OF RENT BASED ON THE TENANT'S RIGHT TO POSSESSION.** If a tenant fails to pay rent based on another tenant's claim of a superior right to possess the leased premises, proceed to Part E.1. For a tenant's nonpayment of rent based on the physical possession of the leased premises by a holdover tenant, proceed to Part E.2. For a tenant's nonpayment of rent based on the destruction of the leased premises, proceed to Part E.3. For a tenant's nonpayment of rent based on an impossibility, illegality, or frustration defense, proceed to Part E.4.

1. **Interference With Tenant's Right To Legal Possession.** The tenant must have the legal right to possession of the premises for the duration of the lease. The mere threat of another tenant's competing claim to legal possession of the premises does not allow the occupying tenant to

terminate the lease or to stop paying rent. Once the tenant has taken possession of the leased premises, the tenant may not terminate the lease and must continue to pay rent unless and until the tenant is actually evicted by a court ruling that another competing tenant has the superior legal right to possession of the leased property.

2. **Interference With The Tenant's Right To Physical Possession (Eviction Of A Holdover Tenant).** Whether the landlord has a duty to put the tenant in physical possession of the leased premises depends on whether the jurisdiction follows the English Rule or the American Rule.

   a. **English Rule Jurisdiction.** The landlord must provide the tenant with actual physical possession of the premises, but only for the first day of the lease term. Thereafter, the tenant is responsible for evicting trespassers.

      i. **Tenant's Remedies Against Landlord.** If the landlord fails to evict a holdover tenant, the incoming tenant may terminate the lease and sue the landlord for damages, or may cease to pay rent to the landlord until the tenant is able to take physical possession.

      ii. **Tenant's Remedies Against Holdover Tenant/Trespasser.** The tenant may evict the holdover tenant/ trespasser and sue for damages.

   b. **American Rule Jurisdiction.** The landlord is not responsible for providing the tenant with actual physical possession of the premises on the first day of the lease term.

      i. **Tenant Has No Remedy Against Landlord.** The tenant cannot terminate the lease and must continue to pay rent to the landlord while evicting the holdover tenant/trespasser.

ii. **Tenant's Remedies Against Holdover Tenant/Trespasser.** The tenant must evict the holdover tenant/trespasser and sue for damages.

3. **Destruction Of The Leased Premises.** When the leased premises are destroyed, the express terms of the lease govern whether the tenant remains liable for rent. If the express terms of the lease do not address the destruction of the leased property, whether the tenant remains liable for rent depends on whether the jurisdiction applies the common law rule or the modern rule.

   a. **Common Law (Minority) Rule.** The tenant remains liable for rent even if the leased property is destroyed.

   b. **Modern (Majority) Rule.** The tenant is not liable for rent if the leased property is destroyed, unless the destruction is caused by the tenant's own negligence.

4. **Illegality, Impossibility And Frustration Defenses.** If circumstances permit, the tenant may assert these defenses to a claim by the landlord for nonpayment of rent.

   a. **The Tenant's Use Has Become Illegal.** A change in the law after the lease is executed that makes the tenant's use of the leased premises illegal relieves the tenant of the further obligation to pay rent.

      i. **Partial Or Alternative Legal Use Still Possible?** If the tenant can still use part of the leased property or the property has an alternative legal use, the tenant remains liable for rent.

   b. **Impossibility of Performance Defense.** Impossibility is closely associated with illegal use or destruction of the property. Mere hardship (e.g., increased inconvenience or financial expense) does not make the tenant's performance under the lease impossible.

  c. **(Commercial Property Only) Frustration Defense.** Have changed circumstances so frustrated the fundamental purposes for which the tenant entered the lease that it is now a hardship for the tenant to continue to perform the tenant's obligations under the lease? Mere financial hardship (making less profit than anticipated) does not frustrate the fundamental purpose of the lease.

F. DISCRIMINATION CLAIMS BY THE TENANT. Have the tenant's federal rights under the Federal Fair Housing Act ("FHA") or the Civil Rights Act of 1866 ("CRA") been violated? For potential violations of the FHA in the selection of a tenant, proceed to Part F.1. For discrimination by the landlord in the terms and conditions of the lease or failure to accommodate a handicapped tenant, proceed to Part F.2. For discrimination in advertising, proceed to Part F.3. For remedies for an FHA violation, proceed to Part F.4. For violations of the CRA, proceed to Part F.5.

  1. **Fair Housing Act: Discrimination In The Selection Of Tenants.** Section 3604 Of the FHA prohibits discrimination in the rental of housing.

    a. **Does An Exception Apply?** Section 3603(b) excepts certain rental properties from the discrimination prohibitions (but not the advertising prohibitions of § 3604(c)) of the FHA. The landlord can discriminate in the selection of tenants if the rental property is:

      i. **A Single Family House** that is rented without the services of a real estate professional, the owner owns three or fewer such houses, and any advertisement of the property does not violate the FHA's advertising prohibition in § 3604(c).

      ii. **A Dwelling Occupied By The Owner** where the owner rents out rooms or units in the rest of the building to no more than three other families who live independently of each other.

b. Is The Tenant A Protected Person? Assuming an exception does not apply, determine if the tenant is protected from housing discrimination under the FHA.

    i. Protected Categories Of Tenants. Under § 3604(a), the landlord cannot refuse to rent to a tenant based on race, color, religion, sex, familial status or national origin. Under § 3604(f)(1), the landlord cannot refuse to rent because of a handicap of the tenant, or the handicap of a person who resides with or is associated with the tenant. Persons who are handicapped include recovering (not current) alcoholics or drug addicts.

        • **Familial Status** is defined as having minor children under age 18. Increasing the monthly rent or the damages deposit over the amount normally charged to other tenants because minor children are residing on the property is familial status discrimination under the FHA.

        • **Recovered Substance Abusers** are protected as handicapped persons under the FHA.

        • **Qualifying Senior Housing** is an exception to the prohibition on discrimination based on familial status.

    ii. Permitted Forms Of Discrimination. The FHA does not prohibit a landlord from refusing to rent to a tenant based on occupation, sexual orientation, whether the tenant is married, numerical occupancy limits designed to maintain the economic value of the property, or based on the tenant's current illegal use of a controlled substance.

c. **Can Tenant Establish A Prima Facie Case?** To establish a prima facie case, the tenant must: (1) be a protected person under the FHA; (2) have offered to lease the property; (3) been rejected by the landlord; and (4) the rental property must have remained available for rent by others.

   i. **Misrepresented As Not Available.** If the property is misrepresented by the landlord or the landlord's agent as not being available for rent when in fact the property is available, § 3604(d) is the source of the FHA violation.

   ii. **Proof Of Discriminatory Intent Not Required.** Proof of discriminatory intent by the landlord is not required to establish a prima facie case under the FHA.

d. **Can Landlord Show A Nondiscriminatory Reason For Rejecting The Tenant?** If no, the tenant wins under the FHA. Proceed to Part F.4 to determine the tenant's remedies. If yes, the burden of proof shifts back to the tenant to prove the landlord's purported nondiscriminatory reason is a pretext for prohibited housing discrimination.

e. **Can Tenant Prove The Landlord's Reason Is A Pretext For Prohibited Discrimination?** Proof of actual discriminatory intent by the landlord is not required. The tenant only must show evidence that the landlord's stated reason for rejecting the tenant is not the real reason. If pretext is proven, proceed to Part F.4 to determine the tenant's remedies.

2. **Fair Housing Act: Discrimination In Terms And Conditions And Reasonable Accommodations For Handicapped Persons.** Section 3604(b) of the FHA prohibits discrimination in the terms and conditions of the tenant's lease based on race, color, religion, sex, familial status or national origin. Section 3604(f)(2) prohibits discrimination in the terms and conditions of the lease based on the handicap of the tenant, or the handicap of a person who resides with or is associated with the tenant. Section 3604(f)(3) requires the landlord to make reasonable accommodations for handicapped persons.

   a. **Does An Exception Apply?** Refer to the exceptions in Part F.1.a. If the rental unit is a qualifying single family house or a dwelling occupied by the owner, then the prohibitions and requirements of §§ 3604(b), 3604(f)(2), and 3604(f)(3) do not apply.

   b. **Discrimination In Terms And Conditions Of The Lease.** Sections 3604(b) and 3604(f)(2) of the FHA prohibit the landlord from discriminating against protected persons in the terms and conditions of the lease. Determine if the tenant is a protected person under Part F.1.b above. **If yes**, the tenant potentially has a prima facie case if the terms and conditions of the protected tenant's lease are different from other tenants.

   c. **Failure To Make Reasonable Accommodations?** Section 3604(f)(3) makes it unlawful discrimination for the landlord to refuse to make reasonable accommodations for a handicapped person who resides on the leased premises.

      i. **Modifications To Premises.** The tenant must be permitted to make reasonable modifications to the leased premises for the handicapped tenant or a handicapped person residing there. The tenant must agree to pay for the modifications and to restore the premises at the end of the lease.

    ii. **Modifications To Landlord's Rules, Policies And Procedures.** The landlord must make reasonable modifications to rules, policies and procedures that are necessary to give a handicapped tenant an equal opportunity to use and enjoy the property.

3. **Fair Housing Act: Discrimination In Advertising.** Section 3604(c) of the FHA prohibits any printed or oral public statement that indicates a preference for or discrimination against a prospective tenant based on race, color, religion, sex, familial status, national origin, or handicap.

    a. **No Exceptions To Prohibition On Discrimatory Advertising.** The prohibition on discrimination in advertising applies to all types of residential properties, even those exempt from the general nondiscrimination provisions of the FHA under § 3603(b) (i.e., a qualifying single family house or dwelling occupied by the owner).

    b. **Standard For Determining Violation.** Would the ordinary listener or ordinary reader think the statement indicates a preference for or discrimination against renting the property to a protected person? Refer to Part F.1.b above to determine the characteristics of a protected person.

4. **Remedies For FHA Violations.** The tenant's possible remedies for a FHA violation are injunctive relief, compensatory damages and punitive damages.

5. **Civil Rights Act Of 1866 (42 U.S.C. § 1982).** The CRA ("§ 1982") prohibits discrimination based solely on "race" in the rental of property. Unlike the FHA, there are no exceptions based on the type of property being rented.

    a. **Was Discrimination Based On Tenant's Race?** Under the CRA, race connotes ancestry or ethnicity. If the discrimination in rental of the property is based on national origin or religion, refer to Part F.1 above for analysis of a possible FHA violation.

    b. **Was Discrimination Limited To The Refusal To Sell Or Lease The Property?** The CRA only applies to the sale or leasing of property. Discrimination in the terms and conditions of the lease and discriminatory advertising are not prohibited by § 1982. Refer to Part F.2 above if the landlord's conduct involves the terms and conditions of the lease, or to Part F.3 if the conduct involves statements or advertising for analysis of a possible FHA violation.

    c. **Remedies For CRA Violations.** Remedies available to the tenant are injunctive relief and damages.

G. **TORT LIABILITY OF THE LANDLORD.** As a general rule, the landlord has no tort liability to the tenant or the tenant's guests for personal injuries incurred on the leased premises.

    1. **Defect Causing Injury Existed Before Lease Began.** If the defect causing the injury existed before the lease began, the landlord has no tort liability under the general rule unless an exception applies under Parts G.1.a or 1.b below.

        a. **Failure To Warn Of Latent (Hidden) Defect.** If the landlord knew of a latent (hidden) defect, but failed to warn the tenant, then the landlord is liable in tort for injuries to the tenant or the tenant's guests caused by the latent defect.

            i. **Landlord Warns Tenant Of The Latent Defect.** Once the landlord has warned the tenant of a latent defect, thereafter the landlord is not liable for injuries to the tenant or the tenant's guests caused by the defect.

b. **Dangerous For Public Use.** If the landlord knows or should know that: (1) the leased premises will be used by the public; (2) a dangerous defect exists that the landlord has not corrected; and (3) the tenant is unlikely to correct the defect, then the landlord is liable in tort for injuries caused by the defect to members of the public.

2. **Defect Arose After Lease Began.** If the defect causing the injury arose after the lease began, under the general rule the landlord has no tort liability unless an exception applies under Parts G.2.a or 2.b below.

a. **Defect Or Dangerous Condition In A Common Area.** If the defect or dangerous condition is located in a common area of the leased property, the landlord's duty to maintain common areas makes the landlord liable in tort for injuries that are caused by breach of this duty.

b. **Landlord's Liability For Injuries Resulting From Criminal Conduct.** The landlord may be liable in tort for injuries caused by the criminal conduct of third parties on the landlord's property if the criminal conduct was reasonably foreseeable and the landlord failed to take reasonable precautions.

c. **Defect Arose From Landlord's Negligent Attempt To Repair.** If landlord promised in the lease or otherwise volunteered to make repairs to the leased property and did so negligently, then the landlord is liable in tort for injuries caused by the negligent repairs.

d. **Residential Property: Landlord's Failure To Repair Under The IWH.** The landlord may be liable in tort if the landlord has an affirmative duty to make repairs under the IWH, the landlord fails to make the repairs, and foreseeable injury results.

3. **Effect Of Exculpatory Clause.** An exculpatory clause in a commercial lease is generally valid. An exculpatory clause in a residential lease is more likely to be void based on unequal bargaining power, public policy favoring safe housing, or by statute (e.g., the Uniform Residential Landlord Tenant Act prohibits exculpatory clauses for residential leases).

H. **LANDLORD CLAIMS AGAINST A SUBTENANT (ASSIGNMENT AND SUBLEASE ISSUES).** The landlord may bring claims against the original tenant or a subtenant who has taken possession of the property under an assignment or sublease. To determine if the original tenant's assignment or sublease is lawful, proceed to Part H.1. For the landlord's claims against the original tenant, proceed to Part H.2. To determine whether the original tenant has assigned or sublet the leased premises, proceed to Part H.3. For the landlord's claims against a sublessee in possession of the leased premises, proceed to Part H.4. For the landlord's claims against an assignee in possession of the leased premises, proceed to Part H.5. For the landlord's claims against intermediate subtenants who are no longer in possession of the leased premises, proceed to Part H.6.

1. **Original Tenant's Right To Assign Or Sublease.** If the original lease is silent, then the original tenant can assign or sublease the leased premises without the landlord's permission or consent.

   a. **Does The Lease Expressly Prohibit Transfer By Original Tenant? If yes**, the prohibition on assignment or sublease by the original tenant is enforceable.

      i. **Does The Prohibition Apply To The Proposed Transfer?** If the prohibition language does not apply to the circumstances of the proposed transfer of the lease, then the transfer is valid (e.g., a prohibition on assignment does not restrict a sublease arrangement and vice versa).

    ii. Did The Landlord Waive The Prohibition? The landlord can waive the prohibition on transfer expressly or implicitly by accepting rent payments from the subtenant.

- **Future Effect Of Express Waiver (*Dumptor's Case*).** Under the rule in *Dumpor's Case*, once the landlord consents to an assignment by the original tenant, the prohibition on assignments in the original lease becomes unenforceable, unless: (1) the prohibition language in the lease is binding on the tenant's assigns; or (2) the landlord's consent expressly is limited so as to exclude transfers in the future.

b. Does The Lease Permit Transfer With The Consent Of The Landlord? If the lease provides that it may be transferred with the consent of the landlord, whether such consent can be arbitrarily withheld depends on the rule the jurisdiction follows.

    i. Majority Rule. The landlord arbitrarily can refuse to consent to a proposed assignment or sublease of the original lease.

    ii. Minority Rule. The landlord can refuse to consent to a proposed assignment or sublease of the original lease only if such refusal is based on objectively reasonable factors.

- **Objectively Reasonable Factors.**

The financial strength of the proposed subtenant, the compatibility of the proposed subtenant's use with the businesses of other tenants, and the need for alterations to the property to accommodate the proposed subtenant's use are all reasonable factors justifying the landlord's refusal to consent to a proposed transfer of the lease to a subtenant.

- **Unreasonable Factors.** Refusing consent to command a higher rent under the original lease is not a reasonable basis for refusing consent. Bias or prejudice is not a reasonable basis to withhold consent (and for a residential property, may be a violation of the FHA).

2. **Landlord Claims Against The Original Tenant.** The original tenant remains liable for satisfying all of the terms of the original lease, unless the landlord grants a novation releasing the original tenant from the obligation to perform under the terms of the original lease.

    a. **Novation Releasing Original Tenant.** Did the landlord *expressly* agree to release the original tenant from further performance under the original lease? If the release is not express, no novation has occurred and the original tenant remains liable.

    b. **Landlord's Consent To Transfer Not Implied Novation.** A novation is not implied merely because the landlord consented to an assignment or sublease of the property by the original tenant.

3. **Landlord Claims Based On Assignment Or Sublease**

Arrangement. The landlord's claims against a subtenant will depend on whether the transfer is classified as an assignment or a sublease.

    a.   **Common Law (Retained Reversion) Test For An Assignment.** Does the subtenant have the right to possession of the leased property on the last day of the original lease term? **If yes**, the original tenant has retained no interest in the property and the transfer is an assignment. **If no**, the original tenant has retained a reversion interest and the transfer is a sublease.

    b.   **Modern Test.** What was the parties' intent? Did the parties intend for the transfer to be an assignment or a sublease? The language of the parties' written agreement (if one exists) is the best evidence of the parties' intent.

    c.   **"Split Decisions."** If the arrangement could be classified as either an assignment or a sublease depending on whether the common law test or the modern test is used, analyze both possibilities. Proceed to Part H.4 for the landlord's claims against a sublessee in possession. Proceed to Part H.5 for the landlord's claims against an assignee in possession.

4. Landlord Claims Against A Sublessee In Possession. Normally, the landlord's only remedy against a sublessee in possession who fails to pay rent is to evict the sublessee. If the sublessee agreed to assume the terms of the original lease, then the landlord may be able to bring a damages claim (either directly or as a third party beneficiary) for the sublessee's breach of the terms of the original lease.

    a.   **Eviction Of Subtenant In Possession For Nonpayment Of Rent.** Eviction is the only claim the landlord can bring against a nonpaying sublessee in possession of the property where there is no privity of contract or privity of estate between the landlord and a sublesse. If the sublessee agreed to assume the original tenant's obligations under the terms of the original lease, proceed to Part H.4.b below for further analysis. For the sublessee's defenses to an eviction claim, proceed to Part B.1 above.

b. **Sublessee Assumed Terms Of Original Lease.** If the sublessee agreed to assume the terms of the original lease, the sublessee is liable for any breach of the terms of the original lease (not merely rent).

    i. **Sublessee Made Direct Assumption Agreement With Landlord.** If the sublessee's assumption agreement is directly with the landlord, privity of contract exists directly between the landlord and the sublessee. The landlord can sue the sublessee based on the breach of any of the contractual terms of the original lease.

    ii. **Sublessee Made Assumption Agreement With Transferring Tenant.** If the sublessee's assumption agreement is with the transferring tenant, the landlord can sue the sublessee as a third party beneficiary of the assumption agreement between the transferring tenant and the sublessee. As a third party beneficiary, the landlord can sue the sublessee based on the breach of any of the contractual terms of the original lease.

    iii. **Effect Of Subsequent Transfer Or Abandonment By Assuming Sublessee.** Once the sublessee assumes the obligations under the original lease, the sublessee remains in privity of contract and is still liable for performing all of the terms of the assumed lease, even if the sublessee later transfers or abandons the leased property.

    iv. Defenses Of Assuming Sublessee. The sublessee who assumes also has all of the defenses that the original tenant has under the terms of the assumed lease. Proceed to Parts B, C, D, E and F above to review possible sublessee defenses.

5. Landlord Claims Against An Assignee In Possession. The landlord may evict or bring a damages claim against an assignee in possession who fails to pay rent due under the lease. The landlord also may be able to bring other damages claims for a commercial assignee's breach of the covenant of good repair, or if the assignee has assumed the terms of the original lease.

    a. Eviction For Nonpayment Of Rent. The landlord always can evict an assignee in possession for nonpayment of rent. For the assignee's defenses to an eviction claim, proceed to Part B.1 above.

    b. Claim For Damages For Unpaid Rent. The landlord always can bring a damages claim for unpaid rent against an assignee in possession because privity of estate exists between the landlord and an assignee.

        i. Extent Of Liability For Unpaid Rent. The assignee is not liable for rent that is unpaid before the lease was assigned to the assignee.

        ii. Assignee Later Subleases The Property. The assignee remains liable for rent if the assignee later subleases the property because privity of estate still exists between the assignee and the landlord.

iii. **Assignee Later Assigns The Property.** The assignee is not liable for rent that accrues after a subsequent assignment. The subsequent assignment extinguishes privity of estate between the first assignee and the landlord and establishes privity of estate between the second assignee and the landlord. The new assignee is liable for unpaid rent that accrues after the subsequent assignment. The old assignee is liable for rent that accrued before the subsequent assignment.

iv. **Assignee Assumed The Terms Of The Original Lease.** If the assignee agreed to assume the terms of the original lease, the assignee is liable for any breach of the terms of the original lease. For a commercial property tenant, beware that the obligations assumed under the original lease are likely to be more extensive than the covenant of good repair that is associated with privity of estate. For a residential property tenant, the landlord's IWH supersedes the tenant's covenant of good repair and requires the landlord to make needed repairs to the leased property. Proceed to Part D of the checklist above for further analysis of the IWH.

• **Assignee Made Direct Assumption Agreement With Landlord.** If the assignee's assumption agreement is directly with the landlord, privity of contract exists directly between the landlord and the assignee and the landlord can sue the assignee directly based on breach of the contractual terms of the original lease.

- **Assignee Made Assumption Agreement With Transferring Tenant.** If the assignee's assumption agreement is with the transferring tenant, the landlord can sue the assignee for a breach of the contractual lease terms as a third party beneficiary of the assumption agreement between the transferring tenant and the assignee.

c. **Claim For Damages For Breach Of Covenant Of Good Repair.** For a commercial property, the assignee is liable for damages for breach of the implied covenant of good repair. This covenant requires the assignee to make any repairs necessary to maintain the condition of the leased premises. The implied covenant of good repair is based on the privity of estate that exists between the assignee and the landlord.

i. **Commercial Property: Assignee Not Liable For Original Tenant's Other Contractual Lease Covenants.** Absent an assumption of the original lease terms by the assignee, privity of contract does not exist between the landlord and an assignee. Therefore, the assignee is not liable for performing any of the original lease terms that are contractual in nature. The commercial property assignee is liable only for paying rent and maintaining the property in good repair.

ii. Residential Property: Assignee Not Liable For Repairs. For a residential property, the assignee's implied covenant of good repair associated with privity of estate is superceded by the landlord's duty to make repairs under the IWH.

6. Landlord Claims Against Intermediate Subtenants. If the intermediate subtenant is a sublessee, proceed to Part H.6.a below. If the intermediate subtenant is an assignee, proceed to Part H.6.b below.

    a. Claims Against An Intermediate Sublessee. Did the intermediate sublessee agree to assume the original lease terms?

        i. No Assumption By Intermediate Sublessee. The landlord cannot bring any claim against an intermediate sublessee who is no longer in possession of the property.

        ii. Assumption Of Original Lease By Intermediate Sublessee. The landlord can sue the intermediate sublessee for all rent due for the duration of the lease and for all damages resulting from any breach of the terms of the original lease. Liability extends until the termination of the lease, even if the assuming sublessee is no longer in possession of the property unless the landlord has granted a novation.

    b. Claims Against An Intermediate Assignee. Did the intermediate assignee later sublease or assign the property?

        i. Intermediate Assignee Later Subleases. An intermediate assignee who later subleases the property remains in privity of estate with the landlord and therefore is liable for rent due for the balance of the lease term.

   ii. Intermediate Assignee Later Assigns. An intermediate assignee who later assigns the property is no longer in privity of estate with the landlord after the assignment occurs.

- **Liability For Rent.** The intermediate assignee is liable for rent accrued and damages incurred while the intermediate assignee was in legal possession of the property.

- **Limitations On Liability For Rent.** The intermediate assignee who later assigns is not liable for rent that accrued before the assignment to the intermediate assignee, or after the intermediate assignee subsequently assigns the property.

   iii. Intermediate Assignee Agreed To Assume The Original Lease Terms. Determine if the intermediate assignee agreed to assume the terms of the original lease.

- **No Assumption.** If the intermediate assignee did not agree to assume the terms of the original lease, the landlord has only privity of estate claims (rent, and for a commercial property only breach of the covenant of good repair) against the intermediate assignee.

- **Assumption Agreement.** Absent a novation, if the intermediate assignee agreed to assume the terms of the original lease, the landlord can sue the intermediate assignee for all rent due for the duration of the lease and all damages resulting from any breach of the terms of the original lease. This liability extends until the termination of the lease, even after the intermediate assignee is no longer in possession of the property.

- **Direct Assumption Agreement With Landlord.** If the assignee's assumption agreement is directly with the landlord, privity of contract exists between the landlord and the assignee. The landlord can sue the intermediate assignee directly for a breach of any of the contractual terms of the original lease.

- **Assumption Agreement With Intermediate Subtenant.** If the intermediate assignee's assumption agreement is with another intermediate subtenant, the landlord can sue the intermediate assignee for breach of the contractual lease terms as a third party beneficiary of the assumption agreement.

ILLUSTRATIVE PROBLEM

Here is a complex problem that illustrates how the Checklist can be used to resolve landlord and tenant questions.

■ PROBLEM 6.1 ■

Larry Landlord owned a duplex in the State of Bliss, which follows the majority common law rules on matters of landlord and tenant law. Larry resided in one unit of the duplex and rented the other unit in the duplex to Tina Tenant. Larry told Tina, "You pay me $5,700 for a six month lease. Rent is $950 a month. Rent is due on the first day of each month. After that, we can agree to go month-to-month." Tina agreed to these terms. As part of the lease arrangement, Tina agreed to mow the lawn and water the flowers and landscaping in exchange for the $50 per month rent discount (Larry normally charged $1,000 a month for the unit). Tina paid the $950 in monthly rent on the first day of the first and second months of the lease.

Two and one-half months after their initial agreement, Larry came home and found the following note taped to his front door:

Larry—

My brother Sam is a recovering drug addict. He just got out of rehab and has no place to live. I've gone to California to get him and bring him here to live with me. My friend Aliza will stay at my place, pay the rent as it comes due for me, and take care of things around my place while I am away.

Tina

Shortly after Tina left, a summer heat wave struck the area. Aliza paid the rent of $950 to Larry on the first day of the third month of the lease. Aliza failed, however, to water the landscaping and the flowers. When Larry asked Aliza when she would water the landscaping and the flowers, Aliza said, "That's not my problem."

Disgusted, Larry watered the landscaping and the flowers himself. When Aliza tried to pay the monthly rent of $950 on the first day of the fourth month after the original lease began, Larry refused the check, saying, "That's not enough. It's $1,000 because I had to do the watering." When Aliza refused to pay Larry $1,000, Larry turned off the water to Tina's unit (the controls were in Larry's side of the duplex). Aliza complained to Larry, "You know, I can't live here without any running water." Larry replied, "You'll get water when I get $1,000." Aliza retorted, "That's it! I am gone for good!" Aliza packed her things and left. Larry began advertising the unit as "For Rent" in the local paper.

When Tina returned with her brother Sam one week later, she found that her unit lacked running water. Tina confronted Larry, who told Tina that he would restore the water only if she paid $1,000 for the monthly rent, paid an additional $1,000 as a damages deposit "for that addict brother of yours," and paid $250 "to replace my dried up flowers and shrubs." Tina refused to pay, saying "That's it, my lease just terminated." Six months later, Larry found another tenant for Tina's unit, who moved in exactly nine months after Larry and Tina's original lease commenced.

Larry has come to you for legal advice. Larry wants to be compensated for the rent he lost prior to reletting the unit. He also wants to recover the $250 he spent to replace his damaged landscaping. How much can Larry recover in damages against Tina or Aliza? What counterclaims may be brought against Larry if he sues Tina or Aliza?

Analysis

The initial lease arrangement between Larry and Tina is a term of years lease for a six month term. Although rent is paid on the first of each month, it is clear from their agreement that only after the initial six month term expires will the lease become a month-to-month periodic tenancy (if both Larry and Tina agree to continue the lease). This is an oral lease, but because the term is only six months, the lease is not subject to the Statute of Frauds and its terms are enforceable in a court of law. Therefore, Larry can bring a damages claim based on a breach of the terms of the lease.

The terms of the oral lease between Larry and Tina are silent concerning transfer of the lease by Tina. Therefore, Tina did not need Larry's permission or consent to transfer the leased premises to Aliza.

Larry can bring a damages claim against Tina only for unpaid rent due for the balance of the six month term, but not beyond. No notice is required for a tenant to terminate a term of years lease. Tina's obligation to pay rent expired automatically at the end of the six month term. The lease rent is $950 per month. Tina paid the rent for the first three months of the lease. Therefore, the maximum amount of Larry's damages claim for unpaid rent is three months times $950, or $2,850.

Larry also can bring a claim against Tina for damages to the landscaping caused by Tina's failure to water the plants. Irrespective of whether the arrangement with Aliza was an assignment or a sublease, Tina remained in privity of contract with Larry by virtue of the original oral lease. There is no evidence that Larry released Tina from her obligations under the lease by granting a novation. Therefore, Tina is liable for damages for any breach of the terms of the original oral lease (here, watering the landscaping).

Larry's claims against Aliza depend on whether the arrangement between Tina and Aliza is characterized as an assignment or a sublease. Based on the language of the note left with Larry, the arrangement appears to be a sublease under both the common law test and the modern test. Under the common law test, the note indicates that Tina intended to return and remain in possession until the end of the lease term (she retained a reversion interest in the unit). Under the modern test, the note indicates that Tina and Aliza intended for this to be a temporary and short-term arrangement, with the implication being that Aliza would only occupy the unit until Tina returned with her brother Sam. As a sublessee, Aliza cannot be sued by Larry for accrued rent or damages to the landscaping because Aliza is neither in privity of contract nor privity of estate with Larry.

Larry may try to argue that Aliza agreed to assume Tina's promises under the original oral lease to pay rent and water the landscaping. If the court finds that Aliza agreed with Tina to assume Tina's promises under the lease with Larry, then Larry can sue Aliza for the rent due and the damages to the landscaping as a third party beneficiary of the assumption agreement between Tina and Aliza. Aliza's response will be that she did not agree to assume the terms of the original lease between Tina and Larry. Tina's note to Larry said that Aliza will pay the rent *"for me"* and will take care of things "around *my* place." The quoted language indicates that Aliza probably did not agree to assume Tina's obligations under the original oral lease, including the obligation to water the landscaping.

Tina's defenses to Larry's damages claim for rent and compensation for the landscaping are that Larry breached the covenant of quiet enjoyment and the implied warranty of habitability by turning off the water to the unit. Tina cannot assert a violation of the Fair Housing Act as a counterclaim against Larry. In the unlikely event that a court finds that Aliza assumed Tina's obligations under the original lease, then Aliza also will assert defenses based on Larry's breach of the covenant of quiet enjoyment and breach of the implied warranty of habitability.

With respect to Tina, the terms of the note clearly indicated that she intended to return and resume living in the unit with her brother Sam. Therefore, Tina was not abandoning and offering to surrender the property to Larry by leaving temporarily for California.

Tina will argue that Larry breached the covenant of quiet enjoyment by cutting off the water to the unit. The covenant of quiet enjoyment is breached if the landlord engaged in wrongful conduct that substantially interfered with the tenant's use and enjoyment of the property. Although lack of running water in the unit is a substantial interference with the use and enjoyment of the property, to establish a breach of the covenant of quiet enjoyment Tina must show that Larry's conduct in turning off the water must be wrongful. At common law, the landlord did not have a duty to furnish or maintain habitable leased premises. Larry's conduct in turning off the water to the leased unit does not appear to have breached an express contractual duty because the terms of the oral lease did not expressly provide that Larry would furnish water to the unit. Larry's conduct was wrongful, however, in that turning off the water to the unit breached the warranty of habitability that modernly is implied by law as a term of every residential lease.

The implied warranty of habitability requires that the landlord must furnish and maintain residential leased premises for the duration of the lease that are fit for human habitation. By cutting off the water to the unit, Larry breached the implied warranty of habitability. Tina did not need to give Larry notice of the problem because Larry was the person who turned off the water. Tina vacated the premises immediately after returning from California and discovering that the unit lacked running water. Under these circumstances, a court is likely to rule that Tina is not liable for the last three months of rent ($2,850) due under the remaining term of the lease based on Larry's breach of the implied warranty of habitability.

Larry is likely to recover from Tina the $250 in damages to his landscaping due to Tina's failure to water the plants (more precisely on these facts, Tina's failure to find a responsible person to water the plants in her absence while she traveled to and from California). Tina breached this material term of the lease *before* Larry turned off the water to the unit. Therefore, Tina is liable for the $250 in damages to Larry's landscaping.

Tina cannot bring a counterclaim for damages against Larry for a violation of the Fair Housing Act based on Larry's demand for an additional deposit because a handicapped person, her brother Sam, is residing with Tina. Tina's unit is part of an owner-occupied dwelling (here, a duplex) where no more than three other families reside. Because the owner Larry resides in the other unit of the duplex, Larry is exempt under Section 3603(b) of the Fair Housing Act from the requirements of Section 3604(f) prohibiting discrimination against handicapped persons.

As discussed earlier, Larry is unlikely to recover any damages against Aliza because Aliza appears to be a sublessee who is neither in privity of contract or privity of estate with Larry. If a court finds, however, that Aliza agreed with Tina to assume the terms of Tina's original oral lease with Larry, then Larry could attempt to enforce those terms as a third party beneficiary of the assumption agreement. Aliza would have the same defenses to Larry's claims as does Tina. Therefore, if the court finds that Aliza assumed the original terms of Tina's oral lease, Aliza would not be liable for the remaining $2,850 in rent, but would be liable for $250 in damages to Larry's landscaping.

POINTS TO REMEMBER

- The tenant's primary obligation is to pay rent. For a commercial property, the tenant must keep the leased premises in good repair. For a residential property, the implied warranty of habitability requires the landlord to maintain and make any repairs to the property throughout the duration of the tenancy.

- The landlord's primary obligation is to avoid disturbing the tenant's quiet enjoyment of the property and, for a residential property only, to maintain the premises in a habitable condition as required by the implied warranty of habitability.

- If the dispute involves a residential property, always consider both a breach of the covenant of quiet enjoyment and a breach of the implied warranty of habitability as potential tenant defenses. If the dispute involves a commercial property, focus only on a breach of the covenant of quiet enjoyment as a potential tenant defense. The implied warranty of habitability does not apply to a commercial property.

- Do not jump to a discussion of potential discrimination under the Fair Housing Act until you first determine that the rental property is subject to the Act and is not except as a qualifying single family house or an owner-occupied dwelling.

- The landlord only can sue a sublessee for damages for nonpayment of rent if the sublessee has assumed the terms of the original lease. Absent such an assumption, all the landlord can do is to evict the nonpaying sublessee.

- Remember that the original tenant always remains liable for the terms of the original lease, even if the landlord has consented to an assignment or sublease of the property. Such consent is *not* a novation that releases the original tenant from compliance with the terms of the original lease.

CHAPTER 7

Real Estate Transactions

C hapter 7 focuses on the transfer of real estate from a seller to a buyer in an arms' length transaction. Issues unique to the transfer of real estate by gift are discussed in Chapter 2.

REAL ESTATE TRANSACTIONS REVIEW

The rules that govern the transfer of real estate and the related rights of the buyer and the seller are a mixture of ancient Property law and modern Contracts law. The key to applying these rules successfully on your Property exam is to have an understanding of the entire real estate transfer process. Each step in the transfer of real estate triggers a specific set of potential legal issues. This Review emphasizes the key steps in the real estate transfer process and the major issues that may arise at each step. These key steps and related legal issues are summarized in the diagram below and described in the Review. The Checklist at the end of Chapter 7 contains the detailed rules that courts use to resolve these issues.

Key Steps In The Transfer Of Real Estate

Listing Agreement	Sales Contract	Transfer of Title	Post-Closing

- Commission Due?
- Fiduciary Duties of Broker/Agent?

- Statute of Frauds?
- Can Buyer Rescind Based on:
  - Seller's inability to convey marketable title?
  - Seller's misrepresentation or nondisclosure?
  - Failure of a precondition to buyer's performance?
- Who Bears the Loss If the Property Is Destroyed?
- Remedies for Breach of Sales Contract?

- Statute of Frauds?
- Valid Delivery of Deed?

- Can Buyer Recover Damages for:
  - Legal title defects (breach of deed covenants)?
  - Physical defects /conditions (seller's misrepresentation or nondisclosure)?
  - Defects in residential construction (breach of IWQ)?

Claims Involving Listing Agreements

Although not required to sell a property, many sellers choose to execute a listing agreement with a real estate broker. There are two major issues associated with listing agreements. The first issue is whether a commission is owed by the seller to the listing broker and any real estate agents who were involved in the sales transaction. The rules that determine whether a commission is owed are described in the Checklist at the end of Chapter 7.

The second major issue involves claims against the listing broker or real estate agents involved in the transaction. Absent an agreement to the contrary, the default rule is that the listing broker, the listing broker's agents, and any other real estate agents who show the property are fiduciary agents of the seller and owe fiduciary duties of loyalty and prudence to the seller alone. These fiduciary duties require the broker/agent to disclose fully to the seller any information obtained about the buyer that may help the seller obtain the best price for the property. Breach of these fiduciary duties gives rise to claims by the seller against the listing broker or agents involved in the breach of fiduciary duty.

As the representative of the seller, brokers and agents have duties of disclosure with respect to prospective buyers. Brokers and agents cannot knowingly make material misrepresentations concerning the property to prospective buyers. Depending on the jurisdiction, the broker or agent showing the property may have an affirmative duty to disclose latent defects that materially affect the value of the property. To protect against these "failure to disclose" claims, brokers and agents typically require the seller to complete a disclosure statement that lists or describes problems or defects that affect the property.

Pre–Closing Claims Involving Real Estate Sales Contracts

The second step in the typical real estate transaction is the execution of a sales contract between the seller and the buyer. The major issues related to sales contracts are:

- whether the sales contract is enforceable under the Statute of Frauds;

- the grounds upon which the buyer successfully can rescind the sales contract prior to the closing and be refunded the buyer's "earnest money" deposit;

- who bears the risk of loss if the property is destroyed between the execution of the sales contract and the closing; and

- the remedies for breach of the sales contract by either party.

Statute Of Frauds For Sales Contracts

Contracts for the sale of real estate are subject to the Statute of Frauds. To be enforceable at law (i.e., for a party to recover damages), the sales contract must be in the form of a writing that satisfies the required elements of the Statute of Frauds. These elements are listed in the Checklist at the end of Chapter 7.

An interesting Statute of Frauds issue can arise when a real estate sales "contract" is formed via a series of e-mails with an electronic signature. Under the federal Electronic Signatures In Global And National Commerce Act ("E–Sign"),[1] a signature cannot

---

1. 15 U.S.C. §§ 7001 et seq.

be invalidated solely because the signature is in an electronic form. A series of e-mails, when read together as a whole, still must meet all of the required elements of the jurisdiction's Statute of Frauds in order to be enforceable at law as a real estate sales contract.

If the alleged sales contract lacks the signature of the party "to be bound" by the contract (i.e., the potential defendant the plaintiff wants to sue), the plaintiff cannot recover damages for breach of the contract. The plaintiff may seek the equitable remedy of specific performance of the contract by relying upon the equitable exceptions of part performance or equitable estoppel.

Buyer's Right Of Rescission

Assuming a valid sales contract exists, the contract imposes obligations upon each party to perform at the closing. The buyer's primary obligation at the closing is to tender the purchase price to the buyer. The seller's primary obligation at the closing is to deliver a properly executed deed to the buyer that conveys marketable title to the property. Performance of these obligations at the closing is subject to various preconditions, particularly for the buyer. If a precondition to the buyer's performance is not satisfied prior to or at the closing, the buyer is entitled to rescind the sales contract and recover the buyer's deposit.

The major grounds for rescission of the sales contract by the buyer are: (1) the seller's inability to convey marketable title to the property at the closing; (2) misrepresentation or nondisclosure by the seller concerning problems or defects that affect the property; or (3) the failure of an express precondition to the buyer's performance that is specified in the sales contract.

Every sales contract (even one that calls for a quitclaim deed[2] to be delivered by the seller at the closing) contains an implied

---

2. The delivery of a quitclaim deed by the seller at the closing does *not* breach the seller's duty to convey marketable title to the buyer. The significance of the buyer's acceptance of a quitclaim deed is that, *after the closing*, the buyer cannot sue the seller for any defects in the legal title to the property that later arise. The buyer who accepts a quitclaim deed may sue the seller for damages after the closing for fraudulent misrepresentation or failure to disclose latent defects or off-site conditions that impair the value of the property.

covenant that the seller's deed will convey marketable title to the buyer. The elements defining marketable title are described in the Checklist at the end of Chapter 7. The seller's obligation to convey "pure and pristine" marketable title usually is limited by an express waiver in the real estate sales contract. In the typical sales contract, the buyer agrees to take title "subject to" certain encumbrances[3] (think of these encumbrances as "blemishes") that otherwise would make the title to the real estate unmarketable.

Disputes often arise concerning whether the waiver in the sales contract covers an encumbrance that is discovered by the buyer prior to the closing. If the waiver covers the encumbrance,[4] the buyer cannot object to the marketability of the seller's title and rescind the sales contract on the ground that the seller has failed to convey marketable title.

The seller's title will be unmarketable if the property is subject to an unreasonable risk of litigation. Normally, the mere existence of various federal, state and municipal laws and private agreements that restrict land use do not make title unmarketable. A *current violation* of such laws or private agreements that *cannot be cured* by the closing date may make title unmarketable because such a violation would subject the buyer to an unreasonable risk of litigation. Examples of violations that may be difficult or impossible for the seller to cure include violations of local zoning ordinances and building codes, federal and state laws and regulations protecting the environment, and violations of privately created real covenants that impose restrictions on the development and use of the property.

---

3. Encumbrances making title unmarketable (unless waived by the buyer in the sales contract) are mortgages and liens that will not be paid off before or at the closing, current easements and real covenants or equitable servitudes that restrict the use of the property.

4. Even if the language of the waiver does not appear to include the encumbrance, if the encumbrance is visible or beneficial to the property being purchased, a court may rule that the buyer has implicitly waived the right to object. This type of dispute arises where the waiver covers only "encumbrances of record" and the property is encumbered by a visible or beneficial easement (such as a sewage drain line) that is not recorded. Even though the easement is not recorded, the seller will argue that the buyer "knew or should have known" of the unrecorded easement and has therefore waived the right to object.

Another major ground for the buyer to rescind the sales contract prior to the closing is the seller's fraudulent misrepresentation or failure to disclose hidden defects that affect the property. In every jurisdiction, the seller cannot knowingly make a false statement concerning the condition of the property. A fraudulent misrepresentation by the seller entitles the buyer to rescind the sales contract.

Jurisdictions are divided concerning whether the seller has an affirmative duty to disclose latent (hidden) material defects that are known to the seller and are not discoverable by the buyer upon a reasonable inspection. Under the common law (minority) rule of caveat emptor, the seller has no duty to disclose hidden defects that are known to the seller. The modern (majority) rule is that the seller has an affirmative duty to disclose material latent defects in the property that are known to the seller and are not discoverable by the buyer upon a reasonable inspection. In a modern rule jurisdiction, the majority rule is that the seller has this affirmative duty of disclosure even if the sales contract provides that the buyer takes the property "as is." Disputes concerning the physical condition of the property usually focus on whether each of the necessary elements for the buyer's nondisclosure claim are satisfied, or whether the seller had a duty to disclose an off-site condition that affects the value of the property.

The third major ground for rescission of the sales contract by the buyer is the failure of an express precondition to the buyer's performance that is specified in the sales contract itself. Here, disputed preconditions typically involve the satisfactory completion of an inspection of the property or the buyer's ability to obtain financing for the purchase of the property.

Destruction Of The Property Prior To Closing

A unique situation arises if the property is destroyed between the time the sales contract is executed and the time of the closing. Absent express language in the sales contract addressing this situation, a default rule will allocate the risk of loss.

The majority common law default rule is based on the doctrine of equitable conversion, which allocates the risk of loss to the buyer. Under the majority rule, the seller can seek specific performance of the sales contract and compel the buyer to purchase the property. If the seller had casualty insurance that covered the loss, the buyer can recover the insurance proceeds that are paid to the seller in a jurisdiction that applies to the majority default rule.

The minority default rule rejects the doctrine of equitable conversion in this situation. Under the minority rule, the seller bears the risk of loss due to destruction of the property prior to the closing. The buyer can rescind the sales contract and recover the buyer's deposit if the property has been destroyed prior to the closing.

Remedies For Breach Of Sales Contract

If all preconditions to performance have been satisfied, but one party refuses to perform as required under the sales contract at the closing, the other party has a variety of remedies for breach of the sales contract. Rescission, damages (including liquidated damages) and specific performance are the remedies available to the nonbreaching party.

The key to quickly and efficiently performing a remedies analysis on the exam is to recognize when loss of bargain damages are the preferred remedy for either the seller or the buyer. For the seller, loss of bargain damages are awarded when the value of the property at the time of the breach[5] is less than the contract sales price. If the property has depreciated in value since the sales contract was executed, the savvy buyer is more likely to breach by refusing to close. The seller's dilemma is to decide between loss of bargain damages, liquidated damages or forfeiture of the buyer's deposit[6] and specific performance.[7]

---

5. If the sales contract contains a time is of the essence clause, the time of the breach is the date the closing is set to occur (unless the breaching party clearly repudiates the sales contract beforehand).

6. If the sales contract contains a liquidated damages clause, the seller can elect the remedy of (greater) liquidated damages in lieu of (lesser) loss of bargain damages if the liquidated damages bear a *reasonable relationship* to the seller's actual damages. If the sales contract does not contain a liquidated damages

For the buyer, loss of bargain damages are awarded if the contract price is less than the value of the property at the time of the breach. In other words, if the property has appreciated in value since the sales contract was executed, the savvy seller is more likely to breach by refusing to close so that the seller can sell the property at a higher price to someone else. The savvy buyer generally will prefer the remedy of specific performance in this situation over the remedy of loss of bargain damages or rescission because the buyer desires to own the appreciated property at the lower contract price.

Claims Involving Transfer Of Title And Delivery Of The Deed

In a purchase and sale transaction, title to the property is transferred at the closing when the seller delivers the deed to the buyer. In a gift transaction, the donor transfers title to the donee by delivery of the deed. In either a sale or a gift situation, recording of the deed is not necessary for the grantor to transfer title to the grantee. The transfer of title becomes effective immediately upon the valid delivery of the deed to the grantee. Major issues that arise in the context of delivery of deeds are:

■ compliance with the Statute of Frauds;

■ the requirements for a valid delivery; and

■ the problem of a void deed in the chain of title.

Statute Of Frauds For Deeds

The transfer of title to real property is accomplished by the grantor's delivery of a written deed to the grantee that satisfies the required elements of the Statute of Frauds. Because the transfer of title is effective immediately upon the valid delivery of the deed to

---

clause, the seller can elect to keep the buyer's (greater) deposit amount in lieu of seeking (lesser) loss of bargain damages, subject to certain limitations imposed by majority and minority rules on the amount of the buyer's forfeiture. Refer to the Checklist at the end of Chapter 7 for the majority and minority rule limitations on forfeiture of the buyer's deposit.

7. Although specific performance is available as a remedy to the nonbreaching seller, from the seller's perspective this remedy is desirable only if the buyer is financially able to pay the purchase price and arbitrarily refuses to do so. The nonbreaching seller often is better served by seeking damages and reselling the property.

the grantee (without recording), a grantee who hands back or tears up the grantor's deed does *not* transfer title back to the grantor. Nor can the grantee transfer title to a third party by striking the grantee's name in the grantor's deed and inserting the name of the third party. Once the grantor's deed is delivered to the grantee, the grantee can *only* convey title by executing and validly delivering as the grantor *another deed* that itself satisfies all of the required elements of the Statute of Frauds.

Delivery Of The Deed

To accomplish a valid delivery of the deed, the grantor must satisfy two requirements. First, the grantor must have the appropriate state of mind by intending to transfer title to (or a partial interest in) the real estate immediately to the grantee. Second, the grantor must irrevocably relinquish physical control over the written deed itself.

Exam questions that raise issues concerning the irrevocable nature of the grantor's physical act usually involve delivery of the deed through the use of a third party escrow agent or a safe deposit box. Delivery issues also arise when it is unclear whether the delivery was completed before the grantor's death. For the delivery to be valid, it must be completed while the grantor is alive. A delivery that is completed after the grantor's death is void as an invalid testamentary transfer.[8]

A common exam question involves the problems associated with a deed that is void, either because the grantor's signature is forged, or because the deed was not validly delivered to the grantee while the grantor was alive and therefore is void as a testamentary transfer. A void deed in the chain of title is problematic because the purported grantor[9] of a deed that is void always maintains superior

---

8. To avoid being invalidated as a testamentary transfer, a deed that is delivered after the grantor's death must satisfy the formal requirements for a valid will. Deeds tend not to satisfy the formal requirements for a will unless the deed is handwritten and the jurisdiction recognizes holographic wills.

9. If the grantor is deceased, then the administrator or executor of the grantor's estate can assert the grantor's claim of superior title.

title to the property, even against a subsequent bona fide purchaser of the property who bought the property without notice of the void deed in the chain of title.

Issues involving a void deed arise because a prudent search of the chain of title by a subsequent bona fide purchaser is unlikely to uncover a forged grantor signature. A prudent title search also may not uncover a deed that is void as testamentary transfer because the grantor's deed does not need to be recorded before the grantor dies to transfer title to the grantee. The grantor's deed only needs to be validly delivered to the grantee (not recorded) prior to the grantor's death in order for title legally to transfer to the grantee. The grantee may record the deed after the grantor's death.

To protect subsequent bona fide purchasers, a majority of jurisdictions by statute create a rebuttable presumption that a recorded deed has been validly delivered. A rebuttable presumption may be refuted by evidence of the actual circumstances of the delivery. A few jurisdictions make this presumption conclusive. In a conclusive presumption jurisdiction, a recorded deed cannot be challenged as void.

For a detailed analysis of void deeds and the distinctions between deeds that are void and those that are merely voidable, refer to Chapter 2.

Post–Closing Claims Involving Defects In Legal Title Or The Physical Condition Of The Property

Post-closing, the universe of major issues divides into two categories:

- claims by an immediate or a more remote grantee based on a legal defect in the title to the property; and

- claims by a buyer based on a physical defect or an off-site condition that impairs the value of the property.

Legal Title Defects And The Role Of The Doctrine Of Merger

Claims based on legal defects in the title to the property are limited by the doctrine of merger to suits based on a breach of deed covenants. The doctrine of merger creates a presumption[10] that any breach of sales contract claims based on defects in the grantee's *legal title* to the property merge into and are extinguished by the deed that is accepted by the buyer at the closing. Consequently, any claim against the grantor based on a defect in the legal title of the property after the grantee has accepted the deed must be based on a breach of the covenants in the grantor's deed.[11]

Claims For Legal Defects Based On Breach Of Deed Covenants

The key to an efficient exam analysis is to recognize the claims that the grantee can bring against the *immediate grantor* for breach of the covenants in the immediate grantor's deed, and to further recognize when the grantee can bring a breach of deed covenant claim against a *more remote grantor* in the chain of title. Deed covenants run with the land and are based on privity of estate. Therefore, direct privity of contract is not necessary for a grantee to sue a more remote grantor based on a breach of the covenants in the more remote grantor's deed.

The grantee always can sue the immediate grantor for breach of the present deed covenants (seisin, right to convey, and the covenant against encumbrances[12]), and for breach of the future

---

10. In the real world, parties can and do contract over and around the doctrine of merger and specify in the sales contract what types of claims by the buyer will survive the closing. The nuances of such contractual "anti-merger" clauses are explored in an advanced course on real estate transactions, leaving the common law doctrine of merger as the "rule" to be followed in the typical first-year Property course.

11. Warranty deeds may contain either general or special (limited) covenants. A general warranty deed makes the grantor potentially liable for title defects that were created before the grantor owned the property (even if *unknown* by the grantor) or during the time the grantor owned the property. A special warranty deed makes the grantor potentially liable only for title defects that were created

during the time the grantor owned the property. A quitclaim deed, by contrast, contains no covenants. The grantor who gives a quitclaim deed is immune from liability if the legal title transferred to the grantee later turns out to be defective.

12. The covenant of seisin is a promise that the grantor actually has the superior ownership right to the property interest that is being conveyed in the grantor's deed. The covenant of right to convey is a promise by the grantor that the grantor has the legal authority or power to transfer the property interest that is being conveyed by the grantor's deed. The covenant against encumbrances is a promise by the grantor that the property is not subject to any encumbrances (mortgages or liens that will not be paid off at the closing, easements, or real covenants or deed covenants (the closely related covenants of quiet enjoyment and warranty,[13] and the covenant of future assurances[14]). The majority rule is that the grantee can sue a more remote grantor only for breach of the future covenants in a deed given by a more remote grantor. Note carefully that the covenants in the more remote grantor's deed may or may not be the same as the deed covenants in the deed the grantee received from the immediate grantor. Major issues involving claims for breach of deed covenants involve when the title defect arose, the statute of limitations for a claim based on a present covenant, what constitutes an eviction that triggers breach of a future covenant, and the amount recoverable by the grantee. The rules and analytical steps for each of these major issues are described in the Checklist at the end of Chapter 7.

Claims For Physical Defects Or Off–Site Conditions

Post-closing claims by the grantee based on physical defects or off-site conditions that impair the value of the property are not extinguished under the doctrine of merger. Although a buyer who accepts the seller's deed at the closing cannot rescind the transaction, the buyer can sue the seller for damages based on the seller's fraudulent misrepresentation.

In a modern rule jurisdiction, the buyer may sue the seller for failure to disclose a latent (hidden) material defect in the physical

---

equitable servitudes). The grantor's deed usually carves out exceptions to the covenant against encumbrances by making this covenant "subject to" various specified encumbrances (e.g., "subject to easements and covenants of record") that are accepted by the grantee.

13. In substance, the covenants of quiet enjoyment and warranty function similarly. These covenants are "a promise by the grantor to compensate the grantee for the loss if the title turns out to be defective or subject to an encumbrance, and the grantee thereby *suffers an eviction*." G. NELSON & D. WHITMAN, REAL ESTATE TRANSFER, FINANCE, AND DEVELOPMENT 189 (7th ed. 2006) (emphasis added) ("Nelson & Whitman"). Note carefully that the covenants of quiet enjoyment

and warranty do *not* impose a duty upon the grantor to *defend* the grantee's title against another person's claim of superior legal title. The grantee must defend his or her own title (and pay the litigation costs, if title was not insured). If the grantee prevails in the title dispute, the covenant of warranty is not breached, and the grantor owes nothing to the grantee. It is only if the grantee *loses* in the title dispute that the covenant of warranty is breached, and the losing grantee can recover damages from the grantor.

14. The covenant of further assurances is a promise by the grantor to execute any other documents that may be necessary to perfect the grantee's title. *See* Nelson & Whitman, *supra*, at 190.

condition of the property. The modern trend is to extend the seller's affirmative duty of disclosure to include off-site conditions that impair the value of the property. If the buyer's property is residential, the buyer can also sue a builder, contractor or developer who constructed or remodeled the property for breach of the implied warranty of quality ("IWQ"). The detailed rules for analysis of these types of claims are contained in the Checklist at the end of Chapter 7.

REAL ESTATE TRANSACTIONS CHECKLIST

With the above Review in mind, the Real Estate Transactions Checklist is presented below.

A. **LISTING AGREEMENT DISPUTES.** If the seller executed a listing agreement for the property with a real estate broker, determine if there are claims related to the listing agreement. If not, proceed to Part B of the checklist.

    1. **Is A Commission Due?** The terms of the listing agreement determine if the seller must pay a commission to the broker/agent. If the listing agreement is silent, the court will apply one of the following default rules.

        a. **Majority Default Rule.** A commission is due if the broker/agent brings an able and willing buyer to the seller, even if the sale fails to close.

            i. **Buyer Cannot Obtain Financing.** If the sales contract contains a financing contingency clause, a buyer who fails to obtain financing to purchase the property is not considered an "able and willing" buyer. Therefore, no commission is due.

        b. **Minority Default Rule.** A commission is not due unless and until the sale actually closes and the seller is paid.

2. **Claims Against Brokers/Agents.** Determine whether the seller or the buyer has a claim against a broker/agent who was involved in the transaction.

    a. **Claims By Seller Against Broker/Agent.** Absent an agreement to the contrary, the broker/agent represents and is a fiduciary of the seller.

        i. **Breach Of Fiduciary Duty Claims.** The seller can sue the broker/agent for breach of the fiduciary duties of prudence and loyalty.

        ii. **Examples Of Breach Of Duty.** Examples of a breach of the fiduciary duty owed to the seller are the failure to disclose information obtained from the buyer that would be relevant to the seller in obtaining the maximum price for the property, the failure to present a buyer's bona fide offer to the seller, or self-dealing or conflicts of interest in the representation of the seller by the broker/agent.

    b. **Claims By Buyer Against Broker/Agent.** As the representative of the seller, the broker/agent is liable for misrepresentation or failure to disclose latent (hidden) material defects that are known to the broker/agent and not discoverable by the buyer through a reasonable inspection of the property. Refer to Part B.2.b for further analysis of misrepresentation or failure to disclose claims.

B. **REAL ESTATE SALES CONTRACTS.** If the sales contract is enforceable, determine the claims and remedies of the buyer and the seller that arise after the execution of the sales contract but before the closing. If there is no sales contract, proceed to Part C to analyze claims arising after the deed has been delivered to the grantee.

1. **Is The Sales Contract Enforceable?** As a contract for the sale of real estate, the sales contract must be in the form of a writing that satisfies the Statute of Frauds. If the sales contract is oral or the writing lacks a required element for enforcement, the sales contract may be enforced in equity through specific performance.

    a. **Written Requirements For Statute Of Frauds.** The sales contract must: (1) describe the real estate to be sold; (2) in the vast majority of jurisdictions, must state the price; and (3) be signed by the party to be bound (the person against whom the contract is being enforced). The elements of the Statute of Frauds can be established through a series of related writings by the parties; a single written document is not required.

        i. **Electronic Compliance: Federal Law.** Under the Electronic Signatures In Global And National Commerce Act ("E–Sign"), a signature for a real estate sales contract cannot be invalidated solely because it is in electronic form. E–Sign does not change the other state law elements necessary to satisfy the Statute of Frauds.

        ii. **Contract By Series Of Writings Or E–Mails.** The parties can satisfy the Statute of Frauds through a series of writings or e-mails. A single writing is not necessary.

    b. **Equitable Exceptions To The Statute Of Frauds.** If the parties' contract fails to satisfy the requirements of the Statute of Frauds, determine if an equitable exception applies that would allow the contract to be enforced in equity through a judicial order of specific performance.

        i. **Part Performance Exception.** The

sales contract is enforceable in equity if the plaintiff can present unequivocal evidence that a contract existed and that the plaintiff relied upon the contract.

- **Unequivocal Evidence** that a contract existed is shown if the buyer paid all or part of the purchase price, and either (1) took possession of the property or (2) made improvements to the property.

- **Admission Of Existence Of Contract** by the defendant can be used to prove that a contract existed.

   ii. **Equitable Estoppel Exception.** If the jurisdiction follows Section 129 of the Restatement (Second) of Contracts, the contract can be enforced in equity if the plaintiff proves the contract existed, the plaintiff reasonably relied on the contract to the plaintiff's detriment, and failure to enforce the contract in equity would result in unjust injury to the plaintiff.

2. **Can The Buyer Rescind And Recover The Deposit?** Determine if a basis for the buyer's rescission of the sales contract exists due to: (1) the seller's inability to convey marketable title; (2) the seller's misrepresentation or nondisclosure concerning the physical condition of the property or an off-site condition that impairs the property's value; or (3) the failure of a contractual precondition to the buyer's performance.

     a. **Rescission Based On Seller's Failure To Convey Marketable Title.** Every sales contract (even one promising to convey title at the closing via a quitclaim deed) contains an implied covenant that the seller will convey marketable title to the property to the buyer at the time of the closing. The seller does *not* need to have marketable title at the time the sales contract is executed.

i. **Definition Of Marketable Title.** Marketable title is title that is (1) free of all encumbrances (unless the encumbrance has been waived by the buyer in the sales contract) and (2) not subject to such reasonable doubt as would create a just apprehension of its validity in the mind of a reasonable and prudent person who, guided by competent legal advice, would be willing to take and pay fair value.

ii. **Encumbrances Making Seller's Title Unmarketable.** Refer to Part B.2.a.ii below to determine if an encumbrance exists that makes the seller's title unmarketable. If so, proceed to Part B.2.a.iv to determine if the buyer has waived the right to object to the encumbrance.

- **Unpaid Mortgages And Liens.** If the sales contract requires that the seller must pay off all mortgages or liens with the sale proceeds from the closing, and the seller is unable to do so, the seller cannot convey marketable title.

- **Current Easements Burdening The Property.** A current express or implied-by-law easement that burdens the property makes title unmarketable. An easement that has been abandoned or terminated does not make title unmarketable. See Chapter 9 for further analysis of how easements are created and terminated.

- **Real Covenants And Equitable Servitudes Burdening The Property.** Any private agreement that affects the owner's use or "touches and concerns" the owner's land makes title unmarketable. See the Checklist at the end of Chapter 9 for further analysis.

- **No Access To Property.** A lack of access to the property does not make title unmarketable. The buyer may try to prove an easement by necessity exists, or may bring a private condemnation action and pay fair market value to acquire a right of way to access the parcel. See the Checklist at the end of Chapter 9 for further analysis.

iii. **Potential Violations Of Law Making Seller's Title Unmarketable.** Is the property in current violation of a federal, state or local law or a private restrictive covenant? **If yes**, title is unmarketable unless the seller can cure the violation prior to the closing date.

iv. **Did The Buyer Waive The Right To Object To An Encumbrance?** If the sales contract states that the buyer agrees to take the property "subject to" certain encumbrances, then the buyer has waived the right to object to any encumbrances described in the "subject to" clause of the sales contract. For example, if the buyer agrees to take title "subject to all easements and covenants of record," the buyer has waived the right to object to any encumbrance that has been recorded prior to the closing.

- **Visible Or Beneficial Easements.** Was an unrecorded easement clearly visible to the buyer, or is the unrecorded easement beneficial to the property? **If yes,** the court may rule that the buyer has waived the right to object to the easement as making title unmarketable.

b. **Rescission Based On Seller's Misrepresentation Or Nondisclosure (Including Seller's Listing Broker Or Agent).** The seller's duties listed below also apply to the seller's listing broker or any agents who were involved in the transaction.

   i. **Did The Seller (Broker/Agent) Knowingly Make A False Statement Concerning The Condition Of the Property? If yes,** the buyer who discovers the fraudulent misrepresentation prior to the closing is entitled to rescind the sales contract and recover the deposit.

   ii. **Did The Seller (Broker/Agent) Fail To Disclose A Hidden Defect?** Liability for nondisclosure depends on the rule the jurisdiction follows.

   - **Common Law (Minority) Rule.**

If the jurisdiction applies the common law rule of caveat emptor, the seller has no duty to disclose hidden defects. The buyer who discovers an undisclosed hidden defect prior to the closing cannot rescind the sales contract.

- **Modern (Majority) Rule.** If the jurisdiction applies the modern rule, the seller must disclose latent (hidden) material defects that are known to the seller and not discoverable by the buyer upon a reasonable inspection. If the buyer discovers the defect prior to the closing, the buyer is entitled to rescind the sales contract and recover the deposit if the buyer can prove that: (1) the seller had actual knowledge of the hidden defect; and (2) the defect is material.

- **Two Tests For Material Defect.** Under the objective test, would a reasonable buyer attach importance to the defect in deciding whether to purchase the property? Under the subjective test, does the defect adversely impact this particular buyer's decision to purchase the property?

- **Obvious Defects.** If the defect is obvious, then the seller had no affirmative duty to disclose the defect. To rescind the sales contract, the buyer must argue that a precondition to the buyer's performance is not satisfied (typically, that due to the obvious defect the property failed to satisfy the precondition imposed by the sales contract's inspection clause).

- **Effect Of An "As Is" Clause.** An "as is" clause in the sales contract prevents the buyer from rescinding based on obvious defects or if a hidden defect is discovered during an inspection of the property. Under the modern rule, an "as is" clause in the sales contract does not relieve the seller of the affirmative duty to disclose latent (hidden) material defects that are not discoverable by a reasonable inspection. An "as is" clause never relieves the seller (even in a common law rule jurisdiction) from the duty not to make fraudulent misrepresentations concerning the physical condition of the property.

iii. **Was An Off–Site Condition Not Disclosed?** Under the common law, the seller has a duty to disclose circumstances or conditions that are not on the property itself that may adversely impact the market value of the property. The modern trend (either by judicial decision or statute) is toward requiring greater disclosure. Off-site conditions or circumstances that are not a matter of public record or are difficult to detect by casual observation present a stronger public policy case for imposing a duty of disclosure on the seller.

c. **Rescission Based On Preconditions To Buyer's Performance In The Sales Contract.** Does the sales contract contain express preconditions to the buyer's performance at the closing? **If yes**, the buyer's failure to tender the purchase price at the closing is not a breach of the sales contract. Failure of a contractual precondition relieves the buyer from performance and entitles the buyer to rescind the sales contract and recover the buyer's deposit.

 i. **Failure Of Inspection Clause Precondition.** If the property fails to satisfy a contractual inspection clause, the buyer may rescind the sales contract and recover the buyer's deposit.

 ii. **Failure Of Buyer's Financing Clause Precondition.** If the sales contract makes the buyer's performance at the closing contingent upon obtaining financing, and the buyer is unable to do so after making a reasonable good faith effort, the buyer may rescind the sales contract and recover the buyer's deposit.

3. **Destruction Of The Property Prior To Closing.** If the property is destroyed after the sales contract is executed, but before the closing has occurred, who bears the risk of loss if the sales contract is silent on the issue?

 a. **Majority Default Rule: Buyer Bears Risk Of Loss.** A majority of jurisdictions apply the doctrine of equitable conversion and hold that the buyer has equitable title to the property as of the moment the sales contract is executed. Under the doctrine of equitable conversion, destruction of the property does not entitle the buyer to rescind the sales contract. The seller can seek specific performance of the contract and compel the buyer to purchase the destroyed property.

    i. Insurance By Seller. If the seller had casualty insurance on the property, the court may order that the insurance proceeds received by the seller before the closing must be credited to reduce the buyer's purchase price. If the insurance proceeds are paid to the seller after the closing, the buyer (who paid full price at the closing) may recover the insurance proceeds from the seller based on the theory the seller holds the insurance proceeds subject to a constructive trust for the benefit of the buyer.

b. Minority Default Rule: Seller Bears Risk of Loss. A minority of jurisdictions reject the doctrine of equitable conversion and allocate to the seller the risk of a substantial loss due to destruction of the property prior to the closing.

    i. Is The Loss Substantial? If the loss is substantial and the terms of the sales contract indicate that the destroyed structure was an integral part of the parties' contract, the buyer may rescind the sales contract and recover the buyer's deposit. If the loss is insubstantial, the buyer is entitled to a reduction (abatement) in the purchase price.

    ii. Is The Seller In Possession? If the seller is in possession of the property, a minority of jurisdictions place the risk of loss on the party in possession as the lowest cost avoider who is best able to insure the property against a casualty loss. If the buyer has not taken possession, the buyer may rescind the sales contract and recover the buyer's deposit.

4. **Remedies For Breach Of Sales Contract.** The seller and the buyer can seek rescission of the sales contract, damages or specific performance as remedies for breach of the sales contract.

   a. **Does The Sales Contract Contain A Time Is Of The Essence Clause?** A time is of the essence clause in the sales contract fixes the time for performance as the closing date.

      i. **Contract Specifies Time Is Of The Essence.** If the contract specifies that time is of the essence in the performance of the contract, then the buyer and the seller must be ready and able to perform on the closing date. Any delay is deemed a material breach of the sales contract by the party who is not ready to perform on the closing date. Although one party may request an extension of time to close, the other party is not required to grant a request for an extension of time, no matter how reasonable the request is.

      ii. **Contract Does Not Specify Time Is Of The Essence.** If the contract does not specify that time is of the essence in the performance of the contract, then either the buyer or the seller can request a reasonable extension of time to close the transaction after the closing date specified in the sales contract without being in material breach of the contract. Merely specifying a date for the closing does not make time of the essence in the performance of the contract.

b. Rescission. Rescission is an equitable remedy that restores the parties to their pre-contractual positions. Rescission requires the seller to refund the buyer's deposit.

c. Seller's Damages Remedy. If the buyer is the breaching party, determine both the seller's loss of bargain damages and damages based on forfeiture of the buyer's deposit to determine the seller's maximum possible damages recovery. Because forfeiture of the buyer's deposit as the seller's liquidated damages substitutes for actual damages where actual damages are difficult to determine, the seller generally cannot obtain both loss of bargain damages and liquidated damages. Moreover, the sales contract itself expressly may limit the seller's remedy for the buyer's breach to only forfeiture of the buyer's deposit as liquidated damages.

> **i. Seller's Loss Of Bargain Damages.** Is the contract price more than the value of the property at the time of the breach? **If yes**, the seller is entitled to the difference as loss of bargain damages. **If no**, determine if the seller can recover more in damages based on the forfeiture of the buyer's deposit.
>
> - **Foreseeable Expenses.** Include as part of the seller's loss of bargain damages other foreseeable expenses incurred as a result of the breach, such as the duplicate costs associated with a second sale of the property.
>
> **ii. Forfeiture Of Buyer's Deposit As**

Damages. Does the sales contract contain a liquidated damages clause?

- **If the sales contract does not contain a liquidated damages clause,** then under the majority common law rule the seller is entitled to keep the buyer's deposit as a forfeiture even if the forfeiture amount exceeds the seller's loss of bargain damages. In general, a forfeiture of 10% of the purchase price is generally upheld. Under the minority common law rule, the forfeiture amount cannot exceed the seller's actual damages. The excess amount is refunded to the buyer to avoid a windfall to the seller and to encourage economically efficient breaches of the sales contract.

- **If the sales contract contains a liquidated damages clause,** then the buyer forfeits the deposit as liquidated damages (generally in lieu of loss of bargain damages under the terms of the sales contract) if the amount bears a reasonable relationship to the seller's foreseeable actual damages. Note that under the reasonable relationship standard for liquidated damages, the buyer's forfeited deposit can exceed 10% of the purchase price.

d. **Buyer's Damages Remedy.** If the seller is the breaching party, is the contract price less than the value of the property at the time of the seller's breach? **If yes**, the buyer is entitled to the difference as loss of bargain damages. In addition, the buyer's loss of bargain damages include any reasonably foreseeable expenses incurred by the buyer as a result of the seller's breach.

e. **Specific Performance.** The equitable remedy of specific performance is available to the non-breaching buyer or seller, but generally courts are more reluctant to award a specific performance remedy against a breaching buyer.

   i. **Evaluate The Equities.** As an equitable remedy in lieu of a damages remedy at law, the court will weigh and evaluate the equitable merits of each party.

   • **Breaching Buyer Who Cannot Pay.** A court is unlikely to award specific performance against a breaching buyer if the buyer cannot pay the purchase price.

   • **Breaching Seller Who Undersold.** A court is likely to award specific performance if the seller's breach is due to a desire to sell the property to someone else for more than the nonbreaching buyer's contract price.

   ii. **Commission May Be Due.** If the seller breaches and arbitrarily refuses to close, in addition to a suit by the buyer for specific performance, the real estate broker/agent who has the listing for the property can sue the seller for the lost commission in a jurisdiction that follows the majority rule on when a commission is due. Refer to Part A.1.a above for further analysis.

C. **TRANSFER OF TITLE AND DELIVERY OF THE DEED.** Title to real property can only be transferred by the grantor's valid delivery of a written deed to the grantee that satisfies the requirements of the Statute of Frauds.

1. **Does The Written Deed Satisfy The Statute Of Frauds?** To satisfy the common law version of the Statute of Frauds, the deed must: (1) identify the grantor and the grantee; (2) provide a legal description of the real estate conveyed; (3) contain words of conveyance; and (4) be signed by the party to be bound.

    a. **Effect Of Forged Signature.** A deed with a forged grantor signature is void and cannot convey good title to the immediate grantee or to any subsequent grantee (including a bona fide purchaser without notice of the forgery) in the chain of title flowing from the void deed.

    b. **Fraudulently Obtained Signature.** A signature obtained from the grantor by trickery, undue influence or fraud is not a forgery making the deed void. A deed with a fraudulently obtained signature is only voidable by the grantor in a suit brought against the immediate grantee. The grantor cannot recover title to the property against a subsequent bona fide purchaser in the chain of title who did not have notice that the grantor's signature was unlawfully obtained.

    c. **Effect Of Grantee Name Left Blank**. The name of the grantee is an essential element for compliance with the Statute of Frauds. Therefore, the deed does not transfer title until the name of the grantee is filled in on the deed.

    d. **Tear Ups, Hand Backs And White Outs/Rewriting Of The Grantor's Deed.** Once title has been transferred to the grantee by valid delivery of a deed that satisfies the requirements of the Statute of Frauds, the grantee must independently execute and validly deliver another deed that itself satisfies the Statute of Frauds in order to convey title back to the grantor (or to someone else).

2. **Was The Deed Validly Delivered?** The transfer of title is effective as between the grantor and the grantee immediately upon delivery. Recording of the deed is not necessary for the transfer of title to become effective.

    a. **Required Elements For A Valid Delivery.** A valid delivery requires that the grantor must: (1) intend to pass title to the property interest described in the deed immediately; and (2) physically relinquish control over the deed by a physical act of manual or constructive delivery. Delivery is completed only when both of these two elements are satisfied.

    b. **Did The Grantor Intend An Immediate "Presently Operative" Transfer Of Title?** Look to the language of the deed and the contemporaneous statements of the grantor to determine whether the grantor intended to transfer title immediately.

        i. **Transfer Of A Future Interest.** A future interest in the property can be conveyed by the deed. The right to present possession of the property by the grantee is not necessary for the grantor to immediately convey a presently operative future interest.

    c. **Did The Grantor Physically Relinquish Control Over The Deed?** Look to the circumstances to determine whether the physical delivery element is satisfied.

        i. **Manual Delivery Directly To Grantee.** Manual delivery of the deed to the grantee is the most perfect form of physical delivery. Focus closely on the grantor's oral statements and the written language of the deed to verify that the grantor intended to make a present transfer when delivering the deed.

ii. **Constructive Delivery To Escrow Agent.** Constructive delivery of the grantor's deed to an escrow agent satisfies the physical delivery element if the grantor cannot revoke the deed and retrieve it from the escrow agent. If the escrow agent later delivers the deed to the grantee, under the relation-back doctrine the moment of the grantor's delivery is deemed to relate back in time to the point in time when the grantor first gave the deed to the escrow agent.

iii. **Constructive Delivery Via Safe Deposit Box.** Determine whether the grantor maintained access to the safe deposit box that contained the deed. If the grantor had the ability to retrieve the deed from the box while the grantor was still alive, the physical delivery element is not satisfied unless and until the grantee removed the deed from the box.

iv. **Delivery Completed After Grantor's Death Renders Deed Void As A Testamentary Transfer.** Did the grantor finally relinquish physical control over the deed only at or after the grantor's death? **If yes**, the deed is void as an attempted testamentary transfer. The attempted transfer of title is ineffective unless the written deed also satisfies all the requirements for a valid will.

- **Relation–Back Doctrine For Escrow Agent Delivery.** The application of the relation-back doctrine will prevent a deed that is delivered to an escrow agent while the grantor is alive from being void as an attempted testamentary transfer if the grantor dies after the deed is delivered to the escrow agent.

v. **Effect Of Recording By Grantee.** Recording of the deed by the grantee in a majority of jurisdictions creates only a rebuttable presumption that the deed has been delivered. In a few jurisdictions, recording of the deed creates a conclusive presumption of a valid delivery of the deed. In a conclusive presumption jurisdiction, recording of the deed trumps all claims of an invalid delivery based on an attempted testamentary transfer.

D. **BUYER'S POST–CLOSING CLAIMS AGAINST SELLER.** Under the doctrine of merger, a presumption arises that the buyer's contract-based claims against the seller that relate to defects in the legal title to the property[15] merge into the deed that is accepted by the seller at the closing and are extinguished. Post-closing, the buyer's remedy for a defect in legal title is limited to claims for damages based on a breach of deed covenants. Claims that are based on a defect in the physical condition of the property do not

---

15. Defective title claims subject to merger and extinguishment also include claims that the quantity (size) of the property conveyed is not consistent with the sales contract. Claims related to the size of the real estate conveyed claims merge based on the legal description of the property in the deed that was accepted by the buyer at the closing.

merge into the deed. The buyer may sue the seller for damages based on the seller's misrepresentation or nondisclosure of a defect in physical condition of the property or an off-site condition that impairs the value of the property. For residential property, the buyer may sue a merchant of housing for damages to residential property based on a breach of the implied warranty of quality ("IWQ"). Proceed to Parts D.1 and D.2 to analyze claims based on breach of deed covenants. Proceed to Part D.3 to analyze claims based on physical defects or a breach of the IWQ.

1. **Claims Against Immediate Grantor Based On Defects In Legal Title (Breach Of Deed Covenants).**

   a. **What Are The Covenants In The Immediate Grantor's Deed?** The grantee potentially can sue an immediate grantor who gave a general warranty or special warranty deed. The grantee cannot sue a grantor who gave a quit-claim deed.

   b. **When Did The Title Defect Arise?** If the grantor gave a special warranty deed, the grantor can only be sued for breach of deed covenants if the title defect arose while the grantor owned the property (not for defects arising before or after the grantor owned the property). If the grantor gave a general warranty deed, the grantor can be sued for breach of deed covenants for any title defect that arose before or while the grantor owned the property (even if the grantor is ignorant of a prior title defect).

   c. **Breach Of Present Deed Covenants?** The present deed covenants of seisin, right to convey, and the covenant against encumbrances are breached, if at all, at the time the deed is delivered by the grantor.

      i. **Statute Of Limitations For Present Deed Covenants.** The statute of limitations for a claim based on breach of a present deed covenant begins to run when the deed is delivered by the seller at the closing.

- **Superior Title Held By Another Person Without Eviction Of Grantee.** The mere fact that another person lawfully holds superior title to the property at the time the grantor's deed is delivered to the grantee breaches the present covenants of seisin and right to convey. Unlike a future covenant, the grantee does not need to be evicted in order to assert a breach of these present covenants.

ii. **Effect Of "Subject To" Waiver On The Covenant Against Encumbrances.** The deed's covenant against encumbrances protects the buyer against unpaid mortgages, liens, easements, and real covenants/ equitable servitudes. The covenant against encumbrances is not breached if the objectionable encumbrance was waived by the buyer in accepting the seller's deed.

- **Examples Of Waiver By Buyer.** The buyer waives the right to sue for any encumbrance that the deed specifies as excluded by a "subject to" caveat in the deed. A deed covenant that is "subject to all encumbrances of record" waives only recorded encumbrances. A deed covenant that is "subject to all easements and private restrictions" waives both recorded and unrecorded encumbrances, such as an implied-by-law easement. Refer to the Checklist at the end of Chapter 9 for further analysis of easements, real covenants and equitable servitudes.

- **Adverse Possession And Prescriptive Easements.** A title defect based on title acquired by adverse possession breaches the present deed covenant of seisin. A title defect based on a prescriptive easement held by another person breaches the present deed covenant against encumbrances (unless unrecorded easement rights are waived by the buyer via a broad "subject to" clause). See the Checklist at the end of Chapter 8 for further analysis of adverse possession claims. See the Checklist at the end of Chapter 9 for further analysis of prescriptive easement claims.

d. **Breach Of Future Deed Covenants?** The future deed covenants of quiet enjoyment and warranty are breached when the grantee is actually or constructively evicted or disturbed in possession of the property by another person who has superior legal title.

   i. **Mere Threat Of Future Eviction.** A mere threat of future eviction is not sufficient to establish a breach of the future deed covenants of quiet enjoyment and warranty. Even if a competing claimant lawfully has superior title and may choose to evict the grantee in the future, the deed covenants of quiet enjoyment and warranty are not breached unless and until the grantee is actually or constructively evicted or disturbed in possession or use of the property.

ii.   **Constructive Eviction.** Constructive eviction occurs if the grantee must pay off the claimant (buy off the claim of superior title) to avoid an eviction from all or part of the property. Constructive eviction triggers a breach of future deed covenants.

iii.   **Disturbance Of Possession.** Disturbance of possession triggers a breach of future deed covenants. If a court enjoins the grantee from using the property as the grantee desires due to the competing claimant's enforcement of a restrictive covenant or an easement right held by the claimant, then the grantee has suffered a disturbance in possession.

iv.   **Future Covenants Do Not Require Grantor To Pay To Defend Grantee's Title.** The covenants of quiet enjoyment and warranty do not require the grantor to defend the grantee's title against a competing claim. The grantee must pay the legal costs of defending title. If the grantee wins, the covenants are not breached and therefore the grantee is not reimbursed for legal expenses. If the grantee loses, then the covenants are breached and the grantee can recover legal expenses as damages for breach of the future covenants.

e. **Amount Recoverable?** The majority rule is that the grantee can recover from the immediate grantor the purchase price paid for the deed. Some courts also will award interest on the grantee's purchase price amount, measured either from the date the deed was delivered (for a breach of a present covenant) or the date the grantee was evicted or disturbed in possession (for a breach of a future covenant).

2. **Claims Against More Remote Grantors In The Grantee's Chain Of Title.** Determine every remote grantor in the grantee's chain of title who can be sued for breach of the covenants in the deed given by the more remote grantor.

   a. **What Are The Covenants In The Remote Grantor's Deed?** The grantee potentially may sue any remote grantor who gave a general warranty or special warranty deed. The grantee cannot sue any remote grantor who gave a quitclaim deed.

   b. **When Did The Title Defect Arise?** If the remote grantor gave a special warranty deed, the remote grantor can only be sued for breach of deed covenants if the title defect arose while the remote grantor owned the property (not for defects arising before or after the remote grantor owned the property). If the grantor gave a general warranty deed, the grantor can be sued for breach of deed covenants for any title defect that arose before or while the grantor owned the property (even if the grantor is ignorant of a prior title defect), but not for title defects that arose after the remote grantor conveyed the property to someone else.

      i. **Relation–Back Of Title Defects Based On Adverse Possession Or**

Prescriptive Easement. If the title defect is based on title acquired by adverse possession or a prescriptive easement, the date of the defect relates back in time to when the statute of limitations began to run to establish title by adverse possession or a prescriptive easement right (not when the statute of limitations expired). See the Checklist at the end of Chapter 8 for further analysis of adverse possession claims. See Checklist at the end of Chapter 9 for additional analysis of prescriptive easement claims.

c. **Breach Of Present Deed Covenants In The Remote Grantor's Deed?** Whether a remote grantor can be sued for breach of the present covenants in the deed given by the remote grantor depends on the rule the jurisdiction follows.

    i. **Majority Rule.** Under the majority rule, a more remote grantor cannot be sued by the grantee for breach of the present deed covenants of seisin, right to convey, and the covenant against encumbrances. The majority rule is based on the theory that present covenants do not run to more remote grantees.

    ii. **Minority Rule.** Under the minority rule, the right to sue (a "chose in action") for a breach of the present covenants in the deed given by a remote grantor is implicitly assigned as title is conveyed by each subsequent grantee. In a minority rule jurisdiction, a remote grantor can be sued by the grantee for breach of the present covenants in the deed given by the remote grantor.

- **Statute Of Limitations For Suits Based On Present Deed Covenants.** The statute of limitations for a claim under the minority rule based on breach of a present deed covenant in the remote grantor's deed begins to run when the remote grantor's deed was delivered (which could be so long ago that the statute of limitations has expired).

- **Effect Of "Subject To" Waivers In The Remote Grantor's Deed On The Covenant Against Encumbrances.** The covenant against encumbrances in the remote grantor's deed is not breached if the objectionable encumbrance was waived by a "subject to" clause in the more remote grantor's deed.

d. **Breach Of Future Deed Covenants?** Future covenants in the deed given by a grantor always run to more remote grantees. Repeat the analysis for breach of future deed covenants in Part D.1.d above to determine if the more remote grantor can be sued by the grantee for breach of the future deed covenants in the remote grantor's deed.

e. **Amount Recoverable?** The majority rule is that the grantee can recover from a remote grantor the purchase price the remote grantor received for the remote grantor's deed (this will likely be less than the amount the grantee paid for the property). Some courts also will award interest on the purchase price amount, measured either from the date the remote grantor's deed was delivered (for a breach of a present covenant) or the date the grantee was evicted or disturbed in possession (a breach of a future covenant).

- **Differing Views If Price of Property Has Declined.** If the grantee paid less for the property than the more remote grantor received for the property, courts are divided concerning the amount the grantee can recover. One view is to permit the grantee to recover only the lesser amount that the grantee actually paid for the property. The other view is to permit the grantee to recover the greater amount that the more remote grantor received for the property.

3. **Claims Based On The Physical Condition Of The Property.** The doctrine of merger does not apply to claims based on the defective physical condition of the property. Post-closing, the buyer can recover damages from the seller for misrepresentation (false statements) or for the failure to disclose a latent (hidden) material defect or an off-site condition that impairs the value of the property. For new residential construction (including remodeling or new improvements), the owner can bring a claim against the builder for breach of the implied warrant of quality ("IWQ").

   a. **Misrepresentation Claims.** Did the seller knowingly make a false statement concerning the physical condition of the property or an off-site condition that impairs the value of the property? **If yes**, the buyer cannot rescind the sale, but may sue the seller for damages for fraudulent misrepresentation.

b. Failure To Disclose Claims. Did the seller fail to disclose a hidden physical defect?

i. Common Law Rule. If the jurisdiction applies the common law rule of caveat emptor, the seller has no duty to disclose hidden defects. Therefore, the buyer who discovers an undisclosed hidden defect after the closing cannot sue the seller for damages.

ii. Modern Rule. If the jurisdiction applies the modern rule, the seller must disclose hidden material defects that are known to the seller and not discoverable by the buyer upon a reasonable inspection. If the buyer discovers a hidden defect after the closing, the buyer cannot rescind the sale, but may sue the seller for breach of the duty to disclose if the buyer can prove that: (1) the seller had actual knowledge of the hidden defect; and (2) the defect is material.

• **Proof Of Actual Knowledge By Seller.** Did the seller hide the defect or previously attempt to fix the defect? **If yes**, a stronger case exists for actual knowledge.

• **Two Tests For Material Defect.** Under the objective test, would a reasonable buyer attach importance to the defect in deciding whether to purchase the property? Under the subjective test, does the defect adversely impact this particular buyer's decision to purchase the property?

- **Obvious Defects Or Defects Discoverable By Reasonable Inspection.** If the defect is obvious or could have been discovered by a reasonable pre-closing inspection by the buyer (who failed to make a pre-closing inspection), then the seller had no affirmative duty to disclose the defect. The buyer has no claim against the seller in these situations if the buyer had the opportunity to inspect the property and declined to do so.

iii. **Duty to Disclose Off–Site Conditions.** Under the common law rule of caveat emptor, there is no duty to disclose circumstances or conditions that are not on the property itself that may adversely impact the market value of the property. The modern trend (either by judicial decision or statute) is toward requiring greater disclosure. Off-site conditions or circumstances that are not a matter of public record or are difficult to detect by casual observation present a stronger public policy case for requiring affirmative seller disclosure.

iv. **Effect Of An "As Is" Clause.** Under the modern rule, an "as is" clause in the sales contract does not relieve the seller of the affirmative duty to disclose hidden defects that are not discoverable by a reasonable inspection.

An "as is" clause never relieves the seller (even in a common law caveat emptor jurisdiction) from the duty not to make fraudulent misrepresentations concerning the physical condition of the property.

c. **Is The Defect Related To New Or Recent Construction (Including Remodeling Or Improvements) (Breach Of IWQ)?** If the construction is flawed or shoddy, the owner of the property may bring a claim for breach of the IWQ.

   i. **Residential Property?** The IWQ applies only to residential property and not to commercial property.

   ii. **Is Defendant A Merchant Of Housing?** The defendant must be a builder, contractor, developer or other commercial vendor of residential housing.

   iii. **Does Privity Of Contract Exist?** Was there a direct contract ("privity of contract") between the first buyer/owner of the property and the defendant? **If yes**, all jurisdictions permit the owner to sue the defendant based on the IWQ. **If no,** the modern trend is to permit a subsequent buyer who is not in direct privity of contract to sue the defendant based on either a tort theory (not to do negligent work) or based on public policy.

   iv. **Standard For Quality?** The standard for quality is that the work must be performed in a workmanlike manner and in accordance with accepted local standards. Violations of local building codes can be used to establish the standard for breach of the IWQ.

v. **Is The Claim Brought Within A Reasonable Time?** The reasonable time limitation is measured from the point in time when the work is originally performed (not when a subsequent buyer later purchases the property).

vi. **Has The IWQ Been Waived?** Courts generally are very reluctant to enforce a written waiver of the IWQ in the parties' contract. If the plaintiff is a subsequent buyer of the property and the defects in workmanship are obvious, a court may rule that the subsequent buyer implicitly has waived the IWQ.

ILLUSTRATIVE PROBLEMS

Here are two problems that illustrate how the Checklist can be used to resolve real estate transactions questions.

■ PROBLEM 7.1 ■

Bob Buyer executed a sales contract ("Contract") with Sam Seller to purchase Sam's farm for $2 million. Buyer gave Seller a deposit of $200,000. The Contract contained a provision stating that "time is of the essence in the closing of this Contract" and set a closing date of April 1st. Paragraph 8 of the Contract further stated:

¶ 8. **Seller hereby promises to convey marketable title**

to the Property, subject to all encumbrances of record, by general warranty deed delivered to the Buyer on the Closing Date.

Paragraph 15 of the Contract stated:

¶ 15.   Buyer's performance under this Contract is pre-conditioned upon obtaining prior to the Closing Date an appraisal of the market value of the Property. Buyer's performance under this Contract is excused if the appraised market value of the Property is less than eighty percent (80%) of the Contract Price.

The Contract did not contain a liquidated damages clause or otherwise limit the remedies available in the event that a party breached the Contract.

Seller's farm was located at the southwest corner of the intersection of two major streets in the suburbs of Pleasantville in the State of Bliss. The State of Bliss follows the common law rules with respect to matters of real property. All of the development surrounding Sam's farm was commercial in nature. Buyer intended to develop the farm property into a small neighborhood retail center.

After Buyer entered into the Contract, Buyer discovered three problems. First, a search of the title revealed that five years ago Seller had given a mortgage on the farm to First State Bank in exchange for a loan of $50,000. The title search did not show that this mortgage had been released by First State Bank. Second, Buyer learned from the Pleasantville Department of Planning that, although the farm currently complied with local zoning law requirements, Buyer's planned neighborhood retail center would violate the local zoning ordinance. It would take at least three months for the Department of Planning to determine whether to recommend a change in the zoning ordinance to accommodate Buyer's proposed retail center. Third, an appraisal of the farm found that the current market value of the property as of March 30 was only $1.9 million.

It is now March 31st. Buyer has come to you seeking legal advice. Buyer no longer desires to purchase the farm property unless he knows he can build the retail center on the property. You have reviewed the Contract and determined that it satisfies the Statute of Frauds. Advise Buyer concerning the potential financial consequences if Buyer refuses to purchase the farm property at the closing on April 1.

Analysis

The Contract contains a time is of the essence clause and establishes April 1 as the closing date. Although Buyer could ask Seller for an extension of time to close, Seller is not required to grant Buyer's request for a reasonable extension of time and can demand that Buyer close on April 1st. Due to the time is of the essence clause, Buyer's refusal to tender the purchase price of $2 million at the closing on April 1st would be a material breach of the Contract unless Buyer is entitled to rescind the Contract.

Buyer can rescind the Contract if: (1) Seller is unable to convey marketable title to the farm property on the closing date; or (2) a precondition to Buyer's obligation to perform on the closing date is excused by the failure of a precondition to Buyer's performance in the Contract.

Buyer is not entitled to rescind the Contract based on Seller's inability to convey marketable title to the farm property. Absent a waiver in a sales contract, the unreleased mortgage is an encumbrance that makes the seller's title to the property unmarketable. Unfortunately, Buyer waived the right to rescind based on the Seller's inability to convey marketable title by agreeing in ¶ 8 of the Contract to take title to the farm property "subject to all encumbrances of record." Encumbrances of record include the recorded and unreleased mortgage held by First State Bank.

Seller's title also is not made unmarketable by the fact that Buyer's prospective change in use of the farm property would violate the local zoning ordinance. The farm property currently is in compliance with the zoning ordinance and therefore is not subject to any risk of litigation concerning the present use of the farm.

Buyer is not entitled to rescind the Contract based on the failure of a contractual precondition. According to the facts, Buyer's only precondition to performance is ¶ 15 of the Contract. Paragraph 15 is satisfied because the appraised value of the Property ($1.9 million) is more than 80% of the purchase price of $2 million.

Thus, if Buyer fails to tender the purchase price of $2 million at the closing on April 1, Buyer will be in material breach of the Contract. Seller's choice of possible remedies are rescission, damages and specific performance. Seller is unlikely to choose rescission because the Contract's purchase price of $2 million is a "good deal" for the Seller. The contract price exceeds the appraised market value of the farm property. Seller is likely to seek either loss of bargain damages or compel Buyer to purchase the farm property by seeking specific performance.

The Contract does not limit Seller's damages remedies or contain a liquidated damages clause. Seller's loss of bargain damages are measured as the difference between the price in the Contract and the value of the farm on the date of Buyer's breach. Here, the Contract price is $2 million. The date of Buyer's breach will be the closing date of April 1. A court would likely use the appraised value of the Property as of March 30 of $1.9 million as the approximate value of the farm on the date of the breach. Seller's loss of bargain damages will be $100,000, plus any other actual expenses which Seller may be able to prove were caused by Buyer's breach.

Although the Contract does not contain a liquidated damages clause, under the common law rule a seller is entitled to keep the buyer's deposit as a forfeiture if the deposit is no more than 10% of the purchase price. Here, the deposit of $200,000 is exactly 10% of the purchase price of $2 million, but it is less than Seller's potential estimated actual damages of $100,000. If the State of Bliss follows the majority common law rule on forfeiture of a breaching buyer's deposit, Seller can keep Buyer's deposit ($200,000) as a damages remedy even though it exceeds Seller's loss of bargain damages and actual expenses ($100,000 plus other actual expenses). If the State of Bliss follows the minority common law rule on forfeiture of a breaching buyer's deposit, Seller must refund to Buyer the amount of the deposit that exceeds Seller's loss of bargain damages and other actual expenses.

Seller's alternative remedy is to seek specific performance of the Contract. Although courts are generally reluctant to award specific performance against a breaching purchaser, here the equities may favor Seller. There is no indication that Buyer cannot afford to purchase the farm under the terms of the Contract. Rather, Buyer appears to be "backing out" of the Contract simply because Buyer struck a "bad" bargain. Buyer executed the Contract waiving all encumbrances of record before doing a title search, failed to investigate the zoning requirements for Buyer's proposed change in use before executing the Contract, and apparently overpaid for the farm. Based on these facts, a court might be persuaded to award specific performance to Seller and force Buyer to purchase the farm for $2 million.

In conclusion, Buyer is not entitled to rescind the Contract. If Buyer refuses to close on April 1, at a minimum Buyer is likely to forfeit approximately $100,000 of Buyer's deposit as damages to Seller, and may be required to forfeit the entire $200,000. Alternatively, Buyer could be forced via a judicial decree of specific performance to purchase the Property as contracted for $2 million.

■ PROBLEM 7.2 ■

Oscar validly conveyed a 10 foot wide strip of his property to Xavier. (Assume that this conveyance was in the form of a quitclaim deed that satisfied the Statute of Frauds.) Xavier planned to pave the 10 foot wide strip and create a more scenic driveway to Xavier's house. Xavier recorded the quitclaim deed he received from Oscar conveying the 10 foot wide strip.

Six months later, Oscar conveyed fee simple absolute title to Oscar's property to Alice by general warranty deed with no exceptions to the six deed covenants of title. Alice did not perform

REAL ESTATE TRANSACTIONS

a title search before purchasing the property. The legal description of the property in Oscar's deed did not exclude the 10 foot wide strip that Oscar previously had conveyed to Xavier. The consideration by Alice for Oscar's general warranty deed was $10,000.

Three months later, Alice conveyed fee simple absolute title to the property to Braden by general warranty deed with no exceptions to the six deed covenants of title. Braden did not perform a title search before purchasing the property. The legal description of the property did not exclude in Alice's deed the 10 foot wide strip that Oscar previously had conveyed to Xavier. The consideration given by Braden for Alice's general warranty deed was $15,000.

Braden decided to build a garden in the area that included the 10 foot wide strip. (Xavier had never cleared and paved his proposed new driveway.) Xavier sought an injunction to prevent Braden from building the garden. One year from the date of Oscar's conveyance of the property to Alice, the court ruled that Xavier had paramount title to the 10 foot wide strip. Due to its location, an appraiser has estimated that the damages to the property (now owned by Braden) as a result of Xavier's 10 foot wide strip are $3,000.

Assume that the statute of limitations for a claim based on a breach of any deed covenant is ten years. Analyze Braden's potential claims against Alice and Oscar.

Analysis

Preliminary Points: When analyzing breach of deed covenant problems, always begin by drawing a diagram. At a minimum, your diagram should list the series of grantors, the type of deed given by each grantor, the price received for each deed, and the point in time when the defect arose. You also may want to add other relevant information. This diagram will virtually lay out the steps for your analysis. In Problem 7.2, your diagram should look something like the diagram on the following page:

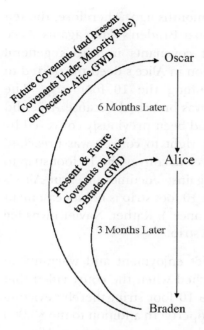

Future Covenants (and Present Covenants Under Minority Rule) on Oscar-to-Alice GWD

→ Oscar
- Title defects arises when Oscar conveys 10' strip to Xavier

6 Months Later

Present & Future Covenants on Alice-to-Braden GWD

→ Alice
- GWD for $10,000
- 6 covenants with no exceptions
- Breach of present covenants of seisin and right to convey due to failure to exclude 10' strip previously conveyed by Oscar to Xavier

3 Months Later

→ Braden
- GWD for $15,000
- 6 covenants with no exceptions
- Breach of present covenants of seisin and right to convey due to failure to exclude 10' strip previously conveyed by Oscar to Xavier

One Year Later
- Braden is disturbed in possession due to court order (triggers breach of future deed covenants)

Analysis of Grantee (Braden) Versus Immediate Grantor (Alice): Braden can sue his immediate grantor Alice for breach of the present covenants in Alice's general warranty deed of seisin and right to convey and the future covenants of quiet enjoyment and warranty. The maximum amount of Braden's recovery against Alice is limited to Braden's actual damages of $3,000.

Alice gave Braden a general warranty deed. The covenants in Alice's general warranty deed extend to the title defect in the property that was created when the prior owner, Oscar, conveyed the 10 foot strip to Xavier. The present covenants of seisin and right to convey were breached when Alice delivered the deed to

Braden. This occurred just three months ago. Therefore, the ten year statute of limitations does not bar Braden's claim against Alice based on breach of the present covenants in Alice's general warranty deed. The legal description in Alice's deed purported to convey the entire property, including the 10 foot strip. The covenant of seisin in Alice's deed was breached because Alice did not own the 10 foot strip, which had been previously conveyed by Oscar to Xavier. The covenant of right to convey was breached because Alice did not have the power to convey the 10 foot strip to Braden. The present covenant against encumbrances in Alice's deed was not breached because the 10 foot strip is not an easement right held by Xavier (an "encumbrance"). Rather, Xavier owns fee simple absolute title to the 10 foot strip.

The future covenants of quiet enjoyment and warranty in Alice's deed to Braden were breached when the court ruled that Xavier had paramount title to the 10 foot strip, thereby evicting Braden from this portion of the property. In addition to the $3,000 in damages to the property, Braden can also recover from Alice his expenses in unsuccessfully litigating the title dispute with Xavier based on this breach of the future covenants of quiet enjoyment and warranty.

Analysis of Grantee (Braden) Versus Remote Grantor (Oscar): Braden also can sue the more remote grantor Oscar for breach of covenants in the general warranty deed that Oscar gave to Alice. Oscar owned the property when the title defect was created by conveying the 10 foot strip to Xavier.

If the jurisdiction follows the majority common law rule, Braden cannot sue Oscar for breach of the present deed covenants of seisin and right to convey because such covenants do not run with the land to a more remote grantee such as Braden. If the jurisdiction follows the minority common law rule, Alice's deed to Braden may be construed by a court as including an implied assignment to Braden of Alice's right to sue Oscar for breach of the present covenants contained in Oscar's deed to Alice. These present covenants were breached when Oscar delivered the deed to Alice, which occurred approximately one year and nine months ago. In a minority rule jurisdiction Braden's claims (based on an implied assignment theory) against Oscar for breach of the present covenants of seisin and right to convey in the Oscar-to-Alice deed are not barred by the ten year statute of limitations.

Even if the jurisdiction follows the majority common law rule, Braden can still bring a claim against Oscar for breach of the future covenants in Oscar's general warranty deed to Alice of quiet enjoyment and warranty. The analysis is the same as for the breach of the future covenants in the general warranty deed that Alice gave to Braden.

Conclusion: Braden cannot receive a "double recovery" by suing both Alice and Oscar. At most, Braden can recover the $3,000 in actual damages to the property and his litigation expenses in unsuccessfully defending title to the property.

Need Additional Practice?

How would your analysis change if Alice had given Braden a special warranty deed instead of a general warranty deed?

If Alice had given Braden a special warranty deed, Braden could not sue Alice for breach of deed covenants because the title defect was created *before* Alice owned the property. Braden could still recover against the more remote grantor Oscar, who created the title defect. The analysis of Braden's claims against Oscar as described above would be unchanged if Alice gave Braden a special warranty deed. Remember that Braden's claims against Oscar are based on the general warranty deed given by Oscar to Alice, not on the special warranty deed that Braden received from Alice.

Author's Note: Preview Of Intersections With Chapter 8 Material

As you move on to read Chapter 8, Problem 7.2 previews a key point of intersection between real estate transactions and the recording act system. If Braden had done a title search prior to purchasing the property, he may have discovered the quitclaim deed conveying the 10 foot wide strip from Oscar to Xavier. Therefore, Braden may not prevail over Xavier in a dispute over who holds paramount title to the 10 foot wide strip because the recording system may have given Braden constructive notice of Oscar's prior conveyance. Problem 8.1 at the end of Chapter 8 provides you with an illustration of an exam question where deed covenant issues are intertwined with recording act issues.

POINTS TO REMEMBER

• Title to real property can only be transferred by the grantor's execution and delivery of a written deed that satisfies the requirements of the Statute of Frauds. Handing back, tearing up, or whiting out parts of another grantor's prior deed does not convey title.

• Beware of the two circumstances that will make a deed void—a forged signature of the grantor or a deed that is not delivered while the grantor is alive. If a deed is void, no one in the chain of title—not the immediate grantee or any subsequent grantees—can prevail in a suit by the grantor or the grantor's estate to reclaim title to the property. Even a bona fide purchaser without notice of a prior void deed in the chain of title loses in a title dispute with the grantor (or the personal representative of the grantor's estate).

• A "subject to" clause in the sales contract that excludes certain encumbrances from the buyer's obligation to convey marketable title waives the buyer's right to rescind the sales contract, but only as to those encumbrances that are described or listed in the "subject to" clause. Scrutinize "subject to" clauses closely and construe their language strictly. Any encumbrance that is discovered by the buyer prior to the closing that is not described or listed in the "subject to" clause of the sales contract makes the seller's title unmarketable, and gives the buyer the right to rescind the sales contract and recover the buyer's deposit. The exception to this rule of strict construction is for implied waivers by the buyer of visible or beneficial easements.

• The covenant against encumbrances in a deed covers any unreleased mortgage or lien, current easement, or real covenant or equitable servitude that burdens the property (unless the deed accepted by the buyer at the closing excepts the encumbrance by a subject to clause).

- A more remote grantor never can be sued for a title defect that arises after the remote grantor has conveyed the property to someone else. The covenants in a general warranty deed only apply to title defects that are created before or while the grantor owned the property. The covenants in a special warranty deed only apply to title defects that arise while the grantor owns the property. A grantor who gives a quitclaim deed never can be sued for title defects.

CHAPTER 8

Recording Acts and Adverse Possession

The material in Chapter 8 addresses the fundamental problem of how to resolve conflicting claims of superior property rights involving the same parcel of real estate. Such conflicts generally arise in two situations. The owner of the property may transfer an interest in the property to more than one grantee, in each instance conveying by a written instrument that is capable of being recorded. Or, a competing claim of superior title may arise by operation of law, as in the case of adverse possession.

RECORDING ACTS AND ADVERSE POSSESSION REVIEW

The classic dispute over superior property rights involves competing claimants who both claim to have acquired their property interests from the owner of the property through a written instrument. The property interests in dispute may be the fee simple absolute title to the property, or a lesser property interest such as a mortgage or an easement. The written instrument that conveys the property interest to the first grantee, although capable of being recorded in the land records system, is not recorded immediately. This omission makes it possible for the owner of the property to convey an interest in the property to a subsequent grantee, who may lack knowledge of the prior conveyance.

The Hierarchy Of Legal Rules

In resolving such disputes, the law employs a hierarchy of legal rules. The baseline default rule for resolving disputes over superior title is the common law rule of **first in time, first in right** ("FTFR"). Under the common law rule, the grantee whose conveyance from the owner occurred first (was "first in time") has paramount title over a later grantee from the same owner. Thus, if O (the proverbial owner of Blackacre) deeds title to Blackacre first to A and later to B, A's claim to title is superior to B's claim if the common law rule of FTFR applies. Similarly, if O grants A a mortgage or easement on Blackacre, and later sells Blackacre to B, under the common law rule of FTFR B takes Blackacre subject to A's prior mortgage or easement right.

The common law rule obviously is unfair if B purchases Blackacre from O without knowing of O's prior transfer of title or a lesser property interest in Blackacre to A. For this reason, every state has enacted a **recording act.** A recording act is a statutory rule that supersedes the common law rule of FTFR if the subsequent grantee B satisfies all of the technical requirements of the statute. If the subsequent grantee B cannot qualify for protection under the recording act statute, the prior grantee (here, A) wins in a title dispute under the common law default rule of FTFR.

Types Of Recording Act Statutes

There are three types of recording act statutes. A **race statute** awards superior rights to the grantee who first records the written deed or other instrument of conveyance from the grantor. In a race statute jurisdiction, notice of a prior transfer of an interest in the property is irrelevant.[1]

A **notice statute** awards superior title to a subsequent grantee who lacked notice of the grantor's prior transfer of another interest in the property. A **race-notice statute** is just like a notice statute in

---

1. Very few states today use a race statute for fee titles. Some states use a race statute for mortgages, but have another type of record- ing statute (notice or race-notice) for conveyances of other property interests.

that it requires the subsequent grantee to lack notice of the grantor's prior transfer of an interest in the property. But a race-notice statute adds an additional requirement—that the subsequent grantee B who lacked notice of the grantor O's prior transfer *also* must record the written deed or other instrument of conveyance from the grantor O *before* the prior grantee A records.

Analyzing Recording Act Problems

Recording act problems raise three potential issues:

■ Whether the subsequent grantee B qualifies for protection under the recording act statute;

■ Whether the subsequent grantee B had notice of the prior conveyance to A; and

■ (For race-notice statutes only), whether the subsequent grantee B recorded first before the prior grantee A.

Subsequent Grantees Eligible For Protection

In analyzing a recording act problem, the first issue is whether the subsequent[2] grantee B qualifies for protection under the statute. Most recording acts require that the grantee must be a purchaser for value. Unless the statute specifies otherwise, a donee is *not* eligible for protection under the recording act. Therefore, absent explicit statutory protection, the claim of a subsequent donee is determined under the common law rule of FTFR.[3]

A void deed in the purchaser's chain of title will eliminate the protection of a recording act. If there is a void deed (i.e., the deed has a forged signature or was a testamentary transfer) in the chain

---

2. Remember, to take advantage of a recording act statute, the grantee's interest must have been acquired after the interest of the competing claimant. In determining which grantee is first and which grantee is second, beware of situations where the actual conveyance is *time-delayed*. For example, the grantee does not acquire a property interest under a deed where the grantee's name has been left blank until the grantee's name is written in on the deed. A deed placed in a safe deposit box accessible by both the grantor and the grantee does not transfer title until the grantee removes the deed from the box. *See supra*, Chapter 7, Real Estate Transactions.

3. *See supra*, Chapter 2, Gifts.

of title, *all* purchasers that follow after a void deed similarly hold void title and are *not* protected by the recording act. (They might, however, have acquired superior title by virtue of adverse possession.)

Jurisdictions are divided concerning the extent of recording act protection for a subsequent purchaser who makes a partial payment,[4] but who does not pay the full purchase price before learning of the prior grantee's competing claim. The **majority rule** is that the subsequent partial payment purchaser is only protected up to the amount actually paid prior to learning of the competing claim. Under the majority rule, generally the court awards title to the property to the prior grantee, but the subsequent purchaser is entitled to receive restitution of the amount paid from the prior grantee.[5] The **minority rule** is to protect fully the subsequent partial payment purchaser, who retains title to the disputed property.[6]

A subsequent purchaser may fail to qualify for protection under the recording act statute if the purchaser accepts a quitclaim deed from the grantor. Again, jurisdictions are divided. The **majority rule** is that a purchaser who accepts a quitclaim deed qualifies for protection under the recording act. The **minority rule**

---

4. The partial payment could result from an installment sale contract arrangement, or from seller financing where the buyer gives the seller a partial payment and a promissory note for the balance of the purchase price.

5. Occasionally, the court will award title to the subsequent purchaser, but subject to a lien for the balance of the purchase price. Or, the court can physically divide the property and award title to a proportionate share of the property to the prior grantee and the subsequent partial payment purchaser.

6. The minority rule has the public policy advantage of placing the risk of loss (here, the loss of title to the unique parcel of real estate that is the subject of the dispute) on the party who is able to avoid the problem at the lowest cost. Here, the lowest cost avoider is the prior grantee, who could have prevented the dispute from arising by promptly recording and thereby providing notice of the conveyance to subsequent purchasers. The minority rule also avoids drawing an arbitrary distinction between a purchaser who finances the purchase from a bank and the purchaser who uses seller financing. In both instances, the subsequent purchaser makes a partial down payment and gives the lender a promissory note for the balance of the price.

is that a subsequent purchaser who accepts a quitclaim is not protected under the recording act.[7]

Recording acts differ concerning whether a creditor who holds a lien[8] or mortgage on the real estate qualifies as a "purchaser" who is protected. Modernly, most jurisdictions protect the creditor's lien or mortgage and give the subsequent lien or mortgage superior priority over a prior unrecorded transfer of title[9] or a prior unrecorded lien or mortgage.

Finally, recording acts only protect a subsequent purchaser against a prior conveyance of title or an encumbrance by a written instrument that is capable of being recorded, but is not recorded. A prior conveyance or encumbrance that is *not* accomplished via a recordable instrument, but rather arises by operation of law, is outside the scope of protection of the recording act system. One example of such an "unrecordable" conveyance is the situation where the lender obtains and records a mortgage on the property, but the borrower's title previously has been transferred by operation of law to an adverse possessor. Other examples are short-term leases (not required to be in writing under the Statute of Frauds), implied-by-law easements and prescriptive easements.[10] If the prior conveyance is accomplished by operation of law without a recordable written instrument, it is outside the scope of protection of the recording act, and the dispute must be resolved under the common law default rule of FTFR.

---

7. The rationale for the minority rule is that the subsequent purchaser who accepts a quitclaim deed from the grantor has *inquiry notice* (based on the quitclaim deed's lack of covenants concerning the title) that something is amiss, and therefore cannot qualify for protection under the recording act.

8. Note that the lien must have "attached" to the real estate for the creditor to be protected by the recording act. *See supra*, Chapter 5, Co–Ownership. A judgment creditor whose lien has not attached to the debtor's real estate is only a general creditor. General creditors are not protected by recording act statutes.

9. The transferee in this situation would hold title subject to repayment of the subsequent creditor's lien or mortgage. If the subsequent creditor's lien or mortgage is not repaid, the subsequent creditor can bring a judicial foreclosure action and force a public sale of the property. *See supra*, Chapter 5, Co–Ownership.

10. For a discussion of implied-by-law easement and prescriptive easements, refer to Chapter 9, Easements, Profits, Real Covenants and Equitable Servitudes.

Notice Of The Prior Conveyance

To qualify for protection under both a notice and a race-notice recording act, the subsequent purchaser must be without actual, constructive, or inquiry notice of the prior conveyance. Of the three possible types of notice, constructive notice is the most problematic.

Issues of constructive notice arise because merely *filing* a document in the records system does not necessarily mean that the document is *recorded* so that a subsequent purchaser is deemed to have notice of the document. The rule of thumb courts use to determine whether a filed document has been validly recorded is whether someone doing a reasonable and prudent title search would find the document. Examples of deeds that are filed in a grantor-grantee index, but are not considered to be "recorded" are:

- Deeds with "Mother Hubbard" clauses;[11]

- Deeds with misspelled names; and

- So-called "wild" deeds that are not connected into the chain of title in a grantor-grantee index system because a prior deed has not been recorded.[12]

If the jurisdiction has a tract index system, deeds and other instruments of conveyance are recorded by the legal description of the affected parcel, not by the names of the grantor and the

---

11. A Mother Hubbard clause is a provision in a deed that purports to convey title to or a lesser property interest in "all of the grantor's property located in" a specific county. A Mother Hubbard clause, which substitutes for a specific description of the property or properties affected by the deed, is not considered recorded because the indexing system used by title searchers relies on specific property descriptions.

12. Generally, a deed is "wild" because a prior deed in the chain of title has not been

recorded. In one case, the court ruled that a prior deed, which *was* filed, was deemed to be *not recorded* due to a missing acknowledgment of the grantor's signature. *See* WILLIAM B. STOEBUCK & DALE A WHITMAN, THE LAW OF PROPERTY 889 (3d ed. 2000) (discussing *Messersmith v. Smith*, 60 N.W.2d 276 (N.D. 1953), as an "extreme" example) ("Stoebuck & Whitman"). Prior conveyances that are recorded too early or too late also may not give notice to a subsequent bona fide purchaser. *See id.* at 895–96.

grantee. Thus, deeds with misspelled names or wild deeds that are filed in a tract index are considered to be recorded.

Deeds that are filed in either a grantor-grantee index or a tract index, but are not considered to be recorded, arise in two situations. First, a deed with a Mother Hubbard-type property description that is filed in a tract index system is not considered to be recorded because the Mother Hubbard clause does not provide the tract-specific property description that is necessary for indexing. Second, a deed that is filed, but that has a missing or obviously defective acknowledgment of the grantor's signature by a notary public, is not considered to be recorded in either a grantor-grantee index or a tract index.

Deeds to adjacent parcels that originate from a common grantor also raise constructive notice issues. When the grantor severs and conveys smaller parcels of the large tract over time, the deeds conveying the smaller parcels may contain covenants that restrict the remaining parcels retained by the grantor. If the grantor later conveys one of these retained parcels, the courts are divided concerning whether the purchaser has constructive notice of the restrictions on the parcel that are absent in the purchaser's deed, but are contained in the prior series of deeds from the common grantor that convey the adjacent parcels.[13]

Issues of inquiry notice can arise based on a physical inspection of the property or references to prior unrecorded conveyances contained in recorded instruments in the subject property's chain of title.[14] Current possession or use of the property by someone other than the purported grantor that is visible, open, exclusive and unambiguous gives inquiry notice to the grantee.[15] This standard for inquiry notice based on the possession or use of the

---

13. *See* Stoebuck & Whitman, *supra*, at 896 & nn. 16–17.

14. Most courts hold that if the instrument containing the reference is itself not entitled to be recorded (perhaps due to a missing or

obviously defective acknowledgment), the instrument does not give inquiry notice of its contents. *See id.* at 886 & n. 47.

15. Stoebuck & Whitman, *supra*, at 885.

property by someone other than the grantor varies widely in application. The outcome in each case depends heavily on the unique factual circumstances.[16]

Recording First By The Subsequent Grantee (Race–Notice Statute Only)

In a race-notice statute jurisdiction, the subsequent purchaser must record his or her deed or other written instrument of conveyance before the prior grantee records in order to prevail under the recording act. Again, a document that is filed in the records system is not necessarily recorded for purposes of satisfying this requirement. If the jurisdiction has only a grantor-grantee index system, a wild deed is not deemed recorded until the last missing link in the chain of title has been recorded.

More Remote Grantees Protected by the Shelter Rule

Title disputes based on recordable written instruments can arise not only between two grantees from a common grantor, but also may involve a more remote grantee in the chain of title that leads back to a common grantor. To illustrate, assume that the grantor O conveyed title to Blackacre first to A and then later to B. B then conveyed title to Blackacre to C. In this example, C is a more remote grantee who is one transaction removed from the original "split" in the chain of title that originated from O.

A more remote grantee such as C who becomes embroiled in a title dispute may independently qualify as a bona fide purchaser ("BFP") whose title is protected under the jurisdiction's recording act from prior unrecorded conveyances. But if C cannot independently qualify for protection as a BFP under the recording act,[17] C's title acquired from B may still be protected under the **shelter rule**. The shelter rule is illustrated by the diagram on the next page.

---

16. *See id.* (contrasting Miller v. Green, 264 Wis. 159, 58 N.W.2d 704 (1953) with Wineberg v. Moore, 194 F.Supp. 12 (N.D. Cal. 1961)).

17. For example, C may not be eligible for protection because C is a donee, or C may not be able to record before a prior grantee in a race-notice jurisdiction.

The Shelter Rule

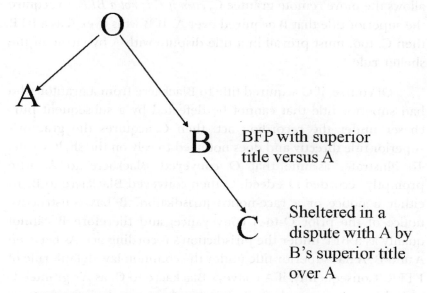

O

A

B BFP with superior title versus A

C Sheltered in a dispute with A by B's superior title over A

The shelter rule provides that a person (here, our more remote grantee C) who acquires the property *from a grantor who qualifies as a BFP* (here, B) acquires the same rights as the grantor B would have in a dispute over title to the property. In other words, if B prevails in a title dispute with A because B qualifies as a BFP under a recording act, then B's superior claim of title "shelters" C in a dispute with A. If B wins over A, then as B's grantee C, too, must win over A.

The shelter rule can be applied in both a notice and a race-notice jurisdiction. The purpose of the shelter rule is fairness to the person who is a BFP protected by the recording act.[18] It does the BFP (here, B) no good to be protected under the recording act if B is not able to pass on paramount title to the property to the more remote grantee, C.

Note carefully that if the shelter rule applies, C can have actual knowledge of a prior adverse conveyance of title to the

---

18. *See* Stoebuck & Whitman, *supra*, at 889.

property (here, the prior conveyance of title from O to A) and yet still prevail in a title dispute with A. In other words, the shelter rule allows the more remote grantee C, *even if C is not a BFP*, to acquire the superior title that B acquired over A. If B wins over A as a BFP, then C, too, must prevail in a title dispute with A by virtue of the shelter rule.

Of course, if C acquired title to Blackacre from a grantor who had superior title that cannot be defeated by a subsequent purchaser under the recording act, then C acquires the grantor's superior title directly and does not need to rely on the shelter rule. To illustrate, assume that O conveyed Blackacre to A, who promptly recorded O's deed. O then conveyed Blackacre to B. In either a notice or a race-notice jurisdiction, B has constructive notice of the prior O-to-A conveyance, and therefore B cannot qualify as a BFP under the jurisdiction's recording act. As between A and B, A has superior title under the common law default rule of FTFR. Consequently, if A conveys Blackacre to C, as A's grantee C must have superior title to B. To keep these two distinct situations straight, remember the following principle: The shelter rule only applies if the person seeking "shelter" has acquired title from a *subsequent* purchaser who has prevailed over a *prior* grantee by *qualifying as a BFP* under the jurisdiction's recording act.

Special Rule: Bona Fide Purchasers Who Buy From Devisees Or Heirs

A special rule applies to protect a bona fide purchaser who buys real estate from a seller who owns the property as a devisee or an intestate heir of the deceased owner's estate. In this unique situation, the devisee or intestate heir is treated as the apparent successor owner of record if there is no prior recorded conveyance of the property made by the deceased owner while the deceased owner was alive. In this situation, because the last owner of record was the deceased owner, a subsequent purchaser may buy the property from the devisee or intestate heir with confidence, knowing that the purchaser is protected from any unknown and unrecorded lifetime conveyances by the deceased prior owner.

Effect Of Marketable Title Acts

A marketable title act is a statute that limits the number of years that a title searcher must search back in time using the records system. The exact number of years varies by jurisdiction.[19] If a prior conveyance of an interest in the property is recorded before the time limit specified by the marketable title act, the subsequent purchaser takes the property free of the prior recorded interest. As a practical matter, a marketable title act requires that interests in real estate must be re-recorded within the time frame described by the statute or else the interest will be extinguished.

Title Insurance

Due to the numerous flaws in the recording act system, purchasers and lenders whose loans are secured by mortgages on real property purchase title insurance. For a one-time premium payment (paid at the closing), title insurance protects the purchaser or mortgage lender against defects in legal title that are not discoverable by a reasonable and prudent search of the records system. For example, title insurance will reimburse the purchaser or mortgage lender if title is void due to a forged deed or a testamentary transfer in the chain of title. Title insurance also protects against defects in legal title that are outside the scope of the recording act system, such as short-term oral leases not required to be in writing by the Statute of Frauds, title acquired by adverse possession, and implied and prescriptive easements.

Adverse Possession

Title acquired by adverse possession is the classic example of a defect in the subsequent purchaser's title that is outside the protection of the recording act system. Title by adverse possession arises by operation of law; therefore, no recordable written document of conveyance is available to be filed in the records system.

If the adverse possessor succeeds in satisfying the elements for acquiring title by adverse possession, the law looks backwards in

---

19. On an exam, you should assume that your title search is *not* limited in duration by a marketable title act unless the exam instructions state otherwise.

time and holds that title passed to the adverse possessor from the moment of the adverse possessor's initial entry onto the land. It is this relation-back feature of title transfer by adverse possession that thwarts the subsequent BFP. The relation-back feature of title by adverse possession can make the adverse possessor "first in time" vis-a-vis the subsequent purchaser, thereby giving the adverse possessor the superior title to the property under the common law default rule of FTFR. The key point to remember is that a recording act does not protect the subsequent BFP against prior title transfers (or encumbrances) that arise by operation of law. Even if the subsequent purchaser was without notice of the adverse possessor's claim of title, under the common law rule of FTFR the prior adverse possessor whose claim to title has been perfected always wins in a title dispute with a subsequent purchaser.

These principles apply equally to a subsequent mortgage lender who loans money to the debtor as the record owner of the property. The lender's loan is secured by a mortgage on the debtor's real estate. If title to the real estate previously has passed (by virtue of the relation-back feature) to the adverse possessor, the lender's mortgage does *not* attach to the property. In this situation, the lender has no mortgage to foreclose as security for the loan. The lender must seek repayment of the loan from the personal assets of the debtor.

The relation-back feature of title acquired by adverse possession also impacts other persons with rights or interests in the property. The adverse possessor takes title to the property subject to all encumbrances (mortgages, liens, easements, real covenants and equitable servitudes) that were already in existence as of the moment of initial entry. The adverse possessor takes title to the property free of any encumbrances that were granted to third parties by the record owner of the property after the moment of initial entry.

The adverse possessor does not acquire the title of any person who holds a future interest in the property. The holder of a future interest by definition is not entitled to present possession and use of the property. Therefore, the statute of limitations for perfection of title due to adverse possession does not run against a future interest holder when the adverse possessor first enters the property. Once the holder of the future interest is entitled to take present possession of the property, then the statute of limitations begins to run against the former future interest holder.

Elements Of Title Acquired By Adverse Possession

To establish title by adverse possession, the adverse possessor must:

- make an *actual entry* onto the property,

- that is *open and notorious*,

- *adverse* (or *"hostile"*), and

- *continuous* for the statute of limitations period.

Each of these elements is explained below.

The first moment of **actual entry** is important because it marks the point in time when the statute of limitations begins to run *and* the point in time that title will transfer if the adverse possessor successfully satisfies all of the required elements. The adverse possessor need not enter onto every inch of the property. Entry onto part of a parcel is deemed constructive entry and claimed possession of the entire parcel. The adverse possessor's entry and occupation of the parcel must, however, be exclusive in the sense that the adverse possessor cannot be sharing possession of the property with the owner or with members of the general public.

The purpose of the **open and notorious** element is to give the owner reasonable notice of the adverse possessor's occupation of the property. Courts look to the nature and type of the property to ascertain whether the actions of the adverse possessor are consistent with how an owner would use and possess the property. If the adverse possessor is using the property in the same manner as a typical owner would, then the true owner has notice of the adverse possessor's potential claim.

Courts differ on how to interpret the **adverse ("hostile")** element. Some jurisdictions apply an objective standard and find that the adverse possessor's actions are hostile if the occupation and use of the property is without the permission of the owner. Under the objective standard, the adverse possessor's state of mind or intent is irrelevant. Other jurisdictions apply a "good faith" subjective standard that, in addition to being without permission from the owner, requires that the adverse possessor must be acting on a subjective good faith belief that the adverse possessor is in fact entitled to possession of the property. A few jurisdictions apply a "bad faith" subjective standard where the adverse possessor must believe that the land belongs to someone else and yet intend to claim and possess it against the owner.

Under either the objective or the good faith subjective standard, an adverse possessor who holds color of title satisfies the hostility element. Color of title is a term of art that describes the situation where the adverse possessor has a written deed that purports to convey title to the property to the adverse possessor, but for some reason the deed does not in fact convey good title.

Occupation of the property **continuously for the statute of limitations period** is not as difficult as it might seem due to the possibility of tacking of the limitations period among successive owners or successive adverse possessors. The key to successful tacking is a voluntary transfer (either during life or at death) of an estate in the land between successive owners, or a voluntary transfer (again, either during life or at death) of an estate in the land or physical possession of the property between successive adverse possessors.

In analyzing the statute of limitations element, beware of the possibility that the statute of limitations may be tolled by statute if the owner is disabled at the moment of initial entry. An unlawful ouster of one adverse possessor by another adverse possessor also tolls the statute of limitations. The Checklist at the end of Chapter 8 elaborates these and other fact-specific, narrow issues that may arise as part of an adverse possession analysis.

Documenting Title Acquired By Adverse Possession

To document the acquisition of title by adverse possession, the adverse possessor must file a quiet title action against the current owner of the property. If the court rules for the adverse possessor, the judicial decree declaring that the adverse possessor holds title to the property is recorded. Again, title acquired by adverse possession is deemed to be transferred back in time as of the initial moment of actual entry by the adverse possessor.

RECORDING ACTS AND ADVERSE POSSESSION CHECKLIST

With the above review in mind, the Recording Acts and Adverse Possession Checklist is presented below.

A. **TITLE ACQUIRED BY A WRITING FROM A COMMON GRANTOR.** If the same grantor conveyed title to or a property interest in the same real estate via a written document to more than one grantee, proceed to Part B. If the dispute involves a remote grantee, proceed to Part C. If a competing claimant's title is based on adverse possession and not a written conveyance from the grantor, proceed to Part D.

B. **DISPUTES BETWEEN TWO IMMEDIATE GRANTEES FROM THE SAME GRANTOR.** Determine which grantee has the superior property right.

   1. **Is A Grantee's Deed Void?** If one grantee's claim is based on a void deed (forged signature or testamentary transfer), the other grantee who has a valid deed from the common grantor automatically has the superior property right.

      a. **Subsequent Purchasers?** Any subsequent purchasers in a chain of title that follows after a void deed similarly hold void title and cannot qualify as BFPs under a recording act.

      b. **Adverse Possession?** Proceed to Part D to determine if the grantee whose claim to title rests on a void deed nevertheless has acquired title by adverse possession.

   2. **Which Grantee Acquired A Property Right First?** Assuming there are no void deeds in either grantee's chain

of title, under the common law rule of FTFR, the grantee who acquired his property right first through a conveyance from the grantor has the superior property right unless the second grantee is protected as a bona fide purchaser under the jurisdiction's recording act.

    a. **Time Of Delivery.** Title (or a lesser property interest) is acquired by a grantee when the deed or other written instrument at conveyance is delivered. Recording is not necessary for or relevant to the determination of when the grantee acquired the property right.

    b. **Deed Omits Grantee's Name.** If the grantee's name in the deed is left blank, title is not conveyed until the grantee's name is inserted on the deed. A delay in inserting the grantee's name could make a prior conveyance second in time.

3. **Is The Second Grantee A Bona Fide Purchaser?** Assuming the first grantee is FTFR, determine if the second grantee from the common grantor qualifies as a BFP who is protected under the jurisdiction's recording act. **If yes**, the subsequent purchaser has the superior property right over the first grantee.

    a. **Is The Second Grantee Eligible For Protection Under The Recording Act?** Determine if the second grantee is eligible for protection using Parts B.3.a.i through 3.a.iv below.

        i. **Donee?** If the second grantee is a donee, determine whether the applicable recording act protects donees. **If no**, the first grantee has the superior property right under the common law rule of FTFR.

        ii. **Partial Payment Subsequent Purchaser?** Protection under the jurisdiction's recording act may not be available for a subsequent purchaser who paid less than the full purchase price, depending on the rule the jurisdiction follows.

- **Majority Rule.** The subsequent partial payment purchaser is protected up to the amount paid, but superior title to the property is awarded to the prior grantee.

- **Minority Rule.** Superior title to the property is awarded to the subsequent partial payment purchaser.

iii. **Subsequent Purchaser Acquires Title By Quitclaim Deed?** Protection under the recording act may not be available if the subsequent purchaser acquired title by a quitclaim deed, depending on the rule the jurisdiction follows.

- **Majority Rule.** A grantee who accepts a quitclaim deed is eligible for protection under the recording act.

- **Minority Rule.** A grantee who accepts a quitclaim deed is not eligible for protection under the recording act because a quitclaim deed's lack of title covenants provides inquiry notice of a potential prior unrecorded conveyance.

iv. **BFP Is A Subsequent Creditor?** A subsequent creditor who is a mortgagee or a judgment lien holder is eligible for protection as a BFP under a recording act. Recording act protection is not limited solely to purchasers of the fee title to the real estate.

b. **Did The Second Grantee Have Notice Of The Prior Unrecorded Conveyance?** In a notice jurisdiction, the second grantee without notice of the prior conveyance holds the superior property right. In a race-notice jurisdiction, the second grantee must record before the first grantee in order to have the superior property right. If the jurisdiction has a race-notice statute, proceed to Part B.3.c of the checklist for further analysis after completing Part B.3.b below.

i. **Actual Notice?** Did the second grantee know of the first unrecorded conveyance prior to the second grantee's acquisition of a property interest in the real estate? **If yes**, the second grantee has actual notice of the prior conveyance and loses in a dispute with the first grantee.

ii. **Constructive (Record) Notice?** If the jurisdiction has only a grantor-grantee index system, the following filed documents are not "recorded" and therefore do not give the second grantee constructive notice of the prior conveyance:

- **A document with a Mother Hubbard clause** that does not provide a legal description of the property.

- **A document with a misspelled name** of the grantor or grantee.

- **A document with a missing or obviously defective acknowledgment** of the grantor's signature by a notary public.

- **A "wild" deed** that is not connected into the chain of grantor-to-grantee title.

- **Covenants in prior deeds to adjacent parcels originating from a common grantor.** Courts are divided whether the covenants in prior recorded deeds to adjacent parcels provide notice of a restriction on the grantee's property. (The split of authority exists regardless of whether the jurisdiction uses a grantor-grantee or a tract index system.)

- **Tract index system.** A deed with a Mother Hubbard clause or a missing or obviously defective acknowledgment of the grantor's signature that is filed in a tract index system is not recorded and does not provide notice to the second grantee.

iii. **Inquiry Notice?** Based on the circumstances, should the second grantee have inquired into the possibility of a prior unrecorded conveyance of title or a lesser property interest in the real estate?

- **Physical inspection?** Would a physical inspection of the property have revealed a visible, open, exclusive and unambiguous use of the premises by someone other than the grantor? **If yes**, inquiry notice exists.

- **References to prior unrecorded conveyances?** Was there a reference in a recorded deed in the chain of title to a prior unrecorded conveyance? **If yes**, inquiry notice of the prior unrecorded conveyance exists.

c. **(Race–Notice Jurisdiction Only) Did The Second Grantee Record First?**

    i. **Filed But Not Recorded?** Determine if the second grantee's deed contains one of the following problems that would prevent the second grantee's deed, even though filed, from being recorded.

- **Mother Hubbard clause** (not recorded in any type of index).

- **Misspelled name of grantor or grantee** (not recorded in a grantor-grantee index system; recorded in a tract index system).

- **Missing or defective acknowledgment** by a notary public of the grantor's signature (not recorded in any type of index).

    ii. **Is The Second Grantee's Deed Wild?** If the jurisdiction has only a grantor-grantee index system, the second grantee's filed deed is not recorded until the last missing link in the chain of title is recorded.

C. **DISPUTES INVOLVING A MORE REMOTE GRANTEE.** If one of the parties to the dispute is a more remote grantee in a chain of title originating from a common grantor, determine first if the more remote grantee independently qualifies as a BFP protected by the jurisdiction's recording act under Part B above. If the more remote grantee does not independently qualify as a BFP, proceed to Part C below.

1. **Who Did The More Remote Grantee Acquire Title From?**

    a. **Title Acquired From Or Through A BFP.** Did the more remote grantee acquire title from or through a BFP who has superior title by virtue of the jurisdiction's recording act? **If yes**, the shelter rule protects the more remote grantee's title against the claim of a prior grantee in another chain of title stemming from a common grantor.

        i. **Shelter Rule Protects Donees.** The shelter rule protects a more remote grantee who is a donee.

        ii. **Shelter Rule Protects Even A More Remote Grantee With Notice Of Another's Claim.** The more remote grantee's title is protected under the shelter rule even if the more remote grantee has notice of a prior grantee's competing claim.

        iii. **Shelter Rule Extends Down The Chain Of Title From A BFP.** The shelter rule applies to any remote grantee in the BFP's subsequent chain of title.

    b. **Title Acquired From Person With Superior Title Under FTFR.** If the more remote grantee acquired title from a grantee who is FTFR and who can defeat the claims of a later purchaser from a common grantor, then the more remote grantee acquires superior title directly from the grantee who has superior title and does not rely on the shelter rule.

D. **CLAIMS BASED ON ADVERSE POSSESSION.** A claim of superior title based on adverse possession cannot be defeated by a recording act statute. Determine if the adverse possessor has satisfied the elements for perfecting title by adverse possession, and if so, when title by adverse possession transferred by operation of law based on the moment of initial entry.

1. Elements For Title By Adverse Possession. To perfect title by adverse possession, the adverse possessor must make an actual entry onto the property that is open and notorious, adverse ("hostile"), and continuous for the statute of limitations period.

    a. Moment Of Actual Entry. Determine when the adverse possessor first entered the owner's property. This begins the statute of limitations and marks the point in time that title is transferred if the adverse possessor's claim is successful.

        i. Constructive Possession. Entry onto part of the owner's land may be treated as constructive possession of all of the owner's land, so long as the adverse possessor is not sharing possession of the property with the owner or members of the general public.

        ii. Joint Adverse Possessors. Two persons acting in concert can jointly acquire title by adverse possession as tenants in common (e.g., a husband and wife).

    b. Open And Notorious. Possession is open and notorious if it is visible and would give a prudent owner reasonable notice of the adverse possessor's occupation of the property. The touchstone test is whether the adverse possessor is acting as an owner. The nature and degree of the adverse possessor's use and occupation of the property as an owner must be consistent with the characteristics of the property.

    c. Adverse ("Hostile"). Jurisdictions are divided over the test used to determine if the hostility element is satisfied. An adverse possessor who acts under color of title satisfies both the objective test and the good faith subjective test.

    i. Objective Test. The objective test for hostility requires only that the adverse possessor's occupation and use of the property be without the owner's permission or consent. The adverse possessor's state of mind is irrelevant.

    ii. Subjective Tests. In addition to lacking the permission or consent of the owner to occupy and use the property under the good faith subjective test, the adverse possessor also must have a good faith belief that he holds title to the property. Knowing trespassers (squatters) can never establish title by adverse possession in a jurisdiction that follows the good faith subjective test. Under the bad faith subjective test, the adverse possessor must be a knowing trespasser.

    iii. Color Of Title. Is the adverse possessor relying in good faith on a written document that purports to convey title to him? **If yes**, the hostility element is satisfied under both the objective and good faith subjective tests.

d. Continuous For The Statute Of Limitations Period. Given the characteristics and nature of the property, did the adverse possessor use and occupy the property as an owner would have done throughout the statute of limitations period?

    i. Tolling For Disability. Does the jurisdiction have a statute that extends the statute of limitations if the owner has a disability when the adverse possessor first enters the property?

- **If owner is disabled under the statute at the moment of initial entry,** then the statute of limitations is tolled.

- **If the owner's disability arose after the initial entry by the adverse possessor,** generally the disability statute will not toll the statute of limitations.

ii. **Tacking Adverse Possessors.** Did one adverse possessor voluntarily transfer (while alive or at death) an estate in land or physical possession of the property to a subsequent adverse possessor? **If yes**, the time of possession by the first adverse possessor is added to the time of possession by the subsequent adverse possessor.

iii. **Tacking Owners.** Did one owner voluntarily transfer an estate in land (either while alive or at death) to a subsequent owner? **If yes**, the time of adverse possession against the first owner is added to the time of adverse possession against the subsequent owner.

- **If the owner interrupts the adverse possessor's occupation of the property,** the statute of limitations is stopped, not tolled. If the adverse possessor later resumes occupying the property after an interruption by the owner, the statute of limitations starts over again from the beginning.

iv. **Effect Of Abandonment By Adverse Possessor.** Abandonment requires both the cessation of physical occupation of the property by the adverse possessor and the mental intent to cease claiming the right to possess the property. A forced interruption of possession caused by another adverse possessor does not cause an abandonment if the displaced adverse possessor still intends to claim possession of the property.

- **Unlawful ouster by another adverse possessor** tolls (but does *not* stop) the ousted adverse possessor's continuous occupation.

- **Abandonment.** Did the adverse possessor intend to abandon occupation of the property? **If yes**, then the statute of limitations is not tolled, but rather starts over again from the beginning if the adverse possessor later changes his mind and resumes occupying the property.

2. **Determine When Title Transferred To The Adverse Possessor.** If the elements for title acquired by adverse possession are satisfied, title transfers by operation of law to the adverse possessor as of the moment of the initial entry onto the owner's land.

   a. **Impact On Easements And Covenants?** The adverse possessor acquires title to the property subject to any easements or covenants that existed at the moment of the initial entry, but free of any easements or covenants that arose after the initial entry.

   b. **Impact On Future Interests?** If ownership of the property is divided into present and future interests, the adverse possessor acquires only the present interest and does not acquire the future interest in the property.

c. **Impact On Mortgagees and Judgment Lien Creditors?** The adverse possessor acquires title to the property subject to any mortgages or judgment liens that were attached to the property at the moment of initial entry, but free of any mortgages or judgment liens that attached to the property after the initial entry.

d. **Impact On Subsequent Purchasers?** Subsequent bona fide purchasers are not protected by the recording act from a prior transfer of title by operation of law to an adverse possessor. The subsequent purchaser's remedy is to sue the immediate or more remote grantors for breach of deed covenants. Refer to the checklist at the end of Chapter 7 for further analysis.

ILLUSTRATIVE PROBLEMS

Here are two problems that illustrate how the Checklist can be used to resolve recording acts and adverse possession questions.

■ PROBLEM 8.1 ■

O owned Blackacre in fee simple absolute. O sold Blackacre, which was a vacant tract of land, to A by a special warranty deed for $100,000. A failed to record the O-to-A deed.

O subsequently sold Blackacre to B by a quitclaim deed for $5,000. B had actual notice of the prior O-to-A deed. B recorded the O-to-B deed.

A began bulldozing the high ground on Blackacre and trucking the excess fill dirt to the low-lying areas of the property. A also began construction on the property.

B sold Blackacre to C by a general warranty deed for $200,000. Prior to purchasing Blackacre, C inspected the property and noticed the fill dirt being removed and relocated and the new construction, but failed to take further investigative action. C recorded the B-to-C deed immediately after the closing.

A then finally recorded the O-to-A deed.

Assume that these events took place in the State of Hanover, which has a grantor-grantee index system and a notice recording act statute. In a title dispute concerning ownership of Blackacre between A and C, who wins? Does the loser have a remedy for damages?

Analysis

In a title dispute between A and C, A is FTFR under the common law rule. Therefore, A prevails over C unless C can either independently qualify as bona fide purchaser without notice under the notice recording act statute, or C is protected by the shelter rule.

On these facts, C did not have actual notice of the prior O-to-A conveyance. The O-to-A deed was not recorded when C purchased from B, so C did not have constructive notice of O's prior conveyance to A. The records system at the time C purchased from B showed a "clean" chain of title from O to B.

A court is likely to find that C had inquiry notice of the prior unrecorded conveyance to A based on two circumstances. First, the excavation and construction on the property by someone other than the grantor B constituted inquiry notice to C. Second, a court may find that the quitclaim deed from O to B gave inquiry notice to C of a prior conveyance. A minority of jurisdictions hold that the grantee of a quitclaim deed has inquiry notice of a possible prior conveyance due to the lack of covenants concerning title to the property in a quitclaim deed. Assuming that C had inquiry notice, C cannot qualify as a bona fide purchaser under the notice recording act statute.

C also cannot prevail in a title dispute with A under the shelter rule. To be protected under the shelter rule, C's grantor B must have been a bona fide purchaser protected under State of Hanover's notice recording act. Here, B is not protected because B had actual notice of the prior O-to-A conveyance. Therefore, the shelter rule does not apply to C's situation.

C's remedy is to bring a claim for damages against C's grantor B based on a breach of the deed covenants contained in the B-to-C general warranty deed. Although the title defect was caused by the prior owner O, who first conveyed Blackacre to A, the covenants in general warranty deed apply to title defects that arose *before* B acquired the property. C can sue B for a maximum of $200,000 in damages (recover the purchase price paid) for breach of the present covenants of seisin and right to convey in the B-to-C general warranty deed. Assuming that C loses in the litigation against A, C also can sue B for breach of the future covenants of warranty and quiet enjoyment in the B-to-C general warranty deed and recover the litigation expenses incurred by C in the title dispute with A.

C has no remedy against O because O gave B a quitclaim deed without any covenants concerning the quality or validity of the title being conveyed to B.

■ PROBLEM 8.2 ■

O, an elderly gentleman with no immediate family, fell and broke his hip. O's hip did not heal correctly. Unable to care for himself, O moved into an assisted living facility. Although limited to a wheelchair, O was mentally sharp as a tack and played bridge with his friends every day in the facility's dining room.

X, who worked as a waiter at the facility, overheard O telling his dining room bridge partners how much he missed spending time at his summer hunting and fishing cabin. X searched the land records system electronically and found the deed by which O originally acquired fee simple absolute title to the cabin property. X prepared a deed conveying the cabin property from O to X and forged O's signature. X's girlfriend, a notary public, acknowledged O's signature on the deed. On the face of the deed, the notary's acknowledgment was flawless. X filed the forged deed in the land records system for the county where the cabin property was located. X then hired a locksmith and changed the locks on the summer cabin so that X had a working set of keys.

X advertised the cabin property for sale on eBay and eventually sold the cabin to B, who had no notice that O's signature on the O-to-X deed was a forgery. B promptly filed the X-to-B deed in the land records system for the county where the cabin was located. B spent every summer between Memorial Day and Labor Day at the cabin. The rest of the year the cabin sat vacant. The cabin was in a remote location and the climate was too cold to enjoy the cabin except during the warm summer months.

Five years after B purchased the cabin from X, O's great-nephew Ned moved into the area. Ned began visiting O every week at the assisted living facility. In gratitude, one year after Ned began his visits O executed a deed conveying fee simple absolute title to the cabin property to Ned. Ned validly recorded the O-to-Ned deed, but did not go to see the cabin. O died eight years after B first purchased the cabin property from X. Ned visited the cabin property for the first time in June following O's death and discovered B occupying the cabin.

Assume that the jurisdiction has a race-notice recording act statute and the statute of limitations to perfect title by adverse possession is seven years. As between Ned and B, who has superior title to the cabin property?

Analysis

The deed purporting to convey title to the cabin property from O to X is void due to the forged signature of the grantor O. Because X acquired title via a void deed, X's grantee B cannot acquire good title, even though B is a bona fide purchaser without notice of the forgery who recorded before Ned under the jurisdiction's race-notice recording act. A recording act statute does not protect purchasers against a void deed in the purchaser's chain of title.

As the grantee of record from the owner O, Ned holds superior title to the cabin property unless B successfully has acquired title by adverse possession. To acquire title by adverse possession, B must actually enter the cabin property, use and possess the property in an open and notorious manner that is hostile to the owner O, and do so continuously for the seven year statute of limitations period. B first entered the cabin property on Memorial Day weekend after purchasing the cabin from X eight years ago. B appears to have used the cabin property in an open and notorious manner by occupying the cabin during the summer months. Given the cold climate and the remote location, B was not required to use and occupy the cabin year-round, but only to occupy the cabin as an owner would under the circumstances.

B occupied the cabin under color of title based on the void X-to-B deed. B's color of title satisfies the hostility requirement necessary to perfect title by adverse possession regardless of whether the jurisdiction applies the objective or the subjective test for the hostility element.

B occupied the cabin property every summer for five years while O owned the property, and for another three years while Ned owned the property. Ned never attempted to interrupt B's use and occupation until after the seven-year statute of limitations period expired. These five-year and three-year periods are tacked together because O voluntarily transferred fee simple absolute title to the cabin from O to Ned. Due to tacking between O and Ned, B is able to show an actual entry and open and notorious use of the cabin property in a hostile manner continuously for the seven year statute of limitations period. A court is likely to rule that B has successfully fulfilled the requirements to acquire title to the cabin property by adverse possession as against Ned, and award superior title to the cabin property to B.

POINTS TO REMEMBER

- If the prior conveyance is not accomplished by a recordable instrument and therefore is outside the scope of protection of the recording act statute, the dispute must be resolved under the common law default rule of FTFR.

- A donee generally is not protected under a recording act statute. Do not waste time performing a recording act analysis unless you first determine that the recording act statute actually covers a donee.

- A deed that is filed is not "recorded" unless the deed would be discoverable by a reasonable title search.

- A tract index eliminates the constructive notice problems associated with misspelled names and wild deeds.

- A recording act statute does not protect a subsequent BFP against a void deed in the BFP's chain of title. A void deed prevents even a BFP without notice of the void deed from acquiring good title to the property.

- The nature and extent of an adverse possessor's use is based on how an owner would use the property under the circumstances. Continuous use and occupation is not necessarily required to satisfy the statute of limitations.

- Knowing trespassers (squatters) can never acquire title by adverse possession in a jurisdiction that applies the subjective test for the hostility element. Adverse possessors acting under color of title can satisfy the hostility element under both the objective test and the subjective test.

CHAPTER 9

Easements, Profits, Real Covenants and Equitable Servitudes

When viewed in isolation, the technical rules governing easements, profits, real covenants and equitable servitudes are not difficult. But the cumulative mass of the rules (and all of their fine distinctions) can be overwhelming at first blush. The main challenge is learning how to recognize each of these property rights. Ask yourself: Is the property right an easement or profit (or is it a defeasible fee simple or a lease or a license instead)? Is the property right a promise that forms a real covenant or equitable servitude (or is it a negative easement instead)?

Once you have classified the property right, exam questions tend to focus on the following four major issues: (1) creation of the property right; (2) transfer of the property right; (3) the scope of use and enforcement of the property right; and (4) termination or equitable nonenforcement of the property right. Given that easements, profits, real covenants and equitable servitudes have unique rules, learning to classify the property right correctly at the outset is crucial to success on the exam.

EASEMENTS, PROFITS, REAL COVENANTS AND EQUITABLE SERVITUDES REVIEW

Initial Classification Of The Property Right

Easements, profits, real covenants and equitable servitudes are subcategories of a more general set of property rights known as servitudes. Fundamentally, servitudes involve a burden on the owner of a particular tract of land (known as the servient or burdened parcel). This burden could restrict the owner's use of his own land, require that the owner affirmatively do something that "touches and concerns" his land, or allow another person to use the owner's land.

To classify the property right at issue, focus initially on whether the right conveyed is the right for one person to enter and/or use land owned by another person, or whether the right conveyed is in the form of a promise by the owner concerning something the owner promises to do that concerns the owner's own land. This promise by the owner could be *negative* (i.e., in the form of a promise not to use the owner's own property in some fashion), or it could be *affirmative* (i.e., a promise by the owner to take action, such as to maintain or repair a wall, or a promise to pay money for services related to the land).

If the property right gives the holder the right to enter and/or use land owned by another person (a "**use right**"), then the use right must be further classified as either an easement, profit, lease or license. If the property right is a promise by the owner of the land that concerns the owner's own conduct (a "**promise-based right**"), then the promise-based right must be further classified as a real covenant or an equitable servitude (or occasionally, as one of the four types of negative easements recognized at common law).[1]

In analyzing a promise-based right that restricts the owner's own use, beware of the situation where the restriction on the owner's use of the land results from a fee simple title that is defeasible if the property is used, or not used, in a certain fashion. If the restriction on the owner's use is due to title held as a fee simple determinable, a fee simple subject to condition subsequent,

---

1. A negative easement at common law was a promise by the owner of the land not to use his own land in a way that interferes with light, air flow, or support of a structure on an adjacent parcel, or the water flow from an artificial stream.

or a fee simple subject to executory limitation, then a present and future interests analysis is required.[2]

This initial classification analysis is illustrated by the diagram below.

Classification of Servitudes

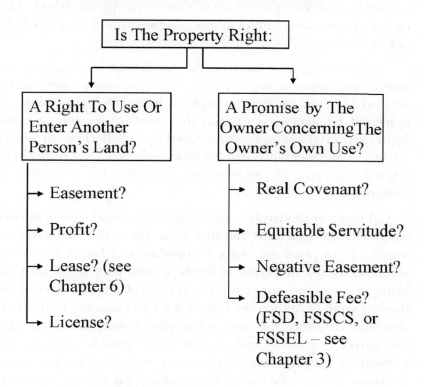

Further Classification Of Use Rights

Use rights are further classified as either an easement, a profit, a lease or a license. An **easement** is the right to enter land owned by another person. An easement right can be for the airspace above, the surface, or the subsurface of the owner's land.

---

2. *See supra*, Chapter 3, Present and Future Interests.

A **profit** is the right to enter and remove something from the owner's land that at common law was considered to be part of the land (e.g., timber, minerals, fish or game).

An express easement or a profit must be created by the parties in the form of a writing that satisfies the Statute of Frauds. To satisfy the Statute of Frauds, the writing must contain the signature of the owner of the burdened parcel as the "party to be bound." Absent a writing that satisfies the Statute of Frauds, the person who has the owner's permission to enter and/or use the owner's property holds only a **license**.

An easement also can be created without a writing by operation of law when a single parcel under common ownership is severed into two or more parcels with separate ownership. An **easement by necessity** arises if the necessity for the easement (generally, a right of ingress and egress to a landlocked parcel) was created by the severance, *and this necessity for access was created by the original severance*. All jurisdictions recognize the easement by necessity.

A majority of jurisdictions recognize a second type of implied easement, the **easement implied from prior use**. An easement implied from prior use arises by operation of law if, before the severance of the single parcel by the owner, part of the land was being used by the owner for the benefit of another part of the owner's land. (A landowner cannot hold an easement right in her own land; therefore, this prior use is called a quasi-easement). After the parcel is severed into two or more parcels with separate ownership, continuation of the prior use must be reasonably necessary for the new owner to use and enjoy the (now severed) parcel.

A **prescriptive easement** is the third type of easement that is created by operation of law. To establish a prescriptive easement right, the claimant must use the owner's land in an open, notorious and adverse (hostile) manner continuously for the statute of limitations period.

A prescriptive easement issue can arise in a stealth-like fashion on an exam. For example, assume the parties attempt to create an express easement or profit, but only create a revocable license. If the owner of the burdened parcel later revokes the license, but the ex-licensee continues to use the owner's property, the statute of limitations begins to run for the establishment of a prescriptive easement right by the ex-licensee.

Express easements and profits are illustrations of rights that are protected by a property rule[3]—a voluntary transfer of property rights between private parties. Normally, an involuntary ("forced") transfer of a property right from the owner to someone else is protected by a liability rule, which requires that the owner must be compensated for the loss of the property right by a judicial award of damages. Easements that arise by operation of law are an exception to the liability rule because no compensation is due to the owner of the parcel that becomes burdened by an easement right that arises by operation of law.

Distinguishing Licenses From Leases

A license is merely a permission given by the person in legal and exclusive possession of the land to allow the licensee to do some act that otherwise would constitute a trespass. A license is characterized by the licensee's right to the nonexclusive use of the property. In a nonexclusive use situation, the licensee shares use of the property with the owner.[4] In contrast, a **lease** transfers to the tenant the *exclusive* right to possess and use the entire property for a fixed or renewable period. If the agreement of the parties creates a lease, then a landlord and tenant analysis is required.[5]

Revocable And Irrevocable Licenses

Unlike an easement, a revocable license does not "run with the land" and bind or benefit subsequent owners. Normally, a license is

---

3. This terminology was introduced into the scholarly literature in Guido Calabresi & A. Douglas Melamed, *Property Rules, Liability Rules and Inalienability: One View of the Cathedral*, 85 Harv. L. Rev. 1089 (1971).

4. Although typically the party who grants the license is the owner of the property, a tenant in exclusive possession of the property

can grant a license for the duration of the tenancy (assuming that the tenant's lease does not expressly prohibit the granting of the license).

5. A lease arrangement incorporates the substantive rights and duties under landlord and tenant law. *See supra*, Chapter 6, Landlord and Tenant.

revocable by the owner who grants the license right. There are two situations where a court may find that a license is irrevocable. The first situation is where a license to enter the owner's property is coupled with a profit right. The profit right is worthless unless the holder of the profit has the ability to enter the land and remove the items of nature that are the subject of the profit right.

The second situation is where a court applies estoppel principles to prevent the owner's revocation of the license based on the licensee's reasonable and detrimental reliance on the license. A license that is irrevocable due to estoppel functions like a permanent easement right, and binds subsequent owners of the burdened parcel.

Further Classification of Promise–Based Rights

Promise-based rights are further classified as either a real covenant, equitable servitude or negative easement. **Real covenants** and **equitable servitudes** are similar in that both involve a *common promise* by and among a group of adjacent landowners that *mutually binds, burdens and benefits* all of the landowners in the group. The differences between a real covenant and an equitable servitude lie in the elements necessary to create each type of property right. The elements necessary to create a real covenant are more numerous and onerous to prove than the required elements for an equitable servitude.

Real covenants and equitable servitudes also differ in the method by which each right is enforced. Real covenants may be enforced by a damages claim. Equitable servitudes can only be enforced by an injunction. These distinctions are discussed in more detail later in Chapter 9.

Negative Easements

Most modern easement rights are "affirmative" in the sense that the holder of the easement has an affirmative right to enter or perform an act on land owned by another person. A so-called **negative easement** forbids the owner of the servient parcel from using his own land in some way.

To distinguish between a negative easement and a real covenant or equitable servitude, focus on whether the promise made by the owner of the burdened parcel is made *unilaterally* by the burdened owner, or whether the promise is *mutually binding on, benefits, and burdens* two or more adjacent landowners. A unilateral promise by the burdened landowner to restrict the use of his own land in a way that benefits only an adjacent landowner is classified as a negative easement.

For exam purposes, the significance of properly distinguishing between a negative easement and a real covenant or equitable servitude lies in the elements necessity for creation and enforcement of the property right. A negative easement is an express easement that must be created by a writing that satisfies the Statute of Frauds. A negative easement is enforceable and the burden is binding on subsequent owners of the servient parcel *without* proving the cumbersome elements for enforcement of the promise as a real covenant or an equitable servitude.

Negative easements arose in response to the Industrial Revolution as part of the English common law. To protect their land from adjacent industrial development, landowners would agree to sell part of their estate only if the portion sold was burdened by a negative easement that prohibited the new owner (or any subsequent owner) from using the property in a way that interfered with the seller's use and enjoyment of the retained adjacent dominant parcel. Eventually, the English common law courts recognized the following four types of negative easements:

- Blocking windows of the dominant parcel owner (interference with light);

- Interfering with air flow in a defined channel (interference with air);

- Removing the lateral or subsurface support of the dominant parcel owner's adjacent building (interference with support); and

- Interfering with the water flow in an artificial stream across the dominant parcel owner's land (interference with an artificial stream flow).

American courts generally have been reluctant to recognize unilateral negative easements[6] beyond the four types recognized by English common law. Unilateral negative easements are viewed as hindering economic development without the perceived benefit of mutually binding restrictions on a group of adjacent landowners.[7]

What appears to be a unilateral negative easement may actually be a situation where the owner of the land holds title in the form of a **defeasible fee simple**. To distinguish between a negative easement and title held as a defeasible fee simple, focus on the consequence of a violation of the use restraint described in the deed. If the violation of the use restraint results in an automatic or discretionary forfeiture of the owner's title, the use restraint is not a servitude at all. Rather, the owner holds some type of defeasible fee simple that requires a present and future interests analysis.[8]

Creation, Transfer and Scope of Easements and Profits

Once a property right is identified as an easement or profit, the next step is to analyze potential issues arising from the:

■ creation of the easement or profit;

■ transfer of the easement or profit right;

■ scope of use of the easement or profit; or

■ termination of the easement or profit.

---

6. Occasionally, a document that creates a real covenant may describe the arrangement as a "reciprocal negative easement agreement." The "reciprocal" reference means that all parties to the agreement are *mutually* agreeing to restrict the use of their land in some way. Do not be fooled by the document's label. A promise that *mutually binds and benefits* a group of adjacent owners is either a real covenant or an equitable servitude, not a negative easement.

7. American courts have recognized the following types of modern negative easements: an unobstructed view of San Francisco Bay; an unobstructed solar panel; facade historical

preservation; primary residence only use; and certain conservation easements where authorized by state statute.

8. Recall that the three types of defeasible fee simples are the fee simple determinable, the fee simple subject to condition subsequent, and the fee simple subject to executory limitation. *See supra*, Chapter 3, Present and Future Interests. If a fee simple subject to executory limitation is created, the future shifting executory interest must be analyzed under the Rule Against Perpetuities. *See supra*, Chapter 4, The Rule Against Perpetuities.

Creation of Express Easements and Profits

An express easement or profit must be created by a writing that satisfies the Statue of Frauds. A grantor may always retain an easement right as part of the deed that conveys the grantor's land to the grantee. If the grantor desires to create an easement right to the property being conveyed in favor of a third party (a so-called "stranger to the deed"), the **majority common law rule** is that two separate deeds must be used. Under the majority common law rule, the grantor must first deed the easement right to the third party. The grantor must use a second deed to convey the parcel, now burdened by the third party's easement right, to the grantee.

Transfer Of Express Easements And Profits

The rules governing the transfer of the burden of an express appurtenant easement,[9] an easement in gross,[10] or a profit are the same. The burden of an express easement or profit transfers automatically with ownership of the burdened parcel. If the new owner of the burdened parcel is a bona fide purchaser, the purchaser acquires title subject to the burden of the easement or profit so long as the purchaser had notice[11] of the express easement or profit right.

The rules governing the transfer of the benefit for an express easement or a profit vary. The benefit of an appurtenant easement transfers automatically with the transfer of title to the benefitted parcel, even if the new owner lacks notice of the benefit. The

9. An appurtenant easement is an easement where the benefit is attached to a particular parcel of land (not to a person). To determine if the easement is appurtenant, look for the "magic words" traditionally associated with the creation of an appurtenant easement. If the writing states that the easement is being conveyed to the grantee *"and [his/its] heirs, successors and assigns"* and that the easement is being conveyed *"for the benefit of"* a specific parcel, then the easement is appurtenant. If

the writing lacks these magic words, the easement can be appurtenant only if the parties' intent to benefit a parcel of land (and not a person) is clearly indicated by the writing that creates the easement.

10. An easement in gross is an easement where the benefit is given to a particular person, and does not attach to a parcel of land.

11. *See supra*, Chapter 8, Recording Acts and Adverse Possession.

benefit of an easement in gross flows to a person (which could be a corporate entity), not to a particular parcel. Therefore, the benefit of an easement in gross must be transferred from one person to another using a written assignment that satisfies the Statute of Frauds.

There is a split of authority concerning whether the owner of the burdened parcel must consent to the assignment of the benefit of an easement in gross. The **majority common law rule** adopted by the *Restatement of Property* is that if the writing creating the easement in gross is silent concerning transfer of the benefit, the benefit is transferrable without the consent of the owner of the burdened parcel only if the benefit is commercial in character.[12] The benefit of an easement in gross is considered to be commercial in character if it has primarily an economic purpose.

The **minority common law rule** adopted by the *Restatement (Third) of Servitudes* is that if the writing is silent, the benefit of the easement in gross is presumed to be assignable. A limited exception applies for the benefit of an easement in gross that is "highly personal" in nature. For example, if the easement in gross is for recreational use of another person's land (such as bird-watching or hunting or fishing), then the easement in gross is presumed *not* to be assignable without the consent of the owner of the burdened parcel.

Although the benefit of a profit always is held in gross by a person, the rule governing the transfer of the benefit of a profit is different than for the benefit of an easement in gross. If the writing creating the profit is silent concerning transfer of the benefit, the benefit is transferrable without the consent of the owner of the burdened parcel. To be validly transferred, the benefit of the profit must be assigned from one person to another in the form of a writing that satisfies the Statute of Frauds.

---

12. Of course, if the writing that created the easement in gross expressly prohibits or per- mits the transfer of the benefit, then the parties' written intent controls.

Division Of Express Easements And Profits

The term "division" refers to the situation where the benefit of an express easement or a profit is being transferred to more than one parcel (appurtenant easement) or person (easement in gross or profit). Again, there are different rules for an appurtenant easement, an easement in gross and a profit. The rules described below are the default rules that apply when the writing that created the express easement or profit is silent concerning the divisibility of the benefit. Of course, if the parties explicitly address the issue of division in the writing that creates the easement or profit right, then the parties' written expression of intent governs.

The benefit of an appurtenant easement can be divided so long as the division is reasonable and foreseeable, the use by the multiple owners is within the scope of the easement and the location of the easement is not changed. The division of an appurtenant easement is illustrated by the situation where a developer acquires a large tract of land together with an easement right across the adjacent owner's land for ingress and egress. Subject to the above criteria, the developer may subdivide the tract and sell off individual lots, with each lot owner receiving the benefit of the appurtenant easement right across the adjacent owner's land for ingress and egress.

The divisibility of an easement in gross depends on whether the holder of the benefit has the exclusive right to use the owner's property for purposes of the easement. If the benefit of the easement in gross is exclusive, then the holder may divide and transfer the benefit to multiple parties, so long as the scope of the easement is not exceeded. If the benefit of the easement in gross is not exclusive (i.e., the owner of the property has retained the right of use covered by the easement in gross), then the holder of the benefit cannot divide and transfer the benefit to multiple persons.

The benefit of a profit may be divided among multiple co-owners. There is a split of authority concerning how multiple co-owners may use the benefit of the profit. Under the **majority common law** rule adopted by the *Restatement of Property* (known as the one-stock rule), each co-owner must consent to how the profit is used and each co-owner may veto a proposed use by another co-owner. The **minority modern rule** adopted by the *Restatement (Third) of Servitudes* eliminates the restraints of the one-stock rule and substitutes a rule of reasonable use. Under the modern rule, each co-owner may use the profit right so long as the use is reasonable under the circumstances.

Scope And Misuse Of Express Easements And Profits

To determine the scope of an express easement or profit, courts look to the description in the written document that created the easement or profit right and the surrounding circumstances at the time of execution. The objective is to ascertain the intent of the parties concerning how the benefit of the easement or profit is to be used. When the use of the benefit of an express easement or profit exceeds its scope, a **misuse** occurs. A misuse is a trespass that entitles the owner of the burdened parcel to damages or injunctive relief.

Special Rules Concerning The Misuse Of Appurtenant Easements

For an appurtenant easement, some degree of change in use over time is permitted without exceeding the scope of the easement. A change in use is not a misuse if the change does not overburden the servient parcel beyond what is foreseeable and reasonable for the normal development of the dominant parcel at the time the easement was created.

Another special rule concerning misuse of an appurtenant easement arises due to the nature of the benefit, which attaches to a particular parcel of land (not a person). It is a per se misuse (regardless of the lightness of the burden on the servient parcel) to use an appurtenant easement right to access or cross any tract of land that is not part of the dominant parcel.[13]

---

13. This special rule has been applied even if the benefitted parcel and the other tract that is being accessed or crossed are held in common ownership and no additional burden is placed on the servient parcel. *See*

WILLIAM B. STOEBUCK & DALE A. WHITMAN, THE LAW OF PROPERTY 461 & nn. 14–15 (3d ed. 2000) ("Stoebuck & Whitman"). *Brown v. Voss,* 105 Wash.2d 366, 715 P.2d 514 (1986), is in accord with this special rule, but in *Voss* the

Any change in the location or width of an appurtenant easement raises potential scope and misuse issues. Under the **majority common law rule** adopted by the *Restatement of Property*, once the location or width of an appurtenant easement is fixed by the writing creating the easement right, the location or width cannot be changed without the consent of both the owner of the servient parcel and the owner of the dominant parcel. If the width of the easement is not specified in the writing, courts apply the general approach to scope issues described above (language and circumstances as indicators of intent) to determine if the expansion in width is a misuse. The **minority common law rule** adopted by the *Restatement (Third) of Servitudes* is that the owner of the servient parcel may change the location of an appurtenant easement subject to certain restrictions.

Easements Arising By Operation Of Law

There are three types of easements that arise automatically by operation of law:

- the easement implied from strict necessity;

- the easement implied from prior use; and

- the prescriptive easement.[14]

All jurisdictions recognize the easement implied from necessity and the prescriptive easement. A majority of jurisdictions recognize the easement implied from prior use.

Before reviewing the elements for creation of easements arising from operation of law, it is important to pause and focus on a key preliminary point. Consider for a moment the significance of an easement *implied by law*. Such an easement is *not* created by a document that can be filed and preserved in the recording system. Therefore, a bona fide purchaser of the servient parcel who lacks notice of an implied-by-law easement nevertheless will take the

---

court refused to grant injunctive relief on other equitable grounds.

14. Note that a negative easement can never be acquired by prescription. *See* Fontainebleau Hotel Corp. v. Forty–Five Twenty–Five, Inc., 114 So.2d 357 (Fla. App. 1959).

servient parcel subject to the burden of the easement under the common law rule of "first in time, first in right."[15]

Creation Of Implied Easements

The easement implied from strict necessity and the easement implied from prior use share the first two elements for creation in common:

- A single parcel of land is originally held in common ownership, and

- The parcel is later severed into two or more parcels with separate ownership.

Assuming these first two elements are satisfied, an easement implied from strict necessity further requires that:

- the strict necessity for the easement must arise as a result of the *original severance* of the parcel claiming the benefit of the easement.

Typically, the necessity for the easement arises because the dominant parcel, once severed, requires a way of ingress and egress across the servient parcel.

An easement implied from prior use is created differently. Assuming the first two elements above are satisfied, an easement implied from prior use requires that:

- *before* the moment of severance, part of the tract was being used[16] by the owner for the benefit of another part of the tract[17]; and

- *after* the moment of severance, continuation of this prior

---

15. *See supra*, Chapter 8, Recording Acts and Adverse Possession.

16. Courts differ on how visible or obvious this prior use by the original owner must be prior to the severance to give rise to an easement implied from prior use.

17. The prior use before the severance is called a quasi-easement because technically an owner cannot hold a true easement right in any part of his or her own land. To be a true easement, the easement right must exist with respect to land owned by someone else.

use must be reasonably[18] necessary for the new owner to enjoy the now-severed parcel.

Creation Of Prescriptive Easements

To establish a prescriptive easement, the person who claims the prescriptive easement right must have engaged in:

- An actual, open and notorious use[19] of another's land that is

- Adverse (hostile) and

- Continuous for the statute of limitations period.

As with adverse possession, to be "adverse" the use must be without the permission of the owner of the servient parcel. Jurisdictions may use either an objective test (without the owner's permission) or a subjective test (without permission and with a good faith belief that the use is lawful and not a trespass) to determine whether the person claiming the prescriptive easement acted adversely.[20] Tacking of use between persons who claim the prescriptive easement right is permitted to establish that the use has been continuous and was not interrupted during the statute of limitations period.

Time Of Creation For Easements Arising By Operation Of Law

If an implied easement is created, the easement right exists as of the moment of severance of the original single parcel into parcels with separate ownership. For a prescriptive easement right, the easement is deemed created as of the moment in time of first use.

---

18. Jurisdictions differ on the degree of necessity required to establish an easement implied from prior use. The modern trend is to require only reasonable necessity.

19. The **majority rule** is that this element is satisfied even if the use is nonexclusive and is shared with the owner of the property (e.g., both the trespasser and the owner share and use a path across the owner's property). The **minority rule** is that use must be exclusive and cannot be shared with the owner of the property. In a majority rule jurisdiction that permits a prescriptive easement right to be created based on the claimant's shared use with the owner of the property, the owner usually argues (based on the fact of shared use) that no prescriptive easement right is perfected because the owner has expressly or implicitly consented and given permission for the use.

20. *See supra*, Chapter 8, Recording Acts and Adverse Possession.

These timing rules often lead to issues on the exam concerning breach of deed covenants by a grantor.[21] For example, assume that the grantor gives a warranty deed to a grantee for a parcel that is burdened by an easement arising by operation of law or a prescriptive easement. If the grantor's deed excepts only "easements of record" from the deed's covenant against encumbrances, then the present covenant against encumbrances is breached when the deed is delivered by the existence of the implied or prescriptive easement. Why would the grantor give a warranty deed that does not exclude the implied or prescriptive easement from the covenant against encumbrances? Because the grantor (particularly the grantor who gives a general warranty deed) probably does not know that a prior severance or a prescriptive use had created an easement right by operation of law.

Transfer Of Easements Arising By Operation Of Law

The rules for transfer of easements arising by operation of law are the same as for express easements. An easement implied from strict necessity and an easement implied from prior use are treated for transfer purposes like express appurtenant easements. A prescriptive easement is treated for transfer purposes as either appurtenant (the use benefits another parcel) or in gross (the use benefits a person).

Scope And Misuse Of Easements Arising By Operation Of Law

The scope of an easement that arises by operation of law turns on how the easement was established. For an easement implied from strict necessity, courts limit the scope to the degree of strict necessity required by the dominant parcel. For an easement implied from prior use, the courts look to the nature and extent of the prior use by the original owner. For a prescriptive easement, scope is determined by the nature and extent of the actual use during the prescriptive period.

---

21. *See supra*, Chapter 7. Real Estate Transactions.

Termination Of All Types Of Easements And Profits

There are two general methods of termination for all types of easements and profits. An easement or profit may be terminated either by a written instrument or by operation of law based on certain circumstances.

An express easement or a profit will terminate according to its written terms if the writing that created the property right contains a termination provision. For example, the writing may limit the duration of the easement or profit right to a specified term of years.

Any type of easement or profit is terminated if the party who holds the benefit of the easement or profit expressly releases the property right in a writing signed by the benefitting party that satisfies the Statute of Frauds. Note that an oral release is ineffective to terminate an easement or profit.

An easement or a profit will terminate automatically by operation of law under the theory of **merger by acquisition of title.** Merger by acquisition of title occurs when the person who holds the benefit of the easement or profit right later acquires title to the burdened parcel. Once a person has superior (fee simple absolute) title to the burdened parcel, the "lesser" easement right is merged into and is permanently extinguished by the owner's "superior" right of fee simple title to the burdened parcel.

Merger by acquisition of title to the burdened parcel extinguishes and thereby terminates all four types of easements (express, implied from prior use, implied from necessity, and prescriptive). Once merged, the easement right is *not* automatically revived if the owner later severs and conveys the parcel that was previously burdened by the easement to someone else. To revive the easement that was previously terminated by merger, the owner must either grant or reserve a new express easement or a profit right by a writing that satisfies the Statute of Frauds, or all of the elements necessary to create an implied or prescriptive easement must be satisfied again as of the moment of the new severance.

An easement or a profit also terminates by operation of law if the person who holds the benefit of the easement or profit

abandons the property right. Termination by abandonment has two required elements. The person who holds the benefit of the easement or profit right must: (1) cease to use the easement or profit right and (2) intend to abandon the easement or profit right. Mere nonuse without proof of the abandoning party's state of mind (intent to abandon) is insufficient to terminate the easement or profit. State of mind may be shown by an oral statement of the abandoning party, such as an oral release by party who holds the benefit of the easement or profit right. Although insufficient to expressly release the property right (due to the failure to satisfy the Statute of Frauds), the oral release coupled with nonuse could be sufficient to prove abandonment.

Special Termination Rules For Easements Implied From Strict Necessity And Prescriptive Easements

Easements implied from strict necessity and prescriptive easements will terminate by operation of law under certain unique circumstances. An easement implied from necessity terminates automatically by operation of law once the necessity giving rise to the implied easement ceases to exist. In contrast, an easement implied from prior use is *not* terminated when circumstances change so that the reasonable necessity for the implied easement no longer exists. This special rule of termination for an easement implied from strict necessity is frequently misunderstood by students, and therefore is frequently tested on exams.

A prescriptive easement right, once perfected, will terminate by operation of law if the owner of the burdened parcel can successfully interrupt the easement holder's use. To successfully terminate the prescriptive easement, the owner must interrupt the use of the prescriptive easement right continuously for the statute of limitations period that applies for the creation of a prescriptive easement.

Summary Of Rules For Easements And Profits

The charts on the following pages summarize the rules governing creation, transfer, scope and termination of easements and profits.

Rules For Express Easements

■**Creation**
- ✓ Only by written instrument
- ✓ Statute of Frauds
- ✓ Conveyance to third party requires two separate deeds

■ **Transfer**

- **Appurtenant Easement**
  - ✓Benefit and burden transfer automatically with ownership of land
  - ✓Notice required if bona fide purchaser acquires burdened parcel
  - ✓Division of benefit among multiple owners permitted if foreseeable and reasonable

- **Easement In Gross**
  - ✓Burden transfers automatically with ownership of land
  - ✓Notice required if bona fide purchaser acquires burdened parcel
  - ✓Benefit transfers from person to person only by written assignment that satisfies Statute of Frauds
  - ✓Consent of owner of burdened parcel may be required to assign the benefit (split of authority)
  - ✓Division of benefit among multiple owners permitted only if easement is exclusive

■**Scope/Misuse**
- ✓Terms of writing
- ✓Unreasonable burden due to change in use
- ✓Per se misuse of appurtenant easement if used to access more than benefitted parcel

■**Termination**

- **By Written Instrument**
  - ✓Express termination provision in original grant
  - ✓Written release by owner of benefitting parcel (appurtenant easement) or person holding benefit (easement in gross) that satisfies Statute of Frauds
- **By Operation Of Law**
  - ✓Merger and extinguishment by acquiring FSA title to both burdened and benefitting parcels
  - ✓No revival if parcel is later re-severed into separate ownership
  - ✓Abandonment of use

Rules For Profits

- **Creation**
    - ✓ Only by written instrument
    - ✓ Statute of Frauds

- **Transfer**
    - ✓ Burden transfers automatically with ownership of land
    - ✓ Notice required if bona fide purchaser acquires burdened parcel
    - ✓ Benefit transfers from person to person only by written assignment that satisfies Statute of Frauds
    - ✓ Consent of owner of burdened parcel not required for assignment of benefit (unless required by the writing that created the profit right)
    - ✓ Division of benefit among multiple co-owners is permitted (subject to one-stock or reasonable use rule)

- **Scope/Misuse**
    - ✓ Terms of writing
    - ✓ Unreasonable burden due to change in use

- **Termination**

    - **By Written Instrument**
        - ✓ Express termination provision in original grant
        - ✓ Written release by person holding benefit that satisfies Statute of Frauds
    - **By Operation Of Law**
        - ✓ Merger and extinguishment by acquiring FSA title to burdened parcel
        - ✓ Abandonment

Rules For Easements Arising By Operation Of Law

- **Creation**
  - **Implied Easement**
    - ✓ One parcel severed into separate ownership
    - ✓ Implied by necessity – strict necessity required at time of severance
    - ✓ Implied from prior use – pre-existing prior use and reasonable necessity required at time of severance
  - **Prescriptive**
    - ✓ Continuous use
    - ✓ Prescriptive easement elements (actual entry, open and notorious, adverse ("hostile"), continuous for statute of limitations)
- **Transfer**
  - **Implied Easement**
    - ✓ Benefit and burden transfer automatically with ownership of parcels
    - ✓ Bona fide purchaser of burdened parcel always takes subject to easement arising by operation of law
  - **Prescriptive**
    - ✓ Burden transfers automatically with ownership of burdened parcel
    - ✓ Bona fide purchaser of burdened parcel always takes subject to implied easement
    - ✓ If appurtenant, benefit transfers automatically with ownership of benefitting parcel
    - ✓ If in gross, benefit transfers from person to person by written assignment that satisfies the Statute of Frauds
- **Scope/Misuse**
  - **Implied From Strict Necessity**
    - ✓ The degree of necessity at the time the parcels were severed
  - **Implied From Prior Use**
    - ✓ The nature of the owner's prior use at the time the parcels were severed
  - **Prescriptive**
    - ✓ Actual use perfecting the prescriptive easement right during the statute of limitations period
- **Termination**
  - **By Written Instrument**
    - ✓ Written release by owner of benefitting parcel (appurtenant easement) or person holding benefit (in gross) that satisfies the Statute of Frauds
  - **By Operation Of Law**
    - ✓ Merger and extinguishment by acquiring FSA title to both burdened and benefitting parcels
    - ✓ No revival if parcel is later re-severed
    - ✓ Abandonment of use
    - ✓ Easement implied by necessity – necessity ends
    - ✓ Prescriptive easement–interruption of use by true owner for statute of limitations period

Real Covenants And Equitable Servitudes: History And The Concepts Of Horizontal And Vertical Privity

Real covenants and equitable servitudes arose as a special type of property right due to the inherent limitations of Contracts law. Under the common law, contractual promises concerning restrictions on land use by two or more adjacent landowners were not enforceable against subsequent owners because there was no direct legal relationship (no "privity" of contract) between the original adjacent landowners and the successor owners.

To illustrate the dilemma faced by landowners, imagine you are back in the days of the Industrial Revolution. There are no municipal zoning laws. A factory owner could purchase a tract of land in the middle of a residential area and build a nasty, pollution-generating facility (or, worse yet, a slaughterhouse or a saloon) right in the middle of the neighborhood. What could the landowners, who wanted to preserve the residential nature of their neighborhood, do to prevent this from occurring? They could, of course, all sign a mutual agreement promising to each other to limit their respective lands to residential use. But once one owner sold her property, the new owner was not bound by the original agreement.[22]

What the landowners wanted was mutual long-term security, namely, the ability to bind subsequent owners to the original agreement to restrict their lands to residential use. Binding subsequent owners also was economically efficient because it eliminated the transaction costs associated with renegotiating the terms of the original agreement with each successive new owner.

The English courts, and later the American courts, responded to these privately created landowner agreements by recognizing a new type of property right—the **real covenant**. A real covenant is enforceable at law through a claim for damages for breach of the

---

22. The modern approach permitting enforcement of a contract by a third party beneficiary did not come into being until long after the real property law of covenants and servitudes was developed. Moreover, even modern Contracts law only permits the benefit to the promisee to run to a third party, not the burden of the promisor.

promises (the "covenants") in the land use agreement. For the common law, the real covenant was a fairly radical development because recognizing this property right allowed one party, who may not have been a party to the original landowners' agreement, to recover damages for breach from another party, who also may not have been a party to the original landowners' agreement.

To illustrate this idea of enforcement of the real covenant by and against persons who are not original parties to the land use agreement, refer to the box diagram below. Assume that A and B each purchase their land from a common owner (O) and that each of their deeds from O contains a real covenant providing that the land can only be used for residential purposes. A and B further agree that their covenant will bind their respective "heirs, successors, and assigns" and will "run with the land" (i.e., the covenant will bind successor owners). A then sells A's land (Whiteacre) to A1, and B sells B's land (Blackacre) to B1. Later, B1 tries to build a saloon on Blackacre in violation of the real covenant. A1 could sue B1 for damages to A1's property, Whiteacre, that result from the violation of the real covenant by B1.

The Box Diagram

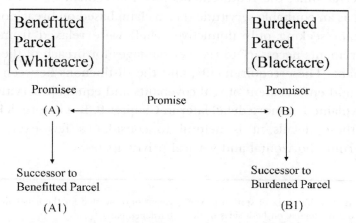

An elaborate set of requirements must be satisfied for A1 to be able to sue B1 for damages for breach of the real covenant. These requirements are based on the concepts of horizontal and vertical privity. **Horizontal privity** refers to the nature of the legal relationship between the original parties to the covenant, A and B. **Vertical privity** refers to the nature of the legal relationship between an original party to the covenant and a subsequent assignee. In the box diagram, assume that the prerequisite vertical privity exists between A and A1, and between B and B1.[23] Once ownership of Blackacre has been assigned from B to B1, B is no longer liable for damages to A (or any assignee of A) for breach of the original covenant by any of B's assignees. Similarly, once ownership of Whiteacre has been assigned from A to A1, A cannot sue to enforce the real covenant against B (or any assignee of B). In short, only current owners[24] can sue and be sued.

The technical requirements for horizontal and vertical privity imposed by the English courts of law made real covenants often difficult to enforce against subsequent owners. In the famous 1848 case of *Tulk v. Moxhay*, the English court of equity eliminated horizontal privity (which was often a sticking point, as discussed below) as a requirement for injunctive relief to enforce a real covenant. The effect of *Tulk v. Moxhay* was to create a "new" property right, known as the **equitable servitude**.

Over time, the requirements for enforcement of a real covenant as an equitable servitude (i.e., a claim based on breach of the covenant seeking only injunctive relief) were relaxed from the requirements necessary to recover damages for breach of the real covenant. These requirements, and the distinctions between creation and enforcement of real covenants and equitable servitudes, are explained in more detail later in Chapter 9. But before delving into these details, it is helpful to consider a few exam tips concerning horizontal and vertical privity issues.

---

23. Note that this chain of vertical privity can go on indefinitely on both sides of the box diagram. Thus, A1 could sell to A2, A2 could sell to A3, and so on. The same is true for B1 and B1's line of assignees. The real covenants "run with the land" down the chains of ownership for the benefitting and burdened parcels.

24. This rule also applies to a person who is not a current owner, but who is entitled to current legal possession, such as a tenant.

Analyzing Covenant And Servitude Problems

Of all the subjects covered in the first year Property course, real covenant and equitable servitude problems require the most careful, precise and meticulous analysis. To avoid becoming lost, follow these two exam tips.

Exam Tip: Memorize And Use The Box Diagram

The box diagram is invaluable as an analytical tool. You must memorize and learn how to use the box diagram by "plugging in" the actual facts of the problem you are analyzing into its format. Always put the original benefitting promisee, the benefitting parcel, and any successors in interest to the benefitting parcel on the left side of the diagram. Always put the original promisor, the burdened parcel, and any successors in interest to the burdened parcel on the right side of the diagram.

By approaching problems using the same methodology each time, you will develop a comfort level with the analytical process. You also will notice patterns in the facts of problems that tend to make real covenants and equitable servitudes either enforceable or unenforceable. Developing these habits as you work practice problems will help you enormously on the exam, where the analysis must be performed under time constraints.

Exam Tip: Analyze The Creation, Burden And Benefit Elements Separately And In Order

The required elements to create and enforce real covenants and equitable servitudes fall into three distinct categories:

- the elements for creation of the covenant or servitude;

- the elements for the burden of the covenant or servitude to run to and bind successors to the original promisor; and

- the elements for the benefit of the covenant or servitude to run to and be enforceable by successors to the original promisee.

You must address these categories of elements separately and in order, beginning with the elements necessary to create the covenant or servitude. If the dispute involves two parties, neither of whom is an original party to the covenant or servitude, after analyzing the creation elements you should first analyze the burden side elements (which are the ones most likely to fail), and then analyze the benefit side elements.

Again, following this tip as you work practice problems will develop your analytical skills and will save you valuable time on the exam.

Creation And Enforcement Of Real Covenants And Equitable Servitudes

The chart on the following page summarizes and compares the elements necessary for the creation and enforcement of real covenants and equitable servitudes. As you review the chart (and before delving into the details of the explanation below), pause and notice the following three major distinctions between real covenants and equitable servitudes:

- **Horizontal Privity.** Horizontal privity between the original parties to the covenant is necessary for the burden of a real covenant to be enforced against a subsequent assignee. But horizontal privity is *not* required for enforcement of the burden of an equitable servitude.

- **Vertical Privity Necessary for Running of the Burden.** For enforcement of a real covenant, traditional vertical privity is required for the burden of a real covenant to be enforced against a subsequent assignee. The traditional vertical privity standard is relaxed so that only minimal vertical privity is necessary for enforcement of the burden of an equitable servitude. The requirements for traditional vertical privity and minimal vertical privity are explained later in Chapter 9.

- **The Gap–Filling Role of a Common Scheme.** The existence of a common scheme can be used to satisfy multiple elements for the creation and enforcement of an equitable servitude. A common scheme can be used to satisfy two of the three elements necessary for creation of the equitable servitude, and can be used to satisfy the notice requirement necessary for the burden of the servitude to run to a subsequent bona fide purchaser of the burdened parcel.- These points are summarized on the chart below

With these three major points of contrast in mind, let's compare the elements of a real covenant with the elements of an equitable servitude.

Comparison of Real Covenants and Equitable Servitudes

Real Covenant	Equitable Servitude
Creation Elements:	**Creation Elements:**
• Writing (Statute of Frauds)	• Writing (Statute of Frauds) or can infer from common scheme
• Intent to run (magic words)	• Intent to run (looser standard – can infer from common scheme)
• Touch and concern	• Touch and concern
Burden Side Elements:	**Burden Side Elements:**
• Horizontal privity	• Not Required
• Traditional vertical privity (transfer of same duration of estate)	• Minimal vertical privity (transfer of any duration of an estate in land)
• Notice to subsequent BFP	• Notice to subsequent BFP (looser standard – can infer from common scheme)
Benefit Side Elements:	**Benefit Side Elements:**
• Minimal vertical privity (transfer of any duration of an estate in land)	• Minimal vertical privity (transfer of any duration of an estate in land)

Elements For The Creation Of Real Covenants

The creation elements for a real covenant must be satisfied for either the burden, the benefit, or both the burden and the benefit of the covenant to bind successors. First, the covenant between the original parties, A and B, can only be created by a writing in a form that satisfies the Statute of Frauds. Recall that deeds are often signed only by the grantor, which creates a potential Statute of Frauds issue if the grantee later is sued for breaching the real covenant in the deed. In this situation, courts hold that if the grantee accepts the grantor's deed containing the real covenant, then the grantee is bound by the real covenant.

Second, the original parties to the real covenant must intend that the benefit and the burden of the covenant will run to subsequent owners of the lands that are subject to the real covenant. This intent to bind successor owners is indicated by using the magic word "assigns" or, better yet, the magic words "heirs, successors and assigns."

The third element for creation of a real covenant is that the covenant must touch and concern the land. "Touch and concern is a concept, and like all concepts has space and content that can be explored and felt better than it can be defined."[25] The touch and concern element always is satisfied by a real covenant that involves the physical touching of the land itself, such as a real covenant to maintain and repair a boundary wall, or a real covenant to use or not use the land in some way, such as to not build any structure except for a single family residence or to not use the land to operate a particular type of business (e.g., a bar or a gas station).

Over time, judicial interpretation of the touch and concern requirement has evolved so that a physical touching or connection to the land itself is *not* strictly necessary. For example, it is not uncommon for commercial properties to be burdened by real covenants that prohibit the sale of a particular type of product (e.g., alcohol or cigarettes or lottery tickets).

Touch and concern issues may involve a promise that involves the payment of money by the burdened landowner. Here, the courts tend to find that a promise to pay money touches and concerns the land "when the payment is for the use of land or to pay for improvements."[26] Thus, a real covenant that requires the

---

25. Stoebuck & Whitman, *supra*, at 475.   26. Stoebuck & Whitman, *supra*, at 476.

landowner to pay dues to a homeowners' association for the maintenance of a common area is held to touch and concern the land.

In difficult touch and concern cases, the court may look to the economic impact of the real covenant on the value of the burdened and benefitted parcels.[27] If the burden of the real covenant makes the burdened parcel less valuable and the benefitted parcel more valuable, a court is likely to rule that the real covenant touches and concerns the land.

On the exam, the touch and concern element for creation of a real covenant offers the opportunity to engage in a policy analysis. If economic impact is the sole or primary basis for arguing that a real covenant touches and concerns the land, you should consider and discuss the policy implications of a judicial ruling that the promise touches and concerns the land. Fundamentally, the policy objective of the touch and concern element is to strike down idiosyncratic restrictions on the use of land while protecting and enforcing restrictions that maximize overall property values. In doing a policy analysis, consider the perspective of future buyers. Would a reasonable future buyer expect or desire that this real covenant be enforced? Would a reasonable future buyer view the benefit of the real covenant as economically valuable? Or is the benefit of the real covenant so unusual or personal in nature to an original owner that it is unreasonable to bind future successors?

Exam Tip: Beware The Benefit In Gross Situation

In analyzing the touch and concern aspects of the real covenant, be careful to determine that the benefit of the promise is to a parcel of land, not merely to a person or class of persons in general. To illustrate, assume that a city grants land to a developer to build a multi-family housing complex in exchange for a promise by the developer to rent a certain number of units to low-income persons at a reduced rental rate. This promise burdens the

---

27. *See* Stoebuck & Whitman, *supra*, at 470 (describing variations of the economic impact test for touch and concern).

developer's land, but who receives the benefit of the promise? Here, the benefit of the promise accrues to a group of persons, not another parcel of land. In this situation, we say that the benefit of the promise is "in gross."

Under the common law, the burden of a real covenant (or an equitable servitude) will not run to successor landowners if the benefit is in gross. Applying this rule to the above illustration, if the developer later sells the multi-family housing complex, the successor owner will not be subject to the burden of the developer's promise to the city. If the successor owner refuses to rent units at a reduced rate to low-income persons, the city cannot enforce the original developer's promise as either a real covenant or as an equitable servitude against the successor owner.

This common law rule is logically inconsistent, of course, with the rule that the burden of an easement in gross runs to successor owners of the parcel that is burdened by the easement. For this reason, the *Restatement (Third) of Servitudes* rejects the common law rule and permits the burden of a covenant or servitude to run when the benefit is in gross. A small minority of jurisdictions follow the *Restatement (Third) of Servitudes* approach. On the exam, if you spot a "benefit in gross" issue you should apply the common law rule, criticize the common law rule as logically inconsistent with the rule for an easement in gross, and discuss the *Restatement (Third) of Servitudes* minority rule as an alternative solution.

Requirements For The Burden Of A Real Covenant To Run

For the burden of the real covenant to run to successors, horizontal privity must exist between the original parties to the covenant, A and B. At common law, the following types of legal relationships between A and B satisfied the horizontal privity requirement:

- A and B are landlord and tenant; or

- A and B are grantor and grantee (seller and buyer); or

- A and B own a "mutual interest in the same land" (e.g., an easement right exists between A and B).

In modern land use planning, horizontal privity is usually established by a grantor-grantee relationship. The modern scenario establishing horizontal privity arises where the grantor is the original common owner of a large tract of land. The owner of the tract develops a subdivision or a commercial project and imposes real covenants on each parcel as it is severed from the larger tract and sold.

For the burden of a real covenant to bind a successor, **traditional vertical privity**[28] must exist between B (the original promisor) and B1, who is B's successor in interest. Traditional vertical privity requires that the duration of the estate B1 acquires from B must be the of exact same duration as B's estate. Typically, the original owner B owns Blackacre (the burdened parcel) in fee simple absolute. In this situation, B1 must acquire fee simple absolute title to Blackacre from B to establish the traditional vertical privity necessary for the burden of the real covenant to run from B to B1.

Finally, if the successor B1 is a bona fide purchaser of Blackacre from B, B1 must have actual or constructive (record) notice of the real covenant in order to be bound by the burden of the covenant. This requirement usually is satisfied by recording the written deed or other document that originally created the real covenant.

Requirements For The Benefit Of The Real Covenant To Run

Assume that the original promisor B still owns the burdened parcel Blackacre, but the original promisee A has conveyed ownership or possession of the benefitting parcel Whiteacre to A1. What is required for the benefit of the real covenant to run to A1 so that A1 can enforce the real covenant against B, the original promisor? To enforce the real covenant against the original promisor B, only **minimal vertical privity** must exist between A and A1.

---

28. Traditional vertical privity requires privity of estate. Therefore, if B1 succeeds to ownership of B's land by adverse possession, the traditional vertical privity element is *not* satisfied for the burden to run.

Minimal vertical privity means that the duration of the estate that
A1 acquires from A does not have to be equal to the duration of A's
estate. For example, A can be a landlord (fee simple absolute estate)
and A1 can be a tenant (term of years estate).

Note carefully that when the burden of the covenant is being
enforced against an original promisor, the elements for the burden
to run (especially the requirement of horizontal privity between the
original parties to the covenant, A and B) do not need to be
satisfied. The plaintiff A1 only must show that the three creation
elements are satisfied, and that minimal vertical privity exists
between A1 and A.

If, however, the original promisor B has conveyed Blackacre
to a successor, B1, then A's successor A1 must show that: (1) the
creation elements are satisfied; (2) the elements for the running of
the burden of the covenant to B1 are satisfied; and (3) the elements
for the running of the benefit of the covenant to A1 are satisfied. If
A1 can prove that all of these elements are satisfied, then A1 can sue
B1 for damages for breach of the real covenant by B1.

Elements For The Creation Of Equitable Servitudes

Due to the number of elements that must be satisfied for
enforcement of a real covenant through a damages claim, more
often the promise reflected in the covenant is enforced as an
equitable servitude through injunctive relief. The creation elements for enforcement of a real covenant as an equitable servitude
must be satisfied for either the burden, the benefit, or both the
burden and the benefit of the equitable servitude to bind
successors. These creation elements are similar, but not identical to,
the elements for a real covenant.

An equitable servitude can be created by a writing where the
parties indicate an intent for the equitable servitude to run to and
bind successor owners. But a court may imply these two creation
elements from the circumstances based on the existence of a

common scheme of development, such as a subdivision that has numerous lots developed only with single family residences.[29]

Like a real covenant, an equitable servitude must touch and concern the land. Although this creation requirement is the same for a real covenant, in practice courts are more willing to engage in an expanded interpretation of the touch and concern element when an equitable servitude is involved because the remedy sought is injunctive relief, not the payment of money damages.

Requirements For The Burden Of The Equitable Servitude To Run

The most significant obstacle to enforcement of the burden of a real covenant against a successor in interest is the requirement of horizontal privity. The burden of an equitable servitude, however, will run to and bind a successor in interest even though horizontal privity does not exist between the original parties, A and B. Elimination of the requirement of horizontal privity makes the creation and enforcement of the burden of an equitable servitude against a successor in interest much more likely.

To illustrate, assume that two or more adjacent landowners acquire their land without any restrictions from a common grantor, or even acquire their land from different grantors. These adjacent landowners can mutually agree to impose restrictions on the use of their respective lands, and a court will enforce these restrictions against successor owners through injunctive relief as an equitable servitude.

For the burden of an equitable servitude to bind a successor, only minimal vertical privity is required[30] between the original

---

29. *See* Sanborn v. McLean, 233 Mich. 227, 206 N.W. 496 (1925).

30. Although at least one casebook states that vertical privity is not necessary for the burden of an equitable servitude to run, this statement obviously cannot be read literally—a complete stranger cannot enforce the burden of the equitable servitude! *See*

JESSE DUKEMINIER ET AL., PROPERTY 748 (6th ed. 2006) ("Nor is vertical privity required for the *burden* to run. All subsequent owners and possessors are bound by the servitude, just as they are bound by an easement.") The reference to "subsequent owners and possessors" in the above quotation makes clear that minimal vertical privity, not traditional vertical promisor, B, and the successor, B1. Again, the more lenient standard for the burden of an equitable servitude to run makes enforcement of the burdensome promise as an equitable servitude much more likely.

Finally, if the successor B1 is a bona fide purchaser[31] of Blackacre from B, B1 must have purchased with actual or constructive notice of the equitable servitude in order to be subject to its burden. This notice requirement may be satisfied by recording the written deed or other document that created the equitable servitude. If the equitable servitude was implied from a common scheme of development, the common scheme can be sufficient to provide notice[32] to a subsequent bona fide purchaser.

Requirements For The Benefit Of The Equitable Servitude To Run

As with a real covenant, horizontal privity between the original parties (A and B) is not required for the benefit of the equitable servitude to run to A's successor A1. When the burden of the equitable servitude is being enforced against an original promisor, the plaintiff A1 only must show that the three creation elements are satisfied, and that minimal vertical privity exists between A and A's successor in interest, A1.

Of course, if the original promisor B has conveyed Blackacre to a successor B1, then A's successor A1 must show that: (1) the creation elements for an equitable servitude are satisfied; (2) the elements for the running of the burden of the equitable servitude to B1 are satisfied; and (3) the elements for the running of the benefit of the equitable servitude to A1 are satisfied. If A1 can prove

---

privity (requiring the transfer of the same duration of estate held by the promisor), is required. The burden of an equitable servitude may be enforced by a successor who acquires either title to the land from the original promisor, or by a successor who acquires a lesser estate with the right of possession, such as a tenant. *See* Stoebuck & Whitman, *supra*, at 499.

31. Note that if B's successor B1 is a donee,

devisee, or inherited Blackacre as an heir, B1 takes ownership subject to the burden of the servitude even though B1 may lack notice of it. *See* Stoebuck & Whitman, *supra*, at 501–502 ("Equitable restrictions are equitable interests in land that are good against subsequent possessors who are not bona fide purchasers.").

32. *See Sanborn, supra* note 29.

that all of these elements are satisfied, then A1 can sue B1 for injunctive relief to enforce the equitable servitude.

Termination Of Real Covenants And Equitable Servitudes

As with easements and profits, covenants and servitudes may be terminated expressly based on a writing, or by operation of law based on changed circumstances.

A covenant or servitude may terminate according to the express terms of the writing that created it. For example, the duration of the burden of the covenant or servitude may be limited by the writing to a certain number of years after its creation. Time restrictions are very common for real covenants that require the landowner to pay money, such as dues owed to a homeowners' association for the maintenance of common areas and amenities.

The second method of termination based on a writing occurs where the owner of the benefitting parcel voluntarily agrees to extinguish the burden of the real covenant or equitable servitude by executing a written release.

Termination by operation of law occurs when the burdened and benefitting parcels come under common ownership. Under the theory of merger by acquisition of title, the "lesser" property right of the benefit of the covenant or servitude is extinguished due to the common owner's "superior" fee simple absolute ownership of the burdened parcel.

A change in the neighborhood effectively can result in termination of an equitable servitude if a court refuses to enforce the servitude. If a court finds that the change in the physical character of the neighborhood "has caused the restriction to become outmoded and to have lost its usefulness, so that the benefits have already been substantially lost,"[33] then the court may refuse to issue

---

33. Stoebuck & Whitman, *supra*, at 488. Although the change in neighborhood doctrine usually arises in the context of a challenge to enforcement of an equitable servi- tude, there is no sound reason that would prohibit the doctrine from applying to a real covenant. *See id.* at 490.

an injunction against a landowner's violation of the servitude. A court also may refuse to enforce a servitude based on equitable principles of estoppel or extreme hardship or abandonment. An exception exists for an affirmative covenant to pay money, such as homeowners' association dues. An affirmative covenant for the payment of money cannot be terminated by abandonment through the refusal by the landowner to pay over an extended period of time.

Exam Tip: Public Policy Obstacles To Enforcement.

A real covenant or equitable servitude may be unenforceable as a matter of law because its enforcement is contrary to federal law or public policy. Examples include racially restrictive covenants, covenants that prohibit group homes for persons who are handicapped under the federal Fair Housing Act, prohibitions on signs that violate freedom of speech under the First Amendment, restrictions on use that violate the federal Religious Land Use and Institutionalized Persons Act, or restrictions on use that violate freedom of religion under the First Amendment. These points of intersection between Property law and federal constitutional and federal statutory law provide fertile grounds for exam questions. On an exam, do not focus so intently on the technical elements for enforcement of a real covenant or an equitable servitude that you overlook these larger public policy issues.

EASEMENTS, PROFITS, REAL COVENANTS AND EQUITABLE SERVITUDES CHECKLIST

With the above Review in mind, the Easements, Profits, Real Covenants and Equitable Servitudes Checklist is presented below.

A. CHARACTERIZE THE NATURE OF THE PROPERTY RIGHT.
Does the property right involve the right to enter and/or use land owned by another person, or does the property right involve a promise by the owner concerning the owner's use of his own land?

1. **Right To Use Land Owned By Another Person?** Determine whether the property right is an easement, profit, lease or license.

    a. **Easement.** An easement is the irrevocable right to enter land owned by another person.

        i. **Created In Writing?** If yes, an express easement may have been created. Proceed to Part B for further analysis.

        ii. **Created By Oral Permission Of Owner?** If yes, the property right is a license. Proceed to Part A.1.d to determine if the license is revocable or irrevocable.

        iii. **Created By Operation Of Law?** Was a single parcel severed? If yes, an implied easement may have been created. Proceed to Parts C.1 and C.2 for further analysis.

        iv. **Created By Prescription?** Did the person asserting the easement right enter the land without the permission of the owner? If yes, a prescriptive easement may have been created. Proceed to Part C.3 for further analysis.

    b. **Profit.** A profit is the right to remove from another's land something that is part of the land (timber, minerals, fish or game).

        i. **Created In Writing?** If yes, a profit may have been created. Proceed to Part B for further analysis.

        ii. **Created By Oral Permission Of Owner?** If yes, the property right is a license. Proceed to Part A.1.d to determine if the license is revocable or irrevocable.

    c. **Lease.** A lease is the right of exclusive and complete possession and use of property owned by another for a fixed or renewable periodic period.

        i. **Shared Possession Or Use With Owner?** If the owner retains the right to possess or use the property, the property right created is either an easement or a license.

        ii. **Landlord And Tenant Relationship Created?** If a lease is created, the parties are in a landlord-tenant relationship. See the checklist at the end of Chapter 6 for further analysis.

    d. **License.** A license is the revocable permission to enter and/or use property owned by another.

        i. **Presumed Revocable.** Normally, a license is revocable at will by the owner of the property.

        ii. **Not Transferrable.** A revocable license does not "run with the land" and does not bind or benefit successors.

        iii. **Irrevocable?** A license may become irrevocable if the license is coupled with a written and irrevocable profit right, or by estoppel based on reasonable detrimental reliance by the licensee.

2. Promise By The Owner Concerning The Owner's Own Use Of The Land? Determine whether the promise: (1) creates a covenant/servitude; (2) creates a negative easement; or (3) the owner holds title as a defeasible fee simple.

    a. **Mutual Burden And Benefit?** Is the owner's promise part of a mutually binding restriction on the use of land that simultaneously burdens and benefits a group of adjacent landowners? **If yes,** a covenant or servitude may have been created. Proceed to Part E for further analysis.

    i. **Owner's Promise To Pay Money.** A promise to pay money is enforceable only as a real covenant. Proceed to Part E for further analysis.

    ii. **Owner's Promise To Take Affirmative Action Concerning The Owner's Land.** The owner's promise may be enforceable as a real covenant or an equitable servitude. Proceed to Part E for further analysis.

  b. **Negative Easement?** Did the owner unilaterally promise to restrict the use of the owner's own land so as to benefit an adjacent parcel?

    i. **English Common Law Rule.** Was the owner's promise not to interfere with light, air flow, artificial stream flow, or building support in order to benefit an adjacent parcel? **If yes,** the English common law recognized a negative easement right that is enforceable against subsequent owners of the burdened parcel without establishing horizontal and vertical privity.

    ii. **Modern American Law Rule.** American courts generally are reluctant to recognize negative easements beyond the traditional four types recognized at English common law.

  c. **Defeasible Fee Simple?** Was the restriction on the owner's use coupled with an express or implied future interest that was retained by the grantor (FSD or FSSCS) or given to a third party (FSSEL)? **If yes,** the current owner holds a defeasible fee simple (FSD, FSSCS, or FSSEL). See the checklist at the end of Chapter 3.

i. **Defeasible Fee In Prior Deeds In Chain Of Title.** If the use restraint creating the defeasible fee simple is in a prior deed in the current owner's chain of title, the current owner remains subject to the restriction and will forfeit fee title to the future interest holder if the restriction is violated (even if the deed delivered to and accepted by the current owner purports to convey FSA title to the current owner).

- **Current Owner's Suit For Breach Of Deed Covenants.** If the current owner's deed purports to convey FSA title to the owner, but does not in fact do so because a prior deed in the chain of title conveyed a defeasible fee, the current owner may be able to bring a claim for breach of deed covenants against immediate and more remote grantors. Refer to the checklist at the end of Chapter 7 for further analysis.

ii. **Invalid Restraints On Alienation.** Determine whether the use restriction created as part of the defeasible fee in the current owner's chain of title is void as an unlawful restraint on alienation. **If yes,** the current owner holds FSA title and is not subject to the restriction on use.

iii. **RAP And A FSSEL.** Determine whether a deed creating a FSSEL in the current owner's chain of title contains a shifting EI that is void under the common law RAP. Refer to the checklist at the end of Chapter 4 for further analysis. **If yes,** after striking the void EI the current owner may hold FSA title and not be subject to any restriction on use.

B. ANALYSIS OF EXPRESS EASEMENTS AND PROFITS. An express easement or a profit must be created in the form of a writing. Once created, the writing governs the terms and conditions by which the easement or profit right is transferred and the scope of use. The writing also may provide for the termination of the easement or profit.

    1. Does The Writing Satisfy The Statute Of Frauds? The writing must describe the easement right and be signed by the owner of the parcel that is burdened by the easement or profit right.

        a. Easement Retained By Grantor? In conveying title to the grantee, the grantor may retain an easement right for himself in the property being conveyed.

        b. Easement Right For A Third Party? Did the grantor use only one deed to simultaneously convey the property to the grantee and create an easement right in the same property being conveyed to a third party? If so, whether the easement is valid depends on the rule the jurisdiction follows.

            i. Majority Common Law Rule. The easement right created by the writing in favor of the third party is void.

            ii. Minority Modern Rule. The easement right created by the writing in favor of the third party is valid.

    2. Did The Owner Retain The Right To Revoke? If the writing is silent concerning the owner's right to revoke, then an express easement or profit right is created. If the owner expressly retained a right to revoke, the writing creates a license. If the writing creates a license, proceed to Part A.1.d above for further analysis.

3. **Is The Express Easement Or Profit Transferrable?** Determine if the burden of the express easement or profit is transferrable to a successor owner of the burdened parcel. To determine if the benefit of the easement or profit is transferrable or assignable, proceed to Part B.3.b. for an appurtenant easement, to Part B.3.c. for an easement in gross, and to Part B.3.d. for a profit.

    a. **Transfer Of Burden Of Easement (All Types) Or Profit.** The burden of an appurtenant easement, an easement in gross, or a profit transfers automatically with the transfer of title to the burdened parcel.

       i. **Bona Fide Purchasers Of The Burdened Parcel** take title subject to the burden of the easement or profit if the purchaser has actual, constructive (record) or inquiry notice of the easement or profit. If the bona fide purchaser lacks notice, the purchaser takes title free of the burden if all of the requirements of the jurisdiction's recording act are satisfied. See the checklist at the end of Chapter 8 for further analysis.

       ii. **Donees, Devisees And Heirs** generally take title subject to the burden of the easement or profit (unless the jurisdiction's recording act also extends protection to donees, devisees and heirs). See the checklist at the end of Chapter 8 for further analysis.

    b. **Appurtenant Easement: Transfer Of Benefit.** The benefit of an appurtenant easement transfers automatically with the transfer of title to the benefitted parcel, even if the new owner lacks notice of it.

c. **Easement In Gross: Transfer Of Benefit.** The benefit of an easement in gross must be assigned by a writing that satisfies the Statute of Frauds.

i. **Can The Benefit Of The Easement In Gross Be Transferred Without Consent By The Owner Of The Burdened Parcel?**

- **Majority Rule (Restatement Of Property).** When the writing that created the easement in gross is silent concerning transfer, the benefit of an easement in gross is transferrable to another person only if it is commercial in character.

- **Minority Rule (Restatement (Third) Of Servitudes).** When the writing that created the easement in gross is silent concerning transfer, the benefit of an easement in gross is presumed to be transferrable.

- **Implied Intent For Highly Personal Recreational Uses.** Under the minority rule, the implied intent of the parties is that the benefit of the easement in gross is not transferrable for recreational uses that are considered highly personal in nature, such as the right to hunt or fish on someone else's land.

ii. **Adjacent Landowner Holds Benefit Of Easement In Gross.** If the holder of the benefit of the easement in gross owns a parcel that is adjacent to the parcel burdened by the easement, the benefit of the easement in gross does not transfer automatically with a change in ownership of the adjacent parcel. To transfer the benefit, the holder of the benefit of the easement in gross must assign the benefit in writing personally to the new owner.

    d. Profit: Transfer Of Benefit. If the writing creating the profit is silent concerning transfer, the benefit of a profit is presumed to be transferrable to another person without the consent of the owner of the burdened parcel. The benefit of the profit must be transferred to another person in the form of a writing that satisfies the Statute of Frauds.

4. Is The Benefit of the Express Easement Or Profit Right Divisible Among Multiple Parties? Is the benefit of the express easement or profit right being transferred to more than one parcel? **If yes**, proceed to Part B.4.a for division of an appurtenant easement, to Part B.4.b for division of an easement in gross, and to Part B.4.c for division of a profit.

    a. Division Of Benefit Of Appurtenant Easement. The benefit can be divided if the benefitting parcel is subdivided into lots so that each lot owner has the benefit of the easement.

        i. Foreseeable And Reasonable? The division of the appurtenant easement cannot overburden the servient parcel beyond what is foreseeable and reasonable for the normal development of the benefitting parcel at the time the easement was created.

        ii. Scope And Location? The division of

the easement cannot exceed the scope of the easement or change its location as fixed by the terms of the writing that created the easement. Proceed to Parts B.5 and B.6 below to analyze scope and location issues.

b. **Division Of Benefit Of Easement In Gross.** Does the holder of the easement in gross have the exclusive right to use the owner's property for the purposes of the easement (or, does the holder share use with the owner of the burdened parcel)?

i. **If The Benefit Is For Exclusive Use,** the easement right may be divided among multiple parties by the holder of the easement in gross, subject to the limitations on the scope of the easement. Proceed to Part B.5 below to analyze scope issues.

ii. **If The Benefit Is Not For Exclusive Use,** then the holder of the benefit of the easement in gross cannot divide the easement in gross among multiple parties.

c. **Division Of Profit.** A profit is presumed to be divisible among multiple co-owners.

i. **Common Law Rule (One–Stock Rule) Limitation.** Under the one stock rule, each co-owner of the profit must agree to how the profit will be used and each co-owner may veto a proposed use by any other co-owner.

ii. **Modern Rule Limitation.** Under the *Restatement (Third) of Servitudes* view, each co-owner's use of the profit must be reasonable under the circumstances. The consent of the other co-owners is not required so long as the use by one co-owner is reasonable.

5. **Is The Use Of The Express Easement Or Profit Within The Scope Of The Writing?** Use that is outside the scope of the express easement or profit right is a misuse. Misuse is a trespass permitting the owner of the burdened parcel to sue the trespasser for damages or injunctive relief.

    a. **Terms Of The Writing Govern.** Look to the language of the written instrument that created the express easement or profit right and the circumstances surrounding its creation to determine if a change in use is beyond the grantor's intended scope of the express easement or profit.

    b. **Change In Use of Appurtenant Easement.** The change in use of an appurtenant easement cannot overburden the servient parcel beyond what is foreseeable and reasonable for the normal development of the benefitting parcel at the time the easement was created.

    c. **Per Se Misuse Of Appurtenant Easement.** An appurtenant easement cannot be used to access or cross any tract of land that is not part of the benefitting parcel, even if the tract and the benefitting parcel are under common ownership and no additional burden is placed on the servient parcel.

6. **Change In Location Or Widening Of Easement.** Does the change involve moving the location or widening the easement?

    a. **Common Law (Majority) Rule.** Once the location of the easement is fixed by the writing, it cannot be changed without the consent of the owners of the dominant and servient parcels. If the width of the easement is specified in the writing, it cannot be widened without the consent of both the owners of the dominant and servient parcels.

    i.   **Indeterminate Width?** If the width of the express easement is not specified in the writing that created the easement, proceed to Parts B.5.a. and B.5.b. above for a scope analysis.

  b. **Modern (Minority) Rule.** The *Restatement (Third) of Servitudes* permits the owner of the burdened parcel to change the location of the easement, at his or her own expense, if the change does not "significantly lessen the utility of the easement, increase the burdens on the owner of the easement in its use and enjoyment, or frustrate the purpose for which the easement was created."

C. ANALYSIS OF EASEMENTS ARISING BY OPERATION OF LAW (CREATION, TRANSFER AND SCOPE OF USE). If the land was originally held in common ownership and later was severed into two or more parcels with separate ownership, determine if an easement implied from strict necessity (Part C.1) or an easement implied from the owner's prior use (Part C.2) has been created. If the circumstances involve an adverse and uninterrupted use of another owner's property, determine whether a prescriptive easement right has been created (Part C.3). To determine the scope and potential misuse of an easement arising by operation of law, proceed to Part C.4.

  1. **Easement Implied From Strict Necessity (All Jurisdictions).** Was the necessity for the easement caused by the original severance of the parcel into two or more parcels?

    a. **If yes,** an easement implied from strict necessity exists.

    b. **If no,** proceed to Part C.3 to determine if a prescriptive easement right exists if there has been an adverse and uninterrupted use.

2. Easement Implied From Prior Use (Majority Rule). Before the moment of original severance, was part of the tract being used by the common owner for the benefit of another part of the owner's tract?

    a. No. Proceed to Part C.3 to determine if a prescriptive easement right exists if there has been an adverse and uninterrupted use.

    b. Yes. After the moment of severance, is continuation of the prior use reasonably necessary for the new owner to enjoy the (now-severed) parcel?

        i. Yes. An easement implied from prior use exists.

        ii. No. Proceed to Part C.3 to determine if a prescriptive easement right exists based on an adverse and uninterrupted use.

3. Prescriptive Easement. To establish a prescriptive easement right, the three elements described in Parts C.3.a through C.3.c below must be satisfied. Did the person claiming the prescriptive easement right engage in:

    a. An Open and Notorious Use?

    b. That Was Adverse (Hostile)? Is the use of the property without the permission or consent of the owner?

        i. Exclusive Or Shared Use? If use of the property is shared with the owner of the property, consider whether the owner has expressly or implicitly given permission for the use (thereby negating the hostility element).

        ii. Objective Or Subjective Test For Hostility? Jurisdictions differ in the test used for the hostility element.

            • **Objective Test.** The objective test requires only that the use of the property be without the owner's consent. The prescriptive user's state of mind is irrelevant.

- **Subjective Test.** In addition to lacking the consent of the owner, the prescriptive user also must have a good faith belief that he is using the property lawfully.

- **Knowing Trespassers** can never establish a prescriptive easement in a jurisdiction that follows the subjective test.

c. **And Continuous and Uninterrupted For The Statute Of Limitations Period?**

    i. **Tacking.** Prescriptive users can tack their use against multiple owners of the burdened property.

    ii. **Interruption By Owner Or Abandonment.** If an owner interrupts the use or the use is abandoned before the statute of limitations period is complete, the statute of limitations is not tolled, but rather starts over again if the use later resumes.

4. **Transfer Of An Implied Easement Right.** The benefit and the burden of an easement implied from strict necessity or prior use transfers automatically with the transfer of ownership to the dominant and servient parcels.

5. **Is The Use Within The Scope Of The Easement Arising By Operation Of Law?** The rules for analyzing scope and potential misuse vary based on the type of easement.

a. **Easement Implied From Strict Necessity.** Look to the degree of necessity required at the time of the original severance to determine scope and misuse.

    b. **Easement Implied From Prior Use.** Look to the nature of the owner's use immediately prior to the original severance to determine scope and misuse.

    c. **Prescriptive Easement.** Look to the actual use during the statute of limitations period to determine scope and misuse.

D. **TERMINATION OF EASEMENTS AND PROFITS.** Termination can occur based on the terms of a written instrument or automatically by operation of law under certain circumstances.

    1. **Termination By Written Instrument.** Does a writing provide for termination at the easement or profit right?

        a. **Termination Provision (Express Easements And Profits Only).** Did the writing that created the express easement or profit right provide expressly for its termination? **If yes**, the express easement or profit expires according to the terms of the writing.

        b. **Release (All Types Of Easements And Profits).** Did the person who holds the benefit of the easement or profit right execute and sign a writing that releases the right to the owner of the burdened parcel? **If yes**, the easement or profit is terminated by the delivery of the written and signed release to the owner of the burdened parcel.

            i. **Oral Release?** An oral release is ineffective because it fails to satisfy the Statute of Frauds. Proceed to Part D.2.b below to determine if the property right has been terminated by abandonment.

    2. **Termination By Operation Of Law?** Determine if any of the following circumstances apply to terminate the easement or profit right automatically by operation of law.

        a. **Merger By Acquisition Of FSA Title?** Did the person who holds the benefit of the easement or profit acquire FSA title to the burdened parcel? **If yes,** the property right is extinguished and terminated based on the merger of the lesser property right into the superior FSA title.

     i.   **No Automatic Revival By Subsequent Transfer Of Burdened Parcel.** Once extinguished by merger into FSA title, the easement or profit right is not automatically revived by the subsequent transfer of the formerly burdened parcel to a new owner. If a new easement or profit right is not created in writing prior to or as part of the subsequent transfer, proceed to Parts C.1 and C.2 above to determine if the severance and transfer of the parcel creates a new implied easement from strict necessity or prior use.

   b.   **Abandonment?** Did the person who holds the benefit of the easement or profit cease using it with the intent to abandon the right? **If yes,** the easement or profit is automatically terminated.

     i.   **Proving Intent.** Did the person who holds the benefit of the easement or profit give an oral release of the benefit of the easement or profit or make other statements indicating an intent to abandon?

     ii.   **Period Of Nonuse.** To constitute abandonment, the period of nonuse by the holder of the benefit of the easement or profit must be consistent with an intent to abandon the use, but does not have to satisfy the statute of limitations required to create a prescriptive easement.

    c. **Necessity Ends (Easements Implied From Necessity Only)?** Did circumstances change so that the easement right is no longer strictly necessary? **If yes,** an easement implied from strict necessity automatically terminates by operation of law.

        i. **Changed Circumstances And Easements Implied From Prior Use.** A change in circumstances does not terminate an easement implied from prior use.

    d. **Interruption By Owner Of Burdened Parcel (Prescriptive Easements Only)?** Did the owner of the burdened parcel interrupt the use of the easement right continuously for the statute of limitations period necessary to establish a prescriptive easement? **If yes,** the prescriptive easement right is terminated.

        i. **Abandonment As Alternative Theory.** If the interruption of use is not sufficient to satisfy the statute of limitations, proceed to Part D.2.b above to determine if the person holding the property right has abandoned it.

E. **ANALYSIS OF REAL COVENANTS AND EQUITABLE SERVITUDES.** To determine if a real covenant or an equitable servitude has been validly created by the promise between the original owners, proceed to Part E.1. To determine whether the burden and benefit of the original promise run to successors, proceed to Parts E.2 through E.3. If enforcement of a real covenant or an equitable servitude is being challenged, proceed to Part E.5.

    1. **Has A Real Covenant Or An Equitable Servitude Been Validly Created?** Determine if the circumstances surrounding the original promise satisfy the three elements for creation below.

a. **Created In Writing.** Is the original promise in the form of a writing that was signed or accepted by the original owner of the burdened parcel (the promisor) so as to satisfy the Statute of Frauds?

    i. **Yes.** The promise forms a real covenant or an equitable servitude if the other creation elements are satisfied.

    ii. **No.** The promise may form an equitable servitude if evidenced by a common scheme and the other creation elements are satisfied.

b. **Intent To Run To Successors.** Does the writing indicate that the benefit and burden of the promise bind and benefit "assigns" or "heirs, successors and assigns" of the original parties?

    i. **Yes.** The promise forms a real covenant or an equitable servitude if the promise touches and concerns the land. Proceed to Part E.1.c. below for further analysis.

    ii. **No.** The promise is merely a contractual agreement that binds only the original parties and does not form a real covenant that runs with the land and binds successors in interest.

    iii. **If There Is No Writing,** intent to apply the promise as an equitable servitude to successors or assigns of the original parties can be inferred from a common scheme. If a common scheme exists, proceed to Part E.1.c. below to determine if the equitable servitude touches and concerns the land.

   c. **Touch And Concern.** The promise touches and concerns the land if you can answer "yes" to any one of the questions in i through iv below. After analyzing touch and concern issues, consider whether the promise contains a benefit that is in gross under Part E.1.c.v. before proceeding to the burden side (Parts E.2 and E.3) and benefit side (Part E.4) analysis.

    i. **Physical Touching Of The Land.** Does the promise involve the physical touching (maintaining, repairing, or building structures) of the land itself?

    ii. **Use Restrictions.** Does the promise relate to using or not using the land in a certain way (only residential use, prohibiting multi-family residential use or commercial use, only a specified type of business)?

    iii. **Payment Of Money.** Does the promise involve the payment of money for the use of land (rent, amenities) or for improvements to the land (homeowners' association dues, maintenance of common areas, or utilities access)? Analyze how the payment of money is connected to the use or improvement of the land.

    iv. **Economic Impact.** Does the promise have an economic impact on the land by making the burdened parcel less valuable and the benefitting parcel more valuable? If the promise touches and concerns solely or primarily due to its economic impact, consider public policy-based arguments.

v. **Benefit In Gross.** Does the benefit of the promise accrue to a person or persons rather than to a parcel? **If yes**, the benefit is in gross. Whether the burden of the promise will be permitted to run to a successor depends on the rule followed by the jurisdiction.

- **Common Law Rule.** The burden of a covenant or servitude with a benefit that is in gross can only be enforced against the original promisor and not against a successor.

- **Minority** (*Restatement (Third) Of Servitudes*) **Rule.** The burden of a covenant or servitude with a benefit that is in gross may be enforced against a successor to the original promisor.

2. **Does The Burden Of The Covenant Run To Successors?** Assuming that the burden is not in gross, determine if the three elements below are satisfied. **If yes**, the burden of the covenant can be enforced against a successor to the original promisor. **If no**, proceed to Part E.3 below to determine if the burden of the promise is enforceable as an equitable servitude against a successor to the original promisor.

   a. **Horizontal Privity?** Horizontal privity exists if the original parties to the promise (A and B in the box diagram) are either landlord and tenant, grantor and grantee, or one party holds an easement right in the other party's land.

   b. **Traditional Vertical Privity?** Traditional vertical privity exists if the original promisor B conveyed his entire estate in the land to the successor B1.

    c. Notice To BFP? If the successor B1 is a bona fide purchaser of the burdened parcel from the original promisor B, the burden of the promise binds the purchaser B1 only if B1 had actual or constructive (record) notice of the real covenant.

3. Does The Burden Of The Servitude Run To Successors? If the burden of a real covenant does not run to a successor, the burden of the original promise may still be enforced via injunctive relief as an equitable servitude. Horizontal privity between the original parties (A and B) is not required for the burden of an equitable servitude to run to a successor B1. If the two elements below are satisfied, the burden of the original promise by B may be enforced against a successor B1 through injunctive relief.

    a. Minimal Vertical Privity? Minimal vertical privity exists if the original promisor B conveyed any part of his estate in the land to the successor B1.

    b. Notice To BFP? If the successor B1 is a bona fide purchaser of the burdened parcel from the original promisor B, the burden of the promise binds the purchaser B1 if B1 had actual or constructive notice of the covenant. For an equitable servitude, constructive notice can be established by a recording or can be inferred from the existence of a common scheme.

4. Does The Benefit Of The Real Covenant Or Equitable Servitude Run To Successors? For either a real covenant or an equitable servitude, the benefit of the promise runs to and is enforceable by the successor A1 if A1 is in minimal vertical privity with the original promisee A. Minimal vertical privity exists if the original promisee A conveyed any part of his estate in the benefitted land to the successor A1.

5. Has The Real Covenant Or Equitable Servitude Been Terminated Or Is It Unenforceable On Public Policy

Grounds? Termination may be by written agreement or by operation of law, or a court may refuse to enforce the covenant or servitude based on public policy.

a. **Termination By Written Agreement?** The real covenant or equitable servitude is terminated if the writing that contains the original promise expressly provides that the promise is binding only for a limited duration. The current owner of the benefitted parcel also can terminate the burden of the covenant or servitude by executing a written release that satisfies the Statute of Frauds.

b. **Termination By Operation Of Law?** Do the following circumstances indicate termination has occurred or that the promise should not be enforced?

i. **Merger Due To Common Ownership?** If a common owner acquires title to the parcels that are burdened by and benefit from the original promise, the real covenant or equitable servitude is terminated with respect to the parcels under common ownership.

ii. **Change In Neighborhood?** A court may refuse to enforce the promise if the physical character of the neighborhood has so changed that the purpose of the real covenant is outdated and its benefits have been substantially reduced or lost.

iii. **Equitable Principles?** A court may (but rarely does) refuse to enforce the burden of an equitable servitude based on equitable principles of estoppel and/or extreme hardship. Financial burden alone is not extreme hardship.

iv. Abandonment? A court may refuse to enforce the original promise if the current owner of the benefitted parcel has clearly indicated an intent to abandon the benefit of the real covenant or equitable servitude.

- **Affirmative Covenant To Pay Money.** The burden of an affirmative covenant to pay money cannot be terminated by abandonment through a refusal by the owner of the burdened parcel to pay over a long period of time.

c. Violation Of Public Policy? Determine if enforcement of the real covenant or equitable servitude would violate a federal, state, or local laws, or would infringe upon federal Constitutional rights. **If yes,** the court will not enforce the promise based on superseding federal, state or local statutory law or on Constitutional grounds.

ILLUSTRATIVE PROBLEMS

Here are three problems that illustrate how the Checklist can be used to resolve questions involving easements, profits, real covenants and equitable servitudes.

■ PROBLEM 9.1 ■

Refer to the diagram below in analyzing Problem 9.1.

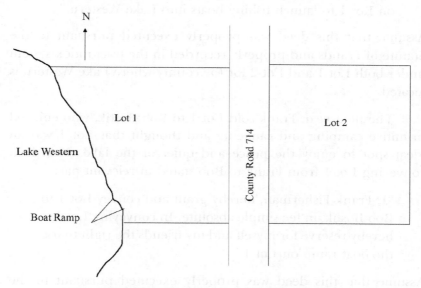

Frank Fisherman owned Lots 1 and 2. Lot 1 was bounded by Lake Western on the west boundary and County Road 714 on the east boundary. Lot 2 was bounded by County Road 714 on the west side. The other boundaries for Lots 1 and 2 are shared with other private landowners.

Frank built a boat ramp on Lot 1 to launch his boat because the nearest public boat ramp was located on the other side of the lake. Frank built a cabin on Lot 2.

Frank told his best friend Larry Longstein, who also was an avid fisherman, that "you can use my boat ramp anytime you want." Larry frequently used the boat ramp on Wednesdays (Larry's day off from work) to launch his boat and fish in Lake Western.

Frank sold Lot 2 and its cabin to Charles Coller. The deed conveying Lot 2 from Frank to Charles stated in relevant part:

"I, Frank Fisherman, hereby grant and convey Lot 2 to
Charles Coller, in fee simple absolute. I further grant
and convey to Charles Coller and his heirs, successors
and assigns an easement for the benefit of Lot 2 to cross
Lot 1 for the sole purpose of using the boat ramp located
on Lot 1 to launch fishing boats into Lake Western."

Assume that this deed was properly executed pursuant to the
Statute of Frauds and properly recorded in the tract index system
under both Lot 1 and Lot 2 for the county where Lake Western is
located.

The next year, Frank sold Lot 1 to Bob Bostik, who enjoyed
primitive camping and canoeing and thought that Lot 1 was an
ideal spot to enjoy the peace and quiet of the lake. The deed
conveying Lot 1 from Frank to Bob stated in relevant part:

"I, Frank Fisherman, hereby grant and convey Lot 1 to
Bob Bostik, in fee simple absolute. In conveying Lot 1, I
hereby reserve for myself and my friends the right to use
the boat ramp on Lot 1."

Assume that this deed was properly executed pursuant to the
Statute of Frauds and properly recorded in the tract index system
under Lot 1 for the county where Lake Western is located.

Frank and his friend Larry continued to use the boat ramp on
Lot 1 to launch their fishing boats. Bob used the boat ramp to
launch his canoe.

The next year, Charles sold Lot 2 with the cabin to another
one of Frank's friends, Jay Jetson. Although Jay was not a fisherman like his friend Frank, Jay did like to jet ski. Jay began using the
boat ramp on Lot 1 to launch his jet ski into Lake Western.

Early one Sunday morning, while Bob was camping on Lot 1,
Jay roared by on his jet ski. Bob emerged from his tent and shook
his fist at Jay. When Jay was through jet skiing for the day, Bob
confronted Jay at the boat ramp as Jay was using his trailer to pull
his jet ski out of the lake. Bob told Jay that "he was a trespasser" and
that he "had better not use my boat ramp again."

The next day, Bob installed a chain link fence around the boat ramp on Lot 1 with a padlocked gate. When Jay, Frank and Larry demanded a key to the gate so that they could use the boat ramp, Bob refused.

Jay, Frank and Larry have each sued Bob in state district court seeking an injunction that prohibits Bob from blocking their access to the boat dock. At trial, Frank argued strenuously that he "gave" his two friends, Larry and Jay, the right to use the boat ramp and that Bob could not interfere with their use of the ramp.

Assume that the jurisdiction follows the majority common law rules on matters involving real property, and that the statute of limitations for prescriptive easements is eight years. You are the judge for these cases. Explain how you will rule on each claim, and briefly explain the reasons for your decisions.

Analysis

Opinion of Judge Student:

In the matter of **Jay versus Bob**, I will grant Jay's injunction request, but will limit the injunction to Jay's use of the boat ramp only to launch fishing boats, not jet skis. When Frank conveyed Lot 2 to Charles, the deed created an appurtenant easement right to use the boat ramp on Lot 1. This appurtenant easement right transferred automatically when ownership of Lot 2 was transferred from Charles to Jay. The scope of the appurtenant easement right created in the deed expressly is limited to use of the boat ramp on Lot 1 to launch fishing boats, not jet skis. Therefore, it is a misuse of the appurtenant easement for Jay to launch jet skis from the boat ramp, and Bob is not required to give Jay access to the boat ramp for this purpose.

In the matter of **Frank versus Bob**, I will grant Frank's injunction request, with the use of the boat ramp not to be limited in nature to fishing boats. When Frank conveyed Lot 1 to Bob, the deed reserved an easement in gross for the benefit of Frank. The language of the deed did not limit the scope of the easement to fishing boats, but rather broadly specified a "right to use."

In the matter of **Larry versus Bob**, I will deny Larry's injunction request. When Frank conveyed Lot 1 to Bob, Frank attempted in the deed to grant an easement in gross to his "friends." Under the majority common law rule, Frank as the grantor of Lot 1 cannot convey an easement right to a third party (his "friends") in the same deed that conveys title to Lot 1. Therefore, Frank's attempt to convey an easement in gross to his friend Larry was void.

With regard to both Jay and Larry, I reject Frank's argument that he "gave" Jay and Larry the right to use the boat dock. Although Frank did validly reserve for himself an easement in gross giving Frank the right to use the boat dock, an easement in gross can only be transferred by a written assignment that satisfies the Statute of Frauds. Here, there is no testimony or evidence that a *written* assignment was made from Frank to "his friends" Jay and Larry.

Even if Frank made a written assignment, Frank cannot transfer or divide his easement in gross right to use the boat dock on Lot 1 and assign it to Jay or Larry. Under the majority common law rule, an easement in gross may only be assigned if it is commercial in character. Here, the easement in gross is for recreational fishing purposes. Moreover, under the majority common law rule an easement in gross may only be divided if the holder of the benefit of the easement in gross has exclusive use of the easement. Here, Frank shares use of the boat ramp with Bob, who uses the ramp to launch his canoe. Therefore, the easement in gross held by Frank cannot be divided among Frank's friends, Jay and Larry.

■ PROBLEM 9.2 ■

Refer to the diagram below in analyzing Problem 9.2.

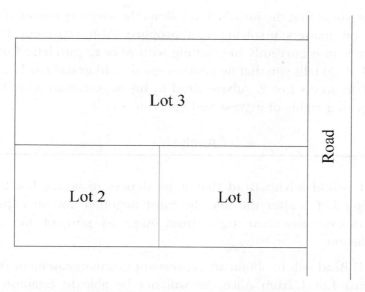

Xavier Xing owned two lots, Lot 1 and Lot 2. Lot 1 had direct access to a public road. Lot 2 was an interior lot with no direct access to a public road. Xavier installed a gravel road across Lot 1 and Lot 2 and used the gravel road to cross Lot 1 and access Lot 2 from the public road.

Xavier sold Lot 1 to Olivia Olong. The deed conveying Lot 1 from Xavier to Olivia stated in relevant part:

"I, Xavier Xing, hereby grant and convey Lot 1 to Olivia Olong in fee simple absolute."

Xavier continued to use the gravel road to access Lot 2 by crossing Lot 1. Olivia did not object, and used the same gravel road to access the house that Olivia constructed on Lot 1.

During this time, Alice Angel owned Lot 3, which abutted Lots 1 and 2 on the northern boundary. Several years after selling Lot 1 to Olivia, Xavier sold Lot 2 to Alice. Alice used her pre-existing road across Lot 3 to access Lot 2, and the gravel road across Lot 1 fell into disrepair. Later, Olivia sold Lot 1 to Alice. At the time of the sale, the former gravel road across Lot 1 was overgrown with weeds and grass and was barely visible.

Assume that the jurisdiction follows the majority common law rules on matters involving real property. You represent Brad Buyer, who is currently negotiating with Alice to purchase Lots 2 and 3. Brad tells you that he plans to use the old gravel road across Lot 1 to access Lot 2. Advise Brad in his negotiations with Alice concerning rights of ingress and egress to Lot 2.

Analysis

I would advise Brad that if he desires to access Lot 2 by crossing Lot 1 after the sale, he must negotiate for an express appurtenant easement right from Alice as part of the sale transaction.

If Brad fails to obtain an express appurtenant easement right to cross Lot 1 from Alice, he will not be able to establish an easement right arising from operation of law to reach Lot 2 by crossing Lot 1. Although the original sale of Lot 1 from Xavier to Olivia created an easement implied from strict necessity and, in a majority jurisdiction, an easement implied from prior use that benefitted Lot 2 and burdened Lot 1, these implied easements have been terminated. The easement implied from strict necessity was terminated when Alice acquired Lot 2 because after acquiring Lot 2 Alice had another way of access to reach the public road by crossing Lot 3 (which Alice also owned). The purchase of Lot 2 by Alice did not, however, extinguish the easement implied from prior use across Lot 1. The easement implied from prior use was terminated under the doctrine of merger by acquisition of title when Alice acquired the fee simple absolute title to both Lot 1 and Lot 2.

In negotiating the express easement right across Lot 1, Brad must describe the easement in a writing that is signed by Alice as the party to be bound. The easement should be made appurtenant by specifying in the writing that the easement "is for the benefit of Lot 2" and shall run to Brad and "his heirs, successors and assigns." By making the easement right appurtenant, it will transfer automatically to the new owner of Lot 2 in the event that Brad decides to sell Lot 2 in the future. In addition, to avoid litigation issues in the future Brad should specify the location and the width of the express easement in the writing that creates the easement. If Brad plans to divide the easement in the future, he should so indicate his intention to divide the easement in the future so that a future division of the easement is reasonably foreseeable to Alice.

■ PROBLEM 9.3 ■

Dan Developer, a builder of residential subdivisions, purchased the entire Block 3 in the Township of Tranquility. After the purchase, Developer validly recorded a development plan for Block 3 ("Development Plan"). The Development Plan called for Block 3 to be subdivided and sold as Lots 1 through 12.

The Development Plan contained in relevant part the following restriction for the proposed development of Block 3:

> **9. Lots 1 through 12 to be restricted to use for single-family residential purposes only. "Single-family" is defined as no more than two persons who are unrelated by blood or marriage.**

Developer began advertising Lots 1 through 12 for sale. Developer sold Lot 1 to Able Adams. The deed from Developer to Adams, which was signed by both parties and recorded, read in relevant part:

> **I, Dan Developer ("Grantor"), hereby convey Lot 1 of Block 3 in the Township of Tranquility to Able Adams in fee simple absolute. Able Adams and his heirs, successors and assigns hereby covenant that the property conveyed by this deed shall be used as**

**a single-family residence only, and further shall be
subject to the restrictions of record contained in the
Development Plan for said Block 3, which is incorporated herein by reference (the "Restrictions").
The parties intend that the burden and benefit of
said Restrictions shall run with the land and bind the
heirs, successors and assigns of Lot 1.**

Later, Developer sold Lots 2 through 11 of Block 3. The deeds
of conveyance, each signed by both parties and recorded, were
identical in substance to the deed set forth above.

Finally, Developer sold Lot 12 to Bob Bender. The deed from
Developer to Bender, which was signed by both parties and
recorded, read in relevant part:

**I, Dan Developer ("Grantor"), hereby convey Lot
#12 of Block 3 in the Township of Tranquility to Bob
Bender in fee simple absolute.**

The deed conveying Lot 12 to Bender did not reference the
Restrictions in the Development Plan or limit Lot 12 to only
single-family residential use.

The original purchasers of Lots 1 through 12 from Developer
all built single-family residences on their respective lots. Bender
died shortly after moving into the residence he built on Lot 12. The
executor of Bender's estate sold Lot 12 and its residence to Sam
Sloan. The executor's deed conveying Lot 12 to Sloan was identical
in substance (except for the name of the grantee) to the deed from
Developer to Bender conveying Lot 12.

After Lots 1 through 12 had been sold, Adams gave a life
estate interest in the residence on Lot 1 to his nephew, Junior.
Adams did not tell Junior about the single-family residential use
restriction in the Development Plan, and the deed conveying the
life estate interest did not mention it. Junior, who was a member of
a retro punk rock band, decided to let all eight band members
(none of whom were related to Junior) live as rent-paying tenants
in the house. The band members practiced loudly every evening.

When Sam Sloan, who was the president of the Block 3 Homeowners Association, complained about the band members living in the
house, Junior told Sloan to "go away and let us jam."

Block 3 of the Township of Tranquility is located in the State
of Mind. The State of Mind follows the traditional common law
rules with respect to real covenants and equitable servitudes. The
State of Mind has a notice recording statute that protects bona fide
purchasers, but the statute does not protect donees of real
property.

Sloan has come to you seeking legal advice. Sloan would like
to bring a lawsuit to "kick out Junior's noisy band members and
make Junior pay for the annoyance." Advise Sloan concerning the
likelihood of success on his stated objectives.

Analysis

Sloan is likely to succeed in enjoining Junior from allowing
more than one of his band member friends from residing in the
house on Lot 1. Sloan is unlikely to succeed in forcing Junior to pay
damages for the annoyance.

My legal advice to Sloan is based on the horizontal and vertical
privity relationships that are illustrated in the diagram on the
following page.

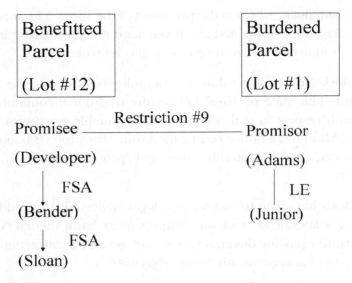

Sloan can obtain injunctive relief against Junior to enforce Restriction #9, the single-family residential use only restriction, as an equitable servitude. The deed conveying Lot 1 from Developer to Adams expressly limited use of Lot 1 to single-family residential use, and further referenced the recorded Development Plan that contained Restriction #9. The written deed conveying Lot 1 from Developer to Adams was signed by Adams as the party bound by the restriction and therefore satisfies the Statute of Frauds. The language of the deed to Lot 1 clearly states the intent of Developer and Adams that the single-family use restriction is intended to run and bind successors to Lot 1. Finally, a single-family residential use restriction touches and concerns the land by restricting how the land is to be used. Such single-family residential use only restrictions are common in residential development and are perceived as desirable for enhancing the economic value of the residences in the development by protecting the character of the neighborhood as residential.

For Restriction #9 to be enforceable by Sloan against Junior, both the burden and the benefit of Restriction #9 must run to Junior (burden side) and Sloan (benefit side) as successors to the original parties, Developer and Adams. Here, the burden of Restriction #9 does not run to Junior as Adam's successor in possession to Lot 1 as a real covenant, but the burden does run as an equitable servitude. Sloan cannot recover damages against Junior ("pay for the annoyance") for breach of Restriction #9 as a real covenant due to a lack of traditional vertical privity between Junior and Adams. Adams owned a fee simple absolute interest in Lot 1, but conveyed an estate of lesser duration (a life estate) to his nephew Junior.

Sloan can enjoin Junior and enforce Restriction #9 as an equitable servitude because only minimal vertical privity between Adams and Junior is necessary for the burden of an equitable servitude to run. Here, minimal vertical privity exists between Adams and Junior due to the conveyance of the life estate interest from Adams to Junior. Junior is a donee, not a purchaser of Lot 1, so notice is irrelevant to the running of the burden of Restriction #9 as an equitable servitude.

The benefit of Restriction #9 runs from Developer to Bender to Sloan because minimal vertical privity exists. Each party, who owned a fee simple absolute interest in Lot 12, conveyed a fee simple absolute interest to his successor. The fact that the single-family residential use restriction is not contained in the original deed conveying Lot 12 from Developer to Bender, or in the deed conveying Lot 12 from Bender to Sloan, is irrelevant to the running of the benefit of Restriction #9 as an equitable servitude. Notice of an equitable servitude is not required for the benefit of the servitude to run to successors.

As written, the deed to Lot 1 does not define the term "single-family," but the deed does reference the recorded Development Plan for Block 3. Restriction #9 defines "single-family" as no more than two unrelated persons. Therefore, Junior can be enjoined from having more than one unrelated band member reside with him in the residence on Lot 1 at any given time.

POINTS TO REMEMBER

- An oral agreement to grant an easement right creates only a license, not an express easement.
- Both the benefit and the burden of an appurtenant easement transfer automatically with title to the real estate.

- The burden of a profit transfers automatically with title to the servient parcel. The benefit of a profit must be assigned in the form of a writing that satisfies the Statute of Frauds.

- A bona fide purchaser of a parcel burdened by an express easement or a profit who lacks notice of the easement or profit can take the property free of the burden only if the requirements of the jurisdiction's recording act are satisfied. A bona fide purchaser always takes property subject to the burden of an easement that arises by operation of law because implied-by-law easements are outside the protection provided by a recording act.

- Watch out for situations where one person acquires fee simple absolute title to both the servient and dominant parcels affected by an easement. Merger by acquisition of title will terminate both express and implied easements for the parcels under common ownership. Any prior easements, once terminated, are not "revived" if the parcels are later "re-severed" into separate ownership.

- When seeking to enforce the burden of a real covenant against a successor, always check for horizontal privity between the original parties first. Real covenants that fail for lack of horizontal privity usually can be enforced as equitable servitudes.

- If the facts suggest that a common scheme exists, use the common scheme to prove the elements of an equitable servitude.

CHAPTER 10

Takings

The Supreme Court's interpretation of what constitutes a "taking" of private property for "public use" has evolved over time. Most professors choose to teach the major Supreme Court decisions in this area in historical sequence. Although the historical approach allows you to see how the law has changed, history does not translate easily into analysis on your Property exam. On the exam, you must apply the law as it currently stands, based on the Supreme Court's most recent pronouncements. Chapter 10 reviews the law of eminent domain and regulatory takings from a current Supreme Court perspective, and highlights those points where older Supreme Court decisions remain viable.

TAKINGS REVIEW

The last part of the Fifth Amendment of the United States Constitution, known as the Takings Clause, states "nor shall private property be taken for public use, without just compensation." The Fifth Amendment on its face applies only to the federal government. But by virtue of the Due Process Clause of the Fourteenth Amendment, the Takings Clause also applies to state and local governments,[1] including administrative agencies and land use planning entities (such as development corporations created by municipalities).

---

1. *See* Chicago, Burlington & Quincy R.R. Co. v. City of Chicago, 166 U.S. 226 (1897).

Overview Of Takings Claims (And Related Issues)

Takings claims generally divide into two main categories—eminent domain claims and inverse condemnation claims. In an **eminent domain claim**, the government brings a condemnation action against a private property owner seeking to force the owner to sell his or her property. In an **inverse condemnation claim**, a property owner sues the government seeking compensation for the alleged taking of the owner's property. Inverse condemnation claims generally are based on the theory of a regulatory taking. A **regulatory taking** occurs when government action or regulation of the owner's land so restricts or limits the use of the land that the owner's property effectively has been "taken" for the public's benefit, thereby entitling the owner to compensation from the government.

For eminent domain claims, the major issues for consideration are whether the government's forced sale of the owner's property is for a public use, and, if so, the amount of just compensation that must be paid to the owner. For inverse condemnation claims, the major issue for consideration is whether the government's regulation in fact constitutes a taking of the owner's property for which compensation is due to the owner.

The diagram on the following page provides a roadmap for navigating takings claims and related issues on the exam. The remainder of the Review explains the key point of the roadmap.

Roadmap For Takings Analysis

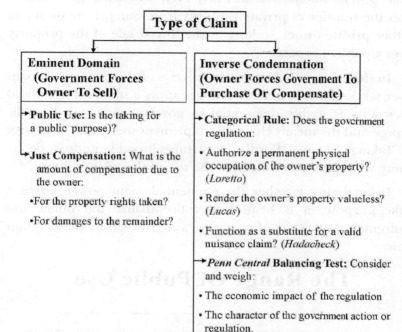

Type of Claim

Eminent Domain (Government Forces Owner To Sell)

→ **Public Use:** Is the taking for a public purpose)?

→ **Just Compensation:** What is the amount of compensation due to the owner:

• For the property rights taken?

• For damages to the remainder?

Inverse Condemnation (Owner Forces Government To Purchase Or Compensate)

→ **Categorical Rule:** Does the government regulation:

• Authorize a permanent physical occupation of the owner's property? (*Loretto*)

• Render the owner's property valueless? (*Lucas*)

• Function as a substitute for a valid nuisance claim? (*Hadacheck*)

→ **Penn Central Balancing Test:** Consider and weigh:

• The economic impact of the regulation

• The character of the government action or regulation.

→ **Exaction:** Is the government demanding that the owner must convey property rights in exchange for approval of a project?

• Is there an essential nexus? (*Nollan*)

• Is the exaction roughly proportional? (*Dolan*)

Analysis Of Eminent Domain Claims

Public Use

The Takings Clause requirement that the power of eminent domain can only be exercised for a public use is satisfied if forcing the sale of the owner's property serves a public purpose. Actual sale to or use of the property by the government, or access and use of the property by the general public is not necessary to satisfy the public use standard of the Fifth Amendment.[2] The public use as public benefit standard is satisfied even when the government forces the transfer of private property from one private owner to another private owner, so long as the forced sale of the property serves a public purpose.

In determining whether the exercise of the eminent domain power serves a public purpose, judges apply a standard of judicial review that is highly deferential to government's stated public purpose and the means chosen to implement that policy objective. The Takings Clause "afford[s] legislatures broad latitude in determining what public needs justify the use of the takings power."[3]

In analyzing whether the eminent domain power serves a public purpose, it is helpful to conceptualize the public use requirement as a range of scenarios, as illustrated by the diagram below.

The Range Of Public Use

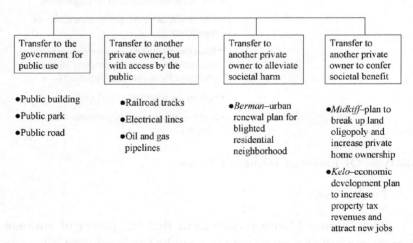

The left side of the range illustrates public use scenarios that are not controversial. It is indisputably a public use when the

---

2. Note that a state constitution or state law may impose a stricter "public use" standard than federal law does under the Fifth Amendment.

3. Kelo v. City of New London, 545 U.S. 469, 483 (2005).

government's power of eminent domain is used to force the sale of private property to the government for its own use or for use by the general public, such as for a public road, public building or a public park. It is also indisputably a public use when the eminent domain power is used to force the sale of private property from one private owner to another private owner, so long as the acquiring owner makes the property available for use by the general public. The typical example of this scenario is the acquisition of private property by a common carrier, such as land or easement rights acquired by a railroad for railway tracks, or by a utility company for electrical or gas lines.

The right side of the range represents Supreme Court interpretations that expand the concept of public use to include a public purpose. Note that in the three Supreme Court decisions of *Berman v. Parker*,[4] *Hawaii Housing Authority v. Midkiff*,[5] and *Kelo v. City of New London*,[6] the government used the power of eminent domain to transfer ownership of private property from one private owner to another private owner. In each case, the Supreme Court found that the government regulation mandating the transfer of ownership was rationally related to a public purpose, and therefore satisfied the public use requirement.

Berman approved a plan of urban renewal and redevelopment enacted by the District of Columbia that addressed a blighted residential neighborhood in Washington, D.C. The redevelopment plan condemned and forced the sale of all properties in the designated blighted area to an urban redevelopment authority for later transfer to other private owners. An individual owner whose commercial property was not blighted challenged the condemnation and forced sale of his property as not being for a public use. The redevelopment plan was approved by the *Berman* Court on the ground that "[i]t is within the power of legislature to determine that the community should be beautiful as well as healthy, spacious as well as clean, well-balanced as well as carefully patrolled. . . . "[7]

---

4.   348 U.S. 26 (1954).   6.   545 U.S. 469 (2005).

5.   467 U.S. 229 (1984).   7.   348 U.S. at 33.

Berman was premised on the fact that the residential housing in the neighborhood was so blighted that it presented a danger to public health and safety. *Midkiff* and *Kelo* were not based on a public health and safety harm, but rather on the perceived benefit to society of a governmental plan that used the power of eminent domain to accomplish a public purpose.

Midkiff approved a plan by the State of Hawaii to address the "societal and economic evils of a land oligopoly."[8] The legislature intended the plan to increase the number of private homeowners in Hawaii by forcing the landlord owners of residential housing to sell their properties to their tenants if certain terms and conditions were satisfied.

Kelo approved an economic development plan by the city of New London, Connecticut. The economic development plan, which condemned properties in an area of the city that was not blighted, forced the sale of these properties to a city-sponsored development corporation. The plan called for the development corporation to resell the properties to private developers, who would then build office buildings and new housing on the sites as well as other public recreational amenities. The public purpose of the economic development plan was to replace the existing non-blighted properties with more expensive commercial and residential properties that would increase the city's property tax revenues and possibly attract new employers and new jobs to the area.

In a 5–4 decision, the *Kelo* Court held that the forced sale of the nonblighted properties pursuant to a comprehensive plan of economic development to the development corporation for later transfer to private developers satisfied the public use requirement. The *Kelo* Court held that "[p]romoting economic development is a traditional and long accepted function of government"[9] and that there was "no principled way of distinguishing economic development from the other public purposes"[10] that the Supreme Court previously had recognized as satisfying the public use requirement in *Berman* and *Midkiff*.

---

8. *Midkiff*, 467 U.S. at 241–42.   **10.** *Id.* at 484.

9. 545 U.S. at 484.

To summarize, *Midkiff* and *Kelo* demonstrate the high degree of judicial deference paid to the legislative body's public purpose objective, and to the use of the governmental power of eminent domain as a rational means of achieving that objective. The prerequisite public purpose is not limited to curing a public harm (e.g., blighted properties), but rather extends to conferring a public benefit (higher tax revenue and better-paying jobs). When the purpose behind the exercise of eminent domain is to confer a public benefit, the government's planning process and use of eminent domain in conjunction with a comprehensive plan for the use of the land are important facts that judges look to when deciding whether the public use requirement is satisfied.

Just Compensation

The property owner is entitled to receive just compensation for the property rights that are taken under the power of eminent domain. Just compensation is an objective standard based on market value. Market value is defined as the price, in cash or on terms equivalent to cash, for which the property rights should sell after reasonable exposure in a competitive market, with the buyer and seller each acting prudently, knowledgeably, and for self-interest, and assuming that neither is under undue duress.[11] In determining market value, the subjective value attached to the property by the owner is *not* taken into consideration.

Market value assumes economically rational buyers and sellers, and further assumes that the market for property rights functions efficiently with perfect information. Consequently, market value takes into consideration a likely increase in the value of the property in the near future due to an anticipated change in zoning that would increase the value of the property.[12] Market value also includes an increase in value if the property's use is changed to an alternative (but still legal) use.[13]

---

11. THE APPRAISAL INSTITUTE, THE APPRAISAL OF REAL ESTATE 23 (13th ed. 2008).

12. Note that municipal authorities cannot "game the system" by first changing zoning to reduce the fair market, and then condemning the property and buying it at the reduced market value.

13. In appraiser parlance, an alternative

The property owner also receives just compensation for a partial taking of property rights, such as the condemnation of only part of the property or an easement right to build or widen a public road or to install a public utility line. In addition to the value of the property rights taken, the property owner may receive compensation for any damages to the remainder. The amount of just compensation for remainder damages is calculated by doing a market value analysis of the property before and after the taking. The difference in the before and after values determines the amount of damages to the remainder.

State law may award compensation to a property owner whose business is lost or disrupted by the taking. State law also may award compensation to a tenant on the property (as opposed to the fee title owner) who is displaced by the taking. These types of damages are *not* available, however, under the Fifth Amendment.

Analysis Of Inverse Condemnation Claims

Analysis of an inverse condemnation claim requires several steps. First, you must address whether one of the Supreme Court's **categorical rules** apply. Categorical (also known as "per se") rules dictate that, if the rule fits the facts, a regulatory taking conclusively has (or has not) occurred.

If a categorical rule does not apply, you must apply a **balancing test** to determine if a regulatory taking has occurred. The balancing test approach originated in the landmark Supreme Court case of *Penn Central Transportation Company v. City of New York*.[14] Applying the *Penn Central* balancing test involves discussing and weighing multiple factors.

To perform a *Penn Central* balancing test analysis successfully on the exam, you must integrate into the test two more important Supreme Court decisions that followed *Penn Central*. These Supreme Court decisions are *Palazzolo v. Rhode Island*[15] and *Tahoe–*

---

legal use that generates a higher market value is known as the property's "highest and best" use.

14. 438 U.S. 104 (1978).

15. 533 U.S. 606 (2001).

Sierra Preservation Council, Inc. v. Tahoe Regional Planning Agency.[16] *Palazzolo* and *Tahoe–Sierra* provide additional insights into how courts should interpret and apply the factors that are weighed in the *Penn Central* balancing test.

Finally, if you conclude that a regulatory taking has occurred, your last analytical step is to determine the amount of compensation that the court should award to an owner who has suffered a regulatory taking.

Categorical Rules

There are three categorical rules that may apply in the context of an inverse condemnation claim. The first two rules are conclusive rules in favor of a regulatory taking. The third rule is a conclusive rule against a regulatory taking. On an exam, you may want to describe all three categorical rules, if only to note that none of the categorical rules apply based on the facts of the problem.

The first categorical rule in favor of a regulatory taking comes from the Supreme Court case of *Loretto v. Teleprompter Manhattan CATV Corporation.*[17] *Loretto* held that if the government regulation authorizes a permanent physical occupation of the owner's property, then a regulatory taking conclusively has occurred and the owner is entitled to just compensation. The occupation may be by a governmental entity, or the regulation may authorize a third party to occupy the owner's property. In *Loretto*, the regulation at issue authorized a cable television company to install boxes and wiring on the owner's building to facilitate access to cable television by tenants of the building.

Note carefully that, under *Loretto*'s categorical rule, the amount of space that is actually occupied, the degree of interference with the owner's current or projected use, and the impact on the market value of the owner's property are irrelevant to the question of whether a regulatory taking has occurred.[18] These facts

---

16. 535 U.S. 302 (2002).

17. 458 U.S. 419 (1982).

18. These facts would be highly relevant if

the *Penn Central* balancing test applied. *See* discussion *infra Penn Central* Balancing Test.

are, however, highly relevant to the question of the amount of just compensation due to the owner. For example, after *Loretto* was remanded, the lower court determined that the amount of just compensation due to the owner for the regulatory taking was only one dollar.

The second categorical rule in favor of a regulatory taking comes from the Supreme Court case of *Lucas v. South Carolina Coastal Council.*[19] *Lucas* held that if a regulation leaves the owner with "*no* productive or economically beneficial use"[20] of the property, then a regulatory taking conclusively has occurred. In *Lucas*, the regulation was a state law that permanently banned the construction of habitable structures on oceanfront lots. The South Carolina state court found, and the Supreme Court accepted as a key fact, that the effect of the law was to render the property owner's two oceanfront lots "valueless."[21]

Several points are noteworthy about the limited application of the *Lucas* rule. First, the *Lucas* rule is limited to the extraordinary situation where the economic effect of the regulation is to reduce the value of the affected property to zero (or only a mere "token" value). According to the majority in *Lucas*, a 95% reduction in value, albeit severe, does not conclusively establish that a regulatory taking has occurred.[22]

Second, in determining whether a regulation has "wiped out" the economic value of the owner's property rights, how those property rights are defined is crucial.[23] The more narrowly the owner's property rights are defined, the more likely that the effect of the regulation will be to eliminate the economic value of those property rights. This threshold definition issue, known as the problem of conceptual severance (or the denominator problem) is discussed in more detail below in the context of the *Penn Central* balancing test.

---

19. 505 U.S. 1003 (1992).

20. *Id.* at 1017 (emphasis in original).

21. *Id.* at 1020.

22. *Id.* at 1019 n. 8.

23. In *Lucas*, the majority described, but did not resolve, the problems involved in defining the scope of the owner's property rights. *See id.* at 1016 n. 7.

Third, the law at issue in *Lucas* was a permanent construction moratorium. The Supreme Court later clarified in *Tahoe–Sierra* that a temporary construction moratorium cannot effect a regulatory taking under the categorical rule of *Lucas* because, when the moratorium is lifted, the economic value of the owner's property rights will be restored.

The Supreme Court's analysis in *Lucas* also greatly narrowed the potential scope of the third and final categorical rule. Unlike the first two categorical rules, this third rule cuts against a regulatory taking. This third categorical rule, known post-*Lucas* as the nuisance control rule, is illustrated by the Supreme Court case of *Hadacheck v. Sebastian*.[24]

In *Hadacheck*, the owner of a brickyard challenged a zoning ordinance that prohibited the operation of a brick kiln on the owner's land. The purpose of the ordinance was to prevent the release of air pollutants from the kiln in a developing residential neighborhood. The *Hadacheck* Court held that the zoning ordinance, which reduced the economic value of the owner's land by an estimated 87½%, conclusively was not a regulatory taking because the law was a valid exercise of the state's police power to regulate to protect the public's health and safety.

Lucas clarified that the nuisance control rule against a regulatory taking is *not* coterminous with the valid exercise of modern state police powers, such as the very broad power to regulate land use under modern zoning laws. Rather, the nuisance control rule against a regulatory taking applies narrowly to situations where, in lieu of enacting a regulation to abate or restrict the owner's use, adjacent landowners or the government instead could successfully bring a private or public nuisance action to enjoin the property owner's use. Significantly, *Lucas* clarified that, under the nuisance control rule, even a regulation that eliminates all economic value of the affected land is not a regulatory taking if the regulation does

---

24. 239 U.S. 394 (1915).

"no more than duplicate the result that could have been achieved in the courts" through a private or public nuisance claim.[25]

Exam Tip: Intertwined Nuisance And Regulatory Taking Issues

Nuisance law is often covered in Torts rather than in the first-year Property course. If, however, your Property professor covers nuisance law in detail, beware a zoning ordinance, environmental law, or other regulation that prohibits or restricts an owner's use based on public health and safety concerns, and thereby decreases the economic value of the property. Such an ordinance or regulation presents the opportunity to test both a nuisance law issue and a regulatory taking issue in a single essay question.

To illustrate, assume that the exam question asks whether the owner may successfully challenge the regulation as a taking by bringing an inverse condemnation claim. Your first analytical step is to run through (and most likely rule out application of) the three categorical rules. In discussing whether the nuisance control rule against a regulatory taking applies, you must determine if a private or public nuisance claim against the owner based on the owner's (now regulated) use would be successful. If the nuisance claim fails, post-*Lucas* so does application of the nuisance control rule against a regulatory taking. Your exam analysis then would shift to a *Penn Central* balancing test (described below) to determine if the ordinance or law constitutes a regulatory taking.

Exam Tip: Avoid Being Too "Categorical"

Generally, an exam question involving a regulatory taking claim is, in basketball parlance, either a slam dunk or a charging/blocking call that can go either way depending on the referee's perspective. A slam dunk question contains facts that clearly and cleanly fit into one of the three categorical rules. Although it is important to be able to recognize a slam dunk question (and not waste time by writing unnecessary words), the

---

25. *Lucas*, 505 U.S. at 1029.

more likely exam scenario is the charging/blocking call-type question. On the exam, you should anticipate a question that will require you to discuss the possible application of a categorical rule (or rules), determine that the facts do not neatly fit any categorical rule, and then engage in a full-blown *Penn Central* balancing test analysis. When evaluating the merits of a private owner's inverse condemnation claim, the better exam strategy is to be cautious of relying exclusively on a categorical rule. Instead, you should anticipate that your professor expects you eventually to consider the *Penn Central* balancing test.

The *Penn Central* Balancing Test

Assuming that one of the three categorical rules does not apply, the *Penn Central* balancing test requires a court to weigh the following two factors against each other:

■ The economic impact of the regulation on the private owner

■ The character or nature of the government action or regulation

Each of these two factors has various components to consider in determining the "weight" of the factor.

Economic Impact Factor Components

There are three major components to the economic impact factor under the *Penn Central* balancing test. These three components are:

- The **diminution in the present market value** of the property caused by the government action or regulation;

- Any **reciprocity of advantage** (i.e., a benefit) accruing to the owner from the government action or regulation, either to the owner's land, to the owner as an individual, or more generally as a member of society; and

- Most importantly, the adverse impact on the property owner's **distinct investment-backed expectations** concerning future development of the property.

The Diminution In Value Component And The Problem Of Conceptual Severance

The Supreme Court case of *Pennsylvania Coal Co. v. Mahon*[26] introduced the concept of diminution in value. Historically, the Supreme Court has tolerated very large percentage decreases in the present market value of the property without finding that a challenged regulation works a taking. For example, the zoning ordinance in *Euclid v. Ambler Realty Co.*[27] resulted in a 75% diminution in value due to a change the zoning for the property from industrial to residential use. In *Hadacheck*, the zoning ordinance that prohibited operation of a brick kiln on the owner's property resulted in an 87½% diminution in value of the present market value of the property. More recently, the majority in *Lucas* indicated that even a 95% diminution in the present market value of an owner's property may not result in a regulatory taking under the *Penn Central* balancing test.[28]

In determining the diminution in the present value of the owner's property as a consequence of the government action or regulation, defining the scope of the property rights that are being devalued is crucial. The dilemma is whether the property rights can be severed into separate and discrete components (e.g., subsurface minerals, surface rights, airspace rights), or whether the diminution in value must be based on the market value of the property as a whole. For example, if the regulation prohibits the mining of all coal underneath the surface, then there is a 100% diminution in value of the subsurface coal rights. But such a regulation would have a much lesser percentage impact if the denominator for the calculation is the value of the property as a whole (subsurface, surface and air space rights).

This issue, known as the problem of conceptual severance (or simply as the "denominator problem"), seems to have been resolved by the Supreme Court's discussions in *Penn Central* and *Tahoe–Sierra*. In *Penn Central*, the historic preservation regulation at

---

26. 260 U.S. 393 (1922).   28. *Lucas*, 505 U.S. at 1016 n. 7.
27. 272 U.S. 365 (1926).

issue prevented the owner from building an office tower on top of a pre-existing historical structure without obtaining approval from a local landmark preservation commission. In upholding the historic preservation regulation, the Supreme Court stated that the focus should be on the extent of the regulation's interference with "rights in the parcel *as a whole*."[29]

In *Tahoe–Sierra*, the Supreme Court rejected the argument that property rights could be severed into a present term of years (the duration of the challenged development moratorium) and the future remainder, with a *Lucas*-type elimination of all economically beneficial use for the term of years interest due to the temporary moratorium. *Tahoe–Sierra* held that the " 'conceptual severance' argument is unavailing because it ignores *Penn Central*'s admonition that in regulatory takings cases we must focus on 'the parcel as a whole.' "[30]

Of course, if only part of the owner's property is impacted by a regulation, the savvy property owner may attempt to divide a single property into affected and unaffected parcels. For example, assume that due to an environmental regulation the property owner is unable to develop part of his land that abuts a protected wetlands area, but still may develop the other part of the property. Can the owner characterize his land as consisting of two distinct parcels, and then claim that the environmental regulation has taken *all* of the portion of the property that cannot be developed because it abuts the wetlands area?

This was the factual situation in *Palazzolo v. Rhode Island*.[31] The property owner in *Palazzolo*, however, presented his severance argument for the first time after the Supreme Court had agreed to take the case. Consequently, the Supreme Court refused to consider the merits of the property owner's severance argument, thus leaving a fascinating issue unresolved (for now).

---

29. *Penn Central*, 438 U.S. at 130–31 (emphasis added); *see also* Keystone Bituminous Coal Ass'n v. DeBenedictis, 480 U.S. 470, 497 (1987) (rejecting inverse condemnation claim based on state law that prohibited under-ground mining of coal in certain areas).

30. *Tahoe–Sierra*, 535 U.S. at 331.

31. 533 U.S. 606 (2001).

Palazzolo openly invites the exam question where a savvy hypothetical owner first divides his property into two or more distinct parcels, and then asserts an inverse condemnation claim regarding only the parcel that is impacted by the regulation. This scenario requires the student to make the proverbial charging/blocking call. On the one hand, a legitimate severance of the fee simple absolute title (perhaps by a conveyance to a straw man and back, or by conveyance into or out of co-ownership)[32] does not appear to be inconsistent with conceptualizing the parcel "as a whole." To the extent that a legitimate severance of the owner's property into affected and unaffected parcels occurred prior to the enactment of the regulation, the property owner's argument based on a regulatory taking of the affected parcel would be a stronger one.

On the other hand, property owners could attempt to manipulate the law of regulatory takings through severing their properties. For example, after the enactment of the regulation, should an owner be permitted to transfer or rearrange legal title to the property in such a manner as to eliminate all economically beneficial use of part of the property, and then argue that the regulation works a categorical taking of the severed part under *Lucas*?

In the above discussion, note that the timing of when title is transferred or rearranged is important. Although *Palazzolo* held that a person who acquires fee title to the property after a regulation has been enacted (a "post-enactment purchaser") may assert that the regulation works a taking of his property, the distinct investment-backed expectations of the post-enactment purchaser are reduced in light of the limitations that the pre-existing regulation places on the owner's property. In contrast, the property owner who acquired title to the property before the challenged regulation was enacted (a "pre-enactment purchaser") has heightened distinct investment-backed expectations that are likely to be adversely affected by the subsequent regulation.

---

32. *See supra*, Chapter 5, Co–Ownership.

Reciprocity Of Advantage

Pennsylvania Coal Co. v. Mahon also introduced the concept of reciprocity of advantage. This term captures the idea that the challenged government action or regulation may provide reciprocal benefits to the property owner that partially offset the diminution in the present market value of the owner's property. Reciprocal benefits may accrue directly to the owner's property, to the owner personally as an individual, or indirectly to the owner as a member of society.

Such reciprocal benefits often are intangible (e.g., aesthetics, cleaner air, preservation of wildlife habitat, historical preservation to attract tourists) and therefore difficult to quantify and weigh against the property owner's dollar-based diminution in present market value. Nevertheless, the *Penn Central* balancing test requires this type of apples-to-oranges comparison and weighing. For exam purposes, merely recognizing and explaining that an offsetting reciprocity of advantage to the property owner may exist as a result of the challenged government action or regulation is sufficient.

Distinct Investment–Backed Expectations

The concept of distinct investment-backed expectations ("DIBE") held by the property owner was introduced earlier in the Review by noting the different DIBE of a pre-enactment purchaser and a post-enactment purchaser. Under the *Penn Central* balancing test, the adverse impact on the property owner's DIBE is a particularly important component for analysis. When analyzing the owner's DIBE, it is important to understand how the DIBE component is different from the diminution in value component.

Diminution in value focuses on the decrease in the present market value of the property using a before-the-regulation and after-the-regulation market valuation. DIBE focuses on how the government action or regulation interferes with the owner's future plans for the property and the future anticipated income that, but for the government's action or regulation, the owner's development would have generated. When discussing the DIBE component on the exam, you should pay close attention to whether the regulation flatly prohibits the property owner's future development plan or whether the owner's plan now must be subjected to supervision as part of a discretionary government approval process. Subjecting the owner's development plan to a governmental approval process has a lesser impact on the owner's DIBE because some form of development may eventually be approved by the government regulator.

In analyzing the impact on the property owner's DIBE, *Penn Central* requires that the owner's expectations must be reasonable. A key fact in assessing reasonableness is whether the property owner is a pre-enactment or post-enactment purchaser of the regulated property. Although *Palazzolo* held that even a post-enactment purchaser may assert that the regulation works a taking of the property, the reasonable post-enactment purchaser naturally should have diminished DIBE concerning the property due to the pre-existing regulation.

Reasonableness is an objective standard. Every person is presumed to know and understand the law. Therefore, a post-enactment purchaser who is subjectively ignorant of the impact of a pre-existing regulation on the property cannot claim to have a higher level of DIBE concerning the property. In evaluating the reasonableness of the property owner's DIBE, *Palazzolo* further noted that background principles of state law based on "common, shared understandings of permissible limitations derived from a State's legal tradition" must be incorporated into the analysis.[33] For example, reasonable DIBE would not include the right to engage in an activity on the property or use the property in such a way as would violate a background principle such as the common law of nuisance.

Exam Tip: Watch For Unresolved Issues

In addition to the unresolved severance issue that arose in *Palazzolo*, the Supreme Court's most recent regulatory taking decision, *Tahoe–Sierra*, suggests several more unresolved issues that

---

33. *Palazzolo*, 533 U.S. at 629–30.

make for interesting exam questions. In *Tahoe–Sierra*, the Supreme Court held that a 32 month moratorium on the development of certain environmentally sensitive properties surrounding Lake Tahoe was not a regulatory taking under the categorical rule of *Lucas*. As discussed above, the *Tahoe–Sierra* Court rejected the notion that the owners' property rights could be severed by time so that, for the 32 month moratorium period, the owners' properties were rendered "valueless" under the categorical rule of *Lucas*. Rather, the Supreme Court in *Tahoe–Sierra* reasoned that economic value had to be assessed over the infinite duration of the owners' fee simple absolute property rights. This economic assessment required using the infinite nature of the fee simple absolute as the denominator for determining the diminution in value suffered by the property owners. Under this approach, the affected properties were not "valueless" because once the temporary moratorium was lifted, the economic value of the affected properties would be restored.

Procedurally, *Tahoe–Sierra* came to the Supreme Court as a class action brought by the property owners based on the categorical rule of *Lucas*. Although application of the categorical rule of *Lucas* was rejected, the *Tahoe–Sierra* Court noted that if the property owners had brought their inverse condemnation claims as individuals rather than as a class, some of the owners "might have prevailed under a *Penn Central* analysis."[34]

The majority opinion in *Tahoe–Sierra* carefully avoided addressing the problem of the so-called "rolling" moratorium—one that purports to be temporary, but that is constantly extended due to delays in the land use planning process. Although normal delays in the planning process are to be expected, at some point even a "temporary" moratorium could work a regulatory taking if the moratorium endures long enough. The Supreme Court acknowledged the limited scope of its holding in *Tahoe–Sierra* by concluding that "[i]n rejecting [the property owners'] per se rule, we do not hold that the temporary nature of a land-use restriction precludes

---

34. *Tahoe–Sierra*, 535 U.S. at 334.

finding that it effects a taking; we simply recognize that it should not be given exclusive significance one way or the other...."[35]

If a temporary regulation does work a taking under a *Penn Central* analysis, then compensation is due to the property owner.[36] The time frame for measuring compensation is the moment of the taking (which logically would come some time after the temporary regulation first was enacted) until the temporary regulation is repealed or amended so that an economically beneficial use of the property becomes possible.

Government Regulation Factor Components

There is less clear-cut guidance for analysis of the character or nature of the challenged government action or regulation under the Supreme Court's decisions. This side of the *Penn Central* balancing test appears to have two major components:

- Whether the regulation authorizes the government or a third party physically to invade or occupy the owner's property; and

- The extent to which the regulation promotes the common good by adjusting the benefits and burdens of economic life.

The invade or occupy component derives from the categorical rule of *Loretto*. If the government-authorized invasion or occupation is only temporary or intermittent or intangible, rather than permanent and physical, then the categorical rule of *Loretto* does not apply. But the nature of the government action or regulation as authorizing a physical invasion or occupation of the owner's property is particularly intrusive, and therefore strengthens the property owner's claim under the *Penn Central* balancing test. Conversely, the absence of a physical invasion or occupation of the owner's property weakens the property owner's inverse condemnation claim.

---

35. *Id.* at 337.

36. *See* First English Evangelical Lutheran Church of Glendale v. County of Los Ange-

les, 482 U.S. 304 (1987) (compensation must be paid for a temporary regulatory taking).

The second major component, promotion of the common good, incorporates judicial deference to the state's exercise of police powers to promote the health, safety and general welfare of society. This deference weights heavily against the property owner's regulatory taking claim. When the burden to one individual property owner is balanced against the benefit to society at large, the scale skews heavily against the claim of the individual property owner. In the historic words of the *Mahon* Court (repeated again in *Penn Central*), "[g]overnment could hardly go on if to some extent values incident to property could not be diminished without paying for every such change in the general law."[37]

A Final Word About Exactions

Many first-year Property courses omit the topic of exactions. Exactions typically are covered in detail in an upper level course on land use planning. If your Property professor skipped exactions, you should now skip to the Checklist at the end of Chapter 10.

An exaction issue is easy to spot because it only arises in a unique *quid pro quo* situation. As a condition for obtaining discretionary government approval for a project, the government demands that the developer must give up specified real property rights without compensation as a condition for government approval of the project.

In *Nollan v. California Coastal Commission*[38] and *Dolan v. City of Tigard*,[39] the Supreme Court held that an exaction is a taking (for which the government must compensate the property owner) if:

- there is no essential nexus between the exaction and a legitimate state interest;[40] or

- the exaction is not roughly proportional to the project's impact.[41]

---

37. *Penn Central*, 438 U.S. at 124 (quoting *Mahon*, 260 U.S. at 413).

38. 483 U.S. 825 (1987).

39. 512 U.S. 374 (1994).

40. *Nollan*, 483 U.S. at 837.

41. *Dolan*, 512 U.S. at 391.

The facts of *Nollan* and *Dolan* illustrate these two alternative tests for when an exaction is a taking. In *Nollan*, the Supreme Court found that an essential nexus was lacking between the government's demand that the owner must convey a public easement right along the beach behind the owner's proposed beach house. The purported state interest was to preserve the public's view of the beach from the road in front of the proposed beach house. On these particular facts, the *Nollan* Court found that an essential nexus was lacking between the exaction and the state interest.

In *Dolan*, the property owner sought approval to expand the physical size of a retail building. The city demanded that, as a condition for approving the store's expansion plan, the property owner had to deed to the city an area of land that was located in the flood plain of an adjacent creek, and deed additional land along the creek for development of a greenway system of walking/bicycle paths. The city did not, however, make any effort to study or quantify its justification for demanding the exaction. The city merely asserted (without proof of a study of traffic patterns) that the expansion of the store would generate additional street traffic that would be alleviated by the greenway system.

On these particular facts, the *Dolan* Court found that the exaction was a taking because the city failed to present any evidence showing that the city's requested exaction was roughly proportional to the traffic impact of the proposed store expansion. In the words of the Supreme Court, although *Dolan*'s rough proportionality test did not require the city to be mathematically precise, the city was required to make "some sort of individualized determination that the required dedication is related in both nature and extent to the impact of the proposed development."[42]

Exam Tip: Analyze Regulatory Takings And Exactions Separately

On the exam, do not confuse a regulatory taking issue with an exaction issue that may be intertwined as part of the same fact pattern. You must analyze each issue separately.

---

42. *Dolan*, 512 U.S. at 391.

For example, assume that a government regulation imposes a development moratorium or a land use restriction. The moratorium or the use restriction, standing alone, may work a regulatory taking of the owner's property under the *Penn Central* balancing test.

Now assume that, as part of the regulation, there is a process by which a governmental regulator has discretion to grant permits to individual owners to develop or use their land in a manner that is otherwise prohibited by the regulation. An individual owner seeks such a permit. The government regulator demands that, as a condition for granting a permit, the owner must deed real property rights to the government for the public's use. The property owner challenges the demand to convey the real property rights (an exaction) as a taking. Now you would apply the essential nexus and rough proportionality tests to determine if the government regulator's exaction works a taking for which compensation is due to the property owner.

TAKINGS CHECKLIST

With the above Review in mind, the Takings Checklist is presented below.

A. EMINENT DOMAIN VERSUS INVERSE CONDEMNATION CLAIM. Who is the plaintiff in the action?

    1. Government As Plaintiff. If the plaintiff is the government, the takings claim is based on the government's power of eminent domain to take private property for public use. Proceed to Part B to determine if the public use requirement is satisfied.

    2. Property Owner As Plaintiff. If the plaintiff is an individual property owner, the claim is one for inverse condemnation based on the theory of a regulatory taking. Proceed to Part C to determine if a regulatory taking has occurred that entitles the owner to compensation.

3. **Just Compensation.** For both eminent domain and inverse condemnation claims, refer to Part D to determine the amount of compensation that is owed to the owner for a taking.

B. IS THE GOVERNMENT TAKING THE PROPERTY FOR A PUBLIC USE? Public use is a question of law decided by the judge.

1. **Transfer To The Government.** If the forced sale of the owner's property is to the government for its own use, the public use requirement is satisfied.

2. **Transfer To A Private Party But With Public Access/Use.** If the forced sale of the owner's property is to another private party, but the public may access or use the property, the public use requirement is satisfied.

3. **Transfer To A Private Party To Alleviate Social Harm Or Confer A Social Benefit.** If the forced sale of the owner's property is to another private party pursuant to a comprehensive government plan or program designed to alleviate a social harm or confer a social benefit, the public use requirement is satisfied.

   a. **Judicial Deference To Legislative Objective And Means Of Implementation.** In determining public use, courts defer to the legislature's means of alleviating a social harm or conferring a social benefit.

   b. **Examples Of Curing Societal Harms.** Is the regulation at issue analogous to a prior Supreme Court decision?

      i. *Berman.* A comprehensive urban renewal plan designed to alleviate blight in a residential neighborhood.

      ii. *Midkiff.* A plan to break up oligopoly ownership of residential housing.

   c. **Examples Of Conferring Social Benefits.** Is the regulation at issue analogous to a prior Supreme Court decision?

        i. *Midkiff.* Plan to provide social benefits resulting from an increase in the number of private home owners.

        ii. *Kelo.* An economic development plan for a non-blighted area designed to boost property tax revenues and attract new jobs to the area.

C. IS THE GOVERNMENT REGULATION A TAKING FOR WHICH COMPENSATION IS DUE? Determine if a categorical rule under Part C.1 applies. If not, proceed to the *Penn Central* balancing test under Part C.2.

    1. Does A Categorical Rule Apply? If one of the categorical rules below applies, the taking issue conclusively is resolved.

        a. Permanent Physical Occupation. Under *Loretto*, if the regulation authorizes a permanent physical occupation of the owner's property, either by the government or by a third party, the regulation is conclusively a taking of the occupied portion of the owner's property. Proceed to Part D to determine the amount of compensation due to the owner.

            i. **Temporary?** A temporary occupation is not a per se taking under *Loretto*.

            ii. **Intangible?** An occupation that is intangible in nature is not a per se taking under *Loretto*.

            iii. **Invasion?** An invasion generally is not an occupation that satisfies *Loretto* unless the invasion is so frequent that it is tantamount to a permanent occupation (e.g., direct overflights by aircraft).

        b. No Remaining Economically Beneficial Use. If the effect of the regulation is to leave the owner's property without *any* productive or economically beneficial use (a *Lucas*-like "total wipe-out"), the regulation is conclusively a taking of the owner's property. Proceed to Part D to determine the amount of the compensation due to the owner.

    i. **Is There Any Remaining Value?** According to the majority in *Lucas*, a 95% reduction in value due to the regulation does not qualify as a per se taking. *Hadacheck* approved a zoning regulation that caused an 87½% reduction in value. *Euclid* approved a zoning regulation that caused a 75% reduction in value.

    ii. **Can The Property Be Severed Into Valuable And Valued Portions?** In *Palazzolo*, the Supreme Court did not address whether an owner could sever his own property into multiple parcels and claim a total wipe-out of economic value for the severed parcel that is affected by the regulation.

  c. **Regulation Substitutes For Private/Public Nuisance Control.** Under *Lucas*, if the government or an adjacent landowner could have successfully brought a nuisance action that has the same effect as the regulation by enjoining the owner's use, then the regulation conclusively does not work a taking of the owner's property, even if the regulation renders the property valueless.

2. *Penn Central* **Balancing Test.** Assuming a categorical rule does not apply, determine if the regulation works a taking by balancing the two factors described in Part C.2 below.

  a. **Economic Impact Of The Regulation On The Private Owner Factor.** Evaluate the economic impact by discussing the three components below.

i. **Diminution In Present Market Value (DIV).** *Mahon* introduced the DIV approach. Determine the regulation's before-and-after impact on the present market value of the property as a percentage reduction of the "before" value.

- **High DIV Percentages.** The Supreme Court has upheld zoning regulations that worked an 87½% (*Hadacheck*) and 75% (*Euclid*) DIV.

- **Scope/Severance Issues.** In determining the DIV, consider how the scope of the property rights affected by the regulation should be defined, and if the affected property rights should be severed.

- **No Severance Of Airspace If FSA.** *Penn Central* held that the airspace rights could not be severed when the owner held a fee simple absolute interest in the property. DIV must be based on the "parcel as a whole."

- **No Severance Of Time If FSA.** *Tahoe–Sierra* held that the owner's fee simple absolute ownership rights could not be severed based on time when determining DIV because the property's value would be restored when the temporary moratorium on development was lifted.

ii. **Offsetting Reciprocity Of Advantage To Property Owner.** *Mahon* indicated that DIV is offset by reciprocity of advantage. Discuss how the owner's property, the owner individually, or the owner more generally as a member of society may benefit from the regulation, thereby reducing the economic impact of the regulation on the private owner.

iii. **Distinct Investment–Backed Expectations For Future Development.** Analyze the owner's future plans for development of the property and the future anticipated income that the owner reasonably may have lost due to the regulation's impact.

- **Pre–Enactment versus Post–Enactment Purchaser.** Did the owner purchase the property before or after the challenged regulation was enacted? A pre-enactment purchaser has stronger DIBE than a post-enactment purchaser. Under *Palazzolo*, a post-enactment purchaser can still challenge the pre-existing regulation as a taking, but the owner's reasonable DIBE are diminished.

- **Objective Reasonableness Of DIBE.** Subjective ignorance of the law is no excuse. Reasonable DIBE do not include the right to use the property in such a way as to violate a background principle of law, such as nuisance law.

- **Amended/New Regulation After Purchase.** A post-enactment purchaser can acquire status as a pre-enactment purchaser if the regulation is significantly amended or superceded by a new regulation.

b. **Character Or Nature Of The Government's Action Or Regulation Factor.** Weigh the economic impact on the private owner against the character or nature of the government's action or regulation by discussing the components below.

    i. **Physical Invasion Or Occupation.** Does the regulation authorize the physical invasion or occupation of the owner's private property, either by the government or by a third party? **If yes**, the regulation is particularly intrusive and strengthens the owner's claim that the regulation works a taking.

    ii. **Promotion Of The Common Good.** Analyze the benefits to society at large from the regulation. Note that courts are highly deferential to the legislative exercise of police powers for the health, safety and general welfare of society.

3. **Is An Exaction A Taking?** Determine if an exaction has occurred and, if so, whether the exaction passes both the *Nollan* and *Dolan* tests.

a. **Exaction.** Did the government demand that the developer must transfer real property rights without compensation as a condition for granting discretionary approval of the developer's project? **If yes**, an exaction has occurred.

b. **Taking Under *Nollan/Dolan* Tests.**

    i. **Essential Nexus?** If there is no essential nexus between the exaction and a legitimate state interest, the exaction is a taking for which compensation is due to the developer (*Nollan* test).

    ii. Rough Proportionality? If the exaction is not roughly proportional to the project's impact, the exaction is a taking for which compensation is due to the developer (*Dolan* test). The government regulator must present some evidence of proportionality.

D. WHAT IS THE AMOUNT OF JUST COMPENSATION? If a categorical taking, a regulatory taking or a taking via an exaction has occurred, determine the amount of compensation due to the owner.

    1. Market Value Of The Property Rights Taken. Determine the amount of "just" compensation due to the property owner by estimating the market value of the property rights taken.

        a. Definition Of Market Value. Market value is the price, in cash or equivalent, for which the property rights should sell after reasonable exposure in a competitive market, with a prudent and knowledgeable buyer and seller each acting without duress.

            i. Subjective Value Not Included. The unique value of the property rights taken to the owner personally is not considered in determining market value.

            ii. Damages To The Remainder. Include as part of compensation any damages to the remaining property caused by the taking.

            iii. Increases In Future Value. Include as part of the owner's compensation any increase value due to anticipated future zoning changes or a legal change in the use of the property that would increase the property's market value.

iv. **Business Losses And Disturbed Tenants.** Just compensation under the Fifth Amendment's Takings Clause is based only on the value of the real estate rights taken and does not include compensation for losses due to disruption of a business or a tenant. Compensation for these losses may be authorized by a state statute.

ILLUSTRATIVE PROBLEMS

Here are two problems that illustrate how the Checklist can be used to resolve takings questions.

■ PROBLEM 10.1 ■

Easy Green Golf Course was developed in the late 1990s ten miles outside of the then-existing limits of the City of Greenville. The City of Greenville is located in the State of Kelo. The state constitution of Kelo contains a "Takings Clause" that is identical to, and interpreted in the same manner as, the Fifth Amendment of the U.S. Constitution.

Over time, the City of Greenville expanded so that by 2011 the Easy Green Golf Course was completely surrounded by residential and commercial development. Around the same time, residents in the area began complaining that during the spring and summer seasonal rains, several key intersections in the area routinely flooded, causing traffic backups and accidents as cars stalled in the high waters at the intersections. Major employers in the area, whose employees were affected by the flooded streets and could not reach their offices, began threatening to relocate their businesses to another town unless the City resolved the street drainage problem.

The City of Greenville commissioned a study to determine the causes of the street drainage problem. The study found that the street drainage problem was caused by the substantial increase in storm water runoff due to the residential and commercial development in the area over the last 20 years. One of the study's recommendations was to preserve the remaining areas of green space, most notably the Easy Green Golf Course.

In 2012, Bob and Sue Miller, the original developers and owners of the Easy Green Golf Course, sold the property to Joe Eden, who was a resident of the City of Greenville. Eden petitioned the Zoning Board for the City of Greenville to rezone the golf course property from recreational use to retail use so that he could build a large regional shopping center on the property. The Zoning Board denied Joe's petition for rezoning.

In 2012, flush with cash from a federal grant for infrastructure improvements, the City of Greenville formed the Greenville Development Corporation ("GDC") to plan, identify and purchase properties that would improve the infrastructure of the City and set the stage for future growth and development. The GDC identified the Easy Green Golf Course property owned by Eden as a "critical component" necessary to control street drainage problems in the area. The GDC condemned the Easy Green Golf Course property. The GDC's infrastructure improvement plan called for the City to lease the Easy Green Golf Course property to a private operator for a 30 year term. Under the GDC's plan, the proposed operating agreement between the City and the private operator would require the operator to give 25% of the net profits from operations to the City of Greenville to pay for the acquisition and maintenance of public parks in the neighborhood. The proposed operating agreement permitted the private operator to operate the golf course as a "members only" club.

Joe Eden has come to you for legal advice. Eden is upset because the City of Greenville has offered to pay him only the purchase price that he paid to the Millers for the Easy Green Golf Course ($2 million). If rezoned for retail use, the golf course property would have a market value of $12 million. Moreover, Eden does not want to sell the property. Rather, he now wants to build a large entertainment and indoor sports complex with a video arcade, bowling, outdoor miniature golf, batting cages, a golf driving range, and indoor soccer fields, basketball courts and an indoor ice skating rink. Eden's proposed entertainment and indoor sports center complies with the existing zoning requirements for recreational use. If developed as an entertainment and indoor sports complex, the property has a present market value of $6 million.

Can Eden prevent the GDC from taking his property? If not, what is the amount of compensation due to Eden?

Analysis

Eden is unlikely to be able to prevent the GDC from acquiring the Easy Green Golf Course, but he may be able to obtain more than the offered $2 million as compensation.

Under the Takings Clause, the GDC can condemn the golf course and force its sale to the GDC if the power of eminent domain is being exercised for a public use. The public use requirement is satisfied if the government's use of the power of eminent domain is for a public purpose. It is not necessary that the government must own or use the property. The power of eminent domain may be used to transfer ownership of property from one private owner to another private owner so long as the transfer of ownership serves a public purpose.

Here, the forced sale of the Easy Green Golf Course to the GDC for lease to a private operator serves a public purpose. The transfer preserves the property as an undeveloped area of green space that the City of Greenville's study identified as a "critical component" of the City's effort to address street flooding problems in the area. Preserving the Easy Green Golf Course as a green space mitigates the harm caused by excess street flooding due to development in the area. In determining whether the power of eminent domain has been exercised for a public use, courts are highly deferential to the legislative means chosen by government to alleviate a public health and safety harm such as severe street flooding. Therefore, a court is likely to hold that the condemnation of the Easy Green Golf Course is for a public use.

The compensation due to Eden as the owner of the Easy Green Golf Course is based on the market value of the property at the time of the taking. Market value is the price in cash or its equivalent that the property should sell for in a competitive market after reasonable exposure assuming a reasonable buyer and seller. Eden is unlikely to receive the market value of $12 million for the property as a retail center because the existing zoning does not permit the property to be used for retail use. Eden has evidence, however, that the market value of the property would increase to $6 million if the recreational use of the property were changed from a golf course to an entertainment and sports complex. An entertainment and sports center is an alternative legal use of the property under current zoning law. A court may award more that $2 million in compensation (the price Eden paid for the property) based on this alternative legal use and the resulting higher market value.

■ PROBLEM 10.2 ■

Refer to the facts in Problem 10.1 above. Assume that Eden acquired the Easy Green Golf Course, unsuccessfully petitioned for the zoning change, and then began making plans to build the entertainment and sports complex on the property. Instead of condemning Eden's property, the Zoning Board for the City of Greenville amended the zoning plan for the area after Eden's petition for rezoning was denied. Under the revised zoning plan, the only type of recreational use permitted for the Easy Green Golf Course was "traditional golf played on natural grass." The reason for the zoning change was to implement the recommendation of the street drainage study that the Easy Green Golf Course must be maintained as a golf course to avoid worsening street drainage problems in the area.

Eden has filed an inverse condemnation claim against the Zoning Board and the City of Greenville, claiming the zoning change is a regulatory taking of his property. At trial, Eden presented evidence that due to the change in zoning the market value of the property has been reduced from $3 million to $2 million. You are the judge for the case. State how you will rule on Eden's claim, and explain the reasoning for your decision.

Analysis

Opinion of Judge Student:

The court rules that plaintiff's claim of inverse condemnation is dismissed. The zoning regulation enacted by the City of Greenville and its Zoning Board does not work a regulatory taking of the plaintiff's property.

The zoning regulation is not a per se regulatory taking under the categorical rule of *Loretto* because the regulation does not authorize a permanent physical occupation of the plaintiff's property. The zoning regulation is not a per se regulatory taking under the categorical rule of *Lucas* because the regulation does not deny the plaintiff *all* productive or economically beneficial use of the property. Under the zoning regulation, the property may continue to operate, as it has been operated in the past, as a traditional golf course.

The zoning regulation is not conclusively a permissible use of the City of Greenville's police power to control nuisances under the Supreme Court's prior decision in *Lucas*. To categorically determine that a regulation of a private landowner's use is not a regulatory taking, *Lucas* held that the regulation must effectively serve as a substitute for a private or public nuisance claim that could successfully enjoin the private landowner's use as a nuisance.

Here, the zoning regulation is not functioning to abate a nuisance. Rather, the regulation is aimed at preserving one of the solutions to the severe street drainage problem by requiring that the property must continue to be used as a traditional golf course.

Given that a categorical rule does not resolve the plaintiff's claim, the court must apply the *Penn Central* balancing test to determine if the zoning regulation works a taking of the plaintiff's property for public use. The *Penn Central* balancing test requires the court to weigh the economic impact of the regulation on the private property owner against the character or nature of the challenged government regulation.

In assessing and weighing the economic impact of the zoning regulation on the plaintiff, the court has considered the diminution in the market value of the property, any offsetting reciprocity of advantage to the owner or the owner's property, and the distinct investment-backed expectations ("DIBE") of the plaintiff in purchasing the Easy Green Golf Course. Based on the evidence, the diminution in value of the property is 75% (from $8 million to $2 million). The plaintiff himself enjoys an offsetting reciprocity of advantage from the continued use of the property as a traditional golf course. The plaintiff as a resident of the City of Greenville will personally benefit if the street drainage problem in the area is prevented from becoming worse as a result of maintaining the property's use as a traditional golf course.

The zoning regulation has reduced the plaintiff's DIBE for the Easy Green Golf Course. It is irrelevant that the Zoning Board rejected plaintiff's petition for a change in zoning for the property to retail use before deciding to change the recreational use of the property to an entertainment and sports complex. The plaintiff is a pre-enactment purchaser of the property with respect to the particular zoning regulation that the plaintiff has challenged, which restricts the permissible recreational use of the property to use as a traditional golf course. The zoning regulation in effect at the time the plaintiff purchased the Easy Green Golf Course would have permitted the plaintiff's proposed change in use of the property from a golf course to an entertainment and sports complex. Plaintiff's DIBE were objectively reasonable because the plaintiff's planned change in the type of recreational use was a legal alternative use of the property when the plaintiff purchased it. The evidence shows that reduction in the plaintiff's DIBE for the future use of the property, measured in present market value dollars, is from $8 million if developed as an entertainment and sports complex to approximately $2 million if continued to be operated as a traditional golf course. This is a reduction in the plaintiff's DIBE of approximately $6 million in present dollars.

In assessing and weighing the character or nature of the zoning regulation, the court has considered that the regulation does not authorize the government or a third party to occupy or invade the plaintiff's property. The zoning regulation is not physically intrusive. The zoning regulation merely limits the plaintiff's use of the property to its current use as a traditional golf course. The court also has considered the benefit to the citizens of the City of Greenville in improving the street drainage problem in the area. The study by the City of Greenville determined that maintaining the plaintiff's property as a traditional golf course was a "critical component" in resolving the street drainage problem. Street drainage problems of the severity experienced in the City of Greenville present a hazard to the public's health and safety, and therefore are weighed heavily by the court in determining whether the zoning regulation works a taking of the plaintiff's property.

Based on the severity of the street drainage problem and the need to maintain the plaintiff's property as a traditional golf course as a "critical component" in resolving the street drainage problem, the court determines that the City of Greenville's zoning regulation is not a taking of the Easy Green Golf Course.

POINTS TO REMEMBER

- Consider the possible application of the three categorical rules for a regulatory taking (*Loretto*, *Lucas*, and the nuisance control rule post-*Lucas*), but do not rely on a categorical rule to resolve an exam question unless the question suggests that a brief answer is appropriate. For an essay question, discuss the *Penn Central* balancing test.

- After *Kelo*, the public use requirement of the Takings Clause conflates with any public purpose that confers an indirect economic benefit to society, such as increased tax revenues or jobs. Under the modern public use standard, the public does not need to use the property. The government can take property from one private owner and transfer it to another private owner, so long as the transfer of private ownership serves a public purpose.

- If the exam question presents specific numerical values in the facts, do not ignore them. Instead, use the numbers to perform a diminution in value percentage calculation if the numbers relate to present market value. If the numbers relate to future anticipated market value, use the numbers to perform a distinct investment-backed expectations analysis.

- Watch for an opportunity to discuss the "hot button" takings issues of the rolling temporary moratorium and the owner who severs his property into two or more parcels and then attempts to claim a *Lucas*-like total wipe-out of the value.

†